THE LANGUAGE OF LITERATURE

THE *InterActive*
READER™ PLUS
for English Learners

McDougal Littell
A HOUGHTON MIFFLIN COMPANY
Evanston, Illinois • Boston • Dallas

Reading Consultant, *The InterActive Reader™ Plus*

Sharon Sicinski-Skeans, Ph.D. Assistant Professor of Reading, University of Houston-Clear Lake; former K-12 Language Arts Program Director, Spring Independent School District, Houston, Texas
The reading consultant guided the conceptual development of the *InterActive Reader*. She participated in the development of prototype materials, the planning and writing of lessons, and the review of completed materials.

Senior Consultants, *The Language of Literature*

Arthur N. Applebee Professor of Education, State University of New York at Albany; Director, National Research Center on English Learning and Achievements; Senior Fellow, Center for Writing and Literacy

Andrea B. Bermúdez Professor of Studies in Language and Culture; Director, Research Center for Language and Culture; Chair, Foundations and Professional Studies, University of Houston-Clear Lake

Sheridan Blau Senior Lecturer in English and Education and former Director of Composition, University of California at Santa Barbara; Director, South Coast Writing Project; Director, Literature Institute for Teachers; Past President, National Council of Teachers of English

Rebekah Caplan Coordinator, English Language Arts K-12, Oakland Unified School District, Oakland, California; Teacher-Consultant, Bay Area Writing Project, University of California at Berkeley; served on the California State English Assessment Development Team for Language Arts

Peter Elbow Professor of English, University of Massachusetts at Amherst; Fellow, Bard Center for Writing and Thinking

Susan Hynds Professor and Director of English Education, Syracuse University, Syracuse, New York

Judith A. Langer Professor of Education, State University of New York at Albany; Director, National Research Center on English Learning and Achievements; Director, Albany Institute for Research on Education

James Marshall Professor of English and English Education, University of Iowa, Iowa City

Acknowledgments can be found on page 527.

ISBN 0-618-31023-1

5 6 7 8 9 -DWI- 08 07 06 05

Table of Contents

Academic and Informational Reading 433

Introducing *The InterActive Reader*™ *Plus*

The InterActive Reader™ Plus is a new kind of literature book. As you will see, this book helps you become an active reader. It is a book to mark on, to write in, and to make your own. You can use it in class *and* take it home.

An Easy-to-Carry Literature Text

This book won't weigh you down—it can fit as comfortably in your hand as it can in your backpack. Yet it contains works by such important authors as . . .

Excerpts from **Geoffrey Chaucer's** beloved *Canterbury Tales*

Jonathan Swift's famous satire "A Modest Proposal"

John Keats's timeless poem "Ode on a Grecian Urn"

D. H. Lawrence's fantastic tale "The Rocking-Horse Winner"

Doris Lessing's contemporary coming-of-age story "A Sunrise on the Veld"

You will read these selections and other great literature—plays, poems, stories, and nonfiction. In addition, you will learn how to understand the texts you use in classes, on tests, and in the real world, and you will study and practice specific strategies for taking standardized tests.

Help for Reading

The InterActive Reader™ *Plus* helps you understand many challenging works of literature. Here's how.

Before-You-Read Activities A prereading page helps you make connections to your everyday life and gives you a key to understanding the selection.

Preview A preview of every selection tells you what to expect.

Reading Tips Reading tips give useful help throughout.

Focus Each longer piece is broken into smaller 'bites' or sections. A focus at the beginning of each section tells you what to look for.

Pause and Reflect At the end of each section, a quick question or two helps you check your understanding.

Read Aloud Specific passages are marked for you to read aloud. You will use your voice and ears to interpret literature.

Reread This feature directs you to passages where a lot of action, change, or meaning is packed in a few lines.

Mark It Up This feature invites you to mark your own notes and questions right on the page.

Vocabulary Support

Words to Know Important new words are underlined. Their definitions appear in a Words to Know section at the bottom of any page where they occur in the selection. You will work with these words in the Words to Know SkillBuilder pages.

Personal Word List As you read, you will want to add some words from the selections to your own vocabulary. Write these words in your Personal Word List on page 508.

SkillBuilder Pages

After each literary selection, you will find these SkillBuilder pages:

    Active Reading SkillBuilder.

    Literary Analysis SkillBuilder.

    Words to Know SkillBuilder (for most selections).

These pages will help you practice and apply important skills.

The InterActive Reader™ Plus for English Learners

The InterActive Reader™ Plus for English Learners provides all of the literature selections and all of the features from the *InterActive Reader™ Plus.* Special additional features include:

Section summaries A brief summary helps get you started with each section or chunk of the text.

More About . . . These notes provide key background information about specific elements of the text such as historical events, scientific concepts, or political situations needed for understanding the selection.

What Does It Mean? These brief notes clearly explain any confusing words, phrases, references, or other constructions.

English Learner Support These notes provide special help with vocabulary, language, and culture issues.

Reading Check These questions at key points in the text help you clarify what is happening in the selection.

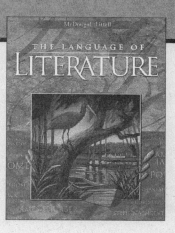

Links to *The Language of Literature*

If you are using McDougal Littell's *The Language of Literature,* you will find *The InterActive Reader™ Plus* to be a perfect companion. The literary selections in the reader can all be found in that book. *The InterActive Reader™ Plus* lets you read certain core selections from *The Language of Literature* more slowly and in greater depth.

Read on to learn more!

Academic and Informational Reading

Here is a special collection of real world examples to help you read every kind of informational material, from textbooks to technical directions. The strategies you learn will help you on tests, in other classes, and in the world outside of school. You will find strategies for the following:

Analyzing Text Features This section will help you read many different types of magazine articles and textbooks. You will learn how titles, subtitles, lists, graphics, many different kinds of visuals, and other special features work in magazines and textbooks. After studying this section you will be ready to read even the most complex material.

Understanding Visuals Tables, charts, graphs, maps, and diagrams all require special reading skills. As you learn the common elements of various visual texts, you will learn to read these materials with accuracy and skill.

Recognizing Text Structures Informational texts can be organized in many different ways. In this section you will study the following structures and learn about special key words that will help you identify the organizational patterns:

- Main idea and supporting details
- Problem and solution
- Sequence
- Cause and Effect
- Comparison and Contrast
- Argument

Reading in the Content Areas You will learn special strategies for reading social studies, science, and mathematics texts.

Reading Beyond the Classroom In this section you will encounter applications, schedules, technical directions, product information, Web pages, and other readings. Learning to analyze these texts will help you in your everyday life and on some standardized tests.

Test Preparation Strategies

In this section, you will find strategies and practice to help you succeed on many different kinds of standardized tests. After closely studying a variety of test formats through annotated examples, you will have an opportunity to practice each format on your own. Additional support will help you think through your answers. You will find strategies for the following:

Successful Test Taking This section provides many suggestions for preparing for and taking tests. The information ranges from analyzing test questions to tips for answering multiple-choice and open-ended test questions.

Reading Tests: Long Selections You will learn how to analyze the structure of a lengthy reading and prepare to answer the comprehension questions that follow it.

Reading Tests: Short Selections These selections may be a paragraph of text, a poem, a chart or graph, or some other item. You will practice the special range of comprehension skills required for these pieces.

Functional Reading These real-world texts present special challenges. You will learn about the various test formats that use applications, product labels, technical directions, Web pages, and more.

Revising and Editing Tests These materials test your understanding of English grammar and usage. You may encounter capitalization and punctuation questions. Sometimes the focus is on usage questions such as verb tenses or pronoun agreement issues. You will become familiar with these formats through the guided practice in this section.

Writing Tests Writing prompts and sample student essays will help you understand how to analyze a prompt and what elements make a successful written response. Scoring rubrics and a prompt for practice will prepare you for the writing tests you will take.

User's Guide

The InterActive Reader™ Plus has an easy-to-follow organization, illustrated by these sample pages from "The Rocking-Horse Winner."

The Rocking-Horse WINNER

D. H. Lawrence

Before You Read

Connect to Your Life

The young boy in this story develops a friendship with his uncle. Think of a relative or family friend with whom you are close. How would you describe him or her? What do you have in common? Write the person's name in the center oval below. Then fill in the other ovals with examples of things you share with this person.

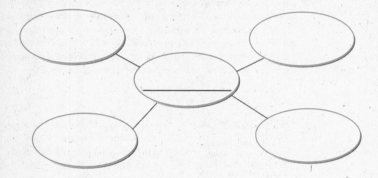

Key to the Story

WHAT'S THE BIG IDEA? In "The Rocking-Horse Winner," luck, or the lack of it, plays an important role. Think about what having good luck or bad luck means to you. Do you believe in luck at all? Then read the story to find out what luck means to the main character and his family.

Connect to Your Life

These activities help you see connections between your own life and what happens in the selection.

Key to the Selection

This section provides a "key" to help you unlock the selection so that you can understand and enjoy it. One of these four kinds of keys will appear:

- **What You Need to Know**— important background information.
- **What's the Big Idea?**—an introduction to key words or concepts in the selection.
- **What Do You Think?**— a preview of an important quotation from the selection.
- **What to Listen For**— a chance to examine the sound and rhythm of a piece.

And there's more

User's Guide continued

Reading Tips

1 These practical strategies will help you gain more from your reading.

PREVIEW

2 This feature tells you what the selection is about, so that you'll know what to expect.

FOCUS

3 Every literary work is broken into sections. Each section is introduced by a Focus that tells you what to look for as you read.

MARK IT UP

4 This feature often appears in the Focus. It may ask you to underline or circle key passages in the text or to take notes in the margin as you read.

As the story . . .

5 This feature provides a brief summary to help you get started with each section of the text.

MARK IT UP KEEP TRACK

6 This easy-to-use marking system will help you track your understanding. Turn to page xiv to see how a model of the system can be used.

SHORT STORY

1 **Reading Tips**

This **short story** is like a fairy tale in that it has an element of magic about it. The characters' problems and **conflicts,** though, are realistic.

- Much of the story is told through **dialogue,** or written conversation. The author usually doesn't tell you why the characters act as they do. You must read between the lines, using what they say to infer their **motives**.

- As you read, think about how the events in the plot are connected. Ask yourself which events cause—or bring about—other events in the story.

As the story begins . . .

5
- The mother of the family realizes that she does not love her children.
- The family lives in style, but they are always in debt.

MARK IT UP KEEP TRACK

6 As you read, you can use these marks to keep track of your understanding.

✔ ..... I understand.

? ..... I don't understand this.

! ..... Interesting or surprising idea

English Learner Support
VOCABULARY

Idiom To read something in someone's eyes means to "see" or understand someone's thoughts.

The InterActive Reader PLUS
280 For English Learners

The Rocking-Horse WINNER

D. H. Lawrence

2 **PREVIEW** In his novels and short stories, D. H. Lawrence (1885–1930) often attacked what he believed were the false values of society—such as the love of money. This story is set in England shortly after World War I. The main character is a boy who bets on horseraces. The amount of money that can be won on a horserace depends on the odds. For example, suppose the odds against a horse are 4 to 1. If that horse wins the race, then everyone who bet on it receives 4 dollars for each dollar bet.

3 **FOCUS**

The narrator describes the mother of a family living beyond its means. Her children sense the tension in the household.

4 MARK IT UP As you read, circle details that help you form impressions of the mother. An example is highlighted.

There was a woman who was beautiful, who started with all the advantages, yet she had no luck. She married for love, and the love turned to dust. She had bonny[1] children, yet she felt they had been thrust upon her, and she could not love them. They looked at her coldly, as if they were finding fault with her. And hurriedly she felt she must cover up some fault in herself. Yet what it was that she

10 must cover up she never knew. Nevertheless, when her children were present, she always felt the center of her heart go hard. This troubled her, and in her manner she was all the more gentle and anxious for her children, as if she loved them very much. Only she herself knew that at the center of her heart was a hard little place that could not feel love, no, not for anybody. Everybody else said of her: "She is such a good mother. She adores her children." Only she herself, and her children themselves, knew it was not so. They read it in each other's eyes.

20 There were a boy and two little girls. They lived in a pleasant house, with a garden, and they had discreet servants, and felt themselves superior to anyone in the neighborhood.

---

1. bonny: pretty.

Although they lived in style, they felt always an anxiety in the house. There was never enough money. The mother had a small income, and the father had a small income, but not nearly enough for the social position which they had to keep up. The father went into town to some office. But though he had good prospects, these prospects never materialized. There was always the grinding sense of the shortage of money, though the style was always kept up.

At last the mother said: "I will see if *I* can't make something." But she did not know where to begin. She racked[2] her brains, and tried this thing and the other, but could not find anything successful. The failure made deep lines come into her face. Her children were growing up, they would have to go to school. There must be more money, there must be more money. The father, who was always very handsome and expensive in his tastes, seemed as if he never *would* be able to do anything worth doing. And the mother, who had a great belief in herself, did not succeed any better, and her tastes were just as expensive.

And so the house came to be haunted by the unspoken phrase: *There must be more money! There must be more money!* The children could hear it all the time, though nobody said it aloud. They heard it at Christmas, when the expensive and splendid toys filled the nursery. Behind the shining modern rocking-horse, behind the smart[3] doll's house, a voice would start whispering: "There *must* be more money! There *must* be more money!" And the children would stop playing, to listen for a moment. They would look into each other's eyes, to see if they had all heard. And each one saw in the eyes of the other two that they too had heard. "There *must* be more money! There *must* be more money!"

It came whispering from the springs of the still-swaying rocking-horse, and even the horse, bending his wooden, champing head, heard it. The big doll, sitting so pink and smirking in her new pram,[4] could hear it quite plainly, and seemed to be smirking all the more self-consciously because of it. The foolish puppy, too, that took the place of the teddy bear, he was looking so extraordinarily foolish for no other reason but that he heard the secret whisper all over the house: "There *must* be more money!"

---

2. **racked:** strained; tortured.
3. **smart:** elegant.
4. **pram:** baby carriage (a shortened form of *perambulator*).

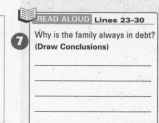

READ ALOUD Lines 23–30

7 Why is the family always in debt? (Draw Conclusions)

_____

_____

_____

_____

Reading Tip

8 Several factors contribute to the tension in this household. This tension is the **effect.** Highlight each **cause** of the tension that you see on pages 280–281. The first cause is that the woman realizes she cannot love her children.

Reading Tip

Writers use italic type to alert readers to words and phrases that they want to emphasize. Find the examples of italic type on this page and think about the reason these words are emphasized.

English Learner Support
LANGUAGE

9 **Metaphor** The house that speaks and whispers is a metaphor for the extreme tension in this family. The house is compared to a person who stands in the shadows and whispers unpleasant and frightening things.

Rocking-Horse Winner **281**

READ ALOUD Lines 23–30

7 From time to time, you'll be asked to read a passage aloud. That's a great way to increase your understanding —and enjoyment.

Reading Tip

8 This feature gives useful and fun tips and strategies for comprehension.

English Learner Support

9 These notes provide help with vocabulary, language, and culture issues.

And there's more

Student Model

These pages show you how one student made use of *The InterActive Reader™ Plus*.

Reading Tip

Line 365 begins a very long sentence. You can read it more easily if you pause after each comma to see what has just taken place. Write a list of events that occur in the sentence, starting with *1. Paul hands over five thousand pounds to his uncle; 2. Paul's uncle deposits the money with the family lawyer*, and so on.

Pause & Reflect

1. Why did Paul start betting on horseraces? Circle the phrase below that tells the answer. **(Clarify)**

   to win Uncle Oscar's respect

   to earn extra money for toys

   to help Bassett support his family

   (to stop the whispering in the house)

2. Do you think Uncle Oscar should keep Paul's gambling a secret from his mother? (Yes) No, because *if she found out about it, she would be upset.*

   (Evaluate)

As the story continues ...

- Paul hears the house "whispering" more and more.
- Paul plans to give the 5,000 pounds to his mother over five years, but she has a different idea.

The InterActive Reader PLUS
290 **For English Learners**

"What does it whisper?"

"Why—why"—the boy fidgeted—"why, I don't know. But it's always short of money, you know, uncle."

"I know it, son, I know it."

350 "You know people send mother writs,[24] don't you, uncle?"

"I'm afraid I do," said the uncle.

"And then the house whispers, like people laughing at you behind your back. It's awful, that is! I thought if I was lucky—"

"You might stop it," added the uncle.

The boy watched him with big blue eyes, that had an uncanny cold fire in them, and he said never a word.

"Well, then!" said the uncle. "What are we doing?"

"I shouldn't like mother to know I was lucky," said the boy.

"Why not, son?"

360 "She'd stop me."

"I don't think she would."

"Oh!"—and the boy (writhed)[25] in an odd way—"I *don't* want her to know, uncle."

"All right, son! We'll manage it without her knowing."

They managed it very easily. Paul, at the other's suggestion, handed over five thousand pounds to his uncle, who deposited it with the family lawyer, who was then to inform Paul's mother that a relative had put five thousand pounds into his hands, which sum was to be paid out a thousand pounds at a

370 time, on the mother's birthday, for the next five years.

"(So she'll have a birthday present of a thousand pounds for five successive years,)" said Uncle Oscar. "I hope it won't make it all the harder for her later."

Pause & Reflect

FOCUS
Read to find out how Paul's mother reacts to her present and what happens to Paul as he bets heavily.

✎ **MARK IT UP** As you read, circle any details that help you understand the mother's reaction.

380

Paul's mother had her birthday in November. The house had been "whispering" worse than ever lately, and, even in spite of his luck, Paul could not bear up against it. He was very anxious to see the effect of the birthday letter, telling his mother about the thousand pounds.

24. **writs:** legal documents (in this case, demands for the payment of debts).

25. **writhed** (ri*th*d): twisted.

When there were no visitors, Paul now took his meals with his parents, as he was beyond the nursery control. His mother went into town nearly every day. She had discovered that she had an odd knack of sketching furs and dress materials, so she worked secretly in the studio of a friend who was the chief "artist" for the leading drapers.[26] She drew the figures of ladies in furs and ladies in silk and sequins for the newspaper advertisements. This young woman artist earned several thousand pounds a year, but Paul's mother only made several hundreds, and she was again dissatisfied. She so wanted to be first in something, and she did not succeed, even in making sketches for drapery advertisements.

She was down to breakfast on the morning of her birthday. Paul watched her face as she read her letters. He knew the lawyer's letter. As his mother read it, her face hardened and became more expressionless. Then a cold, determined look came on her mouth. She hid the letter under the pile of others, and said not a word about it.

"Didn't you have anything nice in the post for your birthday, mother?" said Paul.

"Quite moderately nice," she said, her voice cold and absent. She went away to town without saying more.

But in the afternoon Uncle Oscar appeared. He said Paul's mother had had a long interview with the lawyer, asking if the whole five thousand could not be advanced at once, as she was in debt.

"What do you think, uncle?" said the boy.

"I leave it to you, son."

"Oh, let her have it, then! We can get some more with the other," said the boy.

"A bird in the hand is worth two in the bush, laddie!" said Uncle Oscar.

"But I'm sure to *know* for the Grand National; or the Lincolnshire; or else the Derby. I'm sure to know for *one* of them," said Paul.

So Uncle Oscar signed the agreement, and Paul's mother touched[27] the whole five thousand. Then something very curious happened. The voices in the house suddenly went mad, like a chorus of frogs on a spring evening. There were certain new furnishings, and Paul had a tutor. He was *really* going to Eton, his father's school, in the following autumn.

26. **drapers:** in Britain, dealers in cloth and dry goods.
27. **touched:** received.

Took his meals means "ate his meals."

His mother wanted to be better than other people.

She didn't like her gift.

She wanted all the money at the same time.

Englis
CULT

British
in uppe
often st
other s
tutor, o
began
they att
schools
reason
worry a

Note how this student used the following symbols:

✓ marks a place where something is made clear or understandable

? marks where something is not understood or is confusing

! marks a surprising or interesting place in the text

Also notice how one word is circled, *writhed*. This word was marked by the student for her Personal Word List.

THE LANGUAGE OF LITERATURE

THE *InterActive*
READER™ PLUS
for English Learners

McDougal Littell
A HOUGHTON MIFFLIN COMPANY
Evanston, Illinois • Boston • Dallas

from

BEOWULF

Epic Poetry by the BEOWULF POET

Before You Read

Connect to Your Life

Whom do you consider a hero? Think about real and fictional heroes you admire and then complete the chart by listing the heroic characteristics of those figures.

CHARACTERISTICS OF A HERO	
1.	5.
2.	6.
3.	7.
4.	8.

Key to the Epic Poem

The epic poem *Beowulf,* composed by an unknown author, is the most famous of the early Germanic heroic poems in existence. The version of the poem that has survived was recorded sometime between the eighth and tenth centuries. This epic recounts the heroic conquests of the great warrior Beowulf, defender of the Danes. It was first recited and performed before an audience. The performers were poet-singers called scops (pronounced "shopes"). In the evenings and on special days, people would gather and listen to the scops chant the tale of Beowulf while accompanying themselves on the harp.

Reading Tips

Beowulf is an exciting story told in the form of an **epic poem,** a long narrative poem about a hero. Some parts may be hard to follow, however. The following strategies may help:

- The poem has long sentences that often end in the middle of a line. Try to read the poem one sentence at a time. Also, make use of semicolons and colons as rest stops along the way. Such punctuation marks can help you to divide the sentences into smaller chunks of meaning.

- The names will probably be unfamiliar. Make a list of the **main characters** and their relationship to one another.

As the epic poem begins...

- Hrothgar, king of the Danes, and his warriors listen to poets sing and play the harp.

- The monster Grendel hates the sounds of rejoicing and merriment coming from Herot.

from

BEOWULF

PREVIEW Beowulf is the hero celebrated in this long poem written in England many centuries ago, probably about 700 or 800 A.D. Beowulf is a powerful warrior of the Geats (gēts or gā-əts), a people from what is now Sweden. He is known for his bravery and almost superhuman deeds of strength. When he hears that the neighboring king of the Danes and his men are being terrorized by a vicious monster, the great warrior takes up the challenge. The tales about Beowulf were recited by poets for many years. By the time they were written in the form of an epic, Beowulf was a symbol for the heroic qualities most admired in early England.

> **FOCUS**
> In this section the poet introduces the monster Grendel. He also describes life in the mead hall, a large wooden building where warriors gathered for feasting and entertainment.
> **MARK IT UP** Underline words and phrases that tell what Grendel is like. An example is highlighted.

Hrothgar (hrôth′gär′) is king of the Danes. He has built a wonderful mead hall called Herot (hĕr′ət). As this selection opens, the monster Grendel invades the mead hall, bringing death and destruction.

GRENDEL

A powerful monster, living down
In the darkness, growled in pain, impatient
As day after day the music rang
Loud in that hall, the harp's rejoicing

Use this guide for help with unfamiliar words
and difficult passages.

Reading Tip

This selection is especially challenging
because of the long descriptive sentences
and irregular line breaks. As you read, try
to paraphrase each sentence.

More About...

THE DANES The tribe of Danes living in
Denmark were among several northern
European peoples who came to be known
as Vikings.

4 **harp's rejoicing:** This harp was a small,
hand-held stringed instrument. The poets of
the time played their harps as they told their
stories.

5 Call and the poet's clear songs, sung
Of the ancient beginnings of us all, recalling
The Almighty making the earth, shaping
These beautiful plains marked off by oceans,
Then proudly setting the sun and moon
10 To glow across the land and light it;
The corners of the earth were made lovely with trees
And leaves, made quick with life, with each
Of the nations who now move on its face. And then
As now warriors sang of their pleasure:
15 So Hrothgar's men lived happy in his hall
Till the monster stirred, that demon, that fiend,
Grendel, who haunted the moors, the wild
Marshes, and made his home in a hell
Not hell but earth. He was spawned in that slime,
20 Conceived by a pair of those monsters born
Of Cain, murderous creatures banished
By God, punished forever for the crime
Of Abel's death. The Almighty drove
Those demons out, and their exile was bitter,
25 Shut away from men; they split
Into a thousand forms of evil—spirits
And fiends, goblins, monsters, giants,
A brood forever opposing the Lord's
Will, and again and again defeated.

Pause & Reflect

FOCUS
These lines describe Grendel's first attack on the
hall of Hrothgar. As you read, look for what Grendel
does and what Hrothgar fears.

30 Then, when darkness had dropped, Grendel
Went up to Herot, wondering what the warriors
Would do in that hall when their drinking was done.
He found them sprawled in sleep, suspecting
Nothing, their dreams undisturbed. The monster's
35 Thoughts were as quick as his greed or his claws:
He slipped through the door and there in the silence
Snatched up thirty men, smashed them
Unknowing in their beds and ran out with their bodies,

6–12 The poet sings about the creation of the world.

17 moors (mŏŏrz): wide, open regions with patches of bog.

19 spawned in that slime: born in that dark, horrible den of the monsters.

21 Cain: the eldest son of Adam and Eve. According to the Bible (Genesis 4), he murdered his younger brother Abel. Cain was condemned to wander as an outcast. In lines 20–29, his descendents are pictured as evil creatures forever cut off from God and from humans.

Reading Tip

Draw a slash mark between each sentence as you read. Then if you need to reread a section, it will be easier to find where sentences begin and end.

What Does It Mean?

On its face means "on its surface." The poet is describing the people who live on Earth.

English Learner Support
VOCABULARY

Homonym *Stirred* has two meanings. Here, it means "came awake" or "moved around." It can also mean "mixed with a spoon."

Pause & Reflect

Look at the words and phrases that you underlined as you read. What kind of creature is Grendel? **(Make Judgments)**

_____

_____

_____

_____

As the epic poem continues...

- While the Danes sleep, Grendel sneaks into Herot and kills thirty warriors.
- He returns the next night and kills more warriors.
- The warriors leave Herot.

The blood dripping behind him, back
40   To his lair, delighted with his night's slaughter.
        At daybreak, with the sun's first light, they saw
How well he had worked, and in that gray morning
Broke their long feast with tears and <u>laments</u>
For the dead. Hrothgar, their lord, sat joyless
45   In Herot, a mighty prince mourning
The fate of his lost friends and companions,
Knowing by its tracks that some demon had torn
His followers apart. He wept, fearing
The beginning might not be the end. And that night
50   Grendel came again, so set
On murder that no crime could ever be enough,
No savage assault quench his lust
For evil. Then each warrior tried
To escape him, searched for rest in different
55   Beds, as far from Herot as they could find,
Seeing how Grendel hunted when they slept.
Distance was safety; the only survivors
Were those who fled him. Hate had triumphed.

Pause & Reflect

FOCUS

Read on to learn how much power Grendel has over Hrothgar and his men.

MARK IT UP As you read, underline passages that describe the terrible effects of Grendel's war on the Danes.

So Grendel ruled, fought with the righteous,
60   One against many, and won; so Herot
Stood empty, and stayed deserted for years,
Twelve winters of grief for Hrothgar, king
Of the Danes, sorrow heaped at his door
By hell-forged hands. His misery leaped
65   The seas, was told and sung in all
Men's ears: how Grendel's hatred began,
How the monster <u>relished</u> his savage war

WORDS
TO
KNOW

lament (lə-měnt′) *n.* an audible expression of grief; wail
relish (rěl′ĭsh) *v.* to enjoy keenly

8

40 lair: the den of a wild animal.

52–53 No savage . . . evil: not even the most vicious, brutal attacks on the warriors would be enough to satisfy Grendel's thirst for violence and death.

64 hell-forged hands: hands made in hell. Think about what this phrase suggests about Grendel.

64–65 His misery . . . seas: Hrothgar's grief was so great that people in countries across the seas heard about it.

☑ **Reading Check**

Why is Hrothgar "joyless"?

Pause & Reflect

✎ MARK IT UP **1.** In lines 48–49, the poet says Hrothgar fears that the first attack might not be the last one. Underline the lines that tell whether Hrothgar's fears are proved true. **(Clarify)**

2. How do you think life will change for Hrothgar and his warriors now that Grendel is on the loose? **(Predict)**

_____

_____

_____

_____

As the epic poem continues . . .

• Grendel continues to murder and destroy for twelve years.

• The Danes are powerless to stop him.

• The Danes make offerings to their gods but receive no help.

On the Danes, keeping the bloody feud
Alive, seeking no peace, offering
70 No truce, accepting no settlement, no price
In gold or land, and paying the living
For one crime only with another. No one
Waited for reparation from his plundering claws:
That shadow of death hunted in the darkness,
75 Stalked Hrothgar's warriors, old
And young, lying in waiting, hidden
In mist, invisibly following them from the edge
Of the marsh, always there, unseen.
   So mankind's enemy continued his crimes,
80 Killing as often as he could, coming
Alone, bloodthirsty and horrible. Though he lived
In Herot, when the night hid him, he never
Dared to touch king Hrothgar's glorious
Throne, protected by God—God,
85 Whose love Grendel could not know. But Hrothgar's
Heart was bent. The best and most noble
Of his council debated remedies, sat
In secret sessions, talking of terror
And wondering what the bravest of warriors could do.
90 And sometimes they sacrificed to the old stone gods,
Made heathen vows, hoping for Hell's
Support, the Devil's guidance in driving
Their affliction off. That was their way,
And the heathen's only hope, Hell
95 Always in their hearts, knowing neither God
Nor His passing as He walks through our world,
   the Lord
Of Heaven and earth; their ears could not hear
His praise nor know His glory. Let them
Beware, those who are thrust into danger,
100 Clutched at by trouble, yet can carry no solace
In their hearts, cannot hope to be better! Hail
To those who will rise to God, drop off
Their dead bodies and seek our Father's peace!

Pause & Reflect

WORDS
TO
KNOW

affliction (ə-flĭk'shən) *n.* a cause of pain or distress

73 reparation: something done to make up for loss or suffering. In the society of Beowulf's time, someone who killed another person was expected to make a payment to the victim's family as a way of restoring peace.

84 The mention of God here shows that the poet was a Christian. The Danes at the time of the story were not Christians.

84–85 Grendel's inability to know God's love indicates that he is completely evil.

86 bent: overcome with grief and anguish.

91 heathen (hē′thən): pagan; non-Christian. The characters in the poem still worship "the old stone gods."

93–101 The poet interrupts the story to describe the situation of the pagans. Their old gods give them no comfort **(solace)** in danger.

More About . . .

CHRISTIAN BELIEFS The author of *Beowulf* was a Christian and judged the polytheism (worship of many gods) of the Danes as evil. When the Danes pray and sacrifice to their stone gods to help them defeat Grendel, the author interprets their actions as a plea for the Devil's guidance.

What Does It Mean?

Drop off / their dead bodies and seek our Father's peace means people's souls rise to Heaven to be with God after they die.

Pause & Reflect

1. Look at the passages that you underlined as you read. **Summarize** the power Grendel has over the Danes.

_____

_____

_____

_____

READ ALOUD **2.** Read aloud the boxed passage on page 10. What one part of Herot is protected from Grendel's destruction? **(Clarify)**

_____

_____

MARK IT UP **3.** Are Hrothgar's warriors able to find ways to combat Grendel? *Yes/No* Circle lines on pages 8 and 10 that give support for your conclusion. **(Draw Conclusions)**

from **Beowulf** **11**

FOCUS

Beowulf hears how Grendel attacks the Danes. He sets out with 14 of his men to help them.

MARK IT UP As you read, underline words and phrases that tell what Beowulf is like.

BEOWULF

So the living sorrow of Healfdane's son
105 Simmered, bitter and fresh, and no wisdom
Or strength could break it: that agony hung
On king and people alike, harsh
And unending, violent and cruel, and evil.
    In his far-off home Beowulf, Higlac's
110 Follower and the strongest of the Geats—greater
And stronger than anyone anywhere in this world—
Heard how Grendel filled nights with horror
And quickly commanded a boat fitted out,
Proclaiming that he'd go to that famous king,
115 Would sail across the sea to Hrothgar,
Now when help was needed. None
Of the wise ones regretted his going, much
As he was loved by the Geats: the omens were good,
And they urged the adventure on. So Beowulf
120 Chose the mightiest men he could find,
The bravest and best of the Geats, fourteen
In all, and led them down to their boat;
He knew the sea, would point the prow
Straight to that distant Danish shore.

Beowulf and his men sail over the sea to the land of the Danes to offer help to Hrothgar. They are escorted by a Danish guard to Herot, where Wulfgar, one of Hrothgar's soldiers, tells the king of their arrival. Hrothgar knows of Beowulf and is ready to welcome the young prince and his men.

125   Then Wulfgar went to the door and addressed
The waiting seafarers with soldier's words:
    "My lord, the great king of the Danes, commands me

As the epic poem continues...

- Beowulf hears about Grendel.
- Beowulf gathers fourteen of his strongest warriors and goes to help the Danes.
- Beowulf tells Hrothgar of his past adventures and victories.

104–105 So the living . . . simmered: The deep grief of Hrothgar **(Healfdane's son)** over the loss of his men was with him constantly **(simmered).**

109–110 Higlac's follower: warrior loyal to Higlac (hĭg'lăk'), king of the Geats (and Beowulf's uncle).

English Learner Support
VOCABULARY

Idiom *Fitted out* means "equipped and made ready for the journey."

118 omens were good: signs in nature suggested that Beowulf would have success. People believed that they could tell the future by interpreting various aspects of nature **(omens).**

123 prow: the front part of a ship.

JOT IT DOWN **Reread Lines 116–119**

Did Beowulf's own people, the Geats, support his trip to help Hrothgar? **(Clarify)**

_____

Reading Tip
Read the italicized text carefully. It summarizes what happens in the parts of the original poem that are not excerpted here.

To tell you that he knows of your noble birth
And that having come to him from over the open
130 Sea you have come bravely and are welcome.
Now go to him as you are, in your armor and helmets,
But leave your battle-shields here, and your spears,
Let them lie waiting for the promises your words
May make."
                    Beowulf arose, with his men
135 Around him, ordering a few to remain
With their weapons, leading the others quickly
Along under Herot's steep roof into Hrothgar's
Presence. Standing on that prince's own hearth,
Helmeted, the silvery metal of his mail shirt
140 Gleaming with a smith's high art, he greeted
The Danes' great lord:
                    "Hail, Hrothgar!
Higlac is my cousin and my king; the days
Of my youth have been filled with glory. Now
    Grendel's
Name has echoed in our land: sailors
145 Have brought us stories of Herot, the best
Of all mead-halls, deserted and useless when the moon
Hangs in skies the sun had lit,
Light and life fleeing together.
My people have said, the wisest, most knowing
150 And best of them, that my duty was to go to
    the Danes'
Great king. They have seen my strength for themselves,
Have watched me rise from the darkness of war,
Dripping with my enemies' blood. I drove
Five great giants into chains, chased
155 All of that race from the earth. I swam
In the blackness of night, hunting monsters
Out of the ocean, and killing them one
By one; death was my errand and the fate
They had earned. Now Grendel and I are called
160 Together, and I've come.

Pause & *Reflect*

139 mail shirt: flexible body armor made of metal links.

140 smith's high art: the skilled craft of a blacksmith (a person who makes objects from iron).

142 cousin: here, a general term for a relative. Beowulf is actually Higlac's nephew.

145–148 Herot . . . together: When the sunlight disappears and night falls, the warriors leave Herot because of Grendel.

What Does It Mean?

Wulfgar is asking the Geats to leave their weapons and shields outside until they are needed. The Danes are hoping the Geats will promise to fight Grendel.

What Does It Mean?

Here, *prince* is a general term for a ruler. Hrothgar is actually a king.

English Learner Support
VOCABULARY

Hearth The word *hearth* usually refers to a fireplace and the area right in front of it. Here, it means Hrothgar's home.

Pause & Reflect

1. Look back at the passages that you underlined as you read. Circle the words below that describe Beowulf. **(Infer)**

fearless	respected
hated	proud
strong	sneaky

READ ALOUD 2. Read aloud the boxed passage on page 14, in which Beowulf tells about his past deeds. What victories has he won? **(Clarify)**

_____

_____

_____

_____

FOCUS
Beowulf announces his plans for fighting Grendel,
and Hrothgar responds to Beowulf's offer. As you
read, look for the strengths each leader has.

>   Grant me, then,
> Lord and protector of this noble place,
> A single request! I have come so far,
> Oh shelterer of warriors and your people's
>   loved friend,
> That this one favor you should not refuse me—
>
> 165 That I, alone and with the help of my men,
> May purge all evil from this hall. I have heard,
> Too, that the monster's scorn of men
> Is so great that he needs no weapons and fears none.
> Nor will I. My lord Higlac
>
> 170 Might think less of me if I let my sword
> Go where my feet were afraid to, if I hid
> Behind some broad linden shield: my hands
> Alone shall fight for me, struggle for life
> Against the monster. God must decide
>
> 175 Who will be given to death's cold grip.
> Grendel's plan, I think, will be
> What it has been before, to invade this hall
> And gorge his belly with our bodies. If he can,
> If he can. And I think, if my time will have come,
>
> 180 There'll be nothing to mourn over, no corpse to
>   prepare
> For its grave: Grendel will carry our bloody
> Flesh to the moors, crunch on our bones
> And smear torn scraps of our skin on the walls
> Of his den. No, I expect no Danes
>
> 185 Will fret about sewing our shrouds, if he wins.
> And if death does take me, send the hammered
> Mail of my armor to Higlac, return
> The inheritance I had from Hrethel, and he
> From Wayland. Fate will unwind as it must!"

WORDS
TO
KNOW

purge (pûrj) v. to cleanse or purify
gorge (gôrj) v. to stuff with food

16

As the epic poem continues...

• Beowulf asks Hrothgar's permission to fight Grendel.

• Beowulf says that since Grendel fights without weapons, so will he.

• Hrothgar invites the Geats to a feast in their honor.

English Learner Support

CULTURE

Heroism One of the characteristics of a hero is that he or she is fair and brave. Here, Beowulf wants his fight with Grendel to be fair, so he will fight without weapons. He is also very brave to fight the monster.

✔ **Reading Check**

Who will decide what happens in the fight with Grendel?

172 linden shield: shield made from the wood of a linden tree.

172–174 Beowulf insists on fighting Grendel without weapons.

179 if my time . . . come: if it is time for me to die; a reference to a person's death being controlled by fate. Belief in fate was important to the people of Beowulf's time.

184–185 If Grendel wins, the Danes will not have to worry about making graveclothes **(shrouds)** for the bodies of Beowulf and his men. Grendel will eat up the warriors completely.

188 Hrethel (hrĕ*th*ʹəl): a former king of the Geats—Higlac's father and Beowulf's grandfather.

189 Wayland: a famous blacksmith and magician.

More About...

(WAYLAND) SMITH Wayland was a blacksmith who appears in many Northern European legends. The swords and armor he made were said to be magical, and heroes such as Beowulf often had weapons made by him.

190 Hrothgar replied, protector of the Danes:
"Beowulf, you've come to us in friendship,
    and because
Of the reception your father found at our court.
Edgetho had begun a bitter feud,
Killing Hathlaf, a Wulfing warrior:
195 Your father's countrymen were afraid of war,
If he returned to his home, and they turned him away.
Then he traveled across the curving waves
To the land of the Danes. I was new to the throne,
Then, a young man ruling this wide
200 Kingdom and its golden city: Hergar,
My older brother, a far better man
Than I, had died and dying made me,
Second among Healfdane's sons, first
In this nation. I bought the end of Edgetho's
205 Quarrel, sent ancient treasures through the ocean's
Furrows to the Wulfings; your father swore
He'd keep that peace. My tongue grows heavy,
And my heart, when I try to tell you what Grendel
Has brought us, the damage he's done, here
210 In this hall. You see for yourself how much smaller
Our ranks have become, and can guess what we've lost
To his terror. Surely the Lord Almighty
Could stop his madness, smother his lust!
How many times have my men, glowing
215 With courage drawn from too many cups
Of ale, sworn to stay after dark
And stem that horror with a sweep of their swords.
And then, in the morning, this mead-hall glittering
With new light would be drenched with blood, the
    benches
220 Stained red, the floors, all wet from that fiend's
Savage assault—and my soldiers would be fewer
Still, death taking more and more.

190–207 Hrothgar tells about his relationship to Beowulf's father. Hrothgar helped Edgetho (ĕj'thō) resolve a feud so that Edgetho could return to his homeland.

194 Wulfing: a member of another tribe.

205–206 ocean's furrows: the long, low spaces between two waves that look like the rows plowed in a field **(furrows).**

Inheriting the Kingdom The highlighted words refer to the idea that the eldest son inherits the kingdom. The phrase can be rewritten in this way: "I was the second son. But when my elder brother died, I became king."

What Does It Mean?

In lines 204–205, the poet is saying that Hrothgar paid the *wergild,* or price, for Hathlaf's death. *Wergild* was an amount of money paid to a victim's family by the murderer. The purpose of *wergild* was to stop blood feuds. Once the *wergild* was paid, there was no need for revenge, and Edgetho could return home.

Figurative Language In lines 215–216, the poet is saying that when the men got drunk on ale, they thought they could face Grendel.

 **Reading Check**

Who is the fiend mentioned in line 220?

But to table, Beowulf, a banquet in your honor:
Let us toast your victories, and talk of the future."
225   Then Hrothgar's men gave places to the Geats,
Yielded benches to the brave visitors
And led them to the feast. The keeper of the mead
Came carrying out the carved flasks,
And poured that bright sweetness. A poet
230 Sang, from time to time, in a clear
Pure voice. Danes and visiting Geats
Celebrated as one, drank and rejoiced.

Pause & Reflect

FOCUS

When Grendel makes his next attack on Herot,
Beowulf is there to meet him.
MARK IT UP As you read, circle the lines that tell
how Grendel gets trapped when he gets to Herot.

*After the banquet, Hrothgar and his followers leave Herot,
and Beowulf and his warriors remain to spend the night.
Beowulf repeats his intent to fight Grendel without a sword.
While his followers sleep, he lies waiting, eager for Grendel
to appear.*

THE BATTLE WITH GRENDEL

      Out from the marsh, from the foot of misty
Hills and bogs, bearing God's hatred,
235 Grendel came, hoping to kill
Anyone he could trap on this trip to high Herot.
He moved quickly through the cloudy night,
Up from his swampland, sliding silently
Toward that gold-shining hall. He had visited
    Hrothgar's
240 Home before, knew the way—
But never, before nor after that night,
Found Herot defended so firmly, his reception
So harsh. He journeyed, forever joyless,
Straight to the door, then snapped it open,
245 Tore its iron fasteners with a touch
And rushed angrily over the threshold.

227 mead: an alcoholic drink made of honey and water.

228 carved flasks: richly decorated metal pitchers or large cups.

Toast Here, *toast* means "to take a drink in praise of someone or something."

Pause **&** **Reflect**

What do you learn about Hrothgar and Beowulf as leaders? **(Infer)**

Hrothgar_____

_____ .

Beowulf _____

_____ .

As the epic poem continues . . .

• That night, Grendel leaves his marsh and goes to Herot.

• He breaks into Herot, where Beowulf is waiting.

Alliteration Writers use alliteration, or the repetition of consonant sounds, for dramatic effect. Notice the effect of alliteration in the highlighted words. The *s* sound makes Grendel seem to slither like a snake. Look for other examples of alliteration as you read.

246 threshold: the strip of wood or stone at the bottom of a doorway.

He strode quickly across the inlaid
Floor, snarling and fierce: his eyes
Gleamed in the darkness, burned with a gruesome
250 Light. Then he stopped, seeing the hall
Crowded with sleeping warriors, stuffed
With rows of young soldiers resting together.
And his heart laughed, he relished the sight,
Intended to tear the life from those bodies
255 By morning; the monster's mind was hot
With the thought of food and the feasting his belly
Would soon know. But fate, that night, intended
Grendel to gnaw the broken bones
Of his last human supper. Human
260 Eyes were watching his evil steps,
Waiting to see his swift hard claws.
Grendel snatched at the first Geat
He came to, ripped him apart, cut
His body to bits with powerful jaws,
265 Drank the blood from his veins and bolted
Him down, hands and feet; death
And Grendel's great teeth came together,
Snapping life shut. Then he stepped to another
Still body, clutched at Beowulf with his claws,
270 Grasped at a strong-hearted wakeful sleeper
—And was instantly seized himself, claws
Bent back as Beowulf leaned up on one arm.
　　　　That shepherd of evil, guardian of crime,
Knew at once that nowhere on earth
275 Had he met a man whose hands were harder;
His mind was flooded with fear—but nothing
Could take his talons and himself from that tight
Hard grip. Grendel's one thought was to run
From Beowulf, flee back to his marsh and hide there:
280 This was a different Herot than the hall he
　　had emptied.
But Higlac's follower remembered his final
Boast and, standing erect, stopped

WORDS
TO
KNOW

talon (tăl′ən) *n.* a claw

247–248 inlaid floor: wooden floor made of pieces of wood fitted together in a beautiful pattern.

249 gruesome: terrifying and horrible.

253 relished: took great pleasure in.

257–259 But fate . . . supper: The poet reminds his audience that the outcome of this struggle is determined by fate.

280 Up to this point Grendel has killed his human victims easily.

281–282 Higlac's follower . . . Boast: Beowulf (**Higlac's follower**) will fight Grendel with his bare hands, as he promised.

 READ ALOUD **Lines 250–257**

As you read these lines aloud, try to express Grendel's feelings about the possibility of feasting on the warriors.

Reading Tip

The Beowulf poet doesn't always use the names of characters when referring to them. For example, Grendel is "that shepherd of evil" and Beowulf is "Higlac's follower." In the following chart, list the phrases that refer to Beowulf and Grendel.

Phrases That Refer to Beowulf	Phrases That Refer to Grendel

English Learner Support
VOCABULARY

Idiom *Bolted / Him down* means that Grendel swallowed the man whole.

The monster's flight, fastened those claws
In his fists till they cracked, clutched Grendel

285 Closer. The infamous killer fought
For his freedom, wanting no flesh but retreat,
Desiring nothing but escape; his claws
Had been caught, he was trapped. That trip to Herot
Was a miserable journey for the writhing monster!

Pause & Reflect

FOCUS
In this section, the poet describes the battle
between Grendel and Beowulf. As you read, try to
picture the sights and sounds of the battle.

290   The high hall rang, its roof boards swayed,
And Danes shook with terror. Down
The aisles the battle swept, angry
And wild. Herot trembled, wonderfully
Built to withstand the blows, the struggling
295 Great bodies beating at its beautiful walls;
Shaped and fastened with iron, inside
And out, artfully worked, the building
Stood firm. Its benches rattled, fell
To the floor, gold-covered boards grating
300 As Grendel and Beowulf battled across them.
Hrothgar's wise men had fashioned Herot
To stand forever; only fire,
They had planned, could shatter what such skill
   had put
Together, swallow in hot flames such splendor
305 Of ivory and iron and wood. Suddenly
The sounds changed, the Danes started
In new terror, cowering in their beds as the terrible
Screams of the Almighty's enemy sang
In the darkness, the horrible shrieks of pain
310 And defeat, the tears torn out of Grendel's
Taut throat, hell's captive caught in the arms

WORDS TO KNOW	**infamous** (ĭn'fə-məs) *adj.* having a bad reputation; notorious. **writhing** (rī'thĭng) *adj.* twisting and turning in pain **writhe** v. **cowering** (kou'ə-rĭng) *adj.* cringing in fear **cower** v. **taut** (tôt) *adj.* pulled tight

301–305 **Hrothgar's . . . wood:** Hrothgar's men had built Herot so well that its strength and beauty would not be damaged by anything except a raging fire.

308 **Almighty's enemy:** This is Grendel. The "Almighty" refers to the Christian God.

Pause & **Reflect**

1. What does Grendel think will happen when he gets to Herot? **(Clarify)**

_____

_____

_____

_____

2. Circle the words below that describe Grendel's reactions to Beowulf. **(Infer)**

afraid   brave

confident   cowardly

As the epic poem continues . . .

• Beowulf and Grendel fight.

Reading Tip

Read the boxed lines aloud. Try to put drama into your voice to express the excitement of the battle and how it affects Herot.

✔ Reading Check

What was the only thing people thought could destroy Herot?

Of him who of all the men on earth
Was the strongest.

          That mighty protector of men
Meant to hold the monster till its life
315 Leaped out, knowing the fiend was no use
To anyone in Denmark. All of Beowulf's
Band had jumped from their beds, ancestral
Swords raised and ready, determined
To protect their prince if they could. Their courage
320 Was great but all wasted: they could hack at Grendel
From every side, trying to open
A path for his evil soul, but their points
Could not hurt him, the sharpest and hardest iron
Could not scratch at his skin, for that sin-stained
   demon
325 Had bewitched all men's weapons, laid spells
That blunted every mortal man's blade.
And yet his time had come, his days
Were over, his death near; down
To hell he would go, swept groaning and helpless
330 To the waiting hands of still worse fiends.
Now he discovered—once the afflictor
Of men, tormentor of their days—what it meant
To feud with Almighty God: Grendel
Saw that his strength was deserting him, his claws
335 Bound fast, Higlac's brave follower tearing at
His hands. The monster's hatred rose higher,
But his power had gone. He twisted in pain,
And the bleeding sinews deep in his shoulder
Snapped, muscle and bone split
340 And broke. The battle was over, Beowulf
Had been granted new glory: Grendel escaped,
But wounded as he was could flee to his den,
His miserable hole at the bottom of the marsh,
Only to die, to wait for the end
345 Of all his days.

Pause & *Reflect*

312–313 him . . . strongest: Beowulf.

313 protector of men: Beowulf.

325–326 laid spells . . . blade: Grendel had cast magic powers over men's swords so that the weapons would be useless when used against him.

327 his time had come: the time for him to die; a reference to the control of fate over a person's destiny.

331–332 afflictor . . . tormentor: one who brings great harm and suffering.

338 sinews (sĭn′yo͞oz): the tendons that connect muscles to bones.

English Learner Support

LANGUAGE

Figurative Language *Till its life / Leaped out* means "until he died."

What Does It Mean?

By referring to *a path for his evil soul,* the poet is saying that the warriors were trying to kill Grendel. They were trying to cut him so badly that his soul would find a way out of his body, meaning that he would die.

Pause & Reflect

1. List four details that describe some of the sights and sounds of the battle between Beowulf and Grendel. **(Visualize)**

   _____

   _____

   _____

   _____

2. Are Beowulf's men able to help him in the battle with Grendel? *Yes/No*, because _____

   _____

   _____

   (Draw Conclusions)

   READ ALOUD 3. Read aloud the boxed passage on page 26, which describes the end of the battle. Who wins? _____
   What happens to Grendel when the battle is over? **(Clarify)**

   _____

   _____

   _____

The poet next describes the celebrations following
Beowulf's victory over Grendel. As you read, try to
imagine what the Danes must have felt like.

And after that bloody
Combat the Danes laughed with delight.
He who had come to them from across the sea,
Bold and strong-minded, had driven affliction
Off, purged Herot clean. He was happy,
350   Now, with that night's fierce work; the Danes
Had been served as he'd boasted he'd serve them;
        Beowulf,
A prince of the Geats, had killed Grendel,
Ended the grief, the sorrow, the suffering
Forced on Hrothgar's helpless people
355   By a bloodthirsty fiend. No Dane doubted
The victory, for the proof, hanging high
From the rafters where Beowulf had hung it, was the
        monster's
Arm, claw and shoulder and all.

        And then, in the morning, crowds surrounded
360   Herot, warriors coming to that hall
From faraway lands, princes and leaders
Of men hurrying to behold the monster's
Great staggering tracks. They gaped with no sense
Of sorrow, felt no regret for his suffering,
365   Went tracing his bloody footprints, his beaten
And lonely flight, to the edge of the lake
Where he'd dragged his corpselike way, doomed
And already weary of his vanishing life.
The water was bloody, steaming and boiling
370   In horrible pounding waves, heat
Sucked from his magic veins; but the swirling
Surf had covered his death, hidden
Deep in murky darkness his miserable
End, as hell opened to receive him.

WORDS
TO   **murky** (mur′kē) *adj.* cloudy; gloomy
KNOW

28

As the epic poem ends...

- The Danes celebrate Beowulf's defeat of Grendel.
- People travel from far away to see the evidence of Grendel's death.
- The Danes return to Herot and retell the story of Beowulf's heroic actions.

What Does It Mean?

Purged means "gotten rid of something." Herot is rid of Grendel's terror.

✏️ MARK IT UP   Reread Lines 355–358

What does Beowulf hang from the rafters as a trophy of his victory? Circle the words that tell you. **(Clarify)**

---

363 gaped: stared.

English Learner Support
LANGUAGE

Figurative Language In lines 370–371, the poet is saying that as Grendel died, a powerful heat escaped from his body.

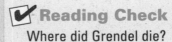
Reading Check

Where did Grendel die?

375　　　　Then old and young rejoiced, turned back
From that happy pilgrimage, mounted their
　　hard-hooved
Horses, high-spirited stallions, and rode them
Slowly toward Herot again, retelling
Beowulf's bravery as they jogged along.

380　And over and over they swore that nowhere
On earth or under the spreading sky
Or between the seas, neither south nor north,
Was there a warrior worthier to rule over men.
(But no one meant Beowulf's praise to belittle

385　Hrothgar, their kind and gracious king!)

　　　　And sometimes, when the path ran straight
　　and clear,
They would let their horses race, red
And brown and pale yellow backs streaming
Down the road. And sometimes a proud old soldier

390　Who had heard songs of the ancient heroes
And could sing them all through, story after story,
Would weave a net of words for Beowulf's
Victory, tying the knot of his verses
Smoothly, swiftly, into place with a poet's

395　Quick skill, singing his new song aloud
While he shaped it, and the old songs as well. . . .

Pause & Reflect

WORDS
TO
KNOW

pilgrimage (pĭl′grə-mĭj) *n.* a journey to a sacred place or
　　with a lofty purpose

392–393 **weave a net . . . into place:** The poet's well-told story is compared to a handmade fishing net made skillfully with many carefully tied knots.

English Learner Support
VOCABULARY

Idiom *Could sing them all through* means "knew all the words."

Pause & Reflect

MARK IT UP **1.** What is the mood at Herot after the battle? Underline words and phrases on pages 28 and 30 that help you to identify that mood. **(Infer)**

_____

_____

2. If you had been one of Hrothgar's warriors, how would you have felt at the sight of Grendel's arm hanging from the rafters? **(Connect)**

_____

_____

_____

_____

READ ALOUD **3.** Read aloud the boxed passage on page 30. Who tells the story of Beowulf's victory over Grendel? **(Clarify)**

_____

_____

CHALLENGE

What is the main message about good and evil in these excerpts from **Beowulf?** Go back and review the excerpts. As you review, use one colored pencil or highlighter to mark passages that show ideas about good and a second color to mark passages that show ideas about evil. **(Analyze)**

Active Reading SkillBuilder

Making Judgments

To **make judgments** about a text, readers need to

- create a set of criteria, or standards, for evaluating a character or a piece of work
- look for any evidence in the text that fulfills the criteria
- compare the evidence with the criteria

Some common characteristics shared by many **epics** are listed below. These characteristics are criteria for judging whether or not a work is an epic. As you read this excerpt from *Beowulf,* record evidence of the presence or absence of the characteristics. Then answer the question below. One example has been done for you.

Criteria for an Epic Poem	Evidence in *Beowulf*
Actions of the hero often set the fate of a nation or group of people.	*Although not a Dane himself, Beowulf saves Denmark by killing Grendel.*
Hero performs courageous deeds.	
Plot has supernatural beings and events, and may involve a long, dangerous journey.	
The characters often give long, formal speeches.	
The poem reflects timeless values, such as courage and honor.	
The poem treats universal ideas such as good and evil, life and death.	

In your judgment, is *Beowulf* a typical epic? Explain your reasoning, based on what you have read so far.

_____

_____

_____

_____

_____

Literary Analysis SkillBuilder

Alliteration

Alliteration is the repetition of consonant sounds at the beginning of words. Poets and writers use alliteration to add emphasis and rhythm to a text. Alliteration can emphasize an image, a mood, or an idea in a poem.

Find examples of alliteration in the *Beowulf* excerpts. Work with a partner to figure out what is emphasized by the alliteration. One example has been done for you.

Alliteration	Image, Mood, Idea Emphasized
Of ale, sworn to stay after dark And stem that horror with a sweep of their swords. (lines 216–217)	The s sound gives a sense of action, and the st of stay and stem emphasizes forcefulness and determination.

Words to Know SkillBuilder

Words to Know

affliction	gorge	livid*	pilgrimage	talon
cowering	infamous	loathsome*	purge	taut
fetter*	lament	murky	relish	writhing

Use words from the word list to fill in the blanks below. Use a word only once.

1. The lake's reflection usually creates a glare, but now the surface is _____.

2. Sad sounds of his _____ show how much he regrets the tragedy.

3. When prey is scarce, a carnivore will _____ whenever it can.

4. The warriors agreed that the attack was hateful, but they carried out their _____ task.

5. A _____ that is too tight can cause pain and bruising.

6. The _____ and frightened beast sought a hiding place.

7. He thought his prey would be tasty, but he did not _____ it at all.

8. The monster clawed at trees with its _____.

9. The beast's prowling was like an _____ that would not end.

10. Where their armor did not protect them, they had _____ marks from the battle.

11. "That creature is _____ for his horrible deeds, but we shall defeat him!"

12. Injured warriors were _____ and calling out for help.

13. The young fighter knew that _____ bandages would help heal his wounds.

14. At dawn, the army made a _____ to a sacred place before they marched home.

15. The older ones said it is wise to _____ the battle from memory.

* These words appear later in *Beowulf.* You can use a dictionary to check the definitions. The words are also defined in the lesson for *Beowulf* found in ***The Language of Literature.***

from The Canterbury Tales

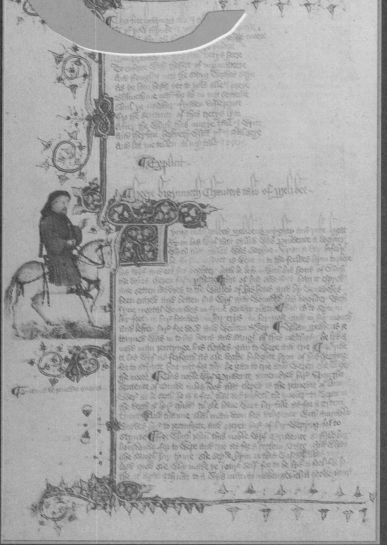

Geoffrey Chaucer

Before You Read

Connect to Your Life

This selection from the prologue of Chaucer's *The Canterbury Tales* provides detailed descriptions of various characters who are all traveling to the same destination. Who are some of the interesting people you have met while traveling either locally or to a more distant location?

Choose one person to describe below.

_____

_____

_____

_____

_____

_____

_____

_____

Key to the Poem

WHAT YOU NEED TO KNOW A *pilgrimage* is a long journey, usually to a holy place. Pilgrims go to holy places to ask for favors or forgiveness or to give thanks. Today, people of many religions still make pilgrimages to sites that are holy to them.

Reading Tips

A **prologue** is a spoken or written introduction to a work of literature. The excerpt from this prologue describes the **setting** of *The Canterbury Tales* and provides **character sketches** of several pilgrim-storytellers.

- At first, the language may seem difficult and old-fashioned. Just be patient and keep reading. Try reading some of the lines and passages aloud to listen to the rhythm and the rhyme. Give your ear time to get used to the verse.

- Pay close attention to marks of punctuation, such as commas and periods. Pause at the end of a line only if you come upon a mark of punctuation.

As the poem begins . . .

- It is spring, a time when many people set off on pilgrimages.
- The narrator joins a group traveling to Canterbury.

MARK IT UP KEEP TRACK

As you read, you can use these marks to keep track of your understanding.

✔ ..... I understand.

? ..... I don't understand this.

! ..... Interesting or surprising idea

from
The Canterbury Tales

Geoffrey Chaucer
Translated by Nevill Coghill

PREVIEW Geoffrey Chaucer (1340–1400) is considered one of the greatest poets of the English language. *The Canterbury Tales* is his masterpiece. It is the story of a group of people who travel together from London to the shrine of Saint Thomas à Becket in the city of Canterbury. These travelers tell stories to pass the time on the road. In the "Prologue," or introduction, the narrator describes these travelers. They come from various walks of life and gather in an inn.

FOCUS

The narrator describes the time of the year when pilgrimages, or journeys to holy places, usually occur. He then tells how he joined a group of pilgrims setting out for Canterbury.

MARK IT UP As you read, circle details that help you form impressions of the narrator. An example is highlighted on page 40.

The Prologue

When in April the sweet showers fall
And pierce the drought of March to the root, and all
The veins are bathed in liquor of such power
As brings about the engendering of the flower,
When also Zephyrus with his sweet breath   5
Exhales an air in every grove and heath
Upon the tender shoots, and the young sun
His half-course in the sign of the *Ram* has run,
And the small fowl are making melody
That sleep away the night with open eye   10
(So nature pricks them and their heart engages)

Use this guide for help with unfamiliar words and difficult passages.

Reading Tip

Because this is a poem, the word order is often changed to fit the rhythm and rhyme. For example, *When in April the sweet showers fall* could be written as "In April, when the sweet showers fall." Take your time in reading. If you have trouble understanding a long phrase or sentence, try breaking it into pieces and then summarizing.

 **Reading Check**

In what month does this story take place?

What Does It Mean?

The engendering of means "the blooming of" or "the birth of."

English Learner Support

VOCABULARY

Fowl *Fowl* are birds.

5 Zephyrus (zĕf′ər-əs): the Greek god of the west wind (the blowing of which is viewed as a sign of spring).

8 the Ram: Aries—one of the 12 groups of stars through which the sun appears to move in the course of the year. The sun completes its passage through Aries in mid-April.

Then people long to go on pilgrimages
And palmers long to seek the stranger strands
Of far-off saints, hallowed in sundry lands,
And specially, from every shire's end
15 Of England, down to Canterbury they wend
To seek the holy blissful martyr, quick
To give his help to them when they were sick.

        It happened in that season that one day
20 In Southwark, at *The Tabard,* as I lay
Ready to go on pilgrimage and start
For Canterbury, most devout at heart,
At night there came into that hostelry
Some nine and twenty in a company
25 Of sundry folk happening then to fall
In fellowship, and they were pilgrims all
That towards Canterbury meant to ride.
The rooms and stables of the inn were wide;
They made us easy, all was of the best.
30 And, briefly, when the sun had gone to rest,
I'd spoken to them all upon the trip
And was soon one with them in fellowship,
Pledged to rise early and to take the way
To Canterbury, as you heard me say.

35   But none the less, while I have time and space,
Before my story takes a further pace,
It seems a reasonable thing to say
What their condition was, the full array
Of each of them, as it appeared to me,
40 According to profession and degree,
And what apparel they were riding in;
And at a Knight I therefore will begin.

Pause & **Reflect**

13 **palmers:** people journeying to religious shrines; pilgrims; **strands:** shores. .

14 **sundry** (sŭn'drē): various.

15 **shire's:** county's.

17 **martyr:** St. Thomas à Becket. He was the archbishop of Canterbury who was murdered in his own cathedral in 1170. Three years later, Becket was declared a saint by the Roman Catholic Church.

20 **Southwark** (sŭ*th*'ərk)**:** in Chaucer's day, a town just south of London (now part of the city itself). The Tabard was an actual inn in Southwark.

23 **hostelry** (hŏs'təl-rē)**:** inn.

27 The route from London to Canterbury is 55 miles. The pilgrims will travel on horseback, and the journey will take three or four days.

35–41 Before describing the journey to Canterbury, the narrator tells about the pilgrims, or the travelers who will make the journey. He intends to tell the social position **(condition)** of each pilgrim and how each is dressed.

40 **degree:** rank.

What Does It Mean?

Wend means "to travel slowly, in a wandering way."

English Learner Support
LANGUAGE

Word Order *Nine and twenty* is another way of saying the number twenty-nine.

What Does It Mean?

Apparel means "clothing."

Pause & Reflect

1. Review the details you circled as you read. Then imagine you are one of the 29 characters at the Tabard Inn. What are your impressions of the narrator? **(Evaluate)**

   _____

   _____

   _____

   _____

2. Travel in the Middle Ages was not as easy as travel today. Why might people want to make this journey in the spring? **(Infer)**

   _____

   _____

The narrator describes the Knight, a member of the
warrior class in the Middle Ages.
MARK IT UP   As you read, circle details that help you
understand the Knight's good qualities.

There was a *Knight,* a most distinguished man,
Who from the day on which he first began
45 To ride abroad had followed (chivalry,)
Truth, honor, generousness and courtesy.
He had done nobly in his sovereign's war
And ridden into battle, no man more,
As well in Christian as in heathen places,
50 And ever honored for his noble graces.

When we took Alexandria, he was there.
He often sat at table in the chair
Of honor, above all nations, when in Prussia.
In Lithuania he had ridden, and Russia,
55 No Christian man so often, of his rank.
When, in Granada, Algeciras sank
Under assault, he had been there, and in
North Africa, raiding Benamarin;
In Anatolia he had been as well
60 And fought when Ayas and Attalia fell,
For all along the Mediterranean coast
He had embarked with many a noble host.
In fifteen mortal battles he had been
And jousted for our faith at Tramissene
65 Thrice in the lists, and always killed his man.
This same distinguished knight had led the van
Once with the Bey of Balat, doing work
For him against another heathen Turk;
He was of sovereign value in all eyes.
70 And though so much distinguished, he was wise
And in his bearing modest as a maid.
He never yet a boorish thing had said
In all his life to any, come what might;
He was a true, a perfect gentle-knight.

75 Speaking of his equipment, he possessed
Fine horses, but he was not gaily dressed.

As the poem continues . . .
• The narrator describes the Knight.

45 chivalry (shǐvʹəl-rē)**:** the qualities regarded as the ideals by which knights should live. These qualities are listed in line 46.

More About . . .

(CHIVALRY) Chivalry was an ideal code of behavior for knights. In addition to the qualities listed on line 46, this code stressed loyalty, courage, and the defense of those who could not defend themselves. Chivalry also encouraged religious devotion, as this knight shows.

51 Alexandria: a city in Egypt, captured by European Christians in 1365. All the places named in lines 51–64 were scenes of conflicts. In these places, Christians in the Middle Ages battled Muslims and other non-Christian peoples.

English Learner Support

VOCABULARY

Homograph The word *sovereign* appears two times in this section of the poem. However, it has a different meaning in each place. On line 47, it refers to the king: his sovereign's war means "his king's war." On line 69, the word describes the value of the Knight. There, it means "the highest."

64 jousted: fought with a lance in an arranged battle against another knight.
65 thrice: three times; **lists:** fenced areas for jousting.
66 van: vanguard—the troops in front in an attack.
67 Bey of Balat: a Turkish ruler.

72 boorish: rude.

What Does It Mean?
Noble host means "great army."

He wore a fustian tunic stained and dark
With smudges where his armor had left mark;
Just home from service, he had joined our ranks
To do his pilgrimage and render thanks.

Pause & *Reflect*

FOCUS
The Squire and the Yeoman go with the Knight on his journey to Canterbury. Read to find out about these characters.

He had his son with him, a fine young *Squire*,
A lover and cadet, a lad of fire
With locks as curly as if they had been pressed.
He was some twenty years of age, I guessed,
In stature he was of a moderate length,
With wonderful agility and strength.
He'd seen some service with the cavalry
In Flanders and Artois and Picardy
And had done valiantly in little space
Of time, in hope to win his lady's grace.
He was embroidered like a meadow bright
And full of freshest flowers, red and white.
Singing he was, or fluting all the day;
He was as fresh as is the month of May.
Short was his gown, the sleeves were long and wide;
He knew the way to sit a horse and ride.
He could make songs and poems and recite,
Knew how to joust and dance, to draw and write.
He loved so hotly that till dawn grew pale
He slept as little as a nightingale.
Courteous he was, lowly and serviceable,
And carved to serve his father at the table.

There was a *Yeoman* with him at his side,
No other servant; so he chose to ride.
This Yeoman wore a coat and hood of green,

80

85

90

95

100

105

WORDS
TO
KNOW

agility (ə-jĭl´ĭ-tē) *n.* an ability to move quickly and easily; nimbleness

44

77 fustian (fŭs'chən)**:** a strong cloth made of linen and cotton.

81 Squire: a young man attending on and receiving training from a knight.
82 cadet: soldier in training.

88 Flanders and Artois (är-twä') and **Picardy** (pĭk'ər-dē)**:** areas in what is now Belgium and northern France.

99–100 The Squire, like many young people today, gets by on very little sleep. Nightingales sing all night long.

103 Yeoman (yō'mən)**:** a servant in a noble household; **him:** the Knight. The Yeoman is a common man in the service of the Knight. The Yeoman is skilled in the knowledge of the woods.

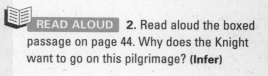

Pause **&** **Reflect**

1. Review the details you circled as you read. Then write a sentence to describe the Knight's good qualities. **(Summarize)**

_____

_____

READ ALOUD **2.** Read aloud the boxed passage on page 44. Why does the Knight want to go on this pilgrimage? **(Infer)**

_____

_____

As the poem continues . . .

• The narrator describes the Squire and the Yeoman.

✔ **Reading Check**

How is the Squire related to the Knight?

English Learner Support
VOCABULARY

Idiom When the narrator says that the Squire was *a lad of fire,* he means that he was passionate.

What Does It Mean?

Lowly and serviceable means that the Squire behaved humbly and served the Knight well.

And peacock-feathered arrows, bright and keen
And neatly sheathed, hung at his belt the while
—For he could dress his gear in yeoman style,
His arrows never drooped their feathers low—
110   And in his hand he bore a mighty bow.
His head was like a nut, his face was brown.
He knew the whole of woodcraft up and down.
A saucy brace was on his arm to ward
It from the bow-string, and a shield and sword
115   Hung at one side, and at the other slipped
A jaunty dirk, spear-sharp and well-equipped.
A medal of St. Christopher he wore
Of shining silver on his breast, and bore
A hunting-horn, well slung and burnished clean,
120   That dangled from a baldrick of bright green.
He was a proper forester, I guess.

Pause & *Reflect*

FOCUS

The narrator next introduces three characters who belong to the church in the Middle Ages. The first character is the Prioress, a nun in authority.

MARK IT UP As you read, circle details that help you get to know this character.

There also was a *Nun*, a Prioress,
Her way of smiling very simple and coy.
Her greatest oath was only "By St. Loy!"
125   And she was known as Madam Eglantyne.
And well she sang a service, with a fine
Intoning through her nose, as was most seemly,
And she spoke daintily in French, extremely,
After the school of Stratford-atte-Bowe;
130   French in the Paris style she did not know.
At meat her manners were well taught withal;
No morsel from her lips did she let fall,
Nor dipped her fingers in the sauce too deep;
But she could carry a morsel up and keep
135   The smallest drop from falling on her breast.

113 saucy: jaunty; stylish; **brace:** a leather arm-guard worn by archers.

116 dirk: small dagger.

117 St. Christopher: the patron saint of foresters and travelers.

120 baldrick: shoulder strap.

122 Prioress: a nun ranking just below the abbess (head) of a convent.

124 St. Loy: St. Eligius (known as St. Eloi in France).

129 Stratford-atte-Bowe: a town (now part of London) near the Prioress's convent.

131-135 In the Middle Ages, eating habits were different from those of today. When dining **(at meat)**, people would dip crusts of bread into a bowl, scoop up bits of food, and then bring the crusts to their mouths. The Prioress does these maneuvers to perfection.

131 withal: moreover.

English Learner Support
VOCABULARY

Archaic Words Today, a *forester* is a person who harvests trees. Here, it refers to someone who is comfortable in or lives in the forest.

Pause **&** Reflect

MARK IT UP   The Squire is young, lively, and love-struck. Underline details on page 44 that support this conclusion. **(Locate Details)**

As the poem continues . . .

• The narrator describes the Prioress.

For <u>courtliness</u> she had a special zest,
And she would wipe her upper lip so clean
That not a trace of grease was to be seen
Upon the cup when she had drunk; to eat,
140 She reached a hand <u>sedately</u> for the meat.
She certainly was very entertaining,
Pleasant and friendly in her ways, and straining
To counterfeit a courtly kind of grace,
A stately bearing fitting to her place,
145 And to seem dignified in all her dealings.
As for her sympathies and tender feelings,
She was so charitably solicitous
She used to weep if she but saw a mouse
Caught in a trap, if it were dead or bleeding.
150 And she had little dogs she would be feeding
With roasted flesh, or milk, or fine (white bread.)
And bitterly she wept if one were dead
Or someone took a stick and made it smart;
She was all sentiment and tender heart.
155 Her veil was gathered in a seemly way,
Her nose was elegant, her eyes glass-grey;
Her mouth was very small, but soft and red,
Her forehead, certainly, was fair of spread,
Almost a span across the brows, I own;
160 She was indeed by no means undergrown.
Her cloak, I noticed, had a graceful charm.
She wore a (coral) trinket on her arm,
A set of beads, the gaudies tricked in green,
Whence hung a golden brooch of brightest sheen
165 On which there first was graven a crowned A,
And lower, *Amor vincit omnia*.

Another *Nun*, the secretary at her cell,
Was riding with her, and *three Priests* as well.

Pause & Reflect

WORDS
TO
KNOW
courtliness (kôrt′lē-nǐs) *n.* refined behavior; elegance
sedately (sǐ-dāt′lē) *adv.* in a composed, dignified manner; calmly

147–154 The narrator describes the Prioress's great concern for animals. The narrator does not tell whether or not she has great concern for suffering people, such as the poor and the sick.

159 span: a unit of length equal to nine inches. A broad forehead was considered a sign of beauty in Chaucer's day.

163 gaudies: the larger beads in a set of prayer beads.

166 *Amor vincit omnia* (ä′môr wĭn′kĭt ôm′ nē-ə)**:** Latin for "Love conquers all things."

More About . . .
(**WHITE BREAD**) In the Middle Ages, most people ate brown, coarse bread made of rye and other grains and seeds. Only rich people could afford white bread made from highly refined flour.

English Learner Support
VOCABULARY

Smart When something *smarts,* it hurts. So, *made it smart* means "hurt it," not "made it intelligent."

More About . . .
(**CORAL**) During Chaucer's time, coral jewelry was considered to be a love charm.

Pause & Reflect

MARK IT UP **1.** Review the details you circled as you read. What details suggest that the Prioress considers herself high-class? Star these details. **(Infer)**

READ ALOUD **2.** Read aloud the boxed passage on page 48. Based on what you know about the Prioress, what kind of love do you think interests her? **(Draw Conclusions)**

_____

_____

_____

_____

FOCUS

The narrator next describes the Monk. Ideally,
monks lived apart from the world. They devoted
themselves to God through prayer, study, and work.
Monks were supposed to live simple and humble
lives. Read to find out whether or not the Monk
follows this ideal.

     A *Monk* there was, one of the finest sort

170   Who rode the country; hunting was his sport.

A manly man, to be an Abbot able;

Many a dainty horse he had in stable.

His bridle, when he rode, a man might hear

Jingling in a whistling wind as clear,

175   Aye, and as loud as does the chapel bell

Where my lord Monk was Prior of the cell.

The Rule of good St. Benet or St. Maur

As old and strict he tended to ignore;

He let go by the things of yesterday

180   And took the modern world's more spacious way.

He did not rate that text at a plucked hen

Which says that hunters are not holy men

And that a monk uncloistered is a mere

Fish out of water, flapping on the pier,

185   That is to say a monk out of his cloister.

That was a text he held not worth an oyster;

And I agreed and said his views were sound;

Was he to study till his head went round

Poring over books in cloisters? Must he toil

190   As Austin bade and till the very soil?

Was he to leave the world upon the shelf?

Let Austin have his labor to himself.

     This Monk was therefore a good man to horse;

Greyhounds he had, as swift as birds, to course.

195   Hunting a hare or riding at a fence

Was all his fun, he spared for no expense.

I saw his sleeves were garnished at the hand

With fine grey fur, the finest in the land,

And on his hood, to fasten it at his chin

200   He had a wrought-gold cunningly fashioned pin;

Into a lover's knot it seemed to pass.

His head was bald and shone like looking-glass;

As the poem continues . . .
- The narrator describes the Monk.

171 .**Abbot:** the head of a monastery.

172 **dainty:** excellent.

176 **Prior:** The Monk was also a Prior, or the male equivalent of a Prioress. In this case, as Prior he was the head of an offshoot of the main monastery.

177 **St. Benet . . . St. Maur:** St. Benedict of Nursia, who created an influential set of rules for monks' behavior. St. Maurus was one of St. Benedict's followers.

What Does It Mean?
He did not rate that text at a plucked hen means that the Monk valued the Benedictine Rule, the set of rules referred to in the Guide For Reading note (line 177), as much as a plucked chicken—meaning not very much.

185 **cloister:** monastery.

English Learner Support
LANGUAGE

Figure of Speech *A good man to horse* means that the Monk was a good horseback rider.

190 **Austin:** St. Augustine of Hippo, who taught that monks should do farm work. **bade:** commanded.

✔ **Reading Check**
What are the Monk's favorite activities?

194 **to course:** for hunting.

197 **garnished:** decorated.

What Does It Mean?
Looking-glass is an old-fashioned term for a mirror.

200 **cunningly:** skillfully.

So did his face, as if it had been greased.
He was a fat and <u>personable</u> priest;
205 His prominent eyeballs never seemed to settle.
They glittered like the flames beneath a kettle;
Supple his boots, his horse in fine condition.
He was a prelate fit for exhibition,
He was not pale like a tormented soul.
210 He liked a fat swan best, and roasted whole.
His palfrey was as brown as is a berry.

Pause & Reflect

FOCUS
Like the Prioress and the Monk, the Friar also belongs to the church. Friars were wandering preachers. They were supposed to teach people about Jesus and live good lives.
MARK IT UP As you read, circle details that help you to evaluate whether the Friar does what he should do.

There was a *Friar,* a wanton one and merry,
A Limiter, a very festive fellow.
In all Four Orders there was none so mellow,
215 So glib with gallant phrase and well-turned speech.
He'd fixed up many a marriage, giving each
Of his young women what he could afford her.
He was a noble pillar to his Order.
Highly beloved and intimate was he
220 With County folk within his boundary,
And city dames of honor and possessions;
For he was qualified to hear confessions,
Or so he said, with more than priestly scope;
He had a special license from the Pope.

WORDS
TO
KNOW

personable (pûr′sə-nə-bəl) *adj.* pleasing in behavior and appearance

52

208 prelate (prĕl'ĭt): high-ranking member of the clergy.

211 palfrey (pôl'frē): saddle horse.

212 Friar: a member of a religious group sworn to poverty and living on charitable donations; **wanton** (wŏn'tən): pleasure-loving.

213 Limiter: a friar licensed to beg for donations in a limited area.

214 Four Orders: the four groups of friars—Dominican, Franciscan, Carmelite, and Augustinian.

218 He was . . . Order: The sentence literally says that the Friar is a good and honorable member of his Order. However, the narrator really means the opposite of what he is saying. This is an example of verbal irony.

222 confessions: church rites in which people confess their sins to members of the clergy. These people usually had to do certain tasks, called penances, as a condition of the forgiveness. Only certain friars were allowed to hear confessions.

✔ **Reading Check**
What does the narrator think about the Monk?

***Pause* & Reflect**
✎ MARK IT UP Monks are often portrayed as lean men in simple robes. This Monk, however, does not look like a typical monk. Underline details on pages 50 and 52 that describe his appearance. **(Locate Details)**

As the poem ends . . .
• The narrator describes the Friar.

What Does It Mean?
Glib means "easy with" or "very good with."

225 Sweetly he heard his penitents at shrift
With pleasant absolution, for a gift.
He was an easy man in penance-giving
Where he could hope to make a decent living;
It's a sure sign whenever gifts are given
230 To a poor Order that a man's well shriven,
And should he give enough he knew in verity
The penitent repented in sincerity.
For many a fellow is so hard of heart
He cannot weep, for all his inward smart.
235 Therefore instead of weeping and of prayer
One should give silver for a poor Friar's care.
He kept his tippet stuffed with pins for curls,
And pocket-knives, to give to pretty girls.
And certainly his voice was gay and sturdy,
240 For he sang well and played the hurdy-gurdy.
At sing-songs he was champion of the hour.
His neck was whiter than a lily-flower
But strong enough to butt a bruiser down.
He knew the taverns well in every town
245 And every innkeeper and barmaid too
Better than lepers, beggars and that crew,
For in so eminent a man as he
It was not fitting with the dignity
Of his position, dealing with a scum
250 Of wretched lepers; nothing good can come
Of commerce with such slum-and-gutter dwellers,
But only with the rich and victual-sellers.
But anywhere a profit might accrue
Courteous he was and lowly of service too.
255 Natural gifts like his were hard to match.
He was the finest beggar of his batch,
And, for his begging-district, paid a rent;
His brethren did no poaching where he went.
For though a widow mightn't have a shoe,
260 So pleasant was his holy how-d'ye-do
He got his farthing from her just the same
Before he left, and so his income came
To more than he laid out. And how he romped,

WORDS
TO
KNOW

eminent (ĕm'ə-nənt) *adj.* standing out above others; high-ranking; prominent

accrue (ə-kroō') *v.* to come as gain; accumulate

225–226 he heard his penitents . . . for a gift: the Friar hears people (penitents) at confession (shrift), where they confess their sins. If they pay him, the Friar then grants them forgiveness (absolution) with few penances.

230 well shriven: completely forgiven through the rite of confession.
231 verity: truth.
232 penitent: one who confesses his or her sins and seeks forgiveness.

237 tippet: an extension of a hood or sleeve, used as a pocket.

240 hurdy-gurdy: a stringed musical instrument, similar to a lute, played by turning a crank while pressing down keys.

252 victual (vĭt'l): food.

258 His brethren . . . went: None of the other friars would dare to preach and beg in the Friar's district.
261 farthing: a coin of small value used in

Reading Check

What can people do to get absolution from the Friar?

More About . . .

(LEPERS) Lepers are people who have a very serious disease called leprosy. Leprosy causes the skin and parts of the body to rot and fall off. Throughout history, lepers have been greatly feared and were social outcasts. Although many clergy devoted their lives to caring for lepers, the friar thought it beneath him to associate himself with such "scum."

English Learner Support

LANGUAGE

Expression *How-d'ye-do* is a short version of the expression "How do you do?" It literally means "How are you?" but is usually just a greeting, like "Hello."

Just like a puppy! He was ever prompt

265 To arbitrate disputes on settling days
(For a small fee) in many helpful ways,
Not then appearing as your cloistered scholar
With threadbare habit hardly worth a dollar,
But much more like a Doctor or a Pope.

270 Of double-worsted was the semi-cope
Upon his shoulders, and the swelling fold
About him, like a bell about its mold
When it is casting, rounded out his dress.
He lisped a little out of wantonness

275 To make his English sweet upon his tongue.
When he had played his harp, or having sung,
His eyes would twinkle in his head as bright
As any star upon a frosty night.
This worthy's name was Hubert, it appeared.

Pause & Reflect

England until recent times.

262–263 his income . . . out: He took in
more money from begging than he had to
pay out in order to beg in that district.

265 settling days: days on which quarrels,
or disputes, were settled out of court. Friars
often acted as judges and charged for their
services, though forbidden by the church to
do so.

270 double-worsted (wŏŏs'tĭd)**:** a
strong, fairly costly fabric made from wool
yarn; **semi-cope:** a short cloak.

274 lisped out of wantonness: spoke in a
sweet way, prompted by lustful desires.

What Does It Mean?
Here, *Doctor* means a professor at a
university, not a medical doctor.

Pause & Reflect

1. Review the details you circled as you read.
Then cross out the phrase below that does
not apply to the Friar. **(Infer)**

   wears an expensive cloak

   takes care of lepers

   gets money even from the poor

   visits taverns

2. Who leads a better moral life, the Friar or the
Monk? Explain. **(Compare and Contrast)**

   _____
   _____
   _____
   _____.

CHALLENGE

Characterization is the way a writer develops a character's personality. A writer can use description of the character's appearance, presentation of the character's speech and actions, and presentation of how other characters relate to that character. Highlight some of the words and phrases that present the personalities of the characters you just met in *The Canterbury Tales.*

Active Reading SkillBuilder

Analyzing Characterization

Characterization is the means by which a writer develops a character's personality. A writer can describe the character's physical appearance and present his or her speech, thoughts, feelings, and actions. Use the chart below to record words and phrases in "The Prologue" that convey each character's personality. As you continue to read "The Prologue," create other charts for the characters you meet. An example is shown.

Character	Character's Appearance	What the Character Says, Thinks, or Does
Knight	*dressed in a stained tunic*	
Squire		
Nun		
Monk		
Friar		

Write words or phrases that describe the narrator's personality. _____

_____

_____

Literary Analysis SkillBuilder

Tone

The **tone** of a literary work expresses the writer's attitude toward the work's subject or characters. An **ironic** tone expresses an attitude toward a subject that is different from what is actually said. In "The Prologue," the narrator's descriptions are detached or understated when he is actually being critical. He may also say the opposite of what he really thinks. Find passages in "The Prologue" that reveal the narrator's tone toward the characters. Record them in the chart below. An example is shown.

Character	What Narrator Says	What Narrator Means
Friar	But anywhere a profit might accrue/ Courteous he was and lowly of service too. (lines 253–254)	He was a greedy flatterer.
Nun		
Monk		

Words to Know SkillBuilder

Words to Know

accrue   defer*   dispatch*   malady*   repine*
agility   diligent*   eminent   mode*   sedately
courtliness disdain*   frugal*   personable wield*

Fill in each set of blanks with the correct word from the Words to Know list.

1. elegant and refined manners

2. acrobat's necessity

3. ranking higher, standing out

4. timeliness and efficiency

5. the style, the fashion

6. to add on and therefore gain

7. so pleasant, easy to like

8. not wasteful of money

9. to express dissatisfaction

10. can lead to a doctor's appointment

11. gets the task done

12. no way to treat a good suggestion

13. to manage or command with skill

14. to put off to another time

15. calmly, steadily, not agitated

The boxed letters, when unscrambled, spell the title of a literary work. Write the name of its author below.

_____

*These words appear later in The Prologue to *The Canterbury Tales*. You can use a dictionary to check the definitions. These words are also defined in the lesson for The Prologue, found in **The Language of Literature.**

WILLIAM SHAKESPEARE

SONNET 29

SONNET 116

SONNET 130

Before You Read

Connect to Your Life

The three sonnets in this selection are about love. What does love mean to you? Write your personal definition of love on the lines below.

_____

_____

_____

_____

_____

_____

Key to the Sonnets

WHAT YOU NEED TO KNOW William Shakespeare (1564–1616) is considered to be the greatest English playwright and among the greatest of poets. Best known for his plays, he also wrote 154 sonnets. Sonnets are poems with 14 lines and a specific rhyme pattern. Each sonnet ends with a couplet, or a rhymed pair of lines. Shakespeare wrote about love—the usual topic for a sonnet—but also about time, change, and death.

PREVIEW Shakespeare wrote a large number of sonnets—154 in all. Most of them are love poems, in which he expresses a great variety of thoughts and feelings. The three sonnets that you will read illustrate that variety. The first one shows the joy that love can bring, and the second one offers a definition of true love. The third one makes fun of the exaggerations that poets sometimes use in describing love.

SONNET 29

WILLIAM SHAKESPEARE

FOCUS

In this sonnet, the speaker begins in a discouraged frame of mind. That changes, however, when he thinks of the person he loves.

MARK IT UP Underline words or phrases in lines 1–8 that describe the speaker's frustration with his life. An example is highlighted.

When in disgrace with Fortune and men's eyes
I all alone beweep my outcast state,[1]
And trouble deaf heaven with my bootless[2] cries,
And look upon myself and curse my fate,
Wishing me like to one more rich in hope,
Featur'd like him,[3] like him with friends possess'd,
Desiring this man's art,[4] and that man's scope,[5]
With what I most enjoy contented least;

5

---

1. **state:** condition.
2. **bootless:** useless.
3. **Featur'd like him:** with his looks—that is, handsome.
4. **art:** skill.
5. **scope:** intelligence.

Reading Tips

These poems are **sonnets,** which have 14 lines. The long sentences and unfamiliar language may give you some trouble at first.

- Read each poem several times—including once or twice aloud—to become more familiar with the words and sounds. After you reread each poem, answer the Pause and Reflect questions.

- Divide long sentences into smaller parts by making breaks wherever punctuation falls.

As the sonnet begins . . .

- The speaker tells about times when he doesn't like himself.

- He then describes the way he feels when he thinks of his beloved.

English Learner Support
LANGUAGE

Figurative Language The speaker says that heaven is *deaf* because he feels that no one hears his cries.

What Does It Mean?

Heaven's gate means "the morning sky."

Usage Here, *wealth* means "a lot of happiness," not "money."

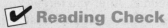

Reading Check

What makes the speaker feel happy again?

Pause & Reflect

1. Look at the passages that you underlined in lines 1–8. The speaker feels he is a (circle one) *success/failure* in life because

_____

_____

_____.

(Infer)

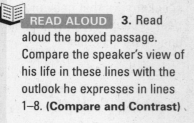

MARK IT UP 2. The speaker uses a comparison from nature to portray his change in mood. Circle the lines that express this comparison. **(Analyze Sensory Language)**

READ ALOUD 3. Read aloud the boxed passage. Compare the speaker's view of his life in these lines with the outlook he expresses in lines 1–8. **(Compare and Contrast)**

_____

_____

_____

_____

Yet in these thoughts myself almost despising,
Haply[6] I think on thee, and then my state,
Like to the lark[7] at break of day arising
From sullen[8] earth, sings hymns[9] at heaven's gate,
For thy sweet love rememb'red such wealth brings,
That then I scorn to change my state with kings.

Pause & Reflect

---

6. **Haply:** by chance.
7. **lark:** the English skylark, noted for its beautiful singing while in flight.
8. **sullen:** dull, gloomy.
9. **hymns:** songs of joy.

SONNET 116

WILLIAM SHAKESPEARE

FOCUS
This sonnet is a kind of definition of true love—what it is and what it is not.
MARK IT UP Underline three statements or comparisons that the speaker makes about love. An example is highlighted.

Let me not to the marriage of true minds,
Admit impediments;[1] love is not love
Which alters when it alteration finds,
Or bends with the remover to remove.
5 O no, it is an ever-fixéd mark[2]
That looks on tempests and is never shaken;
It is the star to every wand'ring bark,[3]
Whose worth's unknown, although his height be taken.[4]
Love's not Time's fool, though rosy lips and cheeks
10 Within his bending sickle's compass[5] come,
Love alters not with his brief hours and weeks,
But bears it out[6] even to the edge of doom.
    If this be error and upon me proved,
    I never writ, nor no man ever loved.

Pause & Reflect

---

1. **impediments:** obstacles. The traditional marriage service reads in part, "If any of you know cause or just impediment why these persons should not be joined together . . ."
2. **mark:** seamark—a landmark that can be seen from the sea and used as a guide in charting the route of a ship.
3. **bark:** sailing ship.
4. **Whose . . . height be taken:** a reference to the star. Its value is measureless even though its altitude (**height**) can be measured.
5. **though . . . come:** although youth (**rosy lips and cheeks**) is cut down by Time (**bending sickle's compass come**) and so gives way to age.
6. **bears it out:** endures; carries on; **doom:** Doomsday; Judgment Day.

As the sonnet begins . . .
• The speaker describes true love.

Reading Tip
In the following chart, write the things the speaker says love *is* and the things the speaker says love *is not*.

Love Is	Love Is Not

More About . . .
 **SICKLE'S COMPASS** A *sickle* is a sharp, curved hand tool used to cut hay or grass. Its *compass* is the area it cuts. Time is often personified as a man with a sickle who eventually "cuts down" all living things.

Pause & Reflect
READ ALOUD 1. Read aloud the boxed passage. In this section of the poem, the speaker compares love to a landmark and to a star. What qualities of love are expressed by these comparisons? Circle two words below. (**Analyzing Sensory Language**)

unmovable   misleading

priceless   changeable

2. In lines 13–14, the speaker shows that he is (circle one) *doubtful/confident* about his views on love. (**Draw Conclusions**)

SONNET 130

WILLIAM SHAKESPEARE

As the sonnet begins...

• The speaker describes the woman he loves as she really is.

 Reading Check

How does the speaker feel about the woman in the poem?

Pause & Reflect

1. Circle the statement below that best describes the woman the speaker loves. **(Infer)**

   She is not an attractive woman.

   She is attractive, but she is a human being, not a goddess.

2. In the final two lines, the speaker defends his love. Why do you think he waits until the end of the poem to do this? **(Evaluate)**

   _____

   _____

   _____

FOCUS

In this sonnet, the speaker is poking fun at the flattering descriptions of women in traditional love poetry. He instead describes the woman he loves as she really is.

MARK IT UP Circle words that tell what the woman is being compared to. An example is highlighted.

My mistress' eyes are nothing like the sun;
Coral[1] is far more red than her lips' red;
If snow be white, why then her breasts are dun;[2]
If hairs be wires,[3] black wires grow on her head.
I have seen roses damask'd,[4] red and white,
But no such roses see I in her cheeks,
And in some perfumes is there more delight
Than in the breath that from my mistress reeks.[5]
I love to hear her speak, yet well I know
That music hath a far more pleasing sound;
I grant I never saw a goddess go,[6]
My mistress when she walks treads on the ground.
   And yet, by heaven, I think my love as rare
   As any she belied with false compare.[7]

Pause & Reflect

1. **Coral:** in Shakespeare's time, a red stone used in jewelry.

2. **dun:** tan.

3. **wires:** in Shakespeare's time, poets often described blond hair as golden wire.

4. **damask'd:** with mixed colors.

5. **reeks:** is breathed out (used here without any negative association with bad smells).

6. **go:** walk.

7. **as rare . . . compare:** as fine (rare) as any of the women described in exaggerated ways.

CHALLENGE

In each of these sonnets, Shakespeare talks about a different side of love. For each sonnet, write words or phrases that state the **theme,** or main message, of the poem.

Active Reading SkillBuilder

Analyzing Sensory Language

In his sonnets, Shakespeare often used **sensory language**—words that appeal to the reader's sense of sight, hearing, touch, smell, and taste. Read each poem. Then use the chart to record words or phrases that appeal to one or more of the senses. Note whether any of the senses are not used.

	Sonnet 29	Sonnet 116	Sonnet 130
Sight		an ever-fixed mark (line 5)	the sun (line 1)
Hearing	beweep (line 2)		
Touch			
Smell			
Taste			

Literary Analysis SkillBuilder

Shakespearean Sonnet

In a **Shakespearean sonnet,** the couplet gives a final comment on the
subject discussed in lines 1–12. There is also usually a **turn,** or shift in thought, in
the poem, occurring most often at the couplet or at line 9. Decide where the turn
occurs in each of the three Shakespeare sonnets. What is the effect of each turn?
Use the chart to record your ideas. The first has been done for you.

	Location of Turn	Effect(s) of Turn
Sonnet 29	between lines 8 and 9	The speaker's thoughts turn from himself to his beloved. He stops criticizing himself. Instead, he thinks that he is rich in love.
Sonnet 116		
Sonnet 130		

Macbeth
William Shakespeare

Before You Read

Connect to Your Life

Ambition is a strong drive to achieve something and an important theme in the play *Macbeth*. Is ambition always a positive character trait? If not, when does it become a character flaw? How can ambition be something to fear rather than to admire? Jot down your ideas on the lines below.

_____

_____

_____

_____

_____

_____

_____

Key to the Play

WHAT YOU NEED TO KNOW Shakespeare's play is based on a real-life ruler of Scotland named Macbeth. Macbeth killed his cousin, King Duncan, in order to seize the throne. Although the play is based on fact, Shakespeare changed some of the names and events.

Reading Tips

Reading Shakespeare is a challenge, but well worth the effort. Use the following strategies to keep your reading on track:

- Remember that you don't have to understand every word in a passage to get the overall sense. Read for general meaning. The more you read, the easier it gets.

- Read entire sentences at a time, pausing at the end of a line only if you come upon a mark of punctuation. Try reading some lines aloud as if they were song lyrics and listen to the rhythmic patterns.

- Use the Guide for Reading, beginning on page 75, to help you understand difficult lines and passages.

- Get involved with the **characters.** Picture them in your imagination—and imagine yourself in their situations.

From *The* **Tragedy** *of*

PREVIEW You are about to read Act One of *Macbeth*. Shakespeare's play is about good and evil and about characters who suffer as a result of their actions. Images of blood and darkness create an eerie mood. As the play begins, the forces of evil set out to trap Macbeth and to ruin Scotland.

THE TIME: THE ELEVENTH CENTURY

THE PLACE: SCOTLAND AND ENGLAND

Macbeth

William Shakespeare

English Learner Support
LANGUAGE

Elizabethan English
Shakespeare lived during the Elizabethan Age, named after Queen Elizabeth I. Elizabethan English and modern English are very different, as you will see. Here are some differences to watch for as you read Act I of *Macbeth*.

• The pronouns *thou, thee, thy, thine,* and *thyself* are often used in place of *you, your,* and *yourself*.

• Verb forms were used that are now outdated, such as *art* for *are* and *cometh* for *comes*.

• Unusual word order such as "O, never shall the sun that morrow see!" instead of "Oh, the sun shall never see that morrow!" are used.

• Many Elizabethan words are no longer used, such as *seeling,* which means "blinding."

CHARACTERS

Duncan, king of Scotland

His sons
  Malcolm
  Donalbain

Noblemen of Scotland
  Macbeth
  Banquo
  Macduff
  Lennox
  Ross
  Menteith (mĕn-tēth´)
  Angus
  Caithness (kāth´nĭs)

Fleance (flā´əns), son to Banquo

Siward (syōō´ərd), earl of Northumberland, general of the English forces

Young Siward, his son

Seyton (sā´tən), an officer attending on Macbeth

Son, to Macduff

An English Doctor

A Scottish Doctor

A Porter

An Old Man

Three Murderers

Lady Macbeth

Lady Macduff

A Gentlewoman attending on Lady Macbeth

Hecate (hĕk´ĭt), goddess of witchcraft

Three Witches

Apparitions

Lords, Officers, Soldiers, Messengers, and Attendants

READ ALOUD

Read aloud the names of the characters in this play. Note that some of the characters—for example, the three witches—are forces of evil.

Act I

SCENE 1

An open place in Scotland.

PREVIEW The play opens in a wild and lonely place in medieval Scotland. Three witches enter and speak of what they know will happen this day: The civil war will end, and they will meet Macbeth, one of the generals. Their meeting ends when their demon companions, in the form of a toad and a cat, call them away.

> **FOCUS**
> The three witches are demons, or forces of evil.
> As you read this brief scene, picture them in your
> imagination.

[*Thunder and lightning. Enter three* Witches.]

First Witch. When shall we three meet again
    In thunder, lightning, or in rain?

Second Witch. When the hurlyburly's done,
    When the battle's lost and won.

5 **Third Witch.** That will be ere the set of sun.

First Witch. Where the place?

Second Witch.   Upon the heath.

Third Witch. There to meet with Macbeth.

First Witch. I come, Graymalkin!

Second Witch. Paddock calls.

Third Witch.   Anon!

10 **All.** Fair is foul, and foul is fair.
    Hover through the fog and filthy air.

[*Exeunt.*]

Pause **&** *Reflect*

Use this guide for help with unfamiliar words and difficult passages.

Reading Tip

You might find it helpful to read the Preview for each section of Act I before you begin to read the text.

As Act I begins . . .

• Three witches meet and hint about what is going to happen.

Reading Tip

As you read, note the italicized stage directions in brackets. These directions will help you picture the setting and the action.

3 hurlyburly: turmoil; uproar.

6 heath: a large area of open land; a moor.

8–9 Graymalkin . . . Paddock: two demon helpers in the form of a cat and a toad.

9 Anon: at once.

10 Fair . . . fair: The witches delight in the confusion of good and bad, beauty and ugliness.
[Stage Direction] ***Exeunt*** *Latin:* They leave (the stage).

Pause & Reflect

1. The witches are the first characters who appear on stage. How would you describe the mood that they create? **(Connect)**

_____

_____

_____

_____

READ ALOUD 2. Read aloud the boxed passage on page 74. The witches sometimes speak in riddles. How can something that is fair, or good, be foul, or evil? **(Analyze)**

_____

_____

_____

_____

SCENE 2

King Duncan's camp near the battlefield.

PREVIEW Duncan, the king of Scotland, waits in his camp for news of the battle. He learns that one of his generals, Macbeth, has been victorious in several battles. Macbeth has defeated the rebel Macdonwald. He has also conquered the armies of the king of Norway, who was aided by the Scottish traitor, the thane of Cawdor. (A thane is a kind of lord or baron in Scotland.) Duncan orders the thane of Cawdor's execution and announces that Macbeth will receive the traitor's title.

FOCUS

King Duncan's forces are fighting both rebels and foreign invaders. Read to find out about Macbeth's deeds in defense of his country.

MARK IT UP As you read, underline details that help you get to know Macbeth as a warrior. An example is highlighted on page 78.

[*Alarum within. Enter* Duncan, Malcolm, Donalbain, Lennox, *with* Attendants, *meeting a bleeding* Captain.]

Duncan. What bloody man is that? He can report,
As seemeth by his plight, of the revolt
The newest state.

Malcolm.   This is the sergeant
Who like a good and hardy soldier fought
5   'Gainst my captivity. Hail, brave friend!
Say to the King the knowledge of the broil
As thou didst leave it.

Captain.   Doubtful it stood,
As two spent swimmers that do cling together
And choke their art. The merciless Macdonwald
10   (Worthy to be a rebel, for to that
The multiplying villainies of nature
Do swarm upon him) from the Western Isles
Of kerns and gallowglasses is supplied;
And Fortune, on his damned quarrel smiling,
15   Showed like a rebel's whore. But all's too weak;
For brave Macbeth (well he deserves that name),

• A wounded Captain tells about Macbeth's brave acts in the recent battle.

[Stage Direction] **Alarum within:** the sound of a trumpet offstage, a signal that soldiers should arm themselves.

What Does It Mean?
'Gainst is a contraction of *against*.

5 **'Gainst my captivity:** to save me from capture.
6 **broil:** battle.
7–9 **Doubtful . . . art:** The two armies are compared to two tired swimmers who cling to each other and thus cannot swim.
9–13 The officer hates Macdonwald, whose evils **(multiplying villainies)** swarm like insects around him. His army consists of soldiers **(kerns and gallowglasses)** from the Hebrides **(Western Isles),** an island group off the coast of Scotland.

English Learner Support
LANGUAGE

Personification In the highlighted lines, Shakespeare describes Fortune, or fate, as a woman who smiled upon, or took the side of, the enemy in the battle.

Disdaining Fortune, with his brandished steel,
Which smoked with bloody execution
(Like valor's minion), carved out his passage

20 Till he faced the slave;
Which ne'er shook hands nor bade farewell to him
Till he unseamed him from the nave to the chops
And fixed his head upon our battlements.

Duncan. O valiant cousin! worthy gentleman!

25 **Captain.** As whence the sun 'gins his reflection
Shipwracking storms and direful thunders break,
So from that spring whence comfort seemed to come
Discomfort swells. Mark, King of Scotland, mark.
No sooner justice had, with valor armed,

30 Compelled these skipping kerns to trust their heels
But the Norweyan lord, surveying vantage,
With furbished arms and new supplies of men,
Began a fresh assault.

Duncan.   Dismayed not this
Our captains, Macbeth and Banquo?

Captain.   Yes,

35 As sparrows eagles, or the hare the lion.
If I say sooth, I must report they were
As cannons overcharged with double cracks, so they
Doubly redoubled strokes upon the foe.
Except they meant to bathe in reeking wounds,

40 Or memorize another Golgotha,
I cannot tell—
But I am faint; my gashes cry for help.

Duncan. So well thy words become thee as thy wounds,
They smack of honor both. Go get him surgeons.

[*Exit* Captain, *attended*.]

[*Enter* Ross *and* Angus.]

45 Who comes here?

Malcolm.   The worthy Thane of Ross.

Lennox. What a haste looks through his eyes! So
should he look
That seems to speak things strange.

19 valor's minion: the favorite of valor, meaning the bravest of all.

22 unseamed him . . . chops: split him open from the navel to the jaw.

25–28 As whence . . . discomfort swells: As the rising sun is sometimes followed by storms, a new assault on Macbeth began.

31–33 the Norweyan . . . assault: The king of Norway took an opportunity to attack.

33 Dismayed: frightened.

35 As sparrows . . . lion: Macbeth and Banquo were as frightened as eagles are of sparrows or as a lion is of a rabbit. In other words, Macbeth and Banquo were not frightened at all by the Norweyan lord's attack.

36 sooth: the truth.

37 double cracks: a double load of ammunition.

39–40 Except . . . memorize another Golgotha: The officer claims he cannot decide whether **(except)** Macbeth and Banquo wanted to bathe in blood or to make the battlefield as famous as Golgotha, the site of Christ's crucifixion.

What Does It Mean?

The slave refers to the rebel Macdonwald.

> 🖊 **JOT IT DOWN** **Reread Lines 22–23**
>
> Macbeth defeats Macdonwald in battle and cuts off his head. What do these deeds suggest about Macbeth? **(Infer)**
>
> _____
>
> _____

What Does It Mean?

Mark is an old-fashioned or archaic way to say "Pay attention to me" or "Listen to me carefully."

English Learner Support
LANGUAGE

Diction If written in modern speech, lines 33–34 might read: "Didn't this frighten our captains Macbeth and Banquo?"

 Reading Check

What did Macbeth do that pleased Duncan?

Ross.   God save the King!

Duncan. Whence cam'st thou, worthy thane?

Ross.   From Fife, great King,
   Where the Norweyan banners flout the sky
50   And fan our people cold. Norway himself,
   With terrible numbers,
   Assisted by that most disloyal traitor
   The Thane of Cawdor, began a dismal conflict,
   Till that Bellona's bridegroom, lapped in proof,
55   Confronted him with self-comparisons,
   Point against point, rebellious arm 'gainst arm,
   Curbing his lavish spirit; and to conclude
   The victory fell on us.

Duncan.   Great happiness!

Ross.   That now
   Sweno, the Norways' king, craves composition;
60   Nor would we deign him burial of his men
   Till he disbursed, at Saint Colme's Inch,
   Ten thousand dollars to our general use.

Duncan. No more that Thane of Cawdor shall deceive
   Our bosom interest. Go pronounce his present death
65   And with his former title greet Macbeth.

Ross. I'll see it done.

Duncan. What he hath lost noble Macbeth hath won.

[*Exeunt.*]

Pause & **Reflect**

47–58 Ross has come from Fife, where Norway's troops invaded and frightened the people. There the king of Norway, aided by the thane of Cawdor, fought with Macbeth (described as the husband of **Bellona,** the goddess of war). Macbeth achieved victory.

59 **craves composition:** wants a treaty.

60 **deign:** allow.

61 **disbursed, at Saint Colme's Inch:** paid at Saint Colme's Inch, an island in the North Sea.

63–64 **deceive our bosom interest:** betray our friendship.

64 **present death:** immediate execution.

67 **he:** the Thane of Cawdor.

Reading Tip

Because Shakespeare's words were meant to be spoken, it is very helpful to read the lines aloud. You may even find it both helpful and fun to read Act I aloud as a group, with each person playing one or more characters.

More About . . .

WAR AND MONEY Here, the Scottish army forces the Norwegian king to pay ten thousand dollars for the right to bury his dead soldiers.

Pause & Reflect

1. Review the details you underlined as you read. How would you describe Macbeth as a warrior? **(Infer)**

_____

_____

_____

READ ALOUD **2.** Read aloud the boxed passage on page 80. What reward does King Duncan decide to give Macbeth? **(Clarify)**

_____

_____

_____

SCENE 3

A bleak place near the battlefield.

PREVIEW While leaving the battlefield, Macbeth and Banquo meet the witches. They are gleefully discussing the trouble they have caused. The witches hail Macbeth by a title he already holds, thane of Glamis. Then they prophesy that he will become both thane of Cawdor and king. When Banquo asks about his future, they speak in riddles. They say that he will be the father of kings but not a king himself.

After the witches vanish, Ross and Angus arrive to tell Macbeth that he has been named thane of Cawdor. The first prophecy has come true, and Macbeth is stunned. He immediately begins to consider the possibility of murdering King Duncan to fulfill the witches' second prophecy. Shaken, he turns his thoughts away from this "horrid image."

FOCUS

Read to find out about the witches' prophecies to Macbeth and Banquo.

MARK IT UP As you read, underline each of these prophecies.

[*Thunder. Enter the three* Witches.]

First Witch. Where hast thou been, sister?

Second Witch. Killing swine.

Third Witch. Sister, where thou?

First Witch. A sailor's wife had chestnuts in her lap
5　　And mounched and mounched and mounched. "Give me," quoth I.
　　"Aroint thee, witch!" the rump-fed ronyon cries.
　　Her husband's to Aleppo gone, master o' the "Tiger";
　　But in a sieve I'll thither sail
　　And, like a rat without a tail,
10　　I'll do, I'll do, and I'll do.

Second Witch. I'll give thee a wind.

First Witch. Th' art kind.

Third Witch. And I another.

First Witch. I myself have all the other,
15　　And the very ports they blow,

2 Killing swine: Witches were often accused of killing pigs.

5 mounched: munched.

6 "Aroint thee, witch!" . . . ronyon cries: "Go away, witch!" the fat-bottomed **(rump-fed)**, ugly creature **(ronyon)** cries.

7–8 The woman's husband, the master of a merchant ship **(the "Tiger")**, has sailed to Aleppo, a famous trading center in the Middle East. The witch will pursue him. Witches, who could change shape at will, were thought to sail on a strainer **(sieve)**.

14–23 The witch is going to torture the woman's husband. She controls where the winds blow, covering all points of a compass. She will make him sleepless, keeping his eyelids **(penthouse lid)** from closing. Thus, he will lead an accursed **(forbid)** life for weeks **(sev'nights)**, wasting away with fatigue.

As Act I continues . . .

• The witches meet Macbeth and Banquo.
• The witches make three prophecies.

English Learner Support
LANGUAGE

Verbs Elizabethan English had slightly different verb and pronoun forms than modern English. In line 1, "Where *hast thou* been, sister?" means "Where *have you* been, sister?" in modern English. Other verb changes to watch for are *hath* for "has" and *doth* for "do."

✔ Reading Check

What is the witch going to do to the master of the "Tiger"?

All the quarters that they know
I' the shipman's card.

> I'll drain him dry as hay.
> Sleep shall neither night nor day
20 Hang upon his penthouse lid.
> He shall live a man forbid.
> Weary sev'nights, nine times nine,
> Shall he dwindle, peak, and pine.
> Though his bark cannot be lost,
25 Yet it shall be tempest-tost.

Look what I have.

Second Witch. Show me! Show me!

First Witch. Here I have a pilot's thumb,
Wracked as homeward he did come.

[*Drum within.*]

30 **Third Witch.** A drum, a drum!
Macbeth doth come.

All. The Weird Sisters, hand in hand,
Posters of the sea and land,
Thus do go about, about,
35 Thrice to thine, and thrice to mine,
And thrice again, to make up nine.
Peace! The charm's wound up.

[*Enter* Macbeth *and* Banquo.]

Macbeth. So foul and fair a day I have not seen.

Banquo. How far is't called to Forres? What are these,
40 So withered, and so wild in their attire,
That look not like the inhabitants o' the earth,
And yet are on't? Live you? or are you aught
That man may question? You seem to understand me,
By each at once her choppy finger laying
45 Upon her skinny lips. You should be women,
And yet your beards forbid me to interpret
That you are so.

Macbeth.   Speak, if you can. What are you?

First Witch. All hail, Macbeth! Hail to thee, Thane of Glamis!

32 Weird: relating to fate, or destiny.

33 Posters: quick riders.

36 Nine was considered a magical number by superstitious people.

42–47 aught: anything; **choppy:** chapped; **your beards:** Beards on women identified them as witches.

READ ALOUD **Lines 18–25**

These short, rhymed lines with their driving rhythms sound like a chant. When offended, the witches punish humans severely.

English Learner Support
LANGUAGE

Homograph *Macbeth* was written about 300 years before the airplane was invented. Here, a *pilot* was either the person who steered the boat or a person who came aboard a ship to help guide it into and out of harbor.

Reading Check

Why does Macbeth describe the day as both "foul and fair"?

MARK IT UP **Reread Lines 39–47**

Banquo vividly describes the witches' appearance. Circle details that help you picture the witches in your imagination. **(Visualize)**

Second Witch. All hail, Macbeth! Hail to thee, Thane of
    Cawdor!

50 **Third Witch.** All hail, Macbeth, that shalt be King hereafter!

Banquo. Good sir, why do you start and seem to fear
    Things that do sound so fair? I' the name of truth,
    Are ye fantastical, or that indeed
    Which outwardly ye show? My noble partner
55   You greet with present grace and great prediction
    Of noble having and of royal hope,
    That he seems rapt withal. To me you speak not.
    If you can look into the seeds of time
    And say which grain will grow and which will not,
60   Speak then to me, who neither beg nor fear
    Your favors nor your hate.

First Witch. Hail!

Second Witch. Hail!

Third Witch. Hail!

65 **First Witch.** Lesser than Macbeth, and greater.

Second Witch. Not so happy, yet much happier.

Third Witch. Thou shalt get kings, though thou be none.
    So all hail, Macbeth and Banquo!

First Witch. Banquo and Macbeth, all hail!

70 **Macbeth.** Stay, you imperfect speakers, tell me more!
    By Sinel's death I know I am Thane of Glamis,
    But how of Cawdor? The Thane of Cawdor lives,
    A prosperous gentleman; and to be King
    Stands not within the prospect of belief,
75   No more than to be Cawdor. Say from whence
    You owe this strange intelligence, or why
    Upon this blasted heath you stop our way
    With such prophetic greeting. Speak, I charge you.

[Witches *vanish*.]

Banquo. The earth hath bubbles, as the water has,
80   And these are of them. Whither are they vanished?

Macbeth. Into the air, and what seemed corporal melted
    As breath into the wind. Would they had stayed!

53 Are ye fantastical: Are you (the witches) imaginary?

54–57 My noble partner . . . . rapt withal: The witches' prophecies of noble possessions **(having)**—the lands and wealth of Cawdor—and kingship **(royal hope)** have left Macbeth dazed **(rapt withal)**.

65–68 The witches speak in riddles. Though Banquo will be less fortunate **(happy)** than Macbeth, he will be father to **(get)** future kings.

75–76 whence: where. Macbeth wants to know where the witches received their knowledge **(strange intelligence)**.

80 Whither: where.
81 corporal: physical; real.

 Reading Check

What title does Macbeth already have? What two does he not already have?

English Learner Support

LANGUAGE

Metaphor In lines 58–59, Banquo is saying that the future is made up of *seeds,* or possible fates, that may or may not *grow,* or happen. He says if the witches can tell which seeds, or possible futures, will grow, they should tell him, as they told Macbeth.

More About . . .

Shakespeare put the witches' prophecies about Banquo in the play to please King James I of England. King James, who was also king of Scotland, was the main supporter of Shakespeare's acting company. The legendary Banquo was said to be James's ancestor. Having the witches tell Banquo that he will be greater and happier than Macbeth and that he will get kings, or have royal descendants, was Shakespeare's way of honoring James I.

JOT IT DOWN **Reread Lines 72–75**

What does the audience know about the thane of Cawdor that Macbeth does not know? **(Clarify)**

_____

_____

_____

_____

Banquo. Were such things here as we do speak about?
Or have we eaten on the insane root
85 That takes the reason prisoner?

Macbeth. Your children shall be kings.

Banquo.   You shall be King.

Macbeth. And Thane of Cawdor too. Went it not so?

Banquo. To the selfsame tune and words. Who's here?

Pause **&** Reflect

FOCUS

After the witches disappear, Ross and Angus—two
other leaders of Duncan's troops—enter with a
message for Macbeth. Read to find out Macbeth's
reaction to the message.

MARK IT UP   As you read, circle words and phrases
that help you understand his reaction.

[*Enter* Ross *and* Angus.]

Ross. The King hath happily received, Macbeth,
90 The news of thy success; and when he reads
Thy personal venture in the rebels' fight,
His wonders and his praises do contend
Which should be thine or his. Silenced with that,
In viewing o'er the rest o' the selfsame day,
95 He finds thee in the stout Norweyan ranks,
Nothing afeard of what thyself didst make,
Strange images of death. As thick as hail
Came post with post, and every one did bear
Thy praises in his kingdom's great defense
100 And poured them down before him.

Angus.   We are sent
To give thee from our royal master thanks;
Only to herald thee into his sight,
Not pay thee.

Ross. And for an earnest of a greater honor,
105 He bade me, from him, call thee Thane of Cawdor;
In which addition, hail, most worthy Thane!
For it is thine.

84 **insane root:** A number of plants were believed to cause insanity when eaten.

92–93 **His wonders . . . Silenced with that:** King Duncan hesitates between awe **(wonders)** and gratitude **(praises)** and is, as a result, speechless.

96–97 **Nothing afeard . . . of death:** Although Macbeth left many dead **(strange images of death)**, he obviously did not fear death himself.

104 **earnest:** partial payment.

106 **addition:** title.

Pause **&** *Reflect*

1. Review the prophecies you underlined as you read. What do the witches prophesy for Macbeth? **(Clarify)**

_____

_____

_____

2. What do the witches prophesy to Banquo about his children? **(Clarify)**

_____

_____

_____

As Act I continues . . .

• Angus and Ross, two of Duncan's men, bring a message to Macbeth.

Banquo. What, can the devil speak true?

Macbeth. The Thane of Cawdor lives. Why do you dress me
In borrowed robes?

Angus. Who was the Thane lives yet,
110 But under heavy judgment bears that life
Which he deserves to lose. Whether he was combined
With those of Norway, or did line the rebel
With hidden help and vantage, or that with both
He labored in his country's wrack, I know not;
115 But treasons capital, confessed and proved,
Have overthrown him.

Macbeth. [*Aside*] Glamis, and Thane of Cawdor!
The greatest is behind.—[*To Ross and Angus*] Thanks for
your pains.

[*Aside to Banquo*] Do you not hope your children shall
be kings,
When those that gave the Thane of Cawdor to me
120 Promised no less to them?

Banquo. [*Aside to Macbeth*] That, trusted home,
Might yet enkindle you unto the crown,
Besides the Thane of Cawdor. But 'tis strange!
And oftentimes, to win us to our harm,
The instruments of darkness tell us truths,
125 Win us with honest trifles, to betray's
In deepest consequence.—
Cousins, a word, I pray you.

Macbeth. [*Aside*] Two truths are told,
As happy prologues to the swelling act
Of the imperial theme.—I thank you, gentlemen.—
130 [*Aside*] This supernatural soliciting
Cannot be ill; cannot be good. If ill,
Why hath it given me earnest of success,
Commencing in a truth? I am Thane of Cawdor.
If good, why do I yield to that suggestion
135 Whose horrid image doth unfix my hair
And make my seated heart knock at my ribs
Against the use of nature? Present fears
Are less than horrible imaginings.
My thought, whose murder yet is but fantastical,

GUIDE FOR READING

108–109 Macbeth accuses Ross of dressing him in "borrowed robes" because he does not know that the thane of Cawdor has been sentenced to execution.

111–116 Whether he was . . . overthrown him: The former thane of Cawdor may have been secretly allied **(combined)** with the king of Norway, or he may have supported the traitor Macdonwald **(did line the rebel)**. But he is guilty of treasons that deserve the death penalty **(treasons capital)**, because he aimed at the country's ruin **(wrack)**.

120 home: fully; completely.

121 enkindle you unto: inflame your ambitions.

123–126 to win us . . . consequence: Banquo warns that evil powers often tell little truths to tempt people. The witches may be lying about what matters most **(in deepest consequence)**.

127–129 Two truths . . . imperial theme: The first two "prophecies" only set the stage for the more important act of becoming king.

130–142 Macbeth walks away from the others, his head spinning. Are the witches' predictions **(supernatural soliciting)** good or evil **(ill)**? If they are evil, why has one of them already proved true? If they are good, why is he suddenly filled with the terrible thought **(suggestion)** of killing King Duncan? This idea **(horrible imaginings)** is frightful. Macbeth is overwhelmed by imagining the future **(surmise)**. Nothing seems real to him but his imaginings **(what is not)**.

English Learner Support
LANGUAGE

Compare and Contrast Banquo and Macbeth are friends, but they are different kinds of men. Use a Venn diagram to compare and contrast these two characters. How are they different? Do they have anything in common?

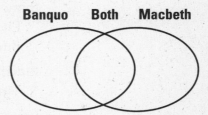

Banquo   Both   Macbeth

More About . . .

ASIDE Shakespeare and other playwrights often have characters speak in an *aside,* or words that are spoken to themselves or to another character. An aside lets the audience hear the character's private thoughts. Some asides are spoken—as if in a whisper—to another character when several others are present on the stage, as Macbeth speaks to Banquo here.

What Does It Mean?

Here, *Cousins* means "fellow lords."

140 Shakes so my single state of man that function
Is smothered in surmise and nothing is
But what is not.

Banquo.   Look how our partner's rapt.

Macbeth. [*Aside*] If chance will have me King, why
       chance may crown me,
Without my stir.

Banquo.   New honors come upon him,
145 Like our strange garments, cleave not to their mold
But with the aid of use.

Macbeth.   [*Aside*] Come what come may,
Time and the hour runs through the roughest day.

Banquo. Worthy Macbeth, we stay upon your leisure.

Macbeth. Give me your favor. My dull brain was wrought
150 With things forgotten. Kind gentlemen, your pains
Are registered where every day I turn
The leaf to read them. Let us toward the King.
[*Aside to* Banquo] Think upon what hath chanced, and, at
       more time,
The interim having weighed it, let us speak
155 Our free hearts each to other.

Banquo.   [*Aside to* Macbeth] Very gladly.

Macbeth. [*Aside to* Banquo] Till then, enough.—Come, friends.

[*Exeunt.*]

Pause & Reflect

144 my stir: my doing anything.

146–147 Come what . . . roughest day: The future will arrive no matter what.

148 stay: wait.

150–152 your pains . . . read them: I will always remember your efforts. The comparison refers to keeping a diary and reading it regularly.

153–155 at more time . . . other: Macbeth wants to discuss the prophecies later, after he and Banquo have had time to think about them.

What Does It Mean?

Strange garments are new clothes. Banquo is saying that just as new clothes eventually become comfortable, Macbeth will get used to his new titles.

Pause & Reflect

1. Review the words and phrases you circled as you read. How does Macbeth react to Ross's message? Underline two phrases below. **(Infer)**

   amazed at the turn of events

   grateful to King Duncan

   angry at the former thane of Cawdor

   horrified at his thoughts of murder

READ ALOUD 2. Read aloud the boxed passage on page 92. How would you **paraphrase,** or put in your own words, this sentence?

_____

_____

_____

_____

3. Do the witches control Macbeth's future, or does he? **(Make Judgments)**

_____

_____

_____

_____

CHALLENGE

One way that Shakespeare shows what Macbeth is like is through the use of a **foil.** A foil is a character who serves as a strong contrast to another character. Banquo is the foil for Macbeth. List details from Scenes 2 and 3 and from your Venn diagram to show how Banquo is a foil for Macbeth. **(Compare and Contrast)**

SCENE 4

A room in the king's palace in Forres.

PREVIEW King Duncan receives news of the execution of the former thane of Cawdor. As the king is admitting his bad judgment concerning the traitor, Macbeth enters with Banquo, Ross, and Angus. Duncan expresses his gratitude to them. Then, he names his own son Malcolm as heir to the throne. To honor Macbeth, Duncan decides to visit Macbeth's castle at Inverness. Macbeth, his thoughts full of dark ambition, leaves to prepare for the king's visit.

> FOCUS
>
> Read to find out how Macbeth reacts to King Duncan and to his surprise announcement.

[*Flourish. Enter* Duncan, Lennox, Malcolm, Donalbain, *and* Attendants.]

Duncan. Is execution done on Cawdor? Are not
　　Those in commission yet returned?

Malcolm.　　　　　　　　　　　　　　My liege,
　　They are not yet come back. But I have spoke
　　With one that saw him die; who did report
5　　That very frankly he confessed his treasons,
　　Implored your Highness' pardon, and set forth
　　A deep repentance. Nothing in his life
　　Became him like the leaving it. He died
　　As one that had been studied in his death
10　　To throw away the dearest thing he owed
　　As 'twere a careless trifle.

Duncan.　　　　　　　　　　　There's no art
　　To find the mind's construction in the face.
　　He was a gentleman on whom I built
　　An absolute trust.

[*Enter* Macbeth, Banquo, Ross, *and* Angus.]

　　　　　　　　　　　　　　O worthiest cousin,
15　　The sin of my ingratitude even now
　　Was heavy on me! Thou art so far before
　　That swiftest wing of recompense is slow
　　To overtake thee. Would thou hadst less deserved,
　　That the proportion both of thanks and payment

2 Those in commission: those who are responsible for Cawdor's execution.

6 set forth: showed.

8–11 He died as . . . trifle: He died as if he had rehearsed **(studied)** the moment of his death. Though losing his life **(the dearest thing he owed)**, he behaved with calm dignity.

13–14 King Duncan tells of his trust in the former thane of Cawdor. Immediately after, Macbeth—who is now the thane of Cawdor—enters.

14–21 O worthiest . . . pay: The king feels that he cannot repay **(recompense)** Macbeth enough. Macbeth's actions are worth more than any thanks or payment Duncan can give.

As Act I continues . . .

- Duncan announces that his son is now the heir to the throne.
- The king says he will honor Macbeth by visiting his castle.

What Does It Mean?
Liege means "lord."

📖 **READ ALOUD** **Lines 11–14**

What can you conclude about Duncan from the fact that he put "absolute trust" in the former thane of Cawdor? **(Draw Conclusions)**

_____

_____

_____

_____

20   Might have been mine! Only I have left to say,
      More is thy due than more than all can pay.

      Macbeth. The service and the loyalty I owe,
      In doing it pays itself. Your Highness' part
      Is to receive our duties; and our duties
25   Are to your throne and state children and servants,
      Which do but what they should by doing everything
      Safe toward your love and honor.

      Duncan.   Welcome hither.
      I have begun to plant thee and will labor
      To make thee full of growing. Noble Banquo,
30   That hast no less deserved, nor must be known
      No less to have done so, let me infold thee
      And hold thee to my heart.

      Banquo.   There if I grow,
      The harvest is your own.

      Duncan.   My plenteous joys,
      Wanton in fullness, seek to hide themselves
35   In drops of sorrow. Sons, kinsmen, thanes,
      And you whose places are the nearest, know
      We will establish our estate upon
      Our eldest, Malcolm, whom we name hereafter
      The Prince of Cumberland; which honor must
40   Not unaccompanied invest him only,
      But signs of nobleness, like stars, shall shine
      On all deservers. From hence to Inverness,
      And bind us further to you.

      Macbeth. The rest is labor, which is not used for you.
45   I'll be myself the harbinger, and make joyful
      The hearing of my wife with your approach;
      So, humbly take my leave.

      Duncan.   My worthy Cawdor!

      Macbeth. [*Aside*] The Prince of Cumberland! That is a step
      On which I must fall down, or else o'erleap,
50   For in my way it lies. Stars, hide your fires!
      Let not light see my black and deep desires.
      The eye wink at the hand; yet let that be,
      Which the eye fears, when it is done, to see. [*Exit.*]

JOT IT DOWN   Reread Lines 28–29

The king says that he plans to give more honors to Macbeth. If you were in Macbeth's situation, what would you be thinking now? (Connect)

_____

_____

33–35 My plenteous . . . sorrow: The king is crying tears of joy.

English Learner Support
LANGUAGE

Pronouns King Duncan uses the first-person plural pronouns *we* and *our* to refer to himself. This usage is known as the regal style, sometimes called "the royal we." The monarch represents both his land and his people.

39 Prince of Cumberland: the title given to the heir to the Scottish throne.

42 Inverness: site of Macbeth's castle, where the king has just invited himself, giving another honor to Macbeth.

45 harbinger: a representative sent before a royal party to make arrangements for its arrival.

What Does It Mean?

In line 44, Macbeth is saying that anything he does for the king does not feel like work.

English Learner Support
LANGUAGE

Contraction *O'erleap* is a short form of *overleap,* meaning "jump over." Macbeth knows to become king he must now get past—or get rid of—Malcolm.

52–53 The eye . . . to see: Macbeth hopes for the king's murder, even though looking at the murdered king would frighten him.

Duncan. True, worthy Banquo: he is full so valiant,
55   And in his commendations I am fed;
    It is a banquet to me. Let's after him,
    Whose care is gone before to bid us welcome.
    It is a peerless kinsman.

[*Flourish. Exeunt.*]

Pause **&** Reflect

SCENE 5

Macbeth's castle at Inverness.

PREVIEW   Lady Macbeth reads a letter from her husband. This
letter tells her of the witches' prophecies, one of which has already
come true. She is determined that Macbeth will be king. However,
she fears that he lacks the cruelty to kill Duncan. After a messenger
tells her the king is coming, she calls on the powers of evil to help
her do what must be done. When Macbeth arrives, she tells him that
the king must die that night. She also tells him that he must pretend
to be a good and loyal host.

FOCUS

In this scene, you meet Lady Macbeth,
Macbeth's wife.
MARK IT UP   As you read, circle details that
help you form impressions of her.

[*Enter* Lady Macbeth *alone, with a letter.*]

Lady Macbeth. [*Reads*] "They met me in the day of
    success; and I have learned by the perfect'st report
    they have more in them than mortal knowledge. When I
    burned in desire to question them further, they made
5   themselves air, into which they vanished. Whiles I stood
    rapt in the wonder of it, came missives from the King,
    who all-hailed me Thane of Cawdor, by which title,
    before, these Weird Sisters saluted me, and referred me
    to the coming on of time with 'Hail, King that shalt
10   be!' This have I thought good to deliver thee, my
    dearest partner of greatness, that thou mightst not lose
    the dues of rejoicing by being ignorant of what
    greatness is promised thee. Lay it to thy heart, and
    farewell."

54–58 Duncan continues an earlier conversation with Banquo about Macbeth's merits.

58 **peerless:** without equal.

1. Without Macbeth's help, Duncan might have lost his entire kingdom. Do you think Duncan rewards Macbeth enough for his deeds in battle? *Yes/No*, because _____

_____

_____

_____.

(Evaluate)

MARK IT UP 2. What is on Macbeth's mind as the scene ends? Write the answer below. Then circle details in lines 48–53 on page 96 that helped you reach your answer. **(Infer)**

_____

_____

_____

_____

As Act I continues . . .

• Lady Macbeth learns about the witches' prophecies.

• She decides that Macbeth must murder Duncan.

English Learner Support
LANGUAGE

Usage Some rules of usage and grammar were different in Elizabethan English. In line 2, *perfect'st* means "most perfect."

1–2 **They met me in the day of success:** The witches met Macbeth on the day that he killed Macdonwald and defeated the King of Norway.

3 **more . . . than mortal knowledge:** The witches know things that mere human beings could not know.

READ ALOUD Lines 10–13

As you read these lines aloud, try to convey Macbeth's feelings for his wife. Consider what the phrase "my dearest partner of greatness" suggests about his view of Lady Macbeth.

15   Glamis thou art, and Cawdor, and shalt be
What thou art promised. Yet do I fear thy nature.
It is too full o' the milk of human kindness
To catch the nearest way. Thou wouldst be great;
Art not without ambition, but without

20   The illness should attend it. What thou wouldst
      highly,
That wouldst thou holily; wouldst not play false,
And yet wouldst wrongly win. Thou'ldst have,
      great Glamis,
That which cries "Thus thou must do," if thou
      have it;
And that which rather thou dost fear to do

25   Than wishest should be undone. Hie thee hither,
That I may pour my spirits in thine ear
And chastise with the valor of my tongue
All that impedes thee from the golden round
Which fate and metaphysical aid doth seem

30   To have thee crowned withal.

[*Enter* Messenger.]

                            What is your tidings?

Messenger. The King comes here tonight.

Lady Macbeth.   Thou'rt mad to say it!
Is not thy master with him? who, were't so,
Would have informed for preparation.

Messenger. So please you, it is true. Our Thane is
      coming.

35   One of my fellows had the speed of him,
Who, almost dead for breath, had scarcely more
Than would make up his message.

Lady Macbeth.   Give him tending;
He brings great news.

[*Exit* Messenger.]

                      The raven himself is hoarse
That croaks the fatal entrance of Duncan

40   Under my battlements. Come, you spirits
That tend on mortal thoughts, unsex me here,
And fill me, from the crown to the toe, top-full
Of direst cruelty! Make thick my blood;
Stop up the access and passage to remorse,

16–30 Lady Macbeth fears her husband is too good **(too full o' the milk of human kindness)** to seize the throne by murder **(the nearest way)**. Lacking the necessary wickedness **(illness)**, he wants to gain power virtuously **(holily)**. But she is convinced he would like to be king, even if becoming king requires murder **(that which rather thou dost fear to do)**. She wishes him home **(Hie thee hither)** so that she can drive out **(chastise)** his fears and anything else that stands in the way of the crown **(golden round)**. Fate and the supernatural seem to be on his side.

35 had the speed of him: rode faster than Macbeth.

38 raven: The harsh cry of the raven, a bird symbolizing evil and misfortune, was supposed to indicate an approaching death.
40–54 Lady Macbeth calls on the spirits of evil to rid her of feminine tenderness **(unsex me)** and to block out guilt. She wants no normal pangs of conscience **(compunctious**

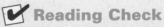
JOT IT DOWN   Reread Lines 16–20

Do you think Lady Macbeth is right about her husband's character? *Yes/No*, because

_____

_____ .

(Infer)

English Learner Support
LANGUAGE

Contraction *Thou'ldst* is a combination and shortening of two words: *thou wouldst*. It means "you would."

Reading Check
What does Lady Macbeth want to talk to her husband about?

45   That no compunctious visitings of nature
   Shake my fell purpose nor keep peace between
   The effect and it! Come to my woman's breasts
   And take my milk for gall, you murd'ring ministers,
   Wherever in your sightless substances
50   You wait on nature's mischief! Come, thick night,
   And pall thee in the dunnest smoke of hell,
   That my keen knife see not the wound it makes,
   Nor heaven peep through the blanket of the dark
   To cry "Hold, hold!"

Pause & Reflect

FOCUS

Macbeth enters, and his wife greets him. Read to find
out what Lady Macbeth advises her husband to do.

   [*Enter* Macbeth.]

                Great Glamis! worthy Cawdor!
55   Greater than both, by the all-hail hereafter!
   Thy letters have transported me beyond
   This ignorant present, and I feel now
   The future in the instant.

Macbeth.   My dearest love,
   Duncan comes here tonight.

Lady Macbeth.   And when goes hence?

60 **Macbeth.** Tomorrow, as he purposes.

Lady Macbeth.   O, never
   Shall sun that morrow see!
   Your face, my Thane, is as a book where men
   May read strange matters. To beguile the time,
   Look like the time; bear welcome in your eye,
65   Your hand, your tongue; look like the innocent
     flower,
   But be the serpent under't. He that's coming
   Must be provided for; and you shall put
   This night's great business into my dispatch,
   Which shall to all our nights and days to come
70   Give solely sovereign sway and masterdom.

visitings of nature) to get in the way of her murderous plan. She asks that her mother's milk be turned to bile **(gall)** by the unseen evil forces **(murd'ring ministers, sightless substances)** in nature. Also, she asks that the night wrap **(pall)** itself in darkness as black as hell so that no one may see or stop the crime.

54–55 Lady Macbeth's greeting to her husband echoes the witches' greeting to him in Scene 3.

58 **in the instant:** at this moment.

63–66 **To beguile . . . under't:** To fool **(beguile)** everyone, act as expected at such a time, that is, as a good host.

68 **my dispatch:** my management.

70 **Give solely sovereign sway:** bring absolute royal power.

What is Lady Macbeth's greatest fear about killing Duncan? (Circle one.)

that she will get caught

that she will be overcome with guilt and won't be able to do it

that she will lose her womanliness and her husband won't love her anymore

As Act I continues . . .

- Lady Macbeth and Macbeth greet each other.
- Lady Macbeth warns her husband not to let his feelings show in his face.

English Learner Support

LANGUAGE

Word Order Lines 60–61 can be reworded as "Oh, tomorrow will never see the sun!"

Macbeth. We will speak further.

Lady Macbeth. Only look up clear.
To alter favor ever is to fear.
Leave all the rest to me.

[*Exeunt.*]

Pause & Reflect

SCENE 6

In front of Macbeth's castle.

PREVIEW King Duncan and his party arrive, and Lady Macbeth
welcomes them. Duncan is generous in his praise of his hosts and
eagerly awaits the arrival of Macbeth.

> **FOCUS**
>
> King Duncan and Banquo admire Macbeth's castle.
> It seems to be a place of "heavenly" peace.
> MARK IT UP As you read, underline details that
> suggest Banquo and Duncan's impressions of
> the castle and of Macbeth and his wife.

[*Hautboys and torches. Enter* Duncan, Malcolm,
Donalbain, Banquo, Lennox, Macduff, Ross,
Angus, *and* Attendants.]

Duncan. This castle hath a pleasant seat. The air
Nimbly and sweetly recommends itself
Unto our gentle senses.

Banquo. This guest of summer,
The temple-haunting martlet, does approve
5   By his loved mansionry that the heaven's breath
Smells wooingly here. No jutty, frieze,
Buttress, nor coign of vantage, but this bird
Hath made his pendent bed and procreant cradle.
Where they most breed and haunt, I have observed
10   The air is delicate.

72 To alter . . . fear: To change your expression **(favor)** is a sign of fear.

[Stage Direction] **Hautboys:** oboes.

1 seat: location.

3–10 This guest . . . delicate: The martin **(martlet)** usually built its nest on a church **(temple)**, where every projection **(jutty)**, sculptured decoration **(frieze)**, support **(buttress)**, and convenient corner **(coign of vantage)** offered a good nesting site. Banquo sees the presence of the martin's hanging **(pendent)** nest as a sign of healthy air.

Pause & *Reflect*

MARK IT UP Who is more in control, Lady Macbeth or her husband? Write the answer below. Then circle details on pages 102 and 104 that led you to your answer. **(Compare and Contrast)**

_____

_____

_____

_____

As Act I continues . . .

• Duncan and others arrive at the castle.

• Lady Macbeth welcomes them.

What Does It Mean?

Procreant cradle refers to the bird's nest where the bird's chicks are conceived.

[*Enter* Lady Macbeth.]

Duncan.　　　　See, see, our honored hostess!
The love that follows us sometime is our trouble,
Which still we thank as love. Herein I teach you
How you shall bid God 'ield us for your pains
And thank us for your trouble.

Lady Macbeth.　　　　All our service
15　In every point twice done, and then done double
Were poor and single business to contend
Against those honors deep and broad wherewith
Your Majesty loads our house. For those of old,
And the late dignities heaped up to them,
20　We rest your hermits.

Duncan.　　　　　　Where's the Thane of Cawdor?
We coursed him at the heels and had a purpose
To be his purveyor; but he rides well,
And his great love, sharp as his spur, hath holp him
To his home before us. Fair and noble hostess,
25　We are your guest tonight.

Lady Macbeth.　　　　Your servants ever
Have theirs, themselves, and what is theirs, in
　　compt,
To make their audit at your Highness' pleasure,
Still to return your own.

Duncan.　　　　　　Give me your hand;
Conduct me to mine host. We love him highly
30　And shall continue our graces towards him.
By your leave, hostess.

[*Exeunt.*]

Pause & Reflect

11–14 The love . . . trouble: Even though love can be troublesome, we should be thankful for it. Duncan, thinking that his visit is a great inconvenience, tells Lady Macbeth that it is a sign of love for which she should be thankful.

16 single business: weak service. Lady Macbeth claims that nothing she or her husband can do will match Duncan's generosity.

20 We rest your hermits: we can only repay you with prayers. The wealthy used to hire hermits to pray for the souls of the dead.

21 coursed him at the heels: followed him closely.

22 purveyor: one who makes advance arrangements for a royal visit.

23 holp: helped.

25–28 Legally, Duncan owned everything in his kingdom. Lady Macbeth politely says that they hold his property in trust **(compt)**, ready to return it **(make their audit)** whenever he wants.

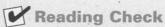

Reading Check

How does Lady Macbeth act toward Duncan? How do you think she feels?

What Does It Mean?

By your leave is an archaic way of saying "with your permission" or "whenever you're ready."

Pause & Reflect

1. Review the details you underlined as you read. How do you think Banquo and Duncan feel about Macbeth and his wife? **(Infer)**

_____

_____

_____

_____

2. How does Duncan feel about Macbeth and Lady Macbeth? **(Infer)**

_____

_____

_____

_____

SCENE 7

A room in Macbeth's castle.

PREVIEW   Macbeth has left Duncan in the middle of dinner. Alone, he begins to have second thoughts about his murderous plan. Lady Macbeth enters and discovers that he has changed his mind. She accuses him of being a coward and tells him that a true man would never back out of a commitment. Then she explains her plan. She will make sure that the king's attendants drink too much. When they are fast asleep, Macbeth will stab the king with the servants' weapons.

FOCUS

Read to find out about Macbeth's state of mind as he thinks about murdering his king.

[*Hautboys. Torches. Enter a* Sewer, *and divers*
   Servants *with dishes and service over the stage.*
   Then enter Macbeth.]

Macbeth. If it were done when 'tis done, then 'twere well
   It were done quickly. If the assassination
   Could trammel up the consequence, and catch,
   With his surcease, success, that but this blow
5   Might be the be-all and the end-all here,
   But here, upon this bank and shoal of time,
   We'd jump the life to come. But in these cases
   We still have judgment here, that we but teach
   Bloody instructions, which, being taught, return
10   To plague the inventor. This even-handed justice
   Commends the ingredience of our poisoned chalice
   To our own lips. He's here in double trust:
   First, as I am his kinsman and his subject,
   Strong both against the deed; then, as his host,
15   Who should against his murderer shut the door,
   Not bear the knife myself. Besides, this Duncan
   Hath borne his faculties so meek, hath been

[Stage Direction] **Sewer:** the butler, the servant in charge of arranging the banquet and overseeing the serving of the food; **divers:** various.

1–10 Again, Macbeth argues with himself about murdering the king. If the murder could be done without causing problems later, then it would be good to do it soon. If Duncan's murder would lead to no bad consequences, then Macbeth would risk eternal damnation. He knows, however, that terrible deeds **(bloody instructions)** often backfire.

12–28 Macbeth reminds himself that he is Duncan's relative, subject, and host and that the king has never abused his royal powers **(faculties)**. In fact, Duncan is such a good king that there is no reason for his murder except Macbeth's own driving ambition. The murder will be such a wicked deed that angels **(cherubin)** will ride the winds **(sightless couriers)** to tell the news to

More About . . .
SOLILOQUIES Macbeth is about to give a *soliloquy,* or a speech that a character makes while alone on the stage. It is used to reveal the character's innermost thoughts and struggles. It is longer than an aside and usually expresses important themes in the play.

As Act I continues . . .

- Macbeth argues with himself about whether or not to murder Duncan.

READ ALOUD **Lines 1–4**

The pronoun *it* refers to the murder of Duncan. Why do you think Macbeth uses a pronoun to refer to his plan for murder? **(Shakespeare's Language)**

_____

_____

English Learner Support
LANGUAGE

Idiom *The be-all and the end-all* means "something that is complete in itself" or "everything." Macbeth means that murdering Duncan might be acceptable if doing so had no consequences.

What Does It Mean?

In lines 10–12, Macbeth is saying that he is afraid that he will have to pay in some way for murdering Duncan.

So clear in his great office, that his virtues
Will plead like angels, trumpet-tongued, against
20 The deep damnation of his taking-off;
And pity, like a naked new-born babe,
Striding the blast, or heaven's cherubin, horsed
Upon the sightless couriers of the air,
Shall blow the horrid deed in every eye,
25 That tears shall drown the wind. I have no spur
To prick the sides of my intent, but only
Vaulting ambition, which o'erleaps itself
And falls on the other—

Pause & Reflect

FOCUS

Lady Macbeth enters and finds her husband lost in
thought. Read to find out how Lady Macbeth prods
her husband to kill the king.

[*Enter* Lady Macbeth.]

How now? What news?

Lady Macbeth. He has almost supped. Why have you
left the chamber?

30 **Macbeth.** Hath he asked for me?

Lady Macbeth.   Know you not he has?

Macbeth. We will proceed no further in this business.
He hath honored me of late, and I have bought
Golden opinions from all sorts of people,
Which would be worn now in their newest gloss,
35 Not cast aside so soon.

Lady Macbeth.   Was the hope drunk
Wherein you dressed yourself? Hath it slept since?
And wakes it now to look so green and pale
At what it did so freely? From this time
Such I account thy love. Art thou afeard
40 To be the same in thine own act and valor
As thou art in desire? Wouldst thou have that

Duncan's subjects and stir great grief.

What Does It Mean?

Taking-off means "murder."

English Learner Support
LANGUAGE

Figurative Language *Sightless couriers* refers to the winds that will carry the cherubin, or angels, as they spread the word about Macbeth's evil deed.

Pause & Reflect

What arguments does Macbeth make *against* murdering Duncan?

_____

_____

As Act I ends . . .

- Lady Macbeth urges her husband to kill the king.
- Macbeth makes a decision.

What Does It Mean?

Supped means "finished eating supper."

32–35 I have . . . so soon: The praises that Macbeth has received are, like new clothes, to be worn, not quickly thrown away.

35–38 Was the hope drunk . . . freely: Lady Macbeth sarcastically suggests that Macbeth's ambition must have been drunk, because it now seems to have a hangover **(to look so green and pale)**.

39–45 Such I . . . adage: Lady Macbeth criticizes Macbeth's weak will to secure the crown **(ornament of life)** and calls him a coward. She compares him to a cat in a proverb **(adage).** This cat wanted to catch fish but did not try because it was afraid to get its feet wet.

JOT IT DOWN Reread Lines 32–35

What has Macbeth decided to do in regard to Duncan? **(Infer)**

_____

_____

_____

Which thou esteem'st the ornament of life,
And live a coward in thine own esteem,
Letting "I dare not" wait upon "I would,"
45   Like the poor cat i' the adage?

Macbeth.   Prithee peace!
I dare do all that may become a man.
Who dares do more is none.

Lady Macbeth.   What beast was't then
That made you break this enterprise to me?
When you durst do it, then you were a man;
50   And to be more than what you were, you would
Be so much more the man. Nor time nor place
Did then adhere, and yet you would make both.
They have made themselves, and that their fitness
      now
Does unmake you. I have given suck, and know
55   How tender 'tis to love the babe that milks me.
I would, while it was smiling in my face,
Have plucked my nipple from his boneless gums
And dashed the brains out, had I so sworn as you
Have done to this.

Macbeth.   If we should fail?

Lady Macbeth.   We fail?
60   But screw your courage to the sticking place,
And we'll not fail. When Duncan is asleep
(Whereto the rather shall his day's hard journey
Soundly invite him), his two chamberlains
Will I with wine and wassail so convince
65   That memory, the warder of the brain,
Shall be a fume, and the receipt of reason
A limbeck only. When in swinish sleep
Their drenched natures lie as in a death,
What cannot you and I perform upon
70   The unguarded Duncan? what not put upon
His spongy officers, who shall bear the guilt
Of our great quell?

Macbeth.   Bring forth men-children only,
For thy undaunted mettle should compose
Nothing but males. Will it not be received,

48 break this enterprise: tell me about your purpose (to kill the king).

49: durst: dared.

51–54 Nor time . . . unmake you: You talked bravely when the time was not right to act. Now that we have the opportunity **(fitness)**, you are afraid.

54 I have given suck: I have nursed a baby.

60 But . . . place: When each string of a guitar or lute is tightened to the peg **(sticking place)**, the instrument is ready to be played.

63 chamberlains: servants: attendants.

64 wassail: drinking.

65–67 That memory . . . a limbeck only: Memory was thought to be located at the base of the brain, to guard against harmful vapors rising from the body. Lady Macbeth will get the guards so drunk that their reason will become like a still **(limbeck)**, producing confused thoughts.

72 quell: murder.

72–74 Bring forth . . . males: Your bold spirit **(undaunted mettle)** is better suited to raising males than females.

What Does It Mean?

Prithee is a short form of *I pray thee,* meaning "please." *Prithee peace!* means "Please be quiet!"

Reading Check

What does Lady Macbeth say she would prefer to do rather than back out of the plan?

What Does It Mean?

Spongy officers is a reference to the two drunken guards. They will be soaked with wine like sponges soaked with water. Lady Macbeth goes on to say that because the guards will be unconscious, she and Macbeth can frame them for Duncan's murder.

75   When we have marked with blood those sleepy two
        Of his own chamber and used their very daggers,
        That they have done't?

Lady Macbeth.   Who dares receive it other,
        As we shall make our griefs and clamor roar
        Upon his death?

Macbeth.   I am settled and bend up
80   Each corporal agent to this terrible feat.
        Away, and mock the time with fairest show;
        False face must hide what the false heart doth know.

        [*Exeunt.*]

Pause & Reflect

79–82 **I am settled . . . know:** Now that Macbeth has made up his mind, every part of his body **(each corporal agent)** is tightened like a bow. He and Lady Macbeth will return to the banquet and trick everyone **(mock the time)**. They will hide their evil intent behind friendly faces.

Pause & Reflect

1. Circle the word below that completes the following sentence.
   Lady Macbeth implies that killing the king is a _____ thing to do. **(Infer)**

   cowardly   foolish

   manly   patriotic

2. How would you **summarize** Lady Macbeth's plan for killing the king and getting away with it?

   _____

   _____

   _____

   _____

3. On the battlefield, Macbeth is a great warrior. How does he act at home with his wife? **(Evaluate)**

   _____

   _____

   _____

   _____

CHALLENGE

Dramatic irony refers to a situation in which the reader or audience knows something that a character doesn't know. For example, the fact that King Duncan calls Macbeth, who is planning murder, "a peerless kinsman" is an instance of dramatic irony. Review Act I to find other examples of dramatic irony. What points do you think Shakespeare was making when he used dramatic irony?

Active Reading SkillBuilder

Shakespeare's Language

The **grammar, word order,** and **vocabulary** of Shakespeare's language are sometimes different from those of today's English. Here are some major differences:

- *Thou, thee, thy, thine,* and *thyself* were used in place of *you.*

- Unfamiliar vocabulary was used.

- Helping verbs were used far less than they are today.

- Sometimes verbs came before subjects, or objects appeared before verbs.

Try to paraphrase Shakespeare's language. In the chart below, Macbeth's opening speech in Act 1, Scene 7 is divided into sections. Record what you think each section is about. Add any questions or comments you have. An example is shown.

Macbeth, Act One, Scene 7

Section	Summary
Lines 1–7	*Macbeth would kill Duncan at once if he could do so without negative consequences.*
Lines 7–12	
Lines 12–16	
Lines 16–25	
Lines 25–28	

Literary Analysis SkillBuilder

Soliloquy/Aside

A **soliloquy** is a speech that reveals a character's private thoughts to the audience.
An **aside** is a remark made by a character that others on stage do not hear. The
soliloquy and the aside allow playwrights to reveal characters' thoughts and motives.
In the chart below, identify soliloquies and asides in Act One of *Macbeth*. Note the
thoughts and motives they reveal.

Act, Scene, and Line Numbers	Soliloquy or Aside?	What It Reveals
Act One, Scene 3, lines 127–142	Aside	Macbeth's belief in the witches' prophecies; his first thoughts of murdering Duncan

from PARADISE LOST

John Milton

Before You Read

Connect to Your Life

According to the Bible, Adam and Eve were the first human beings. They lived in a paradise called the Garden of Eden until they sinned by eating fruit that God had forbidden them to eat. Think about what makes some behavior sinful. Write a definition of sinful behavior below.

_____

_____

_____

_____

_____

_____

_____

_____

_____

Key to the Epic Poem

WHAT'S THE BIG IDEA? In the epic poem *Paradise Lost,* John Milton states that his purpose is to "justify the ways of God to men." This means that Milton wants to clarify and explain God's actions. Do you think that is possible? As you read the excerpt, keep Milton's purpose in mind and think about whether or not he fulfills his purpose.

Reading Tips

Paradise Lost is an **epic poem,** a long poem that tells a story about a serious subject. Though one of the greatest poems in English, it isn't easy to read. Milton uses long sentences, complicated word order, and unfamiliar vocabulary. As you read, try first to get a general idea of what is going on. You can also use the following strategies:

- Look for the main subjects and verbs. Be patient. Often you may have to wait until the end of a long sentence to get to the subject.

- Use punctuation (such as commas, semicolons, and colons) to divide the sentences into smaller chunks.

- Refer to the information in the Guide for Reading to help you understand difficult words and passages.

As the epic poem begins . . .

- The speaker states the topic of the poem.
- He asks the Heavenly Muse for help in writing it.
- He explains his purpose.

from Paradise Lost

John Milton

PREVIEW Everything in *Paradise Lost* is done on a huge scale. The poem deals with the biblical story of how and why evil came into the world. It also explores what part God plays in human life. The setting includes both heaven and hell. The characters are larger than life, especially the fallen angel, Satan. According to the Bible, Satan was the first rebel against God. Satan and his allies were defeated by God's forces and thrown out of heaven. In an act of vengeance, Satan later persuaded Adam and Eve to disobey God. As a result, evil entered the world, and human beings lost paradise. This brief excerpt will introduce you to Milton's purposes and will give you a memorable glimpse of Satan and Hell.

FOCUS

In the opening of the poem, Milton describes his subject. He calls on divine inspiration and announces his purpose in writing.

MARK IT UP As you read, underline phrases that tell how Milton views the great task he is about to begin. An example is highlighted on page 122.

> Of man's first disobedience, and the fruit
> Of that forbidden tree whose mortal taste
> Brought death into the world, and all our woe,
> With loss of Eden, till one greater Man
> 5 Restore us, and regain the blissful seat,
> Sing, Heavenly Muse, that on the secret top
> Of Oreb, or of Sinai, didst inspire
> That shepherd who first taught the chosen seed
> In the beginning how the heavens and earth
> 10 Rose out of Chaos: or, if Sion hill
> Delight thee more, and Siloa's brook that flowed

Use this guide for help with unfamiliar words and difficult passages.

MARK IT UP **KEEP TRACK**

As you read, you can use these marks to keep track of your understanding.

✔ ..... I understand.

? ..... I don't understand this.

! ..... Interesting or surprising idea

1–4 In the biblical story of the Garden of Eden, God told Adam and Eve they could not eat the fruit of one tree. When tempted, however, Eve ate the fruit and then gave some to Adam. They were forced to leave the garden, and their actions brought sin into the world.

4–5 till . . . seat: until Jesus Christ **(one greater Man)** helps us to return to the relationship with God that we had in Eden **(blissful seat).**

6 Heavenly Muse: the divine source of Milton's poetic inspiration. The Muse is the Spirit of God that the Bible says spoke to Moses (the "shepherd" of line 8). Milton is asking the Muse to "sing" the story of how Eden was lost.

7 Oreb (ôr'eb). **. . Sinai** (sī'nī'): Mounts Horeb and Sinai, on which Moses heard the voice of God.

8 the chosen seed: the Jews.

10–11 Sion hill . . . Siloa's brook: places in Jerusalem, the holy city of the Jews.

Reading Tip

Read or reread chapters 1–4 in Genesis, the first book of the Bible. You can use an English translation or a translation in your native language. Knowing what happens in that story will help you better understand *Paradise Lost.*

English Learner Support
CULTURE

Muses The *Muses* were nine daughters of the ancient Greek god Zeus. Each Muse was responsible for a particular art or science. It was her job to help artists and thinkers to do their work. In England at the time Milton was writing, it was customary to ask for the help of a Muse, especially when writing poetry. However, since Milton was a devout Christian, he linked the idea of the Muse to the idea of his God.

Fast by the oracle of God, I thence
Invoke thy aid to my adventurous song,
That with no middle flight intends to soar
Above th' Aonian mount, while it pursues
Things unattempted yet in prose or rhyme.
And chiefly thou, O Spirit, that dost prefer
Before all temples th' upright heart and pure,
Instruct me, for thou know'st; thou from the first
Wast present, and with mighty wings outspread
Dovelike sat'st brooding on the vast abyss,
And mad'st it pregnant: what in me is dark
Illumine; what is low, raise and support;
That to the height of this great argument
I may assert Eternal Providence,
And justify the ways of God to men.

Pause & Reflect

FOCUS

In this section, the poet asks a question: Who tempted Adam and Eve to sin? As the poet answers, he introduces Satan, the enemy of God.

MARK IT UP As you read, circle words and phrases that tell what Satan is like.

Say first (for Heaven hides nothing from thy view,
Nor the deep tract of Hell), say first what cause
Moved our grand parents, in that happy state,
Favored of Heaven so highly, to fall off
From their Creator, and transgress his will
For one restraint, lords of the world besides?
Who first seduced them to that foul revolt?
Th' infernal serpent; he it was, whose guile,
Stirred up with envy and revenge, deceived
The mother of mankind, what time his pride
Had cast him out from Heaven, with all his host
Of rebel angels, by whose aid aspiring
To set himself in glory above his peers,
He trusted to have equaled the Most High,
If he opposed; and with ambitious aim
Against the throne and monarchy of God
Raised impious war in Heaven and battle proud,

GUIDE FOR READING

12 Fast by the oracle of God: near the Jews' temple in Jerusalem.

14 with no middle flight: not in an ordinary or average way.

15 Aonian (ā-ō′nē-ən) **mount:** Mount Helicon in Greece, which in ancient times was considered sacred to the Muses.

20–22 with mighty wings . . . pregnant: In the Bible, the Spirit of God is described as floating over a great empty space **(vast abyss)** during the creation of the universe.

24 argument: subject.

25 Providence: God's plan for the universe.

26 justify: show the justice of. Milton states his purpose in this line.

27–33 The poet asks his Muse for help in understanding Adam and Eve. He asks why they did the one thing that was forbidden them **(one restraint)** and so lost paradise.

29 our grand parents: Adam and Eve.

31 transgress: overstep the limits set by.

32 for: on account of; **besides:** otherwise.

34 th' infernal serpent: Satan, who in the Bible is referred to as "that old serpent" (Revelation 20:2). In the biblical story, Satan took the form of a serpent to tempt Eve to eat the fruit of the Tree of Knowledge; **guile** (gīl): deceit.

36 what time: when.

43 impious (ĭm′pē-əs): showing disrespect for God.

English Learner Support
LANGUAGE

Elision To make the words he wanted to use fit the meter in each line, Milton often cut words short by omitting letters. This is called *elision*. For example, in *th' Aonian*, Milton dropped the *e* sound in the word *the*, so that the *th* and first syllable in *Aonian* run together to make one sound.

What Does It Mean?

John Milton used words that are considered archaic today. An *archaic* word is one that was used in the past but is no longer in general use. Examples include words such as *dost, wast,* and *sat'st*. These words mean "does," "were," and "sat."

Pause & Reflect

In lines 25–26, Milton says his purpose in writing *Paradise Lost* is to "assert Eternal Providence, / And justify the ways of God to men." Circle the phrase below that best expresses this purpose. **(Clarify Meaning)**

to show how God's will and plan for the world works

to show that God cannot be understood by humans

As the epic poem continues . . .

• The speaker introduces Satan and tells how God sent him to Hell.

With vain attempt. Him the Almighty Power
45 Hurled headlong flaming from th' ethereal sky
With hideous ruin and combustion down
To bottomless perdition, there to dwell
In adamantine chains and penal fire,
Who durst defy th' Omnipotent to arms.

Pause & Reflect

FOCUS

Milton now describes the Hell where Satan and his
rebel angels find themselves. As you read, look for
details that tell what Hell is like.

50 Nine times the space that measures day and night
To mortal men, he with his horrid crew
Lay vanquished, rolling in the fiery gulf
Confounded though immortal. But his doom
Reserved him to more wrath; for now the thought
55 Both of lost happiness and lasting pain
Torments him; round he throws his baleful eyes,
That witnessed huge affliction and dismay,
Mixed with obdùrate pride and steadfast hate.
At once, as far as angels ken, he views
60 The dismal situation waste and wild:
A dungeon horrible, on all sides round
As one great furnace flamed; yet from those flames
No light, but rather darkness visible
Served only to discover sights of woe,
65 Regions of sorrow, doleful shades, where peace
And rest can never dwell, hope never comes
That comes to all, but torture without end
Still urges, and a fiery deluge, fed
With ever-burning sulphur unconsumed:
70 Such place Eternal Justice had prepared
For those rebellious; here their prison ordained
In utter darkness and their portion set
As far removed from God and light of Heaven
As from the center thrice to th' utmost pole.
75 O how unlike the place from whence they fell!
There the companions of his fall, o'erwhelmed

GUIDE FOR READING

44 Him: Satan.

45 th' ethereal (ĭ-thîr′ē-əl) **sky:** Heaven.

47 perdition: damnation; Hell.

48 adamantine (ăd′ə-măn′tēn′): indestructible; unbreakable; **penal** (pē′nəl): meant to punish.

49 Who: Satan.

50–52 Nine . . . vanquished: Satan and his allies were stunned by the fall from heaven. For nine days and nights they lay on the floor of Hell.

53 Confounded though immortal: frustrated and brought to ruin even though he is an angel and will never die.

53–54 his doom . . . wrath: fate had more punishment in store for him.

56 baleful: menacing; threatening evil.

58 obdurate (ŏb′dŏŏ-rĭt): stubborn; unyielding.

59 ken: can see.

62–63 Hell is such a terrible place that its flames give no light, only "darkness visible."

65 doleful shades: sorrowful ghosts.

69 sulphur: a chemical that gives off foul-smelling fumes when burning.

73–74 As far . . . utmost pole: The fall from Heaven to Hell is a distance as great as the distance from the earth **(center)** to the outer edge of the universe **(utmost pole).**

76 There: in Hell.

Reading Check

Why has Satan fallen to Hell?

Pause & Reflect

Look at the words you circled as you read. How would you describe Satan? **(Infer)**

_____

_____

_____

As the epic poem continues . . .

• The speaker describes the place where Satan and his allies find themselves.

Reading Tip

Review the excerpt and underline all the names and phrases Milton uses to refer to God. Circle all the names and phrases Milton uses to describe Satan. For example, in line 81, Satan is called "arch-enemy." In line 99, God is called "the Mightiest." Notice that the words that are used to refer to God are capitalized.

Reading Check

What two places is Milton contrasting?

With floods and whirlwinds of tempestuous fire,
He soon discerns; and, weltering by his side,
One next himself in power, and next in crime,
Long after known in (Palestine,) and named
Beëlzebub. To whom th' arch-enemy,
And thence in Heaven called Satan, with bold words
Breaking the horrid silence thus began:

Pause & *Reflect*

FOCUS

This is Satan's first speech in the poem. He recalls
how he led a mighty army against God. He says he
will continue to fight forever. Read to find out how he
feels about God.

"If thou beëst he—but O how fallen! how changed
From him who in the happy realms of light
Clothed with transcendent brightness didst outshine
Myriads, though bright! if he whom mutual league,
United thoughts and counsels, equal hope
And hazard in the glorious enterprise,
Joined with me once, now misery hath joined
In equal ruin; into what pit thou seest
From what height fallen, so much the stronger proved
He with his thunder: and till then who knew
The force of those dire arms? Yet not for those,
Nor what the potent Victor in his rage
Can else inflict, do I repent or change,
Though changed in outward luster, that fixed mind
And high disdain, from sense of injured merit,
That with the Mightiest raised me to contend,
And to the fierce contention brought along
Innumerable force of spirits armed,
That durst dislike his reign, and me preferring,
His utmost power with adverse power opposed
In dubious battle on the plains of Heaven,

78 weltering: twisting and turning.

81 Beëlzebub (bē-ĕl′zə-bŭb): a powerful demon, called "the prince of the devils" in the Bible (Matthew 12:24).

81–82 th' arch-enemy . . . Satan: The name *Satan* comes from a Hebrew word meaning "enemy."

84 If thou beëst he: Satan is seeing his fellow angel Beëlzebub for the first time since the rebel angels were thrown out of heaven.

87–94 if he . . . dire arms: Beëlzebub **(he)** shared Satan's plans and actions in the rebellion against God **(glorious enterprise).** He is now sharing Satan's defeat **(equal ruin).** They have fallen from the greatest height to the lowest depth because God's power was greater than theirs. Until then, they had not realized how strong God was **(the force of those dire arms).**

94–105 Yet not . . . his throne: Satan and his allies are ruined, and God has the power to punish him further. Still, Satan refuses to change his mind. He sticks to his original purpose **(fixed mind and high disdain)** to oppose God. He feels the same sense of injustice **(injured merit)** and dislike of God's authority that led him to organize an army of rebel angels in the first place.

More About . . .

(PALESTINE) *Palestine* here refers to the area of parts of present-day Jordan, Israel, and Egypt, as described in the Bible. It is also known as the "Holy Land."

Reading Check

Who is Beëlzebub?

Pause & Reflect

MARK IT UP What is Hell like? Circle words and phrases in lines 50–83 that describe it. **(Visualize)**

As the epic poem ends . . .

- Satan describes his first battle against God.
- Satan vows to fight God forever.

Reading Tip

Use the following Venn diagram to jot down words, phrases, and your own ideas to compare and contrast Heaven and Hell.

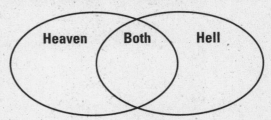

Heaven Both Hell

105 And shook his throne. What though the field be lost?
All is not lost: the unconquerable will,
And study of revenge, immortal hate,
And courage never to submit or yield:
And what is else not to be overcome?
110 That glory never shall his wrath or might
Extort from me. To bow and sue for grace
With suppliant knee, and deify his power
Who from the terror of this arm so late
Doubted his empire—that were low indeed;
115 That were an ignominy and shame beneath
This downfall; since, by fate, the strength of gods
And this empyreal substance cannot fail;
Since, through experience of this great event,
In arms not worse, in foresight much advanced,
120 We may with more successful hope resolve
To wage by force or guile eternal war,
Irreconcilable to our grand Foe,
Who now triùmphs, and in th' excess of joy
Sole reigning holds the tyranny of Heaven."

Pause & Reflect

107 study: pursuit.

110–111 That glory . . . me: Satan will never give glory to God, regardless of God's anger or power.

111–124 To bow . . . Heaven: Satan is speaking. He says that to go begging to God, his worst enemy, would be a disgrace worse than his defeat. Instead, he decides to make the most of what he has left. He is still an immortal angel, and he has not lost his strength. He also has learned a great deal **(in foresight much advanced)** from his battle with God. He declares eternal war against God and vows never to give in, though God is the victorious ruler of Heaven.

112 with suppliant (sŭp'lē-ənt) **knee:** in a begging way.

115 ignominy (ĭg'nə-mĭn'ē)**:** disgrace.

117 this empyreal (ĕm-pîr'ē-əl) **substance:** the heavenly material of which the angels' bodies are made.

What Does It Mean?

Irreconcilable means "refusing to submit or agree with." Satan refuses to give in to God.

Pause & Reflect

READ ALOUD **1.** Read aloud the boxed passage on page 128. Circle the three phrases below that describe Satan. **(Infer)**

strong willpower

hatred of God

ability to overthrow God

desire for revenge against God

MARK IT UP **2.** What does Satan plan for the future? Underline phrases in lines 105–124 that describe his plans. **(Make Judgments)**

CHALLENGE

An **epic hero** is a character who is usually royal or powerful in some other way. He or she often does superhuman things or behaves in a superhuman way. The character's actions also determine the fates of many other characters. Based on this excerpt, do you think Satan could be an epic hero? Why or why not? Star lines in the excerpt that support your ideas. **(Analyze)**

Active Reading SkillBuilder

Clarifying Meaning

As you read this excerpt from Milton's epic poem, use the following suggestions and chart to help you **clarify meaning** in difficult passages. An example is given.

- **Archaic verb and pronoun forms (like *dost* and *thou*):** Replace them with familiar words that make sense. Use a dictionary if necessary.

- **Obsolete or unfamiliar vocabulary:** Use context clues and the Guide for Reading notes. Use a dictionary if necessary.

- **Allusions (mainly to the Bible and mythology):** Use the Guide for Reading notes.

- **Long, sweeping sentences:** Break down each sentence into parts you can understand. Focus on key words, such as the subject and its verb.

- **Unusual word order:** Reorder the words so they sound more natural and make

Passage	My Notes, Definitions, and Paraphrasing
Lines: *1–26* Speaker: *Milton* Speaking to: *Heavenly Muse*	*Milton is asking for divine inspiration to write his great poem. He will explain God's plan to people.*
Lines: Speaker: Speaking to:	
Lines: Speaker: Speaking to:	
Lines: Speaker: Speaking to:	

Literary Analysis SkillBuilder

Diction

In *Paradise Lost,* Milton used the powerful, formal **diction,** or word choice, that his serious subjects and themes demanded. Choose a passage, such as the summary of Satan's fall in lines 34–49 or Satan's speech in lines 84–124. On the chart, list some examples of Milton's diction, and note the lines in which they appear. Then write a synonym for each word. Three examples have been done for you.

	Milton's Words	Synonyms
Nouns	*wrath (l. 54)*	*anger*
Verbs	*invoke (l. 13)*	*ask*
Modifiers	*obdurate (l. 58)*	*stubborn*

A Modest

PROPOSAL

Jonathan Swift

Before You Read

Connect to Your Life

Poverty and hunger exist throughout the world. What are some ways that poverty and hunger might be lessened? How can people and countries who have a lot help those who have little?

_____

_____

_____

_____

_____

Key to the Essay

WHAT YOU NEED TO KNOW "A Modest Proposal" is a satire. Satire attacks society's shortcomings and follies by making fun of them. In this essay, Swift, born to English parents but raised in Ireland, proposes an outrageous "solution" to Ireland's failing economy and widespread poverty. As you read, pay attention to the arguments Swift makes to support his proposal. And don't hesitate to laugh; remember, it's just satire.

A Modest PROPOSAL

Jonathan Swift

PREVIEW With wit and humor, Jonathan Swift attacked injustices. He forced his readers to look at the ugly truth. Swift was 60 when he published this essay in 1729. At that time, England ruled Ireland, and English policies had ruined the Irish economy. Ireland was filled with poor people. In this essay, Swift poses as an official who offers a crazy solution to this problem—namely, to have Irish babies sold for food. Swift, though, really is attacking England and its rich landlords who mistreat the Irish poor.

As the essay begins . . .

- The speaker describes the serious problems of poverty and hunger.

- He says that he has a solution to this problem.

FOCUS

The speaker describes the severe poverty in Ireland. He claims that his solution to the problem will go much further than other proposals.

MARK IT UP As you read, circle details that help you understand the poverty in Ireland. An example is highlighted.

It is a melancholy object to those who walk through this great town[1] or travel in the country, when they see the streets, the roads, and cabin doors, crowded with beggars of the female sex, followed by three, four, or six children, all in rags and importuning[2] every passenger for an alms. These mothers, instead of being able to work for their honest livelihood, are forced to employ all their time in strolling to beg sustenance for their helpless infants, who, as they grow up, either turn thieves for want of work, or

---

1. **this great town:** Dublin.
2. **importuning** (ĭm′ pôr-tōon′ ĭng): begging.

leave their dear native country to fight for the Pretender[3] in Spain, or sell themselves to the Barbadoes.[4]

I think it is agreed by all parties that this <u>prodigious</u> number of children in the arms, or on the backs, or at the heels of their mothers, and frequently of their fathers, is in the present <u>deplorable</u> state of the kingdom a very great

20 additional grievance; and therefore whoever could find out a fair, cheap, and easy method of making these children sound, useful members of the commonwealth would deserve so well of the public as to have his statue set up for a preserver of the nation.

But my intention is very far from being confined to provide only for the children of professed beggars; it is of a much greater extent, and shall take in the whole number of infants at a certain age who are born of parents in effect as little able to support them as those who demand our charity in the

30 streets.

As to my own part, having turned my thoughts for many years upon this important subject, and maturely weighed the several schemes of other projectors, I have always found them grossly mistaken in their computation. It is true, a child just dropped from its dam[5] may be supported by her milk for a solar year, with little other nourishment; at most not above the value of two shillings, which the mother may certainly get, or the value in scraps, by her lawful occupation of begging; and it is exactly at one year old that I propose to provide for

40 them in such a manner as instead of being a charge upon their parents or the parish, or wanting food and raiment for the rest of their lives, they shall on the contrary contribute to the feeding, and partly to the clothing, of many thousands.

There is likewise another great advantage in my scheme, that it will prevent those voluntary abortions, and that horrid practice of women murdering their bastard children, alas, too

---

3. **Pretender:** James Edward Stuart—the "pretender." He claimed to be the rightful King of England. He raised armies to fight against the actual King. The common people of Ireland were loyal to James Stuart.

4. **sell . . . the Barbadoes** (bär-bā′dōz): To escape poverty, some of the Irish sailed to the West Indies. They obtained money for their passage by agreeing to work on plantations there for a set time.

5. **dam:** female parent (often applied to farm animals).

WORDS
TO
KNOW

prodigious (prə-dĭj′əs) *adj.* enormous
deplorable (dĭ-plôr′ə-bəl) *adj.* miserable; woeful

English Learner Support
VOCABULARY

Infants Here, *infants* refers to all small children, not just babies.

✔ **Reading Check**
What is the problem the speaker wants to solve?

English Learner Support
VOCABULARY

Multiple Meanings Here, *charge* means "responsibility," not "an amount of money."

More About . . .

THE PARISH In Ireland, the parish was the community who attended the local church. Before the time of government or private charities, the church was responsible for taking care of people who could not care for themselves.

Pause & Reflect

Which phrase below does *not* apply to the speaker's proposal? Cross out that phrase. **(Main Idea)**

will provide more jobs for adults

will reduce the number of murdered babies

will make poor children useful to the country

As the essay continues . . .

• The speaker uses statistics to describe the problem and to make him sound like an expert.

What Does It Mean?
Maintain means "support."

English Learner Support
LANGUAGE

Tone Notice that this is the second time the speaker refers to the poor as *breeders*. As the footnote explains, the term is usually used to describe farm animals, not people. The fact that the speaker uses the word several times shows that he is not thinking about the poor as human beings.

What Does It Mean?
Reared means "cared for a child or children in the early stages of life."

What Does It Mean?
Probationer refers to a person who undergoes a trial period to determine if he or she can complete given tasks successfully.

frequent among us, sacrificing the poor innocent babes, I doubt, more to avoid the expense than the shame, which would move tears and pity in the most savage and inhuman 50 breast.

Pause & Reflect

FOCUS
The speaker pretends to be an expert who has a solution to the problem of poverty. He uses numbers to show how bad the problem is.

MARK IT UP As you read, circle the numbers used by the speaker.

The number of souls in this kingdom being usually reckoned one million and a half, of these I calculate there may be about two hundred thousand couple whose wives are breeders;[6] from which number I subtract thirty thousand couples who are able to maintain their own children, although I apprehend there cannot be so many under the present distresses of the kingdom; but 60 this being granted, there will remain an hundred and seventy thousand breeders. I again subtract fifty thousand for those women who miscarry,[7] or whose children die by accident or disease within the year. There only remain an hundred and twenty thousand children of poor parents annually born. The question therefore is, how this number shall be reared and provided for, which, as I have already said, under the present situation of affairs, is utterly impossible by all the methods hitherto proposed. For we can neither employ them in 70 handicraft or agriculture; we neither build houses (I mean in the country) nor cultivate land. They can very seldom pick up a livelihood by stealing till they arrive at six years old, except where they are of towardly parts;[8] although I confess they learn the rudiments much earlier, during which time they can however be looked upon only as probationers, as I have been informed by a principal gentleman in the county of Cavan, who protested to me that he never knew above one or two instances under the age of six, even in a part of the kingdom

---

6. **breeders:** animals that can produce young.

7. **miscarry:** fail to carry a baby long enough so that it can live.

8. **are of towardly parts:** have a promising talent.

WORDS
TO
KNOW

rudiment (rōō′də-mənt) *n.* a basic principle or skill

so renowned for the quickest <u>proficiency</u> in that art.

80   I am assured by our merchants that a boy or girl before twelve years old is no salable commodity; and even when they come to this age they will not yield above three pounds, or three pounds and half a crown[9] at most on the Exchange; which cannot turn to account either to the parents or the kingdom, the charge of nutriment[10] and rags having been at least four times that value.

Pause & *Reflect*

FOCUS
In this section the speaker states his proposal. Read to find out why he proposes that Irish babies be sold for food.

90

I shall now therefore humbly propose my own thoughts, which I hope will not be liable to the least objection.

   I have been assured by a very knowing American of my acquaintance in London, that a young healthy child well nursed is at a year old a most delicious, nourishing, and wholesome food, whether stewed, roasted, baked, or boiled; and I make no doubt that it will equally serve in a fricassee or a ragout.[11]

   I do therefore humbly offer it to public consideration that of the hundred and twenty thousand children, already computed, twenty thousand may be reserved for breed,

100 whereof only one fourth part to be males, which is more than we allow to sheep, black cattle, or swine; and my reason is that these children are seldom the fruits of marriage, a circumstance not much regarded by our savages, therefore one male will be sufficient to serve four females. That the remaining hundred thousand may at a year old be offered in sale to the persons of quality and fortune through the kingdom, always advising the mother to let them suck plentifully in the last month, so as to render them plump and

---

9. **crown:** a British coin [no longer in use] worth about sixty-three cents in U.S. currency.

10. **nutriment:** food.

11. **fricassee** (frĭk′e-sē′) . . . **ragout** (ră-gōō′): types of meat stews.

WORDS TO KNOW   **proficiency** (prə-fĭsh′ən-sē) *n.* competence; expertise

---

What Does It Mean?
No salable commodity means "is not worth selling."

Pause & *Reflect*

 READ ALOUD   Read aloud the boxed sentence on this page. What is the speaker's main point? Circle the correct sentence below. **(Main Idea)**

Even if parents sell a child into slavery, they still lose money.

Parents should be glad that children can be sold.

As the essay continues . . .

• The speaker explains his "modest proposal."

English Learner Support
LANGUAGE

Figure of Speech *The fruits of marriage* means "the children of a married couple." The speaker means that most of these poor children are born to single mothers, so there is no reason to have so many males for breeding.

What Does It Mean?
Persons of quality refers to the aristocracy, or the highest social class.

 Reading Check
What is the speaker's "modest"
solution to poverty?

More About . . .

ENGLISH LANDLORDS The vast
majority of the Irish were Roman
Catholics. According to English
law, Catholics could not own
land. Therefore, most people in
Ireland had to pay high rents to
the English landlords.

More About . . .

LENT In Christianity, *Lent* is the
40-day period between Ash
Wednesday and Easter. One of
the observances of this period is
to avoid eating meat. Catholics
ate more fish instead, which
was thought to promote fertility.
This explains the physician's
observation that more children are
born nine months after Lent than
at any other time of the year.

What Does It Mean?

Per annum is a business and
accounting term that means
"each year" or "yearly."

English Learner Support
VOCABULARY

Jargon *Net profit* is an
accounting term. It means
the amount of money a
business makes after paying
its expenses.

fat for a good table. A child will make two dishes at an
110 entertainment for friends; and when the family dines alone,
the fore or hind quarter will make a reasonable dish, and
seasoned with a little pepper or salt will be very good boiled
on the fourth day, especially in winter.

I have reckoned upon a medium[12] that a child just born will
weigh twelve pounds, and in a solar year if tolerably nursed
increaseth to twenty-eight pounds.

I grant this food will be somewhat dear,[13] and therefore
very proper for landlords, who, as they have already devoured
most of the parents, seem to have the best title to the children.
120 Infant's flesh will be in season throughout the year, but
more plentiful in March, and a little before and after. For we
are told by a grave author, an eminent French physician,[14] that
fish being a prolific[15] diet, there are more children born in
Roman Catholic countries about nine months after Lent than
at any other season; therefore, reckoning a year after Lent, the
markets will be more glutted than usual, because the number
of popish[16] infants is at least three to one in this kingdom; and
therefore it will have one other collateral advantage, by
lessening the number of Papists[17] among us.
130 I have already computed the charge of nursing a beggar's
child (in which list I reckon all cottagers, laborers, and four
fifths of the farmers), to be about two shillings per annum,
rags included; and I believe no gentleman would repine[18] to
give ten shillings for the carcass of a good fat child, which, as
I have said, will make four dishes of excellent nutritive meat,
when he hath only some particular friend or his own family to
dine with him. Thus the squire will learn to be a good
landlord, and grow popular among the tenants; the mother
will have eight shillings net profit, and be fit for work till she
140 produces another child.

Those who are more thrifty (as I must confess the times
require) may flay the carcass; the skin of which artificially[19]

---

12. **upon a medium:** on the average.

13. **dear:** costly.

14. **grave . . . physician:** François Rabelais (frăn-swä′ răb′ ə-lā′) (1494?–1553), a
French comic writer.

15. **prolific:** promoting fertility.

16. **popish** (pō′pĭsh): Roman Catholic.

17. **Papists** (pā′pĭsts): Roman Catholics.

18. **repine** (rĭ-pīn′): complain.

19. **artificially:** skillfully.

dressed will make admirable gloves for ladies, and summer boots for fine gentlemen.

As to our city of Dublin, shambles[20] may be appointed for this purpose in the most convenient parts of it, and butchers we may be assured will not be wanting;[21] although I rather recommend buying the children alive, and dressing them hot from the knife as we do roasting pigs.

Pause **&** *Reflect*

150 **FOCUS**
The speaker rejects another plan—one that calls for eating adolescents. Read to find out why.

A very worthy person, a true lover of his country, and whose virtues I highly esteem, was lately pleased in discoursing on this matter to offer a refinement upon my scheme. He said that many gentlemen of this kingdom, having of late destroyed their deer, he conceived that the want of venison might be well supplied by the bodies of young lads and maidens, not exceeding fourteen years of age nor under twelve, so great a number of both sexes in every county being now ready to

160 starve for want of work and service; and these to be disposed of by their parents, if alive, or otherwise by their nearest relations. But with due <u>deference</u> to so excellent a friend and so deserving a patriot, I cannot be altogether in his sentiments; for as to the males, my American acquaintance assured me from frequent experience that their flesh was generally tough and lean, like that of our schoolboys, by continual exercise, and their taste disagreeable; and to fatten them would not answer the charge. Then as to the females, it would, I think with humble submission, be a loss to the public,

170 because they soon would become breeders themselves; and besides, it is not improbable that some scrupulous[22] people might be apt to censure[23] such a practice (although indeed very unjustly) as a little bordering upon cruelty; which, I confess,

---

20. **shambles:** slaughterhouses.
21. **wanting:** lacking.
22. **scrupulous:** too careful.
23. **censure:** find fault with.

WORDS
TO
KNOW   **deference** (děf'ər-əns) *n.* courteous regard or respect

Pause **&** *Reflect*
MARK IT UP Why does the speaker propose that Irish babies be sold for food? Write the answer below. Then circle the details on pages 137 and 138 that led you to your answer. **(Main Idea)**

_____

_____

_____

As the essay continues . . .

• The speaker offers several objections to the idea of eating teenagers.

English Learner Support
LANGUAGE

Irony In the phrase *a true lover of his country,* you can see an example of irony. If the man truly loved his country, he would not want to kill his own countrymen, especially if they were children.

English Learner Support
LANGUAGE

Usage *I cannot be altogether in his sentiments* is another way of saying "I cannot totally agree with him."

What Does It Mean?
Answer the charge means "solve the problem."

FORMOSA *Formosa* was the Portuguese name for the island that is now called Taiwan. Cannibalism was not practiced there, but in Swift's time, people assumed it must a barbaric place because it was far away and foreign.

What Does It Mean?

Prime dainty means "a very tasty snack."

What Does It Mean?

In the highlighted lines, Swift is referring to the mistresses of wealthy men or to prostitutes. He is saying that although they have no money, these girls wear fine clothes that they don't pay for and go to plays and other fun events in sedan chairs, which were closed carriages carried by footmen.

English Learner Support
VOCABULARY

Idiom *Pine away* means "to waste away slowly until death."

Pause & *Reflect*

READ ALOUD Read aloud the boxed sentences on this page. Why do many poor adults die each year? **(Main Idea)**

_____

_____

_____

_____

hath always been with me the strongest objection against any project, how well soever intended.

But in order to justify my friend, he confessed that this expedient was put into his head by the famous Psalmanazar,[24] a native of the island Formosa, who came from thence to London above twenty years ago, and in conversation told my
180 friend that in his country when any young person happened to be put to death, the executioner sold the carcass to persons of quality as a prime dainty; and that in his time the body of a plump girl of fifteen, who was crucified for an attempt to poison the emperor, was sold to his Imperial Majesty's prime minister of state, and other great mandarins of the court, in joints from the gibbet,[25] at four hundred crowns. Neither indeed can I deny that if the same use were made of several plump young girls in this town, who without one single groat[26] to their fortunes cannot stir abroad without a chair,
190 and appear at the playhouse and assemblies in foreign fineries which they never will pay for, the kingdom would not be the worse.

Some persons of a desponding spirit are in great concern about that vast number of poor people who are aged, diseased, or maimed, and I have been desired to employ my thoughts what course may be taken to ease the nation of so grievous an encumbrance. But I am not in the least pain upon that matter, because it is very well known that they are every day dying and rotting by cold and famine, and filth and
200 vermin, as fast as can be reasonably expected. And as to the younger laborers, they are now in almost as hopeful a condition. They cannot get work, and consequently pine away for want of nourishment to a degree that if at any time they are accidentally hired to common labor, they have not strength to perform it; and thus the country and themselves are happily delivered from the evils to come.

Pause & *Reflect*

24. **Psalmanazar** (săl′mə-năz′ər): a French impostor in London. He pretended to be from Formosa (now Taiwan).

25. **gibbet** (jĭb′ĭt): gallows.

26. **groat:** an old British coin worth four pennies.

WORDS
TO
KNOW

expedient (ĭk-spē′dē-ənt) *n.* a means to an end
encumbrance (ĕn-kŭm′brəns) *n.* a burden

FOCUS

The speaker explains six main advantages of his proposal.

210

▲ MARK IT UP As you read, underline these advantages.

I have too long digressed, and therefore shall return to my subject. I think the advantages by the proposal which I have made are obvious and many, as well as of the highest importance.

For first, as I have already observed, it would greatly lessen the number of (Papists,) with whom we are yearly overrun, being the principal breeders of the nation as well as our most dangerous enemies; and who stay at home on purpose to deliver the kingdom to the Pretender, hoping to take their advantage by the absence of so many good Protestants, who have chosen rather to leave their country than stay at home
220 and pay tithes against their conscience to an Episcopal curate.[27]

Secondly, the poorer tenants will have something valuable of their own, which by law may be made liable to distress,[28] and help to pay their landlord's rent, their corn and cattle being already seized and money a thing unknown.

Thirdly, whereas the maintenance of an hundred thousand children, from two years old and upwards, cannot be computed at less than ten shillings a piece per annum, the nation's stock will be thereby increased fifty thousand pounds
230 per annum, besides the profit of a new dish introduced to the tables of all gentlemen of fortune in the kingdom who have any refinement in taste. And the money will circulate among ourselves, the goods being entirely of our own growth and manufacture.

Fourthly, the constant breeders, besides the gain of eight shillings sterling per annum by the sale of their children, will be rid of the charge of maintaining them after the first year.

Fifthly, this food would likewise bring great custom to taverns, where the vintners[29] will certainly be so prudent as to
240 procure the best receipts for dressing it to perfection, and consequently have their houses frequented by all the fine gentlemen, who justly value themselves upon their knowledge

---

27. **Protestants . . . curate:** Swift is referring to Anglo-Irish landowners who lived in England. Much of the poverty in Ireland was caused by these absentee landlords. Swift had once been a curate, or parish priest.

28. **distress:** seizure for unpaid debts.

29. **vintners:** wine merchants.

As the essay continues . . .

• The speaker lists six reasons for adopting his proposal.

More About . . .

(PAPISTS) *Papist* is an offensive term used to refer to a Roman Catholic. Here, Swift uses satire to comment on the pervasive anti-Catholic views among Protestants in Ireland.

What Does It Mean?

In the highlighted sentence, Swift refers to the children, served as food at the tables of gentlemen, as "goods." He explains that by purchasing Irish goods, people will strengthen the Irish economy.

in good eating; and a skillful cook, who understands how to oblige his guests, will contrive to make it as expensive as they please.

Sixthly, this would be a great inducement to marriage, which all wise nations have either encouraged by rewards or enforced by laws and penalties. It would increase the care and tenderness of mothers toward their children, when they were sure of a settlement for life to the poor babes, provided in some sort by the public, to their annual profit instead of expense. We should see an honest emulation among the married women, which of them could bring the fattest child to the market. Men would become as fond of their wives during the time of their pregnancy as they are now of their mares in foal, their cows in calf, or sows when they are ready to farrow; nor offer to beat or kick them (as is too frequent a practice) for fear of a miscarriage.

Many other advantages might be enumerated. For instance, the addition of some thousand carcasses in our exportation of barreled beef, the propagation of swine's flesh, and improvement in the art of making good bacon, so much wanted among us by the great destruction of pigs, too frequent at our tables, which are no way comparable in taste or magnificence to a well-grown, fat, yearling child, which roasted whole will make a considerable figure at a lord mayor's feast[30] or any other public entertainment. But this and many others I omit, being studious of brevity.

> Supposing that one thousand families in this city would be constant customers for infants' flesh, besides others who might have it at merry meetings, particularly weddings and christenings, I compute that Dublin would take off annually about twenty thousand carcasses, and the rest of the kingdom (where probably they will be sold somewhat cheaper) the remaining eighty thousand.

Pause & Reflect

✔ **Reading Check**
What does the speaker think would make women care more for their children and men care more for their wives?

English Learner Support
LANGUAGE

Tone *Yearling* means "an animal between one and two years old." The word is never used to describe people, so by using it here, Swift is again showing that the speaker views these people as animals.

Pause & Reflect

READ ALOUD Read aloud the boxed sentence on this page. Then describe your reaction to the idea of serving cooked baby at "weddings" and "christenings." **(Connect)**

_____
_____
_____
_____

30. **lord mayor's feast:** Lord Mayors held banquets to celebrate their time in office.

WORDS TO KNOW

emulation (ĕm′yə-lā′shən) *n.* an effort to equal or outdo another person; rivalry

FOCUS
Read to find out why
the speaker believes
his plan is the best.

I can think of no one objection that will possibly be raised against this proposal, unless it should be urged that the number of people will be thereby much lessened in the kingdom. This I freely own,[31]

280 and it was indeed one principal design in offering it to the world. I desire the reader will observe, that I calculate my remedy for this one individual kingdom of Ireland and for no other that ever was, is, or I think ever can be upon earth. Therefore let no man talk to me of other expedients: of taxing our absentees at five shillings a pound: of using neither clothes nor household furniture except what is of our own growth and manufacture: of utterly rejecting the materials and instruments that promote foreign luxury: of curing the expensiveness of

290 pride, vanity, idleness, and gaming in our women: of introducing a vein of parsimony,[32] prudence, and temperance: of learning to love our country, in the want of which we differ even from Laplanders and the inhabitants of Topinamboo:[33] of quitting our <u>animosities</u> and factions, nor acting any longer like the Jews, who were murdering one another at the very moment their city was taken:[34] of being a little cautious not to sell our country and conscience for nothing: of teaching landlords to have at least one degree of mercy toward their tenants: lastly, of putting a spirit of honesty, industry, and skill into our shopkeepers;

300 who, if a resolution could now be taken to buy only our native goods, would immediately unite to cheat and exact upon us in the price, the measure, and the goodness, nor could ever yet be brought to make one fair proposal of just dealing, though often and earnestly invited to it.

Therefore I repeat, let no man talk to me of these and the like expedients,[35] till he hath at least some glimpse of hope

As the essay ends . . .

• The speaker lists and rejects other solutions.

• The speaker ends by saying that his proposal wouldn't help him because his children are too old to sell.

What Does It Mean?

Here, *gaming* means "gambling."

 Reading Check

What are the three ideas that the speaker rejects?

---

31. **own:** admit.

32. **parsimony** (pär′sə-mō′nē): thrift.

33. **Topinamboo** (tŏp′ĭ-năm′bōō): an area in Brazil.

34. **Jews . . . taken:** In A.D. 70, during a Jewish revolt against Roman rule, the people of Jerusalem fought among themselves. Their fighting made it easier for the Romas to capture the city.

35. **let no man . . . expedients:** Swift had, in his writings, suggested the "other expedients," or plans, without success.

WORDS
TO   **animosity** (ăn′ə-mŏs′ĭ-tē) *n.* hostility; hatred
KNOW

English Learner Support
LANGUAGE

Archaic Expression At the time Swift was writing, *full in our own power* meant "within our ability" or "something we can do."

More About . . .

SALTING Before refrigeration, meat was preserved by packing it  in salt, or in salty water called brine.

✔ **Reading Check**

What country does the speaker say would be glad to "eat up" Ireland?

What Does It Mean?

Here, *bent* means "committed to."

✔ **Reading Check**

Who are beggars "in effect," or in reality, but not beggars on the street?

---

that there will ever be some hearty and sincere attempt to put them in practice.

But as to myself, having been wearied out for many years 310 with offering vain, idle, visionary thoughts, and at length utterly despairing of success, I fortunately fell upon this proposal, which, as it is wholly new, so it hath something solid and real, of no expense and little trouble, full in our own power, and whereby we can incur no danger in disobliging[36] England. For this kind of commodity will not bear exportation, the flesh being of too tender a consistence to admit a long continuance in salt, although perhaps I could name a country which would be glad to eat up our whole nation without it.[37]

320 After all, I am not so violently bent upon my own opinion as to reject any offer proposed by wise men, which shall be found equally innocent, cheap, easy, and effectual. But before something of that kind shall be advanced in contradiction to my scheme, and offering a better, I desire the author or authors will be pleased maturely to consider two points. First, as things now stand, how they will be able to find food and raiment for an hundred thousand useless mouths and backs. And secondly, there being a round million of creatures in human figure throughout this kingdom, whose sole 330 subsistence put into a common stock would leave them in debt two millions of pounds sterling, adding those who are beggars by profession to the bulk of farmers, cottagers, and laborers, with their wives and children who are beggars in effect; I desire those politicians who dislike my overture, and may perhaps be so bold to attempt an answer, that they will first ask the parents of these mortals whether they would not at this day think it a great happiness to have been sold for food at a year old in the manner I prescribe, and thereby have avoided such a perpetual scene of misfortunes as they have 340 since gone through by the oppression of landlords, the

---

36. **disobliging:** offending.

37. **a country . . . without it:** Swift is accusing England here of "eating up" the Irish.

WORDS
TO
KNOW

perpetual (pər-pĕch′ōō-əl) *adj.* everlasting; continual

impossibility of paying rent without money or trade, the want of common sustenance, with neither house nor clothes to cover them from the inclemencies of the weather, and the most inevitable prospect of entailing the like or greater miseries upon their breed forever.

> I profess, in the sincerity of my heart, that I have not the least personal interest in endeavoring to promote this necessary work, having no other motive than the public good of my country, by advancing our trade, providing for infants, relieving the poor, and giving some pleasure to the rich. I have no children by which I can propose to get a single penny; the youngest being nine years old, and my wife past childbearing.

350

Pause **&** *Reflect*

What Does It Mean?
Common sustenance means "the basic food needed to live."

What Does It Mean?
Inclemencies means "the bad effects." It refers to the kinds of weather that can hurt people, such as extreme cold.

Pause **&** *Reflect*

1. The speaker rejects a plan to teach "landlords to have . . . mercy toward their tenants." What does Swift the author think about these landlords? **(Author's Purpose)**

_____
_____
_____
_____

READ ALOUD **2.** Read aloud the boxed sentences on this page. What is your final impression of the speaker? **(Connect)**

_____
_____
_____
_____

CHALLENGE

Tone is the writer's attitude toward his or her subject. Mark words or phrases in this essay that show Swift's tone. What is his tone like? What are some clues that Swift's attitude is different from the speaker's? Find places in the selection where you can identify Swift's tone. **(Analyze)**

Active Reading SkillBuilder

Drawing Conclusions

You can use information you already know to **draw conclusions** about what an author really means. You can also look for the meaning beneath the surface details. Use the chart below to record your reactions to Swift's statements in "A Modest Proposal." In the first column, write statements that seem important or surprising to you. In the second column, write your response to the statements. An example is shown.

Statements	My Comments/Reactions
"A boy or girl before twelve years old is no salable commodity." (page 125, lines 80–81)	• The Irish didn't have slaves. • Earlier, Swift wrote about "breeders"— as if people were like livestock.

Literary Analysis SkillBuilder

Irony

Irony is a contrast between what is expected to happen and what actually does happen. Verbal irony is a kind of irony in which a writer says one thing but means another. Find two examples of verbal irony in "A Modest Proposal" and record them on the chart below. Then describe the truth that each ironic statement reveals about conditions in Ireland in the 1720s. Examples are shown.

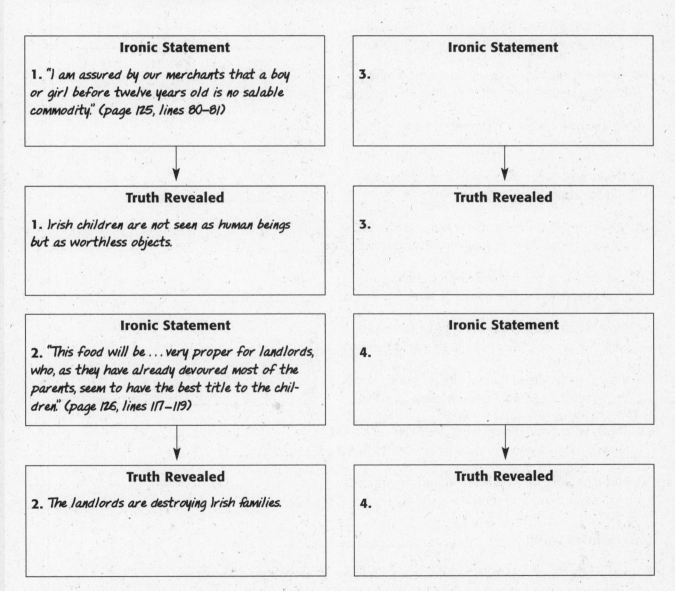

Ironic Statement

1. "I am assured by our merchants that a boy or girl before twelve years old is no salable commodity." (page 125, lines 80–81)

Ironic Statement

3.

Truth Revealed

1. Irish children are not seen as human beings but as worthless objects.

Truth Revealed

3.

Ironic Statement

2. "This food will be . . . very proper for landlords, who, as they have already devoured most of the parents, seem to have the best title to the children." (page 126, lines 117–119)

Ironic Statement

4.

Truth Revealed

2. The landlords are destroying Irish families.

Truth Revealed

4.

Words to Know SkillBuilder

Words to Know

animosity	deplorable	encumbrance	perpetual	proficiency
deference	emulation	expedient	prodigious	rudiment

A. Fill in each set of blanks with the correct word from the word list. Unscramble the boxed letters to spell out what Swift claims his proposal would be to the public.

1. This thing is heavy whether it weighs on your shoulders, on your mind, or on your finances.

   _ _ _ _ _ ☐ _ _ _ _ _

2. An example of this is giving your seat on the bus to a senior citizen or a pregnant woman.

   _ _ ☐ _ _ _ _ _ _

3. An example of this is a prisoner's tying sheets together in order to escape.

   ☐ _ _ _ _ _ _ _ _

4. This describes the number of stars in the sky and the strength of Hercules.

   _ _ _ _ _ _ _ ☐ _ _ _

5. For reading and writing, this is learning the ABC's; for playing the piano, it's learning to find middle C.

   _ _ _ _ _ _ ☐ _

6. This describes the national debt, the situation of the homeless, and the quality of some TV shows.

   _ _ _ _ _ _ _ ☐ _ _ _

7. If the Smiths buy a new car in order to keep up with the Joneses, their purchase represents this.

   ☐ _ _ _ _ _ _ _ _

8. If the Smiths spread hateful, untrue stories about the Joneses, their stories are motivated by this.

   _ _ ☐ _ _ _ _ _ _

9. This is what people have when they can speak a language well enough to communicate effectively.

   _ _ _ _ _ _ ☐ _ _ _ _ _

10. This describes, for all practical purposes, the cycles of the sun, tides, and seasons.

    _ _ _ _ _ _ _ _ ☐

Unscrambled word: _____

B. Imagine that Swift was given a one-paragraph space in a newspaper to respond to angry people who had not realized his essay was ironic. Write the paragraph you think Swift would have written. Use at least **four** of the Words to Know.

FROM A VINDICATION OF THE RIGHTS OF WOMAN

MARY WOLLSTONECRAFT

Before You Read

Connect to Your Life

What does the word *equality* mean to you? Write your responses in the word web below.

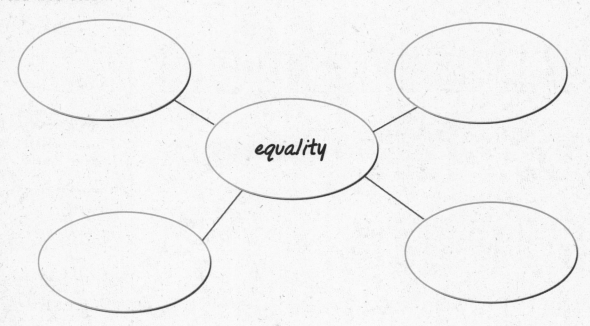

equality

Key to the Essay

WHAT'S THE BIG IDEA? Published in 1792, *A Vindication of the Rights of Woman* is one of the groundbreaking works of feminism. Although the publication caused an uproar, it failed to bring about any major change or reform. It did, however, pave the way for later women's rights pioneers in the 1800s, such as Elizabeth Cady Stanton and Margaret Fuller. The issue of women's rights continues to be debated today.

FROM A VINDICATION OF THE RIGHTS OF WOMAN

MARY WOLLSTONECRAFT

PREVIEW In 18th-century England, it was commonly believed that women were inferior to men. Women were not expected to be independent and had few legal rights. They were supposed to learn only drawing, sewing, dancing, and music. They did not get to study such subjects as history and foreign languages. Mary Wollstonecraft, however, did manage to educate herself and become a writer. *A Vindication of the Rights of Woman*, published in 1792, was the first fully developed argument for women's equality. In this excerpt, you will be introduced to Wollstonecraft's challenging ideas and her criticisms of her society.

ESSAY

Reading Tips

This selection is an excerpt from a nonfiction work. In the excerpt, which takes the form of a **persuasive essay,** the author argues in favor of improved education for women. Some of the sentences are long, and the vocabulary is sometimes difficult. Using the following strategies will help you follow the ideas:

* Read for the **main ideas.** You don't need to understand every passage to get a sense of the author's main points.

* Look for examples that are used to support the main ideas.

What Does It Mean?

A *vindication* is the defense of a point of view and the evidence that supports that view. At the time of this essay, not everyone agreed on what rights women should have.

As the essay begins . . .

* Wollstonecraft says that the way women are educated and taught to behave is wrong.

English Learner Support
VOCABULARY

Figurative Language *The historic page* is another way of saying "history."

FOCUS

Wollstonecraft states that it is wrong to treat women as inferior to men. Instead, women should be educated to develop their mind and character.

MARK IT UP As you read, underline examples that show how women are treated as inferior. An example is highlighted on page 152.

FROM THE INTRODUCTION

After considering the historic page, and viewing the living world with anxious solicitude, the most melancholy emotions of sorrowful indignation have depressed my spirits, and I have sighed when obliged to confess, that either nature has made a great difference between man and man, or that the civilization which has hitherto taken place in the world has been very partial.

WORDS TO KNOW

solicitude (sə-lĭs′ĭ-tōōd′) *n.* care or concern

I have turned over various books written on the subject of education, and patiently observed the conduct of parents and the management of schools; but what has been the result?—a profound conviction that the neglected education of my fellow-creatures is the grand source of the misery I deplore; and that women, in particular, are rendered weak and wretched by a variety of <u>concurring</u> causes, originating from one hasty conclusion.[1] The conduct and manners of women, in fact, evidently prove that their minds are not in a healthy

20 state; for, like the flowers which are planted in too rich a soil, strength and usefulness are sacrificed to beauty; and the flaunting leaves, after having pleased a fastidious eye, fade, disregarded on the stalk, long before the season when they ought to have arrived at maturity. One cause of this barren blooming I attribute to a false system of education, gathered from the books written on this subject by men who, considering females rather as women than human creatures, have been more anxious to make them alluring mistresses than affectionate wives and rational mothers; and the

30 understanding of the sex has been so bubbled[2] by this <u>specious</u> homage, that the civilized women of the present century, with a few exceptions, are only anxious to inspire love, when they ought to cherish a nobler ambition, and by their abilities and virtues exact respect.

In a treatise,[3] therefore, on female rights and manners, the works which have been particularly written for their improvement must not be overlooked; especially when it is asserted, in direct terms, that the minds of women are enfeebled by false refinement; that the books of instruction,

40 written by men of genius, have had the same tendency as more frivolous productions; and that . . . they are treated as a kind of <u>subordinate</u> beings, and not as a part of the human species, when improvable reason is allowed to be the dignified distinction which raises men above the brute creation, and

---

1. **one hasty conclusion:** the conclusion that women are inferior to men.
2. **bubbled:** misled; carried away.
3. **treatise** (trē′tĭs): a formal, detailed article or book on a particular subject; here, referring to this essay.

WORDS
TO
KNOW

concurring (kən-kûr′ĭng) *adj.* occurring at the same time; acting together **concur** *v.*

specious (spē′shəs) *adj.* attractive in a deceptive or insincere way

subordinate (sə-bôr′dn-ĭt) *adj.* less important; lower in rank

puts a natural scepter in a feeble hand.[4]

Yet, because I am a woman, I would not lead my readers to suppose that I mean violently to agitate the contested question respecting the quality or inferiority of the sex; but as the subject lies in my way, and I cannot pass it over without
[50] subjecting the main tendency of my reasoning to misconstruction, I shall stop a moment to deliver, in a few words, my opinion. In the government of the physical world it is observable that the female in point of strength is, in general, inferior to the male. This is the law of nature; and it does not appear to be suspended or abrogated[5] in favor of woman. A degree of physical superiority cannot, therefore, be denied— and it is a noble prerogative! But not content with this natural pre-eminence, men endeavor to sink us still lower merely to render us alluring objects for a moment; and women,
[60] intoxicated by the adoration which men, under the influence of their senses, pay them, do not seek to obtain a durable interest in their hearts, or to become the friends of the fellow creatures who find amusement in their society.

I am aware of an obvious inference: from every quarter have I heard exclamations against masculine women; but where are they to be found? If by this appellation men mean to inveigh against their ardor in hunting, shooting, and gaming, I shall most cordially join in the cry; but if it be against the imitation of manly virtues, or, more properly
[70] speaking, the attainment of those talents and virtues, the exercise of which ennobles the human character, and which raise females in the scale of animal being, when they are comprehensively termed mankind; all those who view them with a philosophic eye must, I should think, wish with me, that they may every day grow more and more masculine. . . .[6]

Pause & *Reflect*

---

4. **they are treated . . . feeble hand:** Wollstonecraft is saying that women are treated as less than human (**subordinate beings**). Men believe that women are not capable of reasoning. Reason is seen as the quality that raises humans above animals (**puts a natural scepter in a feeble hand**).

5. **abrogated** (ăb′rə-gā′tĭd): canceled; repealed.

6. **If by this appellation . . . masculine:** Men criticize women for being masculine. The word *masculine* has two meanings for the author. One relates to the traditionally male activities such as hunting, shooting, and gambling (**gaming**). The other meaning relates to the use of reason to develop one's talents and virtues. Only the second meaning is important to the author.

Pause & *Reflect*

1. Look back at the passages you underlined as you read. Circle three phrases below that describe how women are treated as inferior in Wollstonecraft's society. **(Infer)**

   valued for their beauty, not their minds

   taught to please men

   limited to low-paying jobs

   denied a good education

2. Reread the boxed passage on this page. How does the author want women to become like men? Circle three phrases below that describe her goals. **(Logical Persuasion)**

   practice virtues

   pursue sporting pleasures

   develop talents

   build good character

As the essay continues . . .

• Wollstonecraft explains why women should become stronger in mind and body.

Reading Tip

As you read, fill in the following chart. Write down the problems Wollstonecraft talks about in the first column and the solutions she suggests in the second column.

Problems	Solutions

✔ Reading Check

According to Wollstonecraft, what is the only way that women in her time could improve their lives?

FOCUS

In this section, Wollstonecraft continues her criticism of women's education. As you read, look for changes that she would make.

80

My own sex, I hope, will excuse me, if I treat them like rational creatures, instead of flattering their *fascinating* graces, and viewing them as if they were in a state of perpetual childhood, unable to stand alone. I earnestly wish to point out in what true dignity and human happiness consists—I wish to persuade women to endeavor to acquire strength, both of mind and body, and to convince them that the soft phrases, susceptibility of heart, delicacy of sentiment, and refinement of taste, are almost synonymous with epithets[7] of weakness, and that those beings who are only the objects of pity and that kind of love, which has been termed its sister, will soon become objects of contempt. . . .

90   The education of women has, of late, been more attended to than formerly; yet they are still reckoned a frivolous sex, and ridiculed or pitied by the writers who endeavor by satire or instruction to improve them. It is acknowledged that they spend many of the first years of their lives in acquiring a smattering of accomplishments; meanwhile strength of body and mind are sacrificed to libertine[8] notions of beauty, to the desire of establishing themselves—the only way women can rise in the world—by marriage. And this desire making mere animals of them, when they marry they act as such children

100 may be expected to act: they dress; they paint, and nickname God's creatures. Surely these weak beings are only fit for a seraglio![9] Can they be expected to govern a family with judgment, or take care of the poor babes whom they bring into the world?

     If then it can be fairly deduced from the present conduct of the sex, from the prevalent fondness for pleasure which takes place of ambition and those nobler passions that open and enlarge the soul; that the instruction which women have hitherto received has only tended, with the constitution of

110 civil society, to render them insignificant objects of desire— mere propagators of fools!—if it can be proved that in aiming to accomplish them, without cultivating their understandings, they are taken out of their sphere of duties, and made ridiculous and useless when the short-lived bloom of beauty is

---

7. **epithets** (ĕp′ə-thĕts′): descriptive terms.

8. **libertine** (lĭb′ər-tēn′): indecent or improper.

9. **seraglio** (sə-răl′yō): harem.

over, I presume that *rational* men will excuse me for
endeavoring to persuade them to become more masculine and
respectable.

Indeed the word masculine is only a bugbear:[10] there is little
reason to fear that women will acquire too much courage or
fortitude; for their apparent inferiority with respect to bodily
strength, must render them, in some degree, dependent on
men in the various relations of life; but why should it be
increased by prejudices that give a sex to virtue, and confound
simple truths with sensual reveries?[11]

Pause & Reflect

FROM CHAPTER 2

Youth is the season for love in both sexes;
but in those days of thoughtless
enjoyment provision should be made for
the more important years of life, when
reflection takes place of sensation. But
Rousseau,[12] and most of the male
writers who have followed his steps,
have warmly inculcated[13] that the whole
tendency of female education ought to
be directed to one point: to render them pleasing.

Let me reason with the supporters of this opinion who have
any knowledge of human nature, do they imagine that
marriage can eradicate the habitude of life? The woman who
has only been taught to please will soon find that her charms
are oblique[14] sunbeams, and that they cannot have much effect
on her husband's heart when they are seen every day, when
the summer is passed and gone. Will she then have sufficient
native energy to look into herself for comfort, and cultivate
her dormant faculties? or, is it not more rational to expect
that she will try to please other men; and, in the emotions
raised by the expectation of new conquests, endeavor to forget

---

10. **bugbear:** an object of exaggerated fear.

11. **confound . . . reveries:** confuse simple truths with sexual daydreams.

12. **Rousseau:** 18th-century French philosopher.

13. **inculcated** (ĭn-kŭl′kā′tĭd): taught.

14. **oblique:** slanting; not direct.

FOCUS

Wollstonecraft
describes what
happens to women
who have been
educated only to
please men.

MARK IT UP As you
read, circle passages
that tell what can go
wrong after such a
woman marries.

Pause & Reflect

1. What is wrong with an education that prepares women only
to attract a husband? Circle the
sentence below that states
Wollstonecraft's view. (**Main
Idea**)

Women will focus on raising
their children well.

Women will neglect their minds
and will have poor judgment.

As the essay continues . . .

- Wollstonecraft discusses the
problems caused by the lack
of good education for women.

English Learner Support
LANGUAGE

Metaphor In line 141, the
author is comparing a woman's
charms to summer. Like summer, a woman's charms can
seem new and fresh at the
beginning of a marriage. But
summer soon fades, just as
will the charms of a woman
who has nothing else to bring
to her marriage.

What Does It Mean?

Dormant faculties means
"sleeping or hidden talents."

the mortification her love or pride has received? When the husband ceases to be a lover—and the time will inevitably come, her desire of pleasing will then grow <u>languid</u>, or become a spring of bitterness; and love, perhaps, the most ○150 evanescent[15] of all passions, gives place to jealousy or vanity.

I now speak of women who are restrained by principle or prejudice; such women, though they would shrink from an intrigue with real abhorrence, yet, nevertheless, wish to be convinced by the homage of gallantry that they are cruelly neglected by their husbands;[16] or, days and weeks are spent in dreaming of the happiness enjoyed by congenial souls till their health is undermined and their spirits broken by discontent. How then can the great art of pleasing be such a necessary study? it is only useful to a mistress; the chaste wife, and ○160 serious mother, should only consider her power to please as the polish of her virtues, and the affection of her husband as one of the comforts that render her talk less difficult and her life happier. But, whether she be loved or neglected, her first wish should be to make herself respectable, and not to rely for all her happiness on a being subject to like infirmities with herself.

Pause & Reflect

FOCUS

Wollstonecraft next criticizes a well-known book about the education of women. As you read, ○170 look for her opinion of that book, and notice her goals for women.

The worthy Dr. Gregory[17] fell into a similar error. I respect his heart; but entirely disapprove of his celebrated Legacy to his Daughters. . . .

He actually recommends dissimulation,[18] and advises an innocent girl to give the lie to her feelings, and

---

15. evanescent (ĕv′ə-nĕs′ənt): quickly vanishing; fleeting.

16. **I now . . . husbands:** Women with high moral standards also suffer when their husbands ignore them. Such women would never have an affair. They would, however, enjoy the flattery and honor (**homage of gallantry**) of other men.

17. **Dr. Gregory:** an 18th-century author who wrote *A Father's Legacy to His Daughters.* He advised women to win men's affection by lying. He also advised women to develop a "fondness for dress."

18. **dissimulation:** a hiding of one's true feelings; pretense.

WORDS
TO **languid** (lăng′gwĭd) *adj.* sluggish; weak
KNOW

English Learner Support
LANGUAGE

Usage The highlighted phrase means "on someone who has the same weaknesses as she."

Pause & Reflect

READ ALOUD   Read aloud the boxed passage on this page. What should a woman's "first wish" be? **(Analyze)**

_____

_____

_____

_____

As the essay continues . . .

• The author criticizes a popular book.

• She explains that exercise and energy are healthy for women.

not dance with spirit, when gaiety of heart would make her feet eloquent without making her gestures immodest. In the name of truth and common sense, why should not one woman acknowledge that she can take more exercise than another? or, in other words, that she has a sound constitution; and why, to damp innocent <u>vivacity</u>, is she darkly to be told that men will draw conclusions which she little thinks of? Let the libertine draw what inference he pleases; but, I hope, that no sensible mother will restrain the natural frankness of youth by instilling such indecent cautions.[19] Out of the abundance of the heart the mouth speaketh; and a wiser than Solomon hath said, that the heart should be made clean, and not trivial ceremonies observed, which it is not very difficult to fulfil with scrupulous exactness when vice reigns in the heart.[20]

Women ought to endeavor to purify their heart; but can they do so when their uncultivated understandings make them entirely dependent on their senses for employment and amusement, when no noble pursuit sets them above the little vanities of the day, or enables them to curb the wild emotions that agitate a reed over which every passing breeze has power?[21] To gain the affections of a virtuous man, is affectation necessary? Nature has given woman a weaker frame than man; but, to ensure her husband's affections, must a wife, who by the exercise of her mind and body whilst she was discharging the duties of a daughter, wife, and mother, has allowed her constitution to retain its natural strength, and her nerves a healthy tone, is she, I say, to condescend to use art and <u>feign</u> a sickly delicacy in order to secure her husband's

---

19. **In the name of truth . . . indecent cautions:** The author is critical of Dr. Gregory's advice that girls should lie about how much they like to dance and exercise. He suggests that if they are too lively, or spirited, men will think they are immoral. Wollstonecraft replies that such opinions should be ignored. Natural enthusiasm and energy should be encouraged.

20. **a wiser . . . in the heart:** a reference to Jesus' criticism of religious leaders of his time. They strictly observed rules (**trivial ceremonies**) that made them look good, but they had impure hearts.

21. **Women ought . . . power:** women should try to develop their virtues, but they can't. They lack the education and strength of purpose to control their thoughts and emotions.

WORDS
TO
KNOW

vivacity (vĭ-văs′ĭ-tē) *n.* liveliness

affectation (ăf′ĕk-tā′shən) *n.* unnatural behavior; conduct intended to give a false impression

feign (fān) *v.* to give a false appearance of; simulate or counterfeit

What Does It Mean?

In lines 189–190, Wollstonecraft means that a woman's lack of serious education makes her rely on her *senses*—her physical feelings rather than her mind—for employment. Here, *employment* means "things to do," not "a job."

English Learner Support
VOCABULARY

Usage Although *affections* and *affectation* look alike, they are very different words. *Affections* means "love" or "caring." *Affectation* means "phony, artificial behavior."

✔ Reading Check

According to Wollstonecraft, how can a woman keep her husband's love?

What Does It Mean?
As they respect her means "in relation to her."

What Does It Mean?
Meanly can have related, but different, meanings. Here, the word means "in a lowly, cheap way." It can also mean "cruelly."

Pause & Reflect

1. Dr. Gregory advises young girls to lie about their interest in dancing and exercise. What is Wollstonecraft's opinion of his advice? **(Logical Persuasion)**

_____

_____

MARK IT UP 2. In this section, Wollstonecraft urges women to be strong partners in marriage. Circle words or phrases on this page that describe how she wants a woman to act in marriage. **(Infer)**

As the essay ends . . .

• The speaker argues that women should be free to grow and learn in the same ways that men are.

affection? Weakness may excite tenderness, and gratify the arrogant pride of man; but the lordly caresses of a protector will not gratify a noble mind that pants for, and deserves to be respected. Fondness is a poor substitute for friendship! . . .

Besides, the woman who strengthens her body and exercises her mind will, by managing her family and practicing various virtues, become the friend, and not the humble dependent of her husband; and if she, by possessing such substantial qualities, merit his regard, she will not find it necessary to 210 conceal her affection, nor to pretend to an unnatural coldness of constitution to excite her husband's passions. . . .

If all the faculties of woman's mind are only to be cultivated as they respect her dependence on man; if, when a husband be obtained, she have arrived at her goal, and meanly proud rests satisfied with such a paltry crown, let her grovel contentedly, scarcely raised by her employments above the animal kingdom; but, if, struggling for the prize of her high calling, she look beyond the present scene, let her cultivate her understanding without stopping to consider what character the husband may 220 have whom she is destined to marry. Let her only determine, without being too anxious about present happiness, to acquire the qualities that ennoble a rational being, and a rough inelegant husband may shock her taste without destroying her peace of mind. She will not model her soul to suit the frailties of her companion, but to bear with them: his character may be a trial, but not an impediment to virtue. . . .

Pause & Reflect

FOCUS
Read on to learn Wollstonecraft's conclusions about the "rights of woman."
230

These may be termed Utopian dreams.[22] Thanks to that Being who impressed them on my soul, and gave me sufficient strength of mind to dare to exert my own reason, till, becoming dependent only on him for the support of my virtue, I view, with indignation, the mistaken notions that enslave my sex.

_____

22. **Utopian dreams:** unrealistic dreams of an ideal or perfect society.

WORDS TO KNOW

grovel (grŏv′əl) *v.* to behave with exaggerated submission or humility

I love man as my fellow; but his scepter, real, or usurped, extends not to me, unless the reason of an individual demands my homage; and even then the submission is to reason, and not to man. In fact, the conduct of an accountable being must be regulated by the operations of its own reason; or on what foundation rests the throne of God?

240 It appears to me necessary to dwell on these obvious truths, because females have been insulated, as it were; and, while they have been stripped of the virtues that should clothe humanity, they have been decked with artificial graces[23] that enable them to exercise a short-lived tyranny.[24] Love, in their bosoms, taking place of every nobler passion, their sole ambition is to be fair, to raise emotion instead of inspiring respect; and this ignoble desire, like the servility in absolute monarchies, destroys all strength of character. Liberty is the mother of virtue, and if women be, by their very constitution, 250 slaves, and not allowed to breathe the sharp invigorating air of freedom, they must ever languish like exotics,[25] and be reckoned beautiful flaws in nature.

Pause & Reflect

What Does It Mean?
Here, *fair* means "pretty" rather than "just" or "even-handed."

Pause & Reflect

MARK IT UP **1.** Who or what does Wollstonecraft say is the source of her reason? Circle a word that tells you. **(Clarify)**

READ ALOUD **2.** Read aloud the boxed passage. What have women lost because of their emphasis on beauty and love? **(Analyze)**

_____

_____

_____

_____

3. What must women have if they are to develop virtue? **(Cause and Effect)**

_____

_____

_____

CHALLENGE

According to the author, women should have an education that makes them strong, independent, and good thinkers. Do you think she does a good job with her "vindication"? Has she made her case? Explain why or why not, using phrases from the essay to support your ideas. **(Logical Argument)**

23. **artificial graces:** beauty and charms that are not genuine or natural. Such qualities are developed at the cost of more important ones, such as clear thinking and good judgment.

24. **short-lived tyranny:** the brief period of youth and beauty when a woman can hold sway over men's emotions.

25. **languish like exotics:** be weak like plants grown away from their natural environment.

WORDS
TO
KNOW
    ignoble (ĭg-nō′bəl) *adj.* not noble; degrading; contemptible

Active Reading SkillBuilder

Recognizing Logical Persuasion

In her essay, Wollstonecraft uses **logical persuasion**—persuasive techniques that appeal to logic and reason rather than to emotion. She foresees the opposition's argument and logically responds to it. List the opposing views that Wollstonecraft foresees. Then note how she responds to each view. One set has been done for you.

Opposing Views	Response
Men's physical strength is superior to women's. That shows that men are superior to women.	Being physically superior doesn't mean men are superior to women in other ways.

Literary Analysis SkillBuilder

Argumentation

Argumentation is writing that seeks to convince readers to accept or reject an idea or proposal. Often the writer begins with a statement of an idea or opinion and supports it with logical evidence. On the chart below, list convincing evidence that Wollstonecraft uses to support her argument for women's education. Then note additional points of your own that you think she might have used to strengthen her argument. Two examples have been done for you.

Convincing Evidence	Additional Points
Women do not develop their abilities and virtues.	The pursuit of an education is a basic human right.

Words to Know SkillBuilder

Words to Know

affectation	feign	ignoble	solicitude	subordinate
concurring	grovel	languid	specious	vivacity

A. Decide which word from the word list best completes each verse below.
Then write the word on the blank line on the right.

He says, "I fear I seem an awful pest."
And then, "Of course, of course! For you know best!"
He states, "When you're not here, we're at a loss."
It makes me feel quite sick to hear him (1) to the boss.

_____ (1)

To share what you possess with those in need
Would show (2) for them indeed.

_____ (2)

He has never ventured out beyond the borders of this nation,
So I think his British accent has to be an (3).

_____ (3)

I hate decision making. On the whole,
I function best in a (4) role.

_____ (4)

We fell for everything she said, and then
We realized that it was (5) when,
Despite the fact that she could sound so smart,
The logic she had used all fell apart.

_____ (5)

She spoke in such a (6) tone,
I couldn't hear her on the phone.

_____ (6)

(7) acts are those that make you squirm
When you remember acting like a worm.

_____ (7)

Jitterbugging, to-and-fro-ing,
Jumping rope and do-se-do-ing,
Filling ski-lifts to capacity:
All examples of (8).

_____ (8)

I call up to invite them for a meal
And (9) a friendliness I do not feel.

_____ (9)

A practice that seems to be one quite enduring
Is yelling out "Jinx!" after statements (10).

_____ (10)

B. Imagine that Wollstonecraft were to speak at a modern-day conference on
women's rights. Write a statement that could be used to introduce her to the audience. Use at least **four** of the Words to Know.

FROM

THE LIFE
OF
SAMUEL JOHNSON

JAMES BOSWELL

Before You Read

Connect to Your Life

A biography is the story of someone's life. Whose biography would you like to read? Why? Write your responses in the space below.

I would like to read _____ 's biography because

_____

_____

_____

_____ .

Key to the Biography

WHAT'S THE BIG IDEA? James Boswell first met the famous Samuel Johnson in the back room of a bookseller's shop in 1763. During the next 21 years, Boswell chronicled in great detail his conversations, experiences, and travels with Johnson. In contrast to most biographies, Boswell's biography of Johnson is not structured chronologically, but arranged by subject. In the following excerpt, you will be reading about the kind of man Johnson was rather than about the progression of events that made up his life.

FROM THE LIFE OF SAMUEL JOHNSON

JAMES BOSWELL

Reading Tips

This selection consists of four excerpts from a **biography**, a nonfiction work in which an author tells about the events of another person's life. As you read, keep these points in mind:

- Use the heading of each section as a guide to the content.

- Use the author's **details** to form impressions of the subject. Look for clues about his personality, values, and beliefs.

- When you come upon **dialogue**, read some of the passages aloud—by yourself or with a partner. Listening to these passages will help you understand them better.

PREVIEW *The Life of Samuel Johnson* is considered one of the finest biographies in the English language. James Boswell spent 7 years writing this biography, completing it in 1791. It gives a full and vivid picture of Samuel Johnson, the literary giant of England in the late 18th century. Johnson—poet, essayist, journalist, and critic—created the first complete dictionary in the English language.

Boswell was Johnson's close friend for more than 20 years. Still, he included in this biography negative as well as positive information about Johnson. In defense of this method, Boswell wrote, "In every picture there must be shade as well as light." The following excerpts provide a glimpse of Johnson's personality and beliefs.

As the biography begins . . .

- The author explains that Johnson enjoys food.

Reading Tip

A *fact* is a statement you can prove. An *opinion* is a belief or a feeling. As you read the selection, highlight facts in one color and opinions in another color.

FOCUS

In this excerpt the author describes Samuel Johnson's eating habits.

MARK IT UP As you read, circle details that show you what Johnson was like at the table. An example is highlighted on page 166.

On Eating (1763)

At supper this night he talked of good eating with uncommon satisfaction. "Some people (said he,) have a foolish way of not minding, or pretending not to mind, what they eat. For my part, I mind my belly very studiously, and very carefully; for I look upon it, that he who does not mind his belly will hardly mind anything else."

He now appeared to me *Jean Bull philosophe*,[1] and he was, for the moment, not only serious but <u>vehement</u>. Yet I have

---

1. *Jean Bull philosophe* (zhän′ bool′ fē-lô-zôf′) *French:* John Bull philosopher. (John Bull is a figure representing the typical Englishman—honest, hearty, and gruff.)

WORDS
TO
KNOW

vehement (vē′ə-mənt) *adj.* forceful in expression or feeling; intense

What Does It Mean?

Gratify means "to please." *Palate* is the roof of the mouth and here refers to the sense of taste. The highlighted phrase means "to eat something tasty."

More About . . .

THE (RAMBLER) The *Rambler* was a two-page essay that was published like a newspaper twice a week. There were a total of 208 essays published, and Johnson wrote 203 of them. Each essay gave advice about how to live life properly.

English Learner Support
VOCABULARY

Idiom In Boswell's day, *it must be owned* meant "it must be admitted or confessed."

Reading Tip

After you finish each section in this biography, record Johnson's main opinion or point of view and at least two details that support his view in a chart like the one below.

Section	Point of View	Supporting Details
1		
2		
3		
4		

heard him, upon other occasions, talk with great contempt of people who were anxious to gratify their palates; and the 206th number of his (*Rambler*) is a masterly essay against gulosity.[2] His practice, indeed, I must acknowledge, may be considered as casting the balance of his different opinions upon this subject; for I never knew any man who relished good eating more than he did. When at table, he was totally absorbed in the business of the moment; his looks seemed

20 riveted to his plate; nor would he, unless when in very high company, say one word, or even pay the least attention to what was said by others, till he had satisfied his appetite, which was so fierce, and indulged with such intenseness, that while in the act of eating, the veins of his forehead swelled, and generally a strong perspiration was visible. To those whose sensations were delicate, this could not but be disgusting; and it was doubtless not very suitable to the character of a philosopher, who should be distinguished by self-command. But it must be owned, that Johnson, though he

30 could be rigidly *abstemious*,[3] was not a *temperate* man either in eating or drinking. He could refrain, but he could not use moderately. He told me, that he had fasted two days without inconvenience, and that he had never been hungry but once. They who beheld with wonder how much he ate upon all occasions when his dinner was to his taste, could not easily conceive what he must have meant by hunger; and not only was he remarkable for the extraordinary quantity which he ate, but he was, or affected to be, a man of very nice[4] discernment in the science of cookery. He used to descant[5]

40 critically on the dishes which had been at table where he had dined or supped, and to recollect very minutely what he had liked. . . .

When invited to dine, even with an intimate friend, he was not pleased if something better than a plain dinner was not prepared for him. I have heard him say on such an occasion,

---

2. **gulosity** (gyōō-lŏs′ĭ-tē): excessive appetite; gluttony.
3. **abstemious** (ăb-stē′mē-əs): self-denying; abstinent.
4. **nice**: exacting; particular.
5. **descant** (dĕs′kănt′): speak at length.

WORDS
TO
KNOW

temperate (tĕm′pər-ĭt) *adj.* moderate; restrained
discernment (dĭ-sûrn′mənt) *n.* good judgment

"This was a good dinner enough, to be sure; but it was not a dinner to *ask* a man to." On the other hand, he was wont[6] to express, with great glee, his satisfaction when he had been entertained quite to his mind.

Pause & Reflect

Pause & Reflect
Review the details you circled as you read. How would you describe Johnson's attitude toward food? **(Infer)**

_____

_____

On Equality of the Sexes (1778)

FOCUS
50
This excerpt contains a dialogue about the different standards used to judge men and women at that time. Read to find out Johnson's views on this issue.

Mrs. Knowles affected to complain that men had much more liberty allowed them than women.

JOHNSON. "Why, Madam, women have all the liberty they should wish to have. We have all the labor and the danger, and the women all the advantage. We go to sea, we build houses, we do everything, in short, to pay our court to the women."

MRS. KNOWLES. "The Doctor reasons very wittily, but not

60 convincingly. Now, take the instance of building; the mason's wife, if she is ever seen in liquor, is ruined; the mason may get himself drunk as often as he pleases, with little loss of character; nay, may let his wife and children starve."

JOHNSON. "Madam, you must consider, if the mason does get himself drunk, and let his wife and children starve, the parish will oblige him to find security for their maintenance. We have different modes of restraining evil. Stocks for the men, a ducking-stool for women,[7] and a pound for beasts. If we require more perfection from women than from ourselves,

70 it is doing them honor. And women have not the same temptations that we have: they may always live in virtuous company; men must mix in the world indiscriminately. If a woman has no inclination to do what is wrong being secured from it is no restraint to her. I am at liberty to walk into the Thames; but if I were to try it, my friends would restrain me

As the biography continues...

• Johnson debates with a woman named Mrs. Knowles about equality of the sexes.

What Does It Mean?
Pay our court means "to attract" or "to get the attention of."

READ ALOUD Lines 68–74

Read aloud the boxed passage on this page. How would you **summarize** Johnson's views about the differences between men and women?

_____

_____

More About...
THE THAMES The Thames is a large river that flows through London, the capital of England.

---

6. **wont** (wônt): in the habit; accustomed.

7. **Stocks for the men . . . for women:** These public punishments were common at the time. A man would sit for a designated time with his head, hands, and feet through holes in two hinged boards known as the stocks. A woman would be publicly dunked in the river, in a chair designed for that purpose, for a crime such as gossip.

in Bedlam,[8] and I should be obliged to them."

MRS. KNOWLES. "Still, Doctor, I cannot help thinking it a hardship that more indulgence is allowed to men than to women. It gives a superiority to men, to which I do not see how they are entitled."

JOHNSON. "It is plain, Madam, one or other must have the superiority. As Shakespeare says, 'If two men ride on a horse, one must ride behind.'"

DILLY. "I suppose, Sir, Mrs. Knowles would have them to ride in panniers,[9] one on each side."

JOHNSON. "Then, Sir, the horse would throw them both."

MRS. KNOWLES. "Well, I hope that in another world the sexes will be equal."

BOSWELL. "That is being too ambitious, Madam. *We* might as well desire to be equal with the angels. *We* shall all, I hope, be happy in a future state, but we must not expect to be all happy in the same degree. It is enough if we be happy according to our several capacities. A worthy carman[10] will get to heaven as well as Sir Isaac Newton.[11] Yet, though equally good, they will not have the same degrees of happiness."

JOHNSON. "Probably not."

Pause & *Reflect*

FOCUS
Read to find out about Johnson's attitude toward death.
MARK IT UP   As you read, underline details that reveal his attitude.

On the Fear of Death (1769)

I mentioned to him that I had seen the execution of several convicts at Tyburn,[12] two days before, and that none of them seemed to be under any concern.

JOHNSON. "Most of them, Sir, have never thought at all."

BOSWELL. "But is not the fear of death natural to man?"

JOHNSON. "So much so, Sir, that the whole of life is but

---

8. **Bedlam:** a London institution for the mentally ill.

9. **panniers** (păn′yərz): a pair of baskets hung across the back of a pack animal.

10. **carman:** carriage driver.

11. **Sir Isaac Newton:** a famous English mathematician, who lived from 1642–1727.

12. **Tyburn:** the former site of public hangings in London.

Reading Check

To what does Boswell compare the future equality of men and women?

Pause & *Reflect*

MARK IT UP   Does Johnson believe that women are better than or inferior to men? Write your answer below. Then underline words and phrases on pages 167 and 168 that led you to your answer. **(Draw Conclusions)**

_____

_____

_____

_____

As the biography continues . . .

• Johnson becomes upset during a conversation with the author about death.

keeping away the thoughts of it."

He then, in a low and earnest tone, talked of his meditating upon the awful hour of his own dissolution,[13] and in what manner he should conduct himself upon that occasion: "I know not (said he,) whether I should wish to have a friend by me, or have it all between God and myself." . . .

When we were alone, I introduced the subject of death, and endeavored to maintain that the fear of it might be got over. I told him that David Hume[14] said to me, he was no more uneasy to think he should *not be* after this life, than that he *had not been* before he began to exist.

JOHNSON. "Sir, if he really thinks so, his perceptions are disturbed; he is mad: if he does not think so, he lies. He may tell you, he holds his finger in the flame of a candle, without feeling pain; would you believe him? When he dies, he at least gives up all he has."

BOSWELL. "Foote,[15] Sir, told me, that when he was very ill he was not afraid to die."

JOHNSON. "It is not true, Sir. Hold a pistol to Foote's breast, or to Hume's breast, and threaten to kill them, and you'll see how they behave."

BOSWELL. "But may we not fortify our minds for the approach of death?"

Here I am sensible[16] I was in the wrong, to bring before his view what he ever looked upon with horror; for although when in a celestial frame, in his "Vanity of Human Wishes," he has supposed death to be "kind Nature's signal for retreat," from this state of being to "a happier seat," his thoughts upon this awful change were in general full of dismal apprehensions. His mind resembled the vast amphitheater, the Colosseum at Rome.[17] In the center stood his judgment, which, like a mighty gladiator, combated those apprehensions that, like the wild beasts of the *Arena*, were all around in cells, ready to be let out upon him. After a conflict, he drove them back into their dens; but not killing them, they were still assailing him. To my question, whether we might not fortify

---

13. **awful . . . dissolution:** awe-inspiring hour of his own death.

14. **David Hume:** a Scottish philosopher and historian.

15. **Foote:** Samuel Foote, an actor and dramatist.

16. **sensible:** aware.

17. **Colosseum at Rome:** a large outdoor theater, used for public entertainments such as gladiator shows in ancient Rome.

Reading Check

What does Johnson think of David Hume's opinion of death?

English Learner Support
VOCABULARY

Fortify *Fortify* means "to strengthen."

More About . . .

THE COLOSSEUM 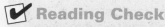 The Colosseum is a huge sports stadium in Rome. One sport the ancient Romans watched there was fighting between gladiators, or enslaved warriors, and wild animals. The animals were kept in dens and cages under the floor of the Colosseum.

What Does It Mean?

Assailing means "attacking." Boswell is saying that Johnson is still struggling with his fears about death.

English Learner Support
LANGUAGE

Diction Here, Johnson is saying "I don't want to meet with you tomorrow."

Pause & *Reflect*

How does Johnson feel about death?

_____

_____

As the biography ends . . .

• Boswell discusses and gives examples of Johnson's courage.

What Does It Mean?

Here, *occasion* is a verb meaning "to cause." It can also be a noun meaning "an event."

English Learner Support
VOCABULARY

Idiom *Kept them all at bay* means that Johnson fought off the men. The idiom *to keep at bay* means "to keep off or at a distance."

our minds for the approach of death, he answered, in a passion, "No, Sir, let it alone. It matters not how a man dies, but how he lives. The act of dying is not of importance, it lasts so short a time." He added, (with an earnest look,) "A man knows it must be so, and submits. It will do him no good to whine."

I attempted to continue the conversation. He was so provoked, that he said, "Give us no more of this"; and was
150 thrown into such a state of agitation, that he expressed himself in a way that alarmed and distressed me; showed an impatience that I should leave him, and when I was going away, called to me sternly, "Don't let us meet to-morrow."

Pause & *Reflect*

FOCUS
Read to find out about Samuel Johnson's personal courage.
✎ MARK IT UP As you read, circle examples that the author gives to show Johnson's courage.

On Johnson's Physical Courage (1775)

. . . **No man was ever** more remarkable for personal courage. He had, indeed, an awful dread of death, or rather, "of something after death"; and what rational man, who seriously thinks of quitting all that he has ever known, and
160 going into a new and unknown state of being, can be without that dread? But his fear was from reflection; his courage natural. His fear, in that one instance, was the result of philosophical and religious consideration. He feared death, but he feared nothing else, not even what might occasion death. Many instances of his resolution may be mentioned. One day, at Mr. Beauclerk's house in the country, when two large dogs were fighting, he went up to them, and beat them till they separated; and at another time, when told of the danger there was that a gun might burst if charged with many
170 balls, he put in six or seven, and fired it off against a wall. Mr. Langton told me, that when they were swimming together near Oxford, he cautioned Dr. Johnson against a pool, which was reckoned particularly dangerous; upon which Johnson directly swam into it. He told me himself that one night he was attacked in the street by four men, to whom he would not yield, but kept them all at bay, till the watch came up, and

carried both him and them to the roundhouse.[18] In the playhouse at Lichfield, as Mr. Garrick informed me, Johnson having for a moment quitted a chair which was placed for him between the side-scenes, a gentleman took possession of it, and when Johnson on his return civilly demanded his seat, rudely refused to give it up; upon which Johnson laid hold of it, and tossed him and the chair into the pit.[19] Foote, who so successfully revived the old comedy, by exhibiting living characters, had resolved to imitate Johnson on the stage, expecting great profits from his ridicule of so celebrated a man. Johnson being informed of his intention, and being at dinner at Mr. Thomas Davies's the bookseller, from whom I had the story, he asked Mr. Davies "what was the common price of an oak stick"; and being answered six-pence, "Why then, Sir, (said he,) give me leave to send your servant to purchase me a shilling one. I'll have a double quantity; for I am told Foote means to *take me off*,[20] as he calls it, and I am determined the fellow shall not do it with <u>impunity</u>." Davies took care to acquaint Foote of this, which effectually checked the wantonness[21] of the mimic. Mr. Macpherson's menaces[22] made Johnson provide himself with the same implement of defense; and had he been attacked, I have no doubt that, old as he was, he would have made his <u>corporal</u> prowess be felt as much as his intellectual.

Pause & Reflect

Reading Tip

Brainstorm a list of words to describe Samuel Johnson. Then make another list to describe James Boswell.

Pause & Reflect

MARK IT UP 1. Review the examples you circled as you read. Place a *T* next to any example that you think shows true courage. Place an *F* next to any example that you think shows foolish conduct. **(Evaluate)**

2. If you had met Samuel Johnson, would you have liked him or not? **(Connect)**

_____

_____

_____

_____

CHALLENGE

The eighteenth century was known as the Age of Enlightenment or the Age of Reason. People believed that reason, logic, and common sense were the best guides for life. Based on this excerpt, do you think Samuel Johnson's personality reflected the ideas of the Enlightenment? Reread the excerpt and mark passages that support your opinion. **(Evaluate)**

---

18. **roundhouse:** jail.

19. **into the pit:** In "playhouses"—or theaters—of Johnson's time, the orchestra sat in a recessed area called the "pit," directly in front of the stage.

20. *take me off:* Foote intends to make a mockery of Johnson.

21. **checked the wantonness:** controlled the playfulness.

22. **Mr. Macpherson's menaces:** the threats of James Macpherson, a Scottish poet whose "translations" of alleged third-century poems had been exposed as frauds by Johnson.

WORDS
TO
KNOW

impunity (ĭm-pyo͞o′nĭ-tē) *n.* freedom from punishment or penalty
corporal (kôr′pər-əl) *adj.* bodily; physical

Active Reading SkillBuilder

Analyzing the Biographer's Perspective

A biographer's **perspective** may be influenced by his or her own views, prejudices, or relationship to the subject. In this selection, Boswell's perspective is signaled by the use of the personal pronoun *I*, by anecdotes and dialogue involving the biographer, and by the writer's tone. Look for evidence of Boswell's perspective in each excerpt. List examples in which Boswell's personal friendship with Johnson influences the writing. An example is shown.

Excerpt	Examples
On Eating	"...I never knew any man who relished good eating more than he did." (p. 150, lines 17–18)
On Equality of the Sexes	
On the Fear of Death	
On Johnson's Physical Courage	

Literary Analysis SkillBuilder

Biography

A **biography** is an account of a person's life written by another person. A biographer strives for a balanced portrayal of the subject through anecdotes, dialogue or conversation, description, quotations, and interpretive passages. A good biography provides a full picture of the subject's personality. Use the graphic to organize examples of details, conversations, or incidents that Boswell presents in his biography of Samuel Johnson. For each example, write an inference that you can make about Johnson. An example is shown.

1. Detail, Conversation, or Incident

Boswell recalls Johnson's huge appetite.

↓

Inference

One of Johnson's personality traits was a love of eating.

2. Detail, Conversation, or Incident

↓

Inference

3. Detail, Conversation, or Incident

↓

Inference

4. Detail, Conversation, or Incident

↓

Inference

Words to Know SkillBuilder

Words to Know

corporal   discernment   impunity   temperate   vehement

A. Fill in each set of blanks with the correct word from the word list.

1. This describes you when you want to make your point (and how you feel about it) absolutely clear.

   ☐ _ _ _ _ _ _ _

2. This is what you show when you obey traffic signals, avoid walking on thin ice, and save money for a rainy day.

   _ _ ☐ _ _ _ _ _ _ _ _

3. A person is this when he or she refuses a second serving, however tempting it may be.

   _ _ _ ☐ _ _ _ _

4. People who think they are above the law also think they deserve this, no matter what they do.

   _ _ _ _ _ ☐ _ _

5. This describes anything that isn't strictly spiritual, mental, emotional, or intellectual.

   _ _ _ _ _ _ _ ☐

Now, unscramble the boxed letters to complete the following saying by Samuel Johnson.

"It matters not how a man dies, but how he _____ ."

B. Fill in each blank with the correct word from the word list.

1. The former addict was _____ in opposing drugs.

2. _____ eaters are less likely to have weight problems than those who eat too little or too much.

3. The court showed _____ in ruling so fairly.

4. Spanking is a kind of _____ punishment.

5. Dictators tend to believe that they can violate even basic human rights

   with _____ .

C. Samuel Johnson was not without enemies. Write a description of him as one of them might have written it, using at least **three** of the Words to Know.

Elegy

WRITTEN IN A COUNTRY CHURCHYARD

Thomas Gray

Before You Read

Connect to Your Life

What do you think of when you see a cemetery or graveyard? Do you feel sad? Do you wonder about the people buried there? Complete the word web below with words that come to your mind when you think of the word *cemetery*.

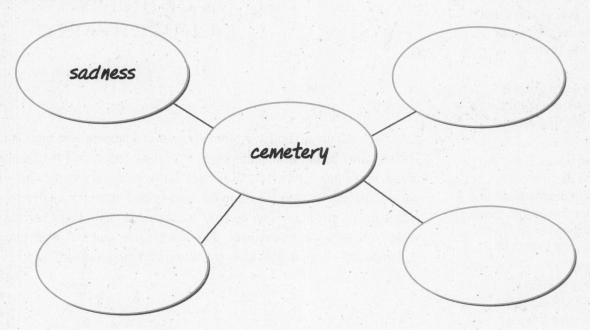

Key to the Poem

WHAT YOU NEED TO KNOW Gray wrote the following in his poem "Elegy Written in a Country Churchyard":

The paths of glory lead but to the grave.

This poem is based on the speaker's belief that death spares no one despite their class, wealth, or achievements.

Reading Tips

This poem is an **elegy,** a reflection on death. It contains detailed descriptions, unusual word order, and difficult words. Try using the following strategies as you read.

• Don't try to understand everything at first. Just try to get the overall ideas and feelings in the poem and visualize the scenes described.

• When the word order is hard to follow, look for the main subject and verb of the sentence.

• Capitalized words in the middle of a line are often examples of **personification.** This is a technique that gives human qualities to an object, animal, or idea. Watch for these words.

• Use the information in the Guide for Reading to help you with confusing passages and difficult words.

As the poem begins . . .

• The speaker describes the sights and sounds of evening.

Elegy
WRITTEN IN A COUNTRY CHURCHYARD

Thomas Gray

PREVIEW An elegy is often written in honor of someone who has died. Thomas Gray began writing this poem after the death at age 26 of a close friend. In the poem, however, Gray does not write about a particular person. Instead he pays tribute to the little-known dead of a country village in England in the 18th century. His thoughts about these humble village folk—their everyday lives, their lost dreams, and their wish to be remembered—have deeply affected readers for more than 200 years.

FOCUS

In the opening stanzas, the poet gives the setting of the poem. The speaker is standing in a churchyard—a cemetery next to a church—at twilight.

MARK IT UP Underline words and phrases that help you picture the time and place of the poem. An example is highlighted.

> The curfew tolls the knell of parting day,
>   The lowing herd wind slowly o'er the lea,
> The plowman homeward plods his weary way,
>   And leaves the world to darkness and to me.

5
> Now fades the glimmering landscape on the sight,
>   And all the air a solemn stillness holds,
> Save where the beetle wheels his droning flight,
>   And drowsy tinklings lull the distant folds;

GUIDE FOR READING

Use this guide for help with unfamiliar words and difficult passages.

1–2 As a bell rings **(curfew tolls)** to signal **(knell)** the end of the day, a herd of mooing **(lowing)** cows slowly makes its way through a meadow, or **lea** (lē).

6–12 Everything is quiet and still except for **(save where)** the following sounds. A beetle can be heard flying around **(wheels his droning flight)**. Sheep and cow bells are softly ringing in far-away valleys **(lull the distant folds)**. An owl in an ivy-covered tower is hooting because she has been disturbed by some creature coming near her hidden home **(secret bower)**.

MARK IT UP **KEEP TRACK**

As you read, you can use these marks to keep track of your understanding.

✔ ..... I understand.

? ..... I don't understand this.

! ..... Interesting or surprising idea

English Learner Support
VOCABULARY

Homograph Here, the word *wind* is pronounced with the long *i* sound as in *find*. It is a verb that means "wander in a zigzag path." The word *wind,* when pronounced with a short *i* sound (as in *pin),* is a noun that means "moving air."

READ ALOUD **Lines 5–8**

Read these lines slowly, pronouncing every word clearly and listening for repeated sounds.

Save that from yonder ivy-mantled tower

10   The moping owl does to the moon complain

Of such, as wandering near her secret bower,

        Molest her ancient solitary reign.

Beneath those rugged elms, that yew tree's shade,

        Where heaves the turf in many a moldering heap,

15 Each in his narrow cell forever laid,

        The rude forefathers of the hamlet sleep.

Pause & *Reflect*

FOCUS

The speaker describes the ordinary lives of the poor who are buried here. Then he reminds the rich and famous that death comes to everyone. As you read, look for clues about how the speaker feels about the poor, the wealthy, and the powerful.

The breezy call of incense-breathing Morn,

        The swallow twittering from the straw-built shed,

The cock's shrill clarion, or the echoing horn,

20   No more shall rouse them from their lowly bed.

For them no more the blazing hearth shall burn,

        Or busy housewife ply her evening care;

No children run to lisp their sire's return,

        Or climb his knees the envied kiss to share.

25 Oft did the harvest to their sickle yield,

        Their furrow oft the stubborn glebe has broke;

How jocund did they drive their team afield!

        How bowed the woods beneath their sturdy
           stroke!

Let not Ambition mock their useful toil,

30   Their homely joys, and destiny obscure;

Nor Grandeur hear with a disdainful smile

        The short and simple annals of the poor.

13–16 Under the large, old trees, there are many graves, marked by mounds of earth **(where heaves the turf in many a moldering heap)**. In these graves **(narrow cell)**, the ordinary, simple country folk **(rude forefathers)** of the village are buried.

17–20 The sights, sounds, and smells of a country morning can no longer greet those who have died; **clarion:** sound like that of a trumpet; **horn:** a hunter's horn.

22 **ply her evening care:** do the jobs that need to be done at the end of every day.
23 **lisp:** to speak imperfectly, as a child learning to talk.
25–28 The speaker describes the work of the poor in the fields and woods; **sickle:** a curved blade used to cut grain; **furrow:** the long row cut in the ground by a plow; **glebe:** soil; **jocund** (jŏ′kənd)**:** merry.
29 **Ambition:** This is an example of personification. *Ambition* here probably refers to people who are ambitious for fame or wealth. Such people might be tempted to make fun of the villagers and their way of life.
30 **homely:** related to the home.
31 **disdainful:** proud and scornful.
32 **annals:** descriptive records; history.

Pause & Reflect

1. Look back at the words and phrases you underlined as you read. What sights and sounds stand out in your impression of the graveyard scene? Star them. **(Visualize)**

2. Circle the phrase below that best expresses the mood of these opening stanzas. **(Infer)**

cheerful and excited

quiet and thoughtful

angry and resentful

As the poem continues . . .

• The speaker describes the lives of the people buried in this churchyard.

Reading Tip

After every stanza, or group of lines, summarize the stanza in your own words.

English Learner Support
LANGUAGE

Diction Poets often reverse word order in sentences to make the words fit the rhythm or rhyme pattern. Line 21 can be reordered as "For them, the blazing hearth shall burn no more." Line 24 can be rewritten as "Or climb his knees to share the envied kiss."

What Does It Mean?

Obscure here means "undistinguished" or "humble." In other words, the people buried here did not become famous.

The boast of heraldry, the pomp of power,
    And all that beauty, all that wealth e'er gave,
35 Awaits alike the inevitable hour.
    The paths of glory lead but to the grave.

Nor you, ye proud, impute to these the fault,
    If Memory o'er their tomb no trophies raise,
Where through the long-drawn aisle and fretted vault
40   The pealing anthem swells the note of praise.

Can storied urn or animated bust
    Back to its mansion call the fleeting breath?
Can Honor's voice provoke the silent dust,
    Or Flattery soothe the dull cold ear of Death?

Pause **&** *Reflect*

FOCUS

The speaker imagines the lives the villagers might
have lived if their circumstances had been different.
As you read, look for both good and bad experiences
they might have had.

45 Perhaps in this neglected spot is laid
    Some heart once pregnant with celestial fire;
Hands that the rod of empire might have swayed,
    Or waked to ecstasy the living lyre.

But Knowledge to their eyes her ample page
50   Rich with the spoils of time did ne'er unroll;
Chill Penury repressed their noble rage,
    And froze the genial current of the soul.

Full many a gem of purest ray serene,
    The dark unfathomed caves of ocean bear:
55 Full many a flower is born to blush unseen,
    And waste its sweetness on the desert air.

33 boast of heraldry: pride in being an aristocrat.

35 inevitable hour: death.

37 impute . . . fault: blame them.

38 trophies: sculptures showing the achievements of the dead person.

39 fretted vault: the decorated arched ceiling of a cathedral.

40 pealing anthem: a majestic piece of music sung by a choir.

41 storied urn: vase used to contain the ashes of a dead person and decorated with scenes from the person's life; **animated bust:** a lifelike sculpture of the deceased person's head. Such memorials of the rich might be found in a palace or a fancy church.

42 mansion: a dead person's body.

43 provoke: call forth.

46 celestial fire: great promise, or potential.

47 hands . . . swayed: someone who might have had the strength, courage, and leadership to conquer and rule a great kingdom.

48 lyre: a small harplike musical instrument. It was used in ancient Greece to accompany the singing of poetry.

51–52 Chill penury (pĕn'yə-rē) **. . . soul:** extreme poverty **(penury)** held back their deep feelings **(noble rage)** and their creativity **(genial current of the soul).**

Reading Tip

Memory, Honor, Flattery, and *Death* are personified, or given human qualities. Memory raises trophies, honor has a voice, flattery can soothe, and death has an ear. As you read, look for other examples of personification.

Pause & Reflect

Reread lines 21–24. How do you think the speaker feels about the villagers and their way of life? **(Infer from Details)**

_____

_____

_____

_____

As the poem continues . . .

• The speaker thinks about what the dead might have done if they had had money and power.

Some village Hampden, that with dauntless breast
    The little tyrant of his fields withstood;
Some mute inglorious Milton here may rest,
60   Some Cromwell guiltless of his country's blood.

The applause of listening senates to command,
    The threats of pain and ruin to despise,
To scatter plenty o'er a smiling land,
    And read their history in a nation's eyes,

65 Their lot forbade: nor circumscribed alone
    Their growing virtues, but their crimes confined;
Forbade to wade through slaughter to a throne,
    And shut the gates of mercy on mankind,

The struggling pangs of conscious truth to hide,
70   To quench the blushes of ingenuous shame,
Or heap the shrine of Luxury and Pride
    With incense kindled at the Muse's flame.

Far from the madding crowd's ignoble strife,
    Their sober wishes never learned to stray;
75 Along the cool sequestered vale of life
    They kept the noiseless tenor of their way.

Pause & *Reflect*

FOCUS

The speaker looks again at the graves in the churchyard. He points out that even the graves of the poor are marked with some kind of memorial. **MARK IT UP** As you read, circle words and phrases that describe the graves.

Yet even these bones from insult to protect
    Some frail memorial still erected nigh,
With uncouth rhymes and shapeless sculpture decked,
80 Implores the passing tribute of a sigh.

57 Hampden: John Hampden, a 17th-century English politician who opposed King Charles I **(little tyrant)** over unjust taxes.

59 mute inglorious Milton: Milton was a great English poet. The reference here is to a villager who might have had Milton's genius but could not write **(mute)** and so remained unknown **(inglorious).**

60 Cromwell: Oliver Cromwell, military leader who helped to overthrow King Charles I in the English Civil War and who then ruled England from 1653 to 1658.

61–65 The villagers never had a chance to become people of national importance.

65–72 The villagers' situation kept them from doing great evil **(crimes)** as well as great good **(growing virtues).** No villager would ever be guilty of killing people to become a ruler **(wade through slaughter to a throne).** They also would never be bad leaders guilty of cruelty, corruption, and greed.

72 incense . . . flame: poetic praise.

73 madding: wildly excited; disorderly.

75 sequestered: isolated.

76 tenor: steady pace.

78 frail memorial: simple gravestone.

79 uncouth: awkward; clumsy.

✔ Reading Check

What are some of the good and bad things the dead never did?

English Learner Support
CULTURE

Muses The Muses were nine daughters of the ancient Greek god Zeus. Each Muse was responsible for a particular art or science. It was their job to help artists—especially poets and musicians—do their work.

Pause & Reflect

From what you have read so far, how would you describe the lives of the villagers? **(Infer from Details)**

_____

_____

_____

_____

As the poem continues . . .

• The speaker talks about the gravestones.

What Does It Mean?

Implores the passing tribute of a sigh means "begs people to stop and sigh."

Their name, their years, spelt by the unlettered Muse,
        The place of fame and elegy supply:
And many a holy text around she strews,
        That teach the rustic moralist to die.

85   For who to dumb Forgetfulness a prey,
        This pleasing anxious being e'er resigned,
Left the warm precincts of the cheerful day,
        Nor cast one longing lingering look behind?

On some fond breast the parting soul relies,
90   Some pious drops the closing eye requires;
Even from the tomb the voice of Nature cries,
        Even in our ashes live their wonted fires.

Pause & *Reflect*

FOCUS

The poem takes an unusual turn at this point. The
speaker seems to address the poet Gray directly. The
speaker also pictures an imaginary poet, seen
through the eyes of an old peasant. The old man
describes this poet walking in the countryside. Then
he tells about the poet's funeral. As you read, form
your own mental pictures of the imaginary poet's life.

For thee, who mindful of the unhonored dead
        Dost in these lines their artless tale relate;
95   If chance, by lonely contemplation led,
        Some kindred spirit shall inquire thy fate,

Haply some hoary-headed swain may say,
        "Oft have we seen him at the peep of dawn
Brushing with hasty steps the dews away
100   To meet the sun upon the upland lawn.

81 unlettered Muse: the "inspiration" of the uneducated stonecutters who carved the words on the tombstones.

83–84 And many . . . die: Passages from the Bible **(holy text)** are carved on many of the gravestones. These passages teach the villagers how to accept death.

85–88 For who . . . behind?: For who has ever accepted that he will be forgotten? Who leaves the warmth of earthly life without any regret?

89–92 On some . . . fires: Those who are dying need to know that someone loves them and will weep **(pious drops)** when they are gone. After we are dead, our tombs are reminders of the human desire to be remembered.

93 thee: that is, Gray himself.

97 haply: perhaps; **hoary-headed swain:** very old peasant or shepherd.

English Learner Support
VOCABULARY

Spelling *Spelt* is an archaic way of writing *spelled.* Today, the past tense of *spell* is *spelled.* When Gray was writing, however, the past tense was *spelt.*

What Does It Mean?

Around she strews means "she spread around." It means that the speaker sees many Bible verses on the gravestones all around the cemetery.

Pause **&** *Reflect*

Look at the words and phrases you circled as you read. How would you describe these graves? **(Infer from Details)**

_____

_____

As the poem continues . . .

- The speaker now addresses the poet Gray.
- The speaker imagines how an old peasant might describe the poet Gray.

✔ Reading Check

To whom is the speaker talking?

English Learner Support
LANGUAGE

Figure of Speech *Kindred spirit* means "a person who likes the same things or feels the same way."

"There at the foot of yonder nodding beech
        That wreathes its old fantastic roots so high,
His listless length at noontide would he stretch,
        And pore upon the brook that babbles by.

105 "Hard by yon wood, now smiling as in scorn,
        Muttering his wayward fancies he would rove,
Now drooping, woeful wan, like one forlorn,
        Or crazed with care, or crossed in hopeless love.

"One morn I missed him on the customed hill,
110   Along the heath and near his favorite tree;
Another came; nor yet beside the rill,
        Nor up the lawn, nor at the wood was he;

"The next with dirges due in sad array
        Slow through the churchway path we saw him
                borne.
115 Approach and read (for thou canst read) the lay,
        Graved on the stone beneath yon aged thorn."

Pause & Reflect

FOCUS

The poem ends with the epitaph that is on the poet's gravestone. The epitaph speaks of the dead poet as a youth. Gray seems to be using an imaginary epitaph for himself to express deep emotions. MARK IT UP As you read, circle details you learn about the poet from these lines.

The Epitaph

Here rests his head upon the lap of Earth
        A youth to fortune and to Fame unknown.
Fair Science frowned not on his humble birth,
120   And Melancholy marked him for her own:

103 His listless length . . . stretch: at noontime he would lie down on the ground, stretched out full-length in a tired way.
104 pore: to look at with concentration.
105–109 The poet wanders **(would rove)** around the woods, talking to himself, as if overcome with sorrow, worry, or hopeless love.

111 rill: stream; creek.

113 next: next morning; **dirges:** funeral hymns.

115 lay: poem.
116 thorn: hawthorn, a small tree with thorns.

Epitaph: the words on a gravestone written in memory of the person buried there.

119 Fair Science . . . birth: Although Gray did not come from a wealthy family, he received an excellent education **(Science)**.
120 Melancholy: sadness; gloominess.

✔ Reading Check
What happened to the poet?

Pause & *Reflect*

The old peasant in lines 98–108 tells what he noticed about the poet. Circle the words and phrases below that apply to the poet. **(Infer from Details)**

kept to himself	enjoyed nature
talkative	busy
carefree	sad

As the poem ends . . .

• The poet's epitaph, or gravestone inscription, describes what he was like..

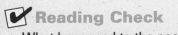

MARK IT UP **Reread Lines 117–120**

Circle examples of **personification** in these lines.

Large was his bounty, and his soul sincere,
　　Heaven did a recompense as largely send:
He gave to Misery all he had, a tear,
　　He gained from Heaven ('twas all he wished) a
　　　friend.

125　　　No farther seek his merits to disclose,
　　Or draw his frailties from their dread abode
(There they alike in trembling hope repose),
　　The bosom of his Father and his God.

Pause & Reflect

121–124 The poet was generous and honest. He sympathized with the sufferings of others. His reward in life—all that he really wanted— was the gift of a friend.

125–128 Don't try to reveal more of his good qualities or to point out his weaknesses. Both his strengths and his faults rest **(repose)** in hope with God.

Pause & Reflect

1. Look at the details you circled as you read. What do you learn about the poet from his epitaph? **(Infer from Details)**

_____

_____

_____

_____

2. In the poem, the poet has been buried in the very churchyard that he has written about. Star the statement below that tells how the poet is like the villagers he has been writing about. **(Evaluate)**

He is an ordinary person, but he wants to be mourned and remembered.

He is proud of his many accomplishments and expects to be honored.

CHALLENGE

What **themes,** or important ideas, about life and death does Gray express in the poem? Review the poem and your notes and mark passages that support your ideas. **(Analyze)**

Active Reading SkillBuilder

Making Inferences from Details

By paying attention to the **descriptive details** that Gray provides, readers can **make inferences** about the people in his poem. Use the chart below to create a list of details and inferences about the villagers. First, identify the details. Then, make inferences about the details. Finally, cite the line or lines of the poem where each detail is found. Try to choose details that show the villagers' values, the conditions of their lives, or their dreams and ambitions. An example is done for you.

Descriptive Details	Inferences	Line(s)
"plowman homeward plods his weary way"	villagers are farmers who work hard	3

Literary Analysis SkillBuilder

Personification

Personification is a type of figurative language in which human qualities are given to an object, animal, or idea. List three examples of personification that Gray uses in "Elegy Written in a Country Churchyard." Write the lines from the poem. Tell what is being personified, and note the human qualities it has. Two examples are given.

Lines	Object, Animal, or Idea	Human Qualities
1. "The moping owl does to the moon complain" (line 10)	owl	moping, complaining
2. "Let not Ambition mock their useful toil," (line 29)	Ambition	mocking
3.		
4.		
5.		

William Wordsworth

Lines Composed
a Few Miles Above
Tintern Abbey

Before You Read

Connect to Your Life

Do you have a favorite place in nature that makes you feel peaceful and contented? In the space below, describe that place or one you would like to find.

_____

_____

_____

_____

_____

Key to the Poem

WHAT'S THE BIG IDEA? William Wordsworth was one of a group of English poets known as the Romantics. Romantic poetry emphasizes the beauty of the natural world and celebrates the important connection between people and nature. As you read the poem, notice the language Wordsworth uses to describe his feelings about nature.

Reading Tips

This poem is one of the author's finest—and one of his most challenging. Most readers have trouble with this poem, so be patient.

- Think of each stanza as a kind of "paragraph" that develops one idea at a time.

- As you read, don't stop at the end of each line. Instead, try to read to the major punctuation marks, such as periods, semi-colons, and dashes. Also, try to identify the major verbs in each sentence.

- Use the Guide for Reading to help you understand unfamiliar words and difficult passages.

As the poem begins . . .

- The speaker talks about how glad he is to be back in a special place.

MARK IT UP **KEEP TRACK**

As you read, you can use these marks to keep track of your understanding.

✔ ..... I understand.

? ..... I don't understand this.

! ..... Interesting or surprising idea

The InterActive Reader PLUS
196 For English Learners

Lines Composed a Few Miles Above Tintern Abbey

William Wordsworth

PREVIEW William Wordsworth wrote this poem when he was 28 years old. Five years earlier, he had visited the ruins of Tintern Abbey. This large building had once been a home for monks. The abbey is located on the banks of the Wye River, near the border between England and Wales.

The **speaker** of the poem is Wordsworth himself. As the poem begins, he again looks out at the beautiful landscape that surrounds the abbey. At his side is Dorothy, his beloved sister. Stirred by the beauty of the scene, he thinks about what it has meant to him over the past five years. He believes that nature has made him a better person.

FOCUS

The speaker stands on a hill a few miles above Tintern Abbey. He provides a word picture of the landscape.

MARK IT UP As you read, underline details that tell you what the speaker hears and sees. An example is highlighted.

Five years have passed; five summers, with the length
Of five long winters! and again I hear
These waters, rolling from their mountain-springs
With a soft inland murmur. Once again
5   Do I behold these steep and lofty cliffs,
That on a wild secluded scene impress
Thoughts of more deep seclusion; and connect
The landscape with the quiet of the sky.

Use this guide for help with unfamiliar words and difficult passages.

MARK IT UP WORD POWER

Mark words that you'd like to add to your **Personal Word List**. After reading, you can record the words and their meanings beginning on page 508.

More About . . .

(TINTERN ABBEY) An *abbey* is home to a religious community. *Tintern Abbey* was established in 1311 and was partially destroyed in the sixteenth century.

MARK IT UP   Reread Lines 4–8

Circle the word that shows the relation between the "landscape" and "the quiet of the sky." **(Clarify)**

English Learner Support
VOCABULARY

Secluded A *secluded* place is private and hidden from view.

Reading Check

What kind of a landscape does the speaker describe?

6–7 That . . . seclusion: No one is present except the speaker and his sister. The speaker is in a quiet, thoughtful mood.

The day is come when I again repose

10 Here, under this dark sycamore, and view
These plots of cottage ground, these orchard tufts,
Which at this season, with their unripe fruits,
Are clad in one green hue, and lose themselves
'Mid groves and copses. Once again I see

15 These hedgerows, hardly hedgerows, little lines
Of sportive wood run wild; these pastoral farms,
Green to the very door; and wreaths of smoke
Sent up, in silence, from among the trees!
With some uncertain notice, as might seem

20 Of vagrant dwellers in the houseless woods,
Or of some Hermit's cave, where by his fire
The Hermit sits alone.

Pause & *Reflect*

FOCUS

The speaker thinks about how his memories of the landscape have helped him. The speaker believes that nature helps humans feel connected to the world. MARK IT UP As you read, underline details that help you understand how the speaker's memories of the landscape have helped him.

These beauteous forms,
Through a long absence, have not been to me
As is a landscape to a blind man's eye;

25 But oft, in lonely rooms, and 'mid the din
Of towns and cities, I have owed to them,
In hours of weariness, sensations sweet,
Felt in the blood, and felt along the heart;
And passing even into my purer mind,

30 With tranquil restoration—feelings too
Of unremembered pleasure; such, perhaps,
As have no slight or trivial influence
On that best portion of a good man's life,
His little, nameless, unremembered, acts

35 Of kindness and of love. Nor less, I trust,
To them I may have owed another gift,
Of aspect more sublime; that blessed mood,
In which the burthen of the mystery,

9 **repose:** lie at rest.

11 **tufts:** clusters or clumps of trees.

13 **hue:** color.

14 **copses** (kŏp'sĭz)**:** thickets of small trees.

15–16 **hedgerows:** rows of shrubs or small trees forming a fence or boundary; **sportive:** playful. The rows of small trees do not seem to follow in straight lines but in "little lines . . . run wild."

16 **pastoral** (păs'tər-əl)**:** rural and peaceful.

19 **With some uncertain notice:** not very noticeable.

20 **vagrant:** wandering.

25–26 **mid the din . . . cities:** mid the noise of city life.

27–29 The speaker describes three stages of his responses to nature. His responses are felt first "in the blood" (physically), then "along the heart" (emotionally), and finally in the "purer mind." These impressions give him calm refreshment **(tranquil restoration).**

35–41 One of nature's best gifts is a sense of inner peace **(that blessed mood).** This gift helps the speaker come to terms with life and raises him to a higher level.

38 **burthen:** burden.

1. Review the details you underlined as you read. Which phrase below names something *not* mentioned by the speaker? Cross out that phrase. **(Visualize)**

rising smoke   cliffs and trees

farms and orchards   workers in the fields

MARK IT UP   **2.** How would you describe the speaker's mood? Write the answer below. Then circle the details on pages 196 and 198 that helped you reach your answer. **(Infer)**

_____

_____

_____

_____

As the poem continues . . .

• Thinking about this place makes the speaker feel happy.

In which the heavy and the weary weight
40 Of all this unintelligible world,
Is lightened—that serene and blessed mood,
In which the affections gently lead us on—

Until, the breath of this corporeal frame
And even the motion of our human blood
45 Almost suspended, we are laid asleep
In body, and become a living soul;
While with an eye made quiet by the power
Of harmony, and the deep power of joy,
We see into the life of things.

                                        If this
50 Be but a vain belief, yet, oh! how oft—
In darkness and amid the many shapes
Of joyless daylight; when the fretful stir
Unprofitable, and the fever of the world,
Have hung upon the beatings of my heart—
55 How oft, in spirit, have I turned to thee,
O sylvan Wye! thou wanderer through the woods,
How often has my spirit turned to thee!

Pause & Reflect

FOCUS

Now the speaker describes his changing view of
nature. As a boy, he took great pleasure in nature.
As a young man, he had intense feelings for nature.
Now, as an adult, he responds to nature is a more
thoughtful way.

MARK IT UP As you read, underline words and
phrases that describe the speaker's various feelings
about nature.

And now, with gleams of half-extinguished thought
With many recognitions dim and faint,
60 And somewhat of a sad perplexity,
The picture of the mind revives again;
While here I stand, not only with the sense
Of present pleasure, but with pleasing thoughts
That in this moment there is life and food
65 For future years. And so I dare to hope,

40 unintelligible: difficult to understand.

42 affections: emotions.

43–46 The speaker feels that he has gone beyond physical existence. He sees the inner qualities of things.

43 corporeal (kôr-pôr′ē-əl)**:** bodily.

53–54 the fretful stir/Unprofitable: useless worries.

56 sylvan: located in a wood or forest; **Wye:** a river in Wales and England.

58–61 The speaker looks at the landscape. His memories of it come back to him.

Pause & Reflect

1. Review the details you underlined as you read. How have the speaker's memories of the landscape helped him? Circle three phrases below. **(Cause and Effect)**

lifted his spirits   gave him wisdom

probably made him   made him wealthy
kinder

▲ MARK IT UP   **2.** Reread the boxed passage on page 200. What two phrases in these lines describe the power of nature? Circle these phrases. **(Evaluate)**

English Learner Support
LANGUAGE

Metaphor *Fever of the world* is a metaphor comparing the bustle of the world to a fever.

As the poem continues . . .

• The speaker compares and contrasts the way he felt about nature when he was a boy and the way he feels about it now.

English Learner Support
LANGUAGE

Figurative Language The highlighted phrase means that the speaker's vision of this landscape will give him strength —like food does—in years to come.

Though changed, no doubt, from what I was when
   first
I came among these hills; when like a roe
I bounded o'er the mountains, by the sides
Of the deep rivers, and the lonely streams,
70 Wherever nature led—more like a man
Flying from something that he dreads than one
Who sought the thing he loved. For nature then
(The coarser pleasures of my boyish days,
And their glad animal movements all gone by)
75 To me was all in all.—I cannot paint
What then I was. The sounding cataract
Haunted me like a passion; the tall rock,
The mountain, and the deep and gloomy wood,
Their colors and their forms, were then to me
80 An appetite; a feeling and a love,
That had no need of a remoter charm,
By thought supplied, nor any interest
Unborrowed from the eye.—That time is past,
And all its aching joys are now no more,
85 And all its dizzy raptures. Not for this
Faint I, nor mourn nor murmur; other gifts
Have followed; for such loss, I would believe,
Abundant recompense. For I have learned
To look on nature, not as in the hour
90 Of thoughtless youth; but hearing oftentimes
The still, sad music of humanity,
Nor harsh nor grating, though of ample power
To chasten and subdue. And I have felt
A presence that disturbs me with the joy
95 Of elevated thoughts; a sense sublime
Of something far more deeply interfused,
Whose dwelling is the light of setting suns,
And the round ocean and the living air,
And the blue sky, and in the mind of man:
100 A motion and a spirit, that impels
All thinking things, all objects of all thought,
And rolls through all things. Therefore am I still
A lover of the meadows and the woods,
And mountains; and of all that we behold
105 From this green earth; of all the mighty world
Of eye, and ear—both what they half create,

66–72 Though . . . loved: When the speaker was younger, he was overcome by the power of the scene's natural beauty. He was "led" by nature, but he did not understand it.

67 roe: deer.

73–74 These lines refer to an even earlier time when the speaker was a boy.

75 paint: describe.

76 cataract: waterfall.

80–83 The speaker had a fierce love for nature. He loved without even thinking about it.

86 faint: lose heart.

88 recompense: compensation or payment. Here the speaker begins to describe the "other gifts" that have taken the place of the thrills he knew in his younger days.

90–93 When the speaker looks upon nature now as an adult, he hears the "still, sad music of humanity." The joy of nature is now mixed with the pains and sorrows of human life.

93 chasten (chā´sən): make modest.

105–107 When we respond to nature, we don't simply notice it—we help to create it.

What Does It Mean?

Glad animal means "happy, carefree, unrestrained."

English Learner Support

LANGUAGE

Diction In the highlighted lines 85–86, the poet changes the word order of a sentence. Usually, the subject *I* would go before the verbs *faint, mourn,* and *murmur* in this way: "I do not faint, mourn, or murmur for this. "

What Does It Mean?

Here, *man* refers to all humankind, not just one male person.

And what perceive; well pleased to recognize
In nature and the language of the sense
The anchor of my purest thoughts, the nurse,
110   The guide, the guardian of my heart, and soul
Of all my moral being.

Pause & Reflect

FOCUS

The speaker now turns to his sister, standing beside him on the banks of the river. He offers a prayer for her, asking that nature guide her.
MARK IT UP   As you read, underline the details that help you understand nature's gifts.

Nor perchance,
If I were not thus taught, should I the more
Suffer my genial spirits to decay:
For thou art with me here upon the banks
115   Of this fair river; thou my dearest Friend,
My dear, dear Friend; and in thy voice I catch
The language of my former heart, and read
My former pleasures in the shooting lights
Of thy wild eyes. Oh! yet a little while
120   May I behold in thee what I was once,
My dear, dear Sister! and this prayer I make,
Knowing that Nature never did betray
The heart that loved her; 'tis her privilege,
Through all the years of this our life, to lead
125   From joy to joy: for she can so inform
The mind that is within us, so impress
With quietness and beauty, and so feed
With lofty thoughts, that neither evil tongues,
Rash judgments, nor the sneers of selfish men,
130   Nor greetings where no kindness is, nor all
The dreary intercourse of daily life,
Shall e'er prevail against us, or disturb
Our cheerful faith, that all which we behold
Is full of blessings. Therefore let the moon
135   Shine on thee in thy solitary walk;

How is the speaker's response to nature different now from the way it was in his younger days? Circle the answer below. **(Compare and Contrast)**

He no longer takes pleasure in nature's beauty.

He now can sense the spiritual power of nature.

As the poem ends . . .

• The speaker hopes his sister will love nature as he does.

111–120 The speaker is talking to his sister. Her voice and her eyes remind him of his own feelings for nature five years ago.

English Learner Support

LANGUAGE

Personification The poet describes Nature as a woman who brings joy to those who love her.

125–134 According to the speaker, the love of nature can help people rise above these bad experiences of city life.

131 dreary intercourse: sad dealings with people.

And let the misty mountain winds be free
To blow against thee: and, in after years,
When these wild ecstasies shall be matured
Into a sober pleasure; when thy mind
140 Shall be a mansion for all lovely forms,
Thy memory be as a dwelling place
For all sweet sounds and harmonies; oh! then,
If solitude, or fear, or pain, or grief
Should be thy portion, with what healing thoughts
145 Of tender joy wilt thou remember me,
And these my exhortations! Nor, perchance—
If I should be where I no more can hear
Thy voice, nor catch from thy wild eyes these gleams
Of past existence—wilt thou then forget
150 That on the banks of this delightful stream
We stood together; and that I, so long
A worshiper of Nature, hither came
Unwearied in that service; rather say
With warmer love—oh! with far deeper zeal
155 Of holier love. Nor wilt thou then forget,
That after many wanderings, many years
Of absence, these steep woods and lofty cliffs,
And this green pastoral landscape, were to me
More dear, both for themselves and for thy sake!

Pause & *Reflect*

139–143 when . . . harmonies: When his sister is older, her mind will be filled with beautiful memories about nature.

144 portion: lot or fate.

146 exhortations: words of encouraging advice.

147–149 In the future the speaker and his sister might be apart.

English Learner Support

VOCABULARY

Perchance *Perchance* means "maybe" or "possibly."

Pause **&** *Reflect*

1. Review the details you underlined as you read. Which of the following quotations from the poem describe a gift of nature? Circle three of them. **(Evaluate)**

   "lead from joy to joy"

   "feed with lofty thoughts"

   "disturb our cheerful faith"

   "impress with quietness and beauty"

2. Reread lines 116–121 on page 204. Then complete the following sentence by circling one of the phrases below.

   The speaker's sister views nature the way he _____. **(Clarify)**

   never could   now does   once did

3. What does the speaker want his sister to remember? **(Clarify)**

   _____

   _____

   _____

   _____

CHALLENGE

A **theme** is a main idea or message in a work of literature. What do you think the theme of this poem is? Think about what the poet says he has gotten from nature and what his life would be like if he had grown up without it. Mark lines and passages in the poem that you think support your idea of the theme.

Active Reading SkillBuilder

Drawing Conclusions

You can use details in a poem—especially the imagery—as well as your own experiences to **draw conclusions.** For example, in "Tintern Abbey," you might draw conclusions about Wordsworth's attitude toward nature at different stages of his life. On the chart below, jot down details about his attitude toward nature as a young man and as an adult. Then write your conclusions in the "View of Nature" column. An example is shown.

Stages of Life	Details	View of Nature
Young man (lines 67–85)	"nature then ... To me was all in all" (lines 72–75)	The speaker lost himself in the beauty and wonder of nature.
Adult (lines 88–102)		

Literary Analysis SkillBuilder

Imagery

Imagery is the use of words and phrases that create a vivid sensory experience for the reader. Images can appeal to any of the five senses: sight, hearing, smell, touch, and taste. Some images appeal to several senses.

On the chart, list three examples of images from "Tintern Abbey." Identify the sense or senses the image appeals to. An example is shown.

Images	Sense(s) Appealed To
"These waters, rolling from their mountain springs With a soft inland murmur" (lines 3–4)	sight, hearing

The RIME of the ANCIENT MARINER

Samuel Taylor Coleridge

Before You Read

Connect to Your Life

In this poem, the poet uses a variety of elements—colors, settings, images—to symbolize good and evil. Think of stories you have read or movies you have seen that involve the forces of good and evil. What common imagery is used to represent each of them? List your ideas below. Some examples have been provided.

GOOD	EVIL
Angel	Snake

Key to the Poem

WHAT YOU NEED TO KNOW Samuel Taylor Coleridge was a leading figure in the *Romantic* movement. He worked with William Wordsworth to create the book *Lyrical Ballads* which was published in 1798. "The Rime of the Ancient Mariner" was the first poem in the collection. Coleridge described poetry as different from science because its goal was pleasure—not truth. He thought imagination, the spirit, and emotions were more important than reason and the material world. "The Rime of the Ancient Mariner" is an imaginative work that uses figurative language and vivid imagery to tell a supernatural tale.

Reading Tips

"The Rime of the Ancient Mariner" is a **narrative poem,** a poem that tells a story. It is also a **literary ballad.** This excerpt will set up the story and introduce some of its main elements. As you read, try using the following strategies:

- Look for details of **setting** and **character** that the poet introduces in this excerpt.

- Use the notes in orange to follow the **plot.** These notes were written by Coleridge himself.

- There are two characters who speak in this excerpt, the ancient Mariner and the Wedding-Guest. Pay close attention to the use of quotation marks to keep track of who is speaking. The Wedding-Guest is the first speaker quoted (line 3).

- Use the information in the Guide for Reading to help you with unfamiliar words and difficult passages.

As the poem begins...

- The ancient Mariner and a young man who is on his way to a wedding feast are introduced.

---

from

The RIME
of the ANCIENT
MARINER

Samuel Taylor Coleridge

PREVIEW "The Rime of the Ancient Mariner" was written at the end of the 18th century. It is the story of a long, dangerous, and strange sea voyage. The "ancient Mariner" is an old sailor who had been on the voyage when he was young. At the beginning of the poem, he meets a young man who is on his way to a wedding celebration. The old Mariner stops the "Wedding-Guest" and begins to tell him his story. He describes the beginning of the voyage and dangers that arose. Then he tells about a large bird, an albatross, that appeared near the ship and seemed to bring good fortune. In a shocking moment, the Mariner reveals that he killed the albatross.

FOCUS

On his way to a wedding feast, a Wedding-Guest is stopped by an old man, the ancient Mariner. The Mariner insists on telling his story to the reluctant listener.

MARK IT UP Underline words and phrases that describe the Mariner. An example is highlighted on page 214.

How a Ship, having first sailed to the Equator, was driven by storms to the cold Country towards the South Pole; how the Ancient Mariner cruelly and in contempt of the laws of hospitality killed a Seabird and how he was followed by many strange Judgments; and in what manner he came back to his own Country.

GUIDE FOR READING

Use this guide for help with unfamiliar words and difficult passages.

English Learner Support

VOCABULARY

Mariner A *Mariner* is a sailor. The word comes from the word *marine,* which means "of the sea."

Reading Tip

As you read, fill in the word web below with details that describe the Mariner.

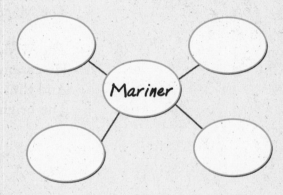

MARK IT UP **KEEP TRACK**

As you read, you can use these marks to keep track of your understanding.

✔..... I understand.

?..... I don't understand this.

!..... Interesting or surprising idea

This paragraph is Coleridge's own brief summary of the entire poem.

P A R T   I

It is an ancient Mariner,
And he stoppeth one of three.
"By thy long grey beard and glittering eye,
Now wherefore stopp'st thou me?

5   The Bridegroom's doors are opened wide,
And I am next of kin;
The guests are met, the feast is set:
May'st hear the merry din."

He holds him with his skinny hand,
10   "There was a ship," quoth he.
"Hold off! unhand me, grey-beard loon!"
Eftsoons his hand dropped he.

He holds him with his glittering eye—
The Wedding-Guest stood still,
15   And listens like a three years' child:
The Mariner hath his will.

The Wedding-Guest sat on a stone:
He cannot choose but hear;
And thus spake on that ancient man,
20   The bright-eyed Mariner.

Pause & *Reflect*

FOCUS

The Mariner describes the ship leaving its port, probably in Scotland. It sails south toward the Equator. The Wedding-Guest wants to get away from the old man but cannot break his spell. As you read, look for what distracts the Wedding-Guest's attention.

"The ship was cheered, the harbor cleared,
Merrily did we drop
Below the kirk, below the hill,
Below the lighthouse top.

*An ancient Mariner meeteth three Gallants
bidden to a wedding feast, and detaineth
one.* (A gallant was a fashionable young
gentleman.)

4 wherefore: why.

6 next of kin: the closest relative.

8 din: loud noise going on.

11 loon: crazy person.
12 Eftsoons: quickly.

*The Wedding-Guest is spellbound by the eye
of the old seafaring man, and constrained to
hear his tale.*

13 holds him with his glittering eye:
The Mariner seems to control the Wedding-
Guest by a spell.

23 kirk: church.

*The Mariner tells how the ship sailed south-
ward with a good wind and fair weather, till
it reached the Line* (the equator).

English Learner Support

Verbs This poem includes many verb
forms that are no longer used. Verbs such
as *stoppeth* (stopped) and *quoth* (said) that
end in *-th* or *-eth* are a few examples.

☑ Reading Check

Where is the young man going?

Pause & Reflect

1. How does the Wedding-Guest respond to
the Mariner when the old man stops him?
(Clarify)

_____

_____

_____

_____

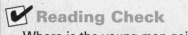 **2.** How does the Mariner
convince the Wedding-Guest to listen to his
tale? Circle the passage on page 214 that
tells you. **(Infer)**

As the poem continues . . .

• The ancient Mariner tells about the start
of his ship's voyage.

• The Wedding-Guest wants to get away,
but he is too curious about the old man's
story.

25 The Sun came up upon the left,
    Out of the sea came he!
    And he shone bright, and on the right
    Went down into the sea.

    Higher and higher every day,
30 Till over the mast at noon—"
    The Wedding-Guest here beat his breast,
    For he heard the loud bassoon.

    The bride hath paced into the hall,
    Red as a rose is she;
35 Nodding their heads before her goes
    The merry minstrelsy.

    The Wedding-Guest he beat his breast,
    Yet he cannot choose but hear;
    And thus spake on that ancient man,
40 The bright-eyed Mariner.

Pause & Reflect

FOCUS

As the ship sails south past the Equator, it is
attacked by wild storms that drive it toward the icy
South Pole. Just as things are at their worst, a large
sea bird appears.

MARK IT UP As you read, underline words that
describe the weather conditions the ship
encounters.

    "And now the Storm-blast came, and he
    Was tyrannous and strong:
    He struck with his o'ertaking wings,
    And chased us south along.

45 With sloping masts and dipping prow,
    As who pursued with yell and blow
    Still treads the shadow of his foe,
    And forward bends his head,
    The ship drove fast, loud roared the blast,
50 And southward aye we fled.

30 over . . . noon: The ship has reached the equator.

The Wedding-Guest heareth the bridal music; but the Mariner continueth his tale.

32 bassoon: a large, low-pitched musical instrument in the woodwind family.
36 minstrelsy: group of musicians.

The ship driven by a storm toward the South Pole.

45 sloping masts and dipping prow: The wind is blowing so hard that the poles **(masts)** that hold the sails are leaning at an angle **(sloping)**. The front part of the ship **(prow)** is pitching up and down in the water.

46–50 As . . . fled: The ship is like someone who is being chased by an attacker close behind. The ship plunges ahead trying to escape the storm.

Pause & Reflect

MARK IT UP **1.** How does the voyage begin? Circle words and phrases that describe the **mood** when the ship sets sail. **(Infer)**

2. Why does the Wedding-Guest stop paying attention to the Mariner's story? **(Clarify)**

_____
_____
_____
_____

3. How would you react if you were in the Wedding-Guest's situation? **(Connect)**

_____
_____
_____
_____

As the poem ends . . .

• The ancient Mariner's ship sails to Antarctica, and a storm begins.

• A large sea bird called an albatross appears.

English Learner Support
LANGUAGE

Personification The speaker personifies, or gives human qualities to, the wind. The wind (he) struck, chased, and pursued.

And now there came both mist and snow,
And it grew wondrous cold:
And ice, mast-high, came floating by,
As green as emerald.

55 And through the drifts the snowy clifts
Did send a dismal sheen:
Nor shapes of men nor beasts we ken—
The ice was all between.

The ice was here, the ice was there,
60 The ice was all around:
It cracked and growled, and roared and howled,
Like noises in a swound!

At length did cross an (Albatross,)
Thorough the fog it came;
65 As if it had been a Christian soul,
We hailed it in God's name.

It ate the food it ne'er had eat,
And round and round it flew.
The ice did split with a thunder-fit;
70 The helmsman steered us through!

And a good south wind sprung up behind;
The Albatross did follow,
And every day, for food or play,
Came to the mariners' hollo!

75 In mist or cloud, on mast or shroud,
It perched for vespers nine;
Whiles all the night, through fog-smoke white,
Glimmered the white moonshine."

"God save thee, ancient Mariner,
80 From the fiends, that plague thee thus!—
Why look'st thou so?"—With my crossbow
I shot the Albatross.

Pause & Reflect

53 ice, mast-high: icebergs.

55 clifts: cliffs.

The land of ice, and of fearful sounds where no living thing was to be seen.

56 dismal sheen: depressing brightness. The sailors could see nothing but shining snow and ice.

57 ken: perceive.

62 swound: swoon; fainting fit.

Till a great sea bird, called the Albatross, came through the snow-fog, and was received with great joy and hospitality.

63 Albatross (ăl′bə-trôs′): a large, web-footed ocean bird common in the Southern Hemisphere.

And lo! the Albatross proveth a bird of good omen, and followeth the ship as it returned northward through fog and floating ice.

71 south wind: A south wind blows *from* the south, and so it would move the ship northward, away from the South Pole.

74 hollo (hä′lō): call.

75 shroud: one of the ropes that support a ship's mast.

76 vespers nine: nine evenings.

80 fiends . . . thus: evil spirits, or demons, that torment you in this way.

The ancient Mariner inhospitably killeth the pious bird of good omen.

More About . . .

(ALBATROSS) Birds are often used as symbols. Here, the albatross may symbolize hope, salvation, and good fortune.

Pause & Reflect

1. Look at the words you underlined as you read. Cross out the one phrase below that does *not* describe this part of the sea voyage. **(Read Narrative Poetry)**

blasting winds and high waves

ice everywhere

hot and windless

gray and foggy

MARK IT UP **2.** The great sea bird, the albatross, is welcomed by the sailors. What happens to save the ship soon after the albatross has made its appearance? Circle the passage that tells you. **(Infer)**

READ ALOUD **3.** Read aloud the boxed passage on page 218. Why do you think the Wedding-Guest says "God save thee" to the Mariner? **(Clarify)**

_____

_____

_____

CHALLENGE

Coleridge uses many sound devices in this poem. They include **alliteration** (repetition of consonant sounds at the beginning of words), **repetition** of words, and **internal rhyme** (rhyming within a line). Mark one example of each of these devices. Explain why you think Coleridge used each one. **(Sound Devices)**

Active Reading SkillBuilder

Reading Narrative Poetry

"The Rime of the Ancient Mariner" is a **narrative poem**—a poem that tells a story. It has many of the basic elements of a prose story: plot, conflict, setting, character, point of view, and theme. In the opening of the poem, several details of the **setting** are introduced. In the chart below, list details of the setting and the lines where these details are found. (Look for details of the voyage, not of the scene with the Mariner and the Wedding-Guest.) An example is given.

Detail of Setting	Line number (s)
The ship starts out sailing south on a sunny sea.	*lines 25–28*

Literary Analysis SkillBuilder

Literary Ballad

"The Rime of the Ancient Mariner" is a **literary ballad**, a poem by a known writer who imitates the style of an anonymous **folk ballad.** Study the characteristics of a folk ballad on the chart below. Based on the excerpt you have read, decide how much "The Rime of the Ancient Mariner" matches typical folk ballad style. Then record your findings on the chart. A sample answer is given. If the excerpt does not include enough information for you to reach a conclusion, write a question mark in the box.

As you go on to read the rest of the poem, try to replace the question marks with conclusions you can reach based on other parts of the poem.

Folk Ballad	"The Rime of the Ancient Mariner"
Brief narrative poem (story poem) set to music	*a long poem; not set to music*
Opens abruptly	
Recounts a single dramatic, often tragic, episode	
Includes supernatural elements	
Has dialogue, often without directly stating who is speaking	
Some lines and stanzas repeat (with slight variations)	
Has four-line stanzas with regular rhythms and with the second and fourth lines rhyming	

Percy Bysshe

Shelley

Ozymandias

Before You Read

Connect to Your Life

Think about monuments or memorials you have seen. Was there one that really impressed you? Write the name of the memorial or monument in the center oval. Then fill in the web with words to describe the memorial or monument.

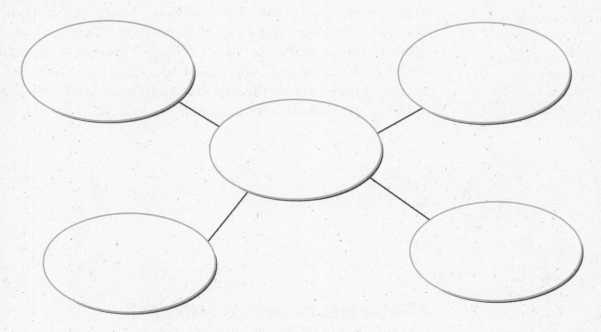

Key to the Poem

WHAT'S THE BIG IDEA? Powerful rulers often build monuments to themselves. What purposes do the monuments serve? Write your ideas on the lines below.

_____

_____

_____

_____

Reading Tips

This poem is a **sonnet,** or a lyric poem of 14 lines that follows a set rhythm. The poem teaches a lesson about power and pride.

- As you read, consider the feelings about the king that the poem stirs in you.
- Ask yourself what lesson the author wants to teach.
- Use the Guide for Reading to help you understand unfamiliar words and difficult lines and passages.

Ozymandias

Percy Bysshe Shelley

PREVIEW Percy Bysshe Shelley (1792–1822) was fascinated by the ancient world. "Ozymandias" (ŏz′ĭ-măn′dē-əs), the title of this poem, is the Greek name for one of the kings of ancient Egypt. This king, or pharoah, was Rameses II (răm′ĭ-sēz′). Known as "Rameses the Great," he ruled Egypt for a long time—from about 1290 to 1224 B.C. He built rock temples in many cities. He also built many huge statues to honor himself. Their size was meant to reflect his power.

As the poem begins . . .

- A traveler tells the speaker a story about a huge statue.

FOCUS

A traveler tells the speaker about a ruined statue he saw in the desert. This statue is of the Egyptian king Ozymandias.

MARK IT UP As you read, circle details that describe the ruined statue. An example is highlighted.

I met a traveler from an antique land
Who said: Two vast and trunkless legs of stone
Stand in the desert . . . Near them, on the sand,
Half sunk, a shattered visage lies, whose frown,
5   And wrinkled lip, and sneer of cold command,
Tell that its sculptor well those passions read
Which yet survive, stamped on these lifeless things,
The hand that mocked them, and the heart that fed:

Pause & Reflect

MARK IT UP **KEEP TRACK**

As you read, you can use these marks to keep track of your understanding.

✔ ..... I understand.

? ..... I don't understand this.

! ..... Interesting or surprising idea

Use this guide for help with unfamiliar words and difficult passages.

1 **antique:** ancient; old.

2 **trunkless legs:** legs separated from the rest of the body.

4 **shattered visage** (vĭz'ĭj)**:** broken face.

5 **sneer:** a look of disapproval made by raising one corner of the upper lip.

6 **those passions:** that is, Ozymandias' passions.

7–8 The sculptor's hand captured in stone **(mocked)** the passions of the king, and the king's heart fed those passions. These passions have survived both the sculptor and Ozymandias.

Reading Tip

As you read this poem, use the web below to record words and phrases that describe what Ozymandias, the ancient ruler, was like.

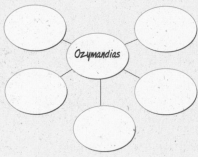

What Does It Mean?

Vast means "huge."

Pause & Reflect

Review the details you circled as you read. The king's facial looks are carved on the pieces of the statue. What do these expressions tell you about the king? **(Infer)**

_____

_____

_____

_____

English Learner Support
LANGUAGE

Word Order The highlighted words in line 6 are in an unusual order. The words could also be written as "read those passions well."

And on the pedestal these words appear:

10 "My name is Ozymandias, king of kings:
Look on my works, ye Mighty, and despair!"
Nothing beside remains. Round the decay
Of that colossal wreck, boundless and bare
The lone and level sands stretch far away.

Pause & Reflect

9 **pedestal:** the base of the statue.

12–14 These lines describe the ruined statue surrounded by the endless sands of the desert.
13 **colossal:** huge.

As the poem ends . . .

- The speaker talks about the words on the ruined statue.

- He describes the lonely surroundings.

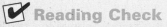

Reading Check

In your own words, repeat the message that Ozymandias left on his statue.

Pause & Reflect

READ ALOUD Read aloud lines 12–14. What do these lines suggest about pride? Check the correct sentence below. **(Draw Conclusions About Theme)**

Great works of pride can outlast time itself.

Time defeats even great works of pride.

CHALLENGE

Situational irony is when a character or the reader thinks one thing is going to happen, but something else does. What is ironic about the words on the statue? Think about the fact that the statue is ruined and alone in the desert. What point do you think Shelley is making by using irony here? **(Analyze)**

Active Reading SkillBuilder

Drawing Conclusions About Theme

You can draw conclusions about the **theme** of a poem by using these strategies:

- Think about why the poet chose the **subject** of the poem.
- Analyze the speaker's **tone,** or attitude, toward the subject.
- Describe the **mood,** or feeling, that the poem inspires in you.
- Note the **rhythmic pattern,** which can enhance a poem's meaning.

Record notes about the subject, tone, mood, and rhythmic pattern in "Ozymandias." Then write your conclusions about the poem's theme. Notes about the rhythmic pattern are shown.

	Notes
Subject	
Tone	
Mood	
Rhythmic Pattern	*iambic pentameter (like speech: regular, predictable)*

	Conclusions
Theme	

Literary Analysis SkillBuilder

Rhythmic Patterns in Poetry

In poetry, **meter** is the repetition of regular rhythmic units. Each unit of meter, or foot, has one stressed and one or two unstressed syllables. In **iambic pentameter,** a line of poetry has five feet. Each foot consists of an unstressed syllable followed by a stressed syllable. Poets may vary the meter by adding an extra syllable or reversing the stressed and unstressed syllables.

On the chart below, two lines from "Ozymandias" are shown. In the first line, the meter is regular; in the second line, a variation is found. Copy two more lines from "Ozymandias" onto the chart. Mark the stressed and unstressed syllables. Then describe the meter of each line.

Lines	Notes About Meter
The lone and level sands stretch far away.	regular iambic pentameter
Stand in the desert . . . Near them, on the sand,	reversed stress in the first foot

ODE

ON A GRECIAN URN

John Keats

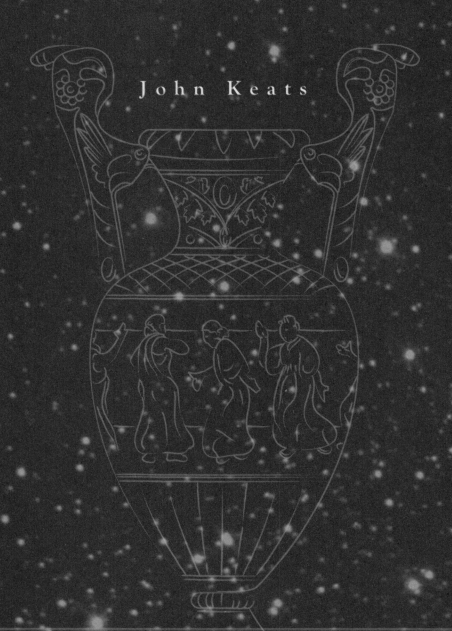

Before You Read

Connect to Your Life

What words or images come to mind when you hear the word *beauty*? Jot down your thoughts in the word web below.

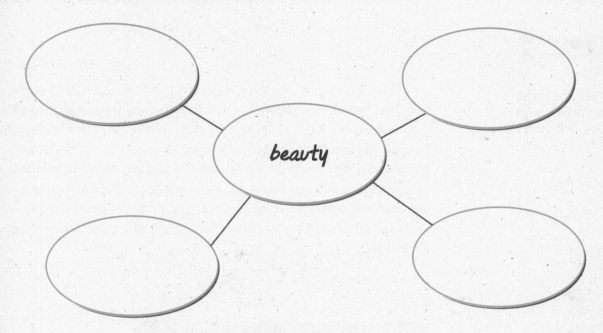

beauty

Key to the Poem

WHAT DO YOU THINK? An ode is a poem of praise. In this poem, the poet praises the beauty of a large urn, or vase, from ancient Greece. No actual Greek vase has been found that is identical to the one the poet describes. The vase in the poem is most likely based on similar vases the poet saw in the British Museum.

Reading Tips

An ode is a complicated poem. That means you will need to be especially patient as you read.

- Think about why the poet is so interested in the painting on the urn.

- Consider how the picture of life on the urn is different from real life.

- As you read, use the information in the Guide for Reading for help with unfamiliar words and difficult passages.

ODE
ON A GRECIAN URN

John Keats

PREVIEW Greek urns, or vases, became an art form about 2,500 years ago. They usually had scenes of gods, humans, and animals painted all around the sides. Keats probably saw such urns in the British Museum in London. The fact that such beautiful objects had existed for centuries fascinated him. His own ill health made him painfully aware of the passing of time and the changes it brings. The people and actions portrayed on an urn, however, would never be changed, never die. The possibility of immortality through beauty held out hope to the young poet, who would die at age 25.

As the poem begins...

- The speaker talks to the urn.

- He asks questions about the figures and pictures on the urn.

FOCUS

In this first stanza, the speaker talks directly to the urn itself. He asks a series of questions about the country scene painted on the vase. In the scene, musicians are playing, and male figures are chasing female figures.

MARK IT UP As you read, underline words and phrases that describe details on the urn. An example is highlighted.

MARK IT UP **KEEP TRACK**

As you read, you can use these marks to keep track of your understanding.

✔ ..... I understand.

? ..... I don't understand this.

! ..... Interesting or surprising idea

Thou still unravish'd bride of quietness,
    Thou foster-child of silence and slow time,
Sylvan historian, who canst thus express
    A flowery tale more sweetly than our rhyme:
5 What leaf-fring'd legend haunts about thy shape
    Of deities or mortals, or of both,
      In Tempe or the dales of Arcady?
    What men or gods are these? What maidens loath?
What mad pursuit? What struggle to escape?
10   What pipes and timbrels? What wild ecstasy?

Pause & Reflect

Use this guide for help with unfamiliar words and difficult passages.

1–3 The speaker calls the urn an **unravish'd bride** because the urn is perfectly preserved. The urn is a **foster-child of silence and slow time** because it has been hidden for centuries. It is a **sylvan historian** because it tells a story that takes place in a forest **(sylvan)** setting.

5 leaf-fring'd legend: Urns often showed scenes from famous stories about the gods. The speaker is wondering what this story, or legend, is about. **Leaf-fring'd** relates to both the country setting of the legend and to the leafy border design painted on the urn; **haunts about:** surrounds.

7 Tempe (tĕm'pē') **. . . Arcady** (är'kə-dē): two places in Greece that were often used as settings in literary works. Tempe is a beautiful valley; Arcady (Arcadia) is a mountain region.

8 loath: unwilling; reluctant.

10 pipes and timbrels: flutes and tambourines.

Reading Tip
After you finish each stanza, summarize its meaning in your own words.

What Does It Mean?
Deities are gods or goddesses.

✔ Reading Check
What do the pictures on the urn show?

Pause & Reflect

1. According to lines 3–4, what kind of story does the urn tell? Circle the description below that tells you. **(Clarify)**

   a pleasing story that is better than any that the poet can tell

   a dull story that will not interest others

2. Look back at the words and phrases that you underlined as you read. Why do you think the speaker asks so many questions about the scene? **(Analyze)**

   _____

   _____

   _____

In these stanzas, the speaker makes a comparison. He contrasts the beauty and happiness shown in the scene on the urn with what is possible in real life. As you read, look for the conclusions he reaches.

Heard melodies are sweet, but those unheard
    Are sweeter; therefore, ye soft pipes, play on;
Not to the sensual ear, but, more endear'd,
    Pipe to the spirit ditties of no tone:
15   Fair youth, beneath the trees, thou canst not leave
    Thy song, nor ever can those trees be bare;
      Bold lover, never, never canst thou kiss,
Though winning near the goal—yet, do not grieve;
    She cannot fade, though thou hast not thy bliss,
20 For ever wilt thou love, and she be fair!

Ah, happy, happy boughs! that cannot shed
    Your leaves, nor ever bid the spring adieu;
And, happy melodist, unweariéd,
    For ever piping songs for ever new;
25 More happy love! more happy, happy love!
    For ever warm and still to be enjoyed,
      For ever panting, and for ever young;
All breathing human passion far above,
    That leaves a heart high-sorrowful and cloy'd,
30   A burning forehead, and a parching tongue.

Pause & *Reflect*

As the poem continues...

• The speaker compares the scene on the urn to real life.

11–12 Heard . . . sweeter: Silent melodies that go on forever in a painting are sweeter than actual music that ends quickly.

12–14 therefore . . . no tone: The speaker says that the musicians should keep on playing the silent, "unheard" melodies **(ditties of no tone).** This music appeals to the **spirit,** or imagination.

English Learner Support

LANGUAGE

Usage The highlighted sentence means: "Although you won't ever get to be with her, you will always love her, and she will always be beautiful."

What Does It Mean?
Adieu means goodbye.

28–30 The love portrayed on the urn is far superior to the love experienced in real life. In real life, love brings sorrow and other extremes of emotion.

29 cloy'd: having had too much of something; oversatisfied.

Pause & Reflect

READ ALOUD Read aloud the boxed passage on page 234. Which of the following statements is *not* true about the lovers shown on the vase? Circle that statement. **(Clarify)**

The lovers can never kiss.

The man will always love the woman.

The woman's beauty will fade.

The speaker next describes a second scene painted
on the other side of the urn. The scene shows people
on their way to an outdoor religious ceremony.
   In the final stanza, the speaker contrasts the
timeless beauty of art with the changes that come to
all people in real life.
MARK IT UP   Underline the statement that expresses
what beauty means to the speaker.

Who are these coming to the sacrifice?
        To what green altar, O mysterious priest,
Lead'st thou that heifer lowing at the skies,
        And all her silken flanks with garlands drest?
35 What little town by river or sea shore,
        Or mountain-built with peaceful citadel,
            Is emptied of this folk, this pious morn?
And, little town, thy streets for evermore
        Will silent be; and not a soul to tell
40   Why thou art desolate, can e'er return.

O Attic shape! Fair attitude! with brede
        Of marble men and maidens overwrought,
With forest branches and the trodden weed;
        Thou, silent form, dost tease us out of thought
45 As doth eternity: Cold Pastoral!
        When old age shall this generation waste,
            Thou shalt remain, in midst of other woe
        Than ours, a friend to man, to whom thou say'st,
"Beauty is truth, truth beauty,"—that is all
50   Ye know on earth, and all ye need to know.

Pause & Reflect

As the poem ends . . .

• The speaker describes another scene on the urn.

• He compares art with life.

☑ **Reading Check**

What is in the second scene on the urn?

Pause & Reflect

1. Why do you think Keats includes this scene from the urn in the poem? **(Analyze Author's Motivation)**

_____
_____
_____

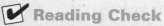 **2.** Reread the boxed passage on page 236. What does the speaker say will happen to the urn when his generation dies? Circle the phrase that tells you. **(Clarify)**

3. Look again at the statement you underlined as you read. Circle the sentence below that expresses its meaning. **(Clarify)**

It's impossible to tell the difference between truth and beauty.

Beauty expresses truth, and truth contains beauty.

CHALLENGE

An **ode** is written in formal language. Mark several examples of formal language in this poem. How does the type of language give the ode a special tone? **(Analyze Diction)**

31–37 This scene shows an ancient religious procession. A priest and worshippers are on their way to make a sacrifice to the gods. The sacrifice will be a young cow, or **heifer** (hĕf'ər). This cow has been carefully brushed and decorated with ropes of flowers **(her silken flanks with garlands drest)**. The "little town" is empty because all the people have left to attend the sacrifice.

41 Attic: simple and elegant, in the style of Athens; **brede:** interwoven design.

44–45 Thou . . . eternity: The speaker says the urn's beauty is as forceful as the idea of eternity; **Cold:** still, unmoving; **Pastoral** (păs'tər-əl): an artistic work that portrays country life in a beautiful way.

48–49 thou: the urn. The speaker presents the statement in quotation marks in line 49 as a message spoken by the urn.

Active Reading SkillBuilder

Analyzing an Author's Motivation

All authors have a **motivation,** or reason, for writing a work. In the chart below, identify the tone and theme in Keats's "Ode on a Grecian Urn." Then write a sentence explaining what you think Keats's motivation for writing the poem is.

Subject of the poem:	*a painted vase from ancient Greece*
Tone, or attitude toward the subject:	
Theme, or message, of the poem:	
Motivation for writing the poem:	

Literary Analysis SkillBuilder

Sound Devices

In poetry, **sound devices** can emphasize words, give a musical quality, create a mood, or unify a passage. **Assonance** is the repetition of similar vowel sounds within words; **consonance** is the repetition of similar consonant sounds within and at the ends of words. Find examples of assonance and consonance in "Ode on a Grecian Urn" and list them on the chart. Sample answers are given.

Assonance	Consonance
Thou foster-child of silence and slow time, (line 2)	Sylvan historian, who canst thus express (line 3)

My Last Duchess

Robert Browning

Before You Read

Connect to Your Life

Do you think jealousy is a normal part of love? Why or why not?
Explain below.

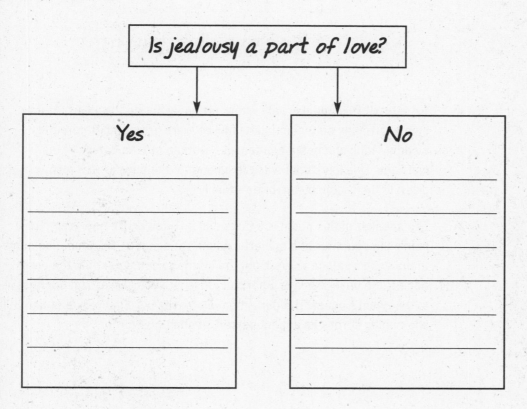

Is jealousy a part of love?

Yes

No

Key to the Poem

WHAT'S THE BIG IDEA? Robert Browning is a master of the dramatic
monologue. A dramatic monologue is a poem in which a fictional speaker
talks to a silent listener about an important experience in his or her life. In a
dramatic monologue, you learn about a character from his or her own words.

Reading Tips

The speaker of this poem tells his listener about the faults of his late wife.

- Read between the lines to discover what the speaker's words reveal about his late wife and about his own personality.

- This poem is written in **rhymed couplets,** or pairs of rhyming lines. Still, it is important that you use the punctuation to guide your reading. Stop at the end of a line only if you come upon a mark of punctuation.

- Use the Guide for Reading to help you understand unfamiliar words and difficult lines and passages.

My Last Duchess

Robert Browning

PREVIEW This poem is set in Italy, probably during the 1500s. At that time, marriages between noble families were arranged. Before the wedding took place, the two families worked out the details of the marriage. One key detail was the amount of the dowry—the money given to the groom by the bride's family.

The speaker of this poem is a duke and a widower. He now wants to marry the daughter of a powerful count. An agent of the count has come to the duke's palace to work out the marriage settlement. As the poem begins, the duke displays a portrait of his late wife—his "last duchess"— to the count's agent. The duke then expresses his disapproval of her. Still, she comes across as a good person, even in *his* words.

As the poem begins . . .

- The speaker shows his visitor a painting.

FOCUS

The duke shows the count's agent a painting of his late wife. This painting has captured her personality. As the duke displays the painting, he describes his late wife's "faults."

MARK IT UP As you read, circle details that help you form impressions of the last duchess. An example is highlighted on page 244.

That's my last Duchess painted on the wall,
Looking as if she were alive. I call
That piece a wonder, now: Frà Pandolf's hands
Worked busily a day, and there she stands.

Use this guide for help with unfamiliar words and difficult passages.

Reading Tip

As you read, note the details that the speaker gives about his former wife. Record the details you find in the word web below.

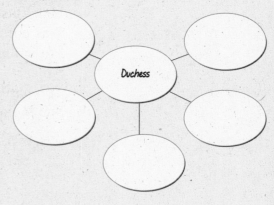

1 That's a painting of my late wife on the wall.

3 **Frà Pandolf's:** of Brother Pandolf, the made-up name of a painter who is also a friar.

4 **a day:** each day for many days.

More About . . .

RENAISSANCE PAINTING Renaissance painters typically portrayed their subjects as realistically as possible. In this portrait, therefore, the Duchess looks (as if she) (were alive.)

5 Will't please you sit and look at her? I said
"Frà Pandolf" by design, for never read
Strangers like you that pictured countenance,
The depth and passion of its earnest glance,
But to myself they turned (since none puts by
10 The curtain I have drawn for you, but I)
And seemed as they would ask me, if they durst,
How such a glance came there; so, not the first
Are you to turn and ask thus. Sir, 'twas not
Her husband's presence only, called that spot
15 Of joy into the Duchess' cheek: perhaps
Frà Pandolf chanced to say "Her mantle laps
Over my lady's wrist too much," or "Paint
Must never hope to reproduce the faint
Half-flush that dies along her throat": such stuff
20 Was courtesy, she thought, and cause enough
For calling up that spot of joy. She had
A heart—how shall I say?—too soon made glad,
Too easily impressed; she liked whate'er
She looked on, and her looks went everywhere.

Pause & Reflect

FOCUS

The duke continues to explain why he was not
happy with his late wife. Read to find out what she
did that displeased him and how he feels about his
bride-to-be—his "next" duchess.

25 Sir, 'twas all one! My favor at her breast,
The dropping of the daylight in the West,
The bough of cherries some officious fool
Broke in the orchard for her, the white mule
She rode with round the terrace—all and each
30 Would draw from her alike the approving speech,
Or blush, at least. She thanked men—good! but thanked
Somehow—I know not how—as if she ranked
My gift of a nine-hundred-years-old name
With anybody's gift. Who'd stoop to blame

6 by design: on purpose.

6–12 for never . . . came there: strangers who look at the painting always want to ask the duke about his wife's expression.

7 countenance: face.

11 durst: dared. Note the hint that the strangers feel afraid to question the duke.

16–21 The duke recalls Frà Pandolf's portrait sessions with his wife. He is irritated that his wife blushed **(that spot of joy)** when the artist complimented her. The artist portrayed that blush in his painting.

16 mantle: cloak.

23 impressed: moved in a favorable way.

25 all one: of the same importance to her; **favor:** jewel, or other rich gift.

25–34 The duke is annoyed that his late wife found equal joy in everything. He wanted her to place himself far above all else in her life. But she treated him in the same friendly way that she treated others.

27 officious: offering unwanted services; meddling.

English Learner Support

LANGUAGE

Contraction *Will't* is a contraction of the words "will" and "it." The words are contracted to make them fit the meter of the line.

Pause **&** *Reflect*

1. Review the details you circled as you read. What are your impressions of the last duchess? **(Connect)**

_____

_____

READ ALOUD **2.** Read aloud the boxed passage on page 244. Why was the duke annoyed at his wife? **(Cause and Effect)**

_____

_____

As the poem ends . . .

- The Duke explains why he was unhappy with his last Duchess.
- He says he is ready to marry his "next Duchess."

What Does It Mean?

Nine-hundred-years-old name means that the speaker has ancestors who can be traced as far back as nine hundred years. He believes he gave his wife a gift—his last name—when they married, and he is upset that she didn't seem to value the gift.

35 This sort of trifling? Even had you skill
In speech—(which I have not)—to make your will
Quite clear to such an one, and say, "Just this
Or that in you disgusts me; here you miss,
Or there exceed the mark"—and if she let
40 Herself be lessoned so, nor plainly set
Her wits to yours, forsooth, and made excuse
—E'en then would be some stooping; and I choose
Never to stoop. Oh sir, she smiled, no doubt,
Whene'er I passed her; but who passed without
45 Much the same smile? This grew; I gave commands;
Then all smiles stopped together. There she stands
As if alive. Will't please you rise? We'll meet
The company below, then. I repeat,
The Count your master's known munificence
50 Is ample warrant that no just pretense
Of mine for dowry will be disallowed;
Though his fair daughter's self, as I avowed
At starting, is my object. Nay, we'll go
Together down, sir. Notice Neptune, though,
55 Taming a sea horse, thought a rarity,
Which Claus of Innsbruck cast in bronze for me!

Pause & Reflect

35 trifling: unimportant actions.

41 forsooth: in truth; indeed.

45–46 The duke strongly hints that he had a hand in his late wife's death.

49–53 These lines might be paraphrased as follows: The Count, your master, is known for his generosity **(munificence).** I am sure that he will not reject my just claim **(pretense)** for the money due to me for marrying his daughter. As I said at the start of the negotiations, his beautiful daughter is my goal—not the money.

53–54 The count's agent has gestured for the duke to go down the stairs first. The duke responds that they will go down together.

54–55 Notice Neptune . . . sea horse: The duke points out a sculpture of Neptune (in Roman mythology, the god of the sea) and a sea horse.

56 Claus of Innsbruck: a made-up name for an Austrian sculptor.

56 The last two words of the poem, "for me," suggest the duke's pride.

Reading Check
Why did the Duchess stop smiling?

Pause & Reflect

MARK IT UP **1.** The duchess enjoyed the simple things of life. Circle details in lines 25–31 on page 244 that support this view. **(Locate Details)**

READ ALOUD **2.** Read aloud the boxed passage on page 246. The duke never told his late wife that she upset him. Why not? Check one sentence below. **(Analyze)**

He didn't want to hurt her feelings.

He was too proud to say he was upset.

CHALLENGE

Situational irony is when something happens that is different from what you expected. What is ironic about the Duke's future marriage? What about his last marriage makes it ironic that he is marrying again? Find lines in the poem to support your ideas. **(Analyze)**

Active Reading SkillBuilder

Making Inferences

An **inference** is a logical guess based on evidence. Often you need to make
inferences to figure out what is unstated yet implied in a literary work. Use the chart
below to record your inferences about the speaker, his late wife, the setting, or past
events in "My Last Duchess." An example is shown.

Inferences	
Speaker	*the duke: very proud*
His Late Wife	
Setting	
Past Events	

Literary Analysis SkillBuilder

Dramatic Monologue

A **dramatic monologue** is a lyric poem in which a speaker describes a crucial experience to a silent or absent listener. A dramatic monologue allows the poet to take the reader inside the speaker's mind by revealing his or her feelings, personality, and motivations. On the following Venn diagram, compare your own opinion of the speaker in "My Last Duchess" with his view of himself. In the overlapping section, record any opinions that you and he share.

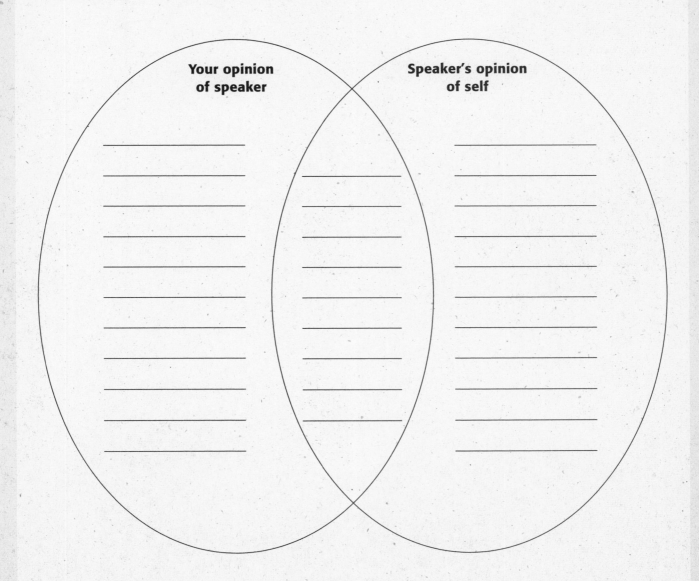

Your opinion of speaker

Speaker's opinion of self

Dover Beach

Matthew Arnold

Before You Read

Connect to Your Life

Is there a part of the natural world that you have strong feelings about?
Fill in the chart below to list one or more things in your natural
surroundings and the thoughts and feelings you have about them.

ASPECT OF NATURE	FEELINGS I HAVE
eagle	sad because it is endangered, happy because it is beautiful and free

Key to the Poem

WHAT'S THE BIG IDEA? The sea is the main image in this poem. What
comes to your mind when you think of the sea? Write your responses in
the word web below.

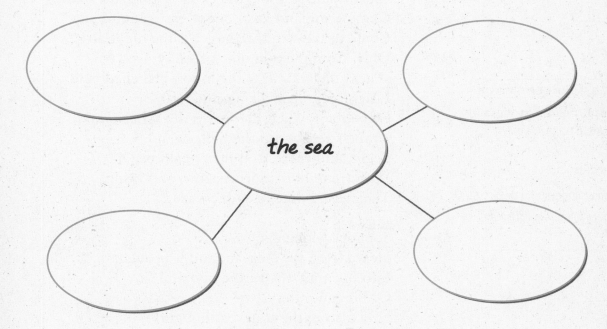

Reading Tips

This poem focuses on a single **image**—the sea at night.

- Picture the details of the sea scene.

- Read each stanza as if it were a paragraph in an essay. Find each stanza's main idea and consider how each stanza relates to the next.

As the poem begins...

- The speaker describes looking out over a calm sea at night.

- He describes the moon's light on the water.

- The constant movement of the water starts to sound sad to the poet.

MARK IT UP **KEEP TRACK**

As you read, you can use these marks to keep track of your understanding.

✔ ..... I understand.

? ..... I don't understand this.

! ..... Interesting or surprising idea

Dover
Beach
Matthew Arnold

PREVIEW This poem is both a love poem and a reflection on the uncertainties of life. It was written in England in the mid-19th century, when many traditional beliefs were being questioned. On a calm evening, the speaker is looking out a window toward the sea and the French coast. His enjoyment of the scene is broken by disturbing thoughts.

FOCUS

The speaker begins by describing a peaceful, pleasant scene of a beautiful moonlit sea. He soon shifts to a sadder mood, however.

MARK IT UP As you read, underline words and phrases that help create the mood of sadness. An example is highlighted.

The sea is calm tonight.
The tide is full, the moon lies fair
Upon the straits—on the French coast the light
Gleams and is gone; the cliffs of England stand,
Glimmering and vast, out in the tranquil bay.   5
Come to the window, sweet is the night air!
Only, from the long line of spray
Where the sea meets the moon-blanched land,
Listen! you hear the grating roar
Of pebbles which the waves draw back, and fling,   10
At their return, up the high strand,
Begin, and cease, and then again begin,
With tremulous cadence slow, and bring
The eternal note of sadness in.

Sophocles long ago   15
Heard it on the Aegean, and it brought
Into his mind the turbid ebb and flow
Of human misery; we
Find also in the sound a thought,
Hearing it by this distant northern sea.   20

Pause & Reflect

Use this guide for help with unfamiliar words
and difficult passages.

3 straits: the Strait of Dover, a narrow
channel of water separating England and
France, at the northern end of the English
Channel.

8 moon-blanched: shining palely in the
moonlight.

11 strand: beach.

13 tremulous cadence: trembling rhythm.

15 Sophocles (sŏf′ə-klēz′)**:** an ancient Greek
writer of tragic plays.

16 Aegean (ĭ-jē′ən)**:** the Aegean Sea—part
of the Mediterranean Sea, between Greece
and Turkey.

17 turbid: in a state of unrest; disturbed.

Reading Tip

Use the punctuation to help you read
complete thoughts rather than pausing
at the end of each line. For example, there
is no punctuation at the end of line 2. So
you can read "the moon lies fair / Upon
the straits" as a single, complete thought.
Identify other places in the first stanza
where a thought continues on to the
next line.

More About . . .

(SOPHOCLES) The Greek playwright
Sophocles lived more than 2,000 years
ago. By referring to Sophocles' writings
that mention the sea, Arnold shows that
people in very different places and at very
different times can have similar images,
thoughts, and concerns.

Pause & Reflect

1. What sights does the speaker describe in
lines 1–6? List at least three details that he
mentions. (**Visualize**)

_____

_____

_____

_____

READ ALOUD **2.** Read aloud the boxed
passage on page 252. What does the
speaker hear? (**Clarify**)

_____

_____

MARK IT UP **3.** Look at the words and
phrases you underlined as you read. Star
one or two phrases that seem especially
important in creating the mood. (**Draw
Conclusions About Mood**)

The speaker goes on to compare the sea to the
religious beliefs that once gave certainty and
comfort to people. The "Sea of Faith" is withdrawing,
however, like the outgoing tide of an ocean. The
speaker asks his beloved to be faithful to him in this
troubled world.

MARK IT UP   As you read, underline passages that
show the speaker's uncertainties and sorrows.

The Sea of Faith
Was once, too, at the full, and round earth's shore
Lay like the folds of a bright girdle furled.
But now I only hear
25   Its melancholy, long, withdrawing roar,
Retreating, to the breath
Of the night wind, down the vast edges drear
And naked shingles of the world.

Ah, love, let us be true
30   To one another! for the world, which seems
To lie before us like a land of dreams,
So various, so beautiful, so new,
Hath really neither joy, nor love, nor light,
Nor certitude, nor peace, nor help for pain;
35   And we are here as on a darkling plain
Swept with confused alarms of struggle and flight,
Where ignorant armies clash by night.

Pause & *Reflect*

GUIDE FOR READING

21 Sea of Faith: traditional religious beliefs about God and the world, long viewed as true and unshakable.

23 girdle: a belt or sash worn around the waist.

27 drear: dreary; gloomy.

28 shingles: pebbly beaches.

35–37 And we . . . night: The world is now in chaos like a battlefield at night. In such a place, signals and directions are confused. Armies fight without knowing what they are doing.

As the poem ends . . .

• The speaker sees the world as an uncertain and painful place.

• He asks that he and his beloved be true to each other in this disturbing world.

Reading Check

"The Sea of Faith" refers to traditional religious beliefs. What does the speaker say is happening to this "Sea"?

English Learner Support
LANGUAGE

Diction *At the full* means "filled to the highest degree."

What Does It Mean?

Darkling is a poetic way to say "dark."

Pause & Reflect

Look back at the passages that you underlined as you read. According to the speaker, what is missing from the world? Check the four words below that apply. **(Analyze)**

joy	ignorance
confusion	peace
certainty	comfort

CHALLENGE

Do you think the speaker believes that the power of love can overcome the confusion and uncertainty he sees in the world? Star the place in the poem that supports what you think. **(Evaluate)**

Active Reading SkillBuilder

Drawing Conclusions about Mood

Mood is the feeling, or atmosphere, that a writer creates for the reader. The mood of a poem may be happy, sad, lonely, angry, and so on. Descriptive details and careful word choice help a writer create a particular mood. Record in the diagram below any descriptive details that are particularly striking in "Dover Beach." Use those details to draw conclusions about the mood of the poem, and describe the mood in the central circle. An example is given.

"Dover Beach"

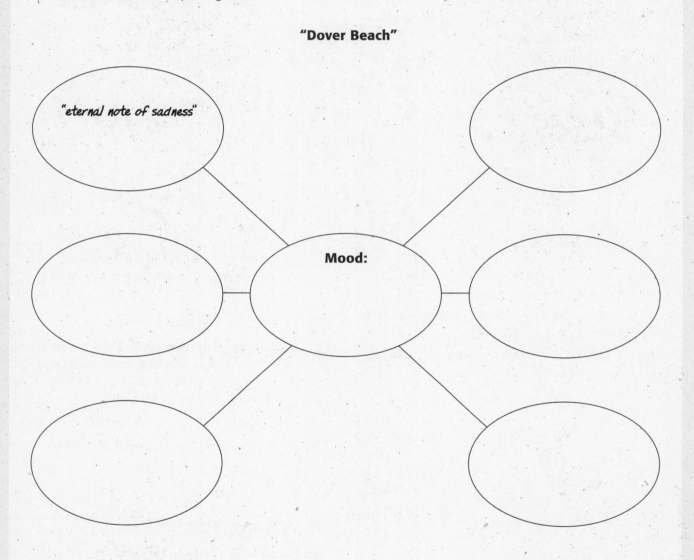

Literary Analysis SkillBuilder

Controlling Image

A **controlling image** is a single image or comparison that continues throughout a literary work and shapes its meaning. Poets often use a controlling image to express their thoughts or feelings. In "Dover Beach," the controlling image is the sea at night. In the chart below, list details in the poem that develop the controlling image. Then describe the thoughts and feelings those details express. Two examples are given.

Details in Poem	Thoughts and Feelings
"sea is calm," "tide is full," "moon lies fair" (lines 1–2)	a sense of peace, calmness
"grating roar / Of pebbles which the waves draw back, and fling" (lines 9–10)	power of ocean, awe

Pied Beauty

Spring
and
Fall:
To a Young Child

GERARD MANLEY HOPKINS

Before You Read

Connect to Your Life

Think about what made you sad when you were a child. Compare these to the things that make you sad now. Fill in the chart below with your thoughts.

WHAT MADE ME SAD AS A CHILD	WHAT MAKES ME SAD NOW
being scolded	people suffering

Key to the Poem

WHAT DO YOU THINK? The poet and Jesuit priest Gerard Manley Hopkins wrote about the beauty of the natural world in new ways. For many years, he kept a journal in which he recorded his reflections on nature and his philosophy of life. As you read his poems, look for imagery that might be based on Hopkins's journal entries.

Reading Tips

Hopkins played with language to find new ways to express feelings and ideas.

- When you first read each poem, look for its overall meaning. When you approach it again, read some lines aloud. Sometimes listening to the sound and **rhythm** of a line can help you to determine the meaning.

- Use the Guide for Reading to help with unfamiliar words and difficult passages.

As the poem begins . . .

- The poet praises God for creating beautiful, speckled, and spotted things.

More About . . .

COINING WORDS Hopkins coined, or made up, compound words such as couple-color and rose-moles to describe the things he saw in the world. You can figure out many such compound words by first looking at the individual words, and then combining their meanings.

What Does It Mean?

Plotted and pieced refers to the plots of British farmland pieced together like the parts of a quilt.

PREVIEW Gerard Manley Hopkins lived in the 19th century. His poetry, however, belongs to the 20th. Hopkins as a poet was far ahead of his time. He used language in bold new ways to create dazzling effects.

The poems you are about to read are two of his finest. "Pied Beauty" praises God for his unusual creations. The word *pied* means "spotted with color." "Spring and Fall: To a Young Child" is about a child who senses a grim truth about life.

Pied Beauty

GERARD MANLEY HOPKINS

FOCUS

This poem begins like a prayer. The speaker then lists several dappled, or spotted, things for which God deserves praise.

MARK IT UP As you read, circle examples of these dappled things. An example is highlighted.

Glory be to God for dappled things—
    For skies of couple-color as a brinded cow;
      For rose-moles all in stipple upon trout that swim;
Fresh-firecoal chestnut-falls; finches' wings;
5   Landscape plotted and pieced—fold, fallow, and plough;
      And áll trádes, their gear and tackle and trim.

All things counter, original, spare, strange;
    Whatever is fickle, freckled (who knows how?)
      With swift, slow; sweet, sour; adazzle, dim;
10 He fathers-forth whose beauty is past change:
    Praise him.

Pause & Reflect

GUIDE FOR READING

Use this guide for help with unfamiliar words and difficult passages.

1 **dappled:** spotted or splashed with color.
2 **brinded:** brindled—streaked or spotted with a darker color.
3 **rose-moles . . . stipple:** spots of pink in flecks or speckles.
4 **fresh-firecoal chestnut-falls:** fallen chestnuts that are the color of glowing coals.
5 **fold:** a pen for animals; **fallow:** land left unseeded.
6 **trim:** equipment.
7 **counter:** opposing; **spare:** unusual.
8 **fickle:** changeable.
10 **fathers-forth:** creates; **past:** beyond.

Pause **&** *Reflect*

1. Review the examples you circled as you read. What qualities does the speaker admire in created things? Circle two words below. **(Infer)**

sameness   variety

order   contrast

READ ALOUD 2. Read aloud the boxed line on page 260. This line has three pairs of words with opposite meanings. What do these word pairs tell you about the dappled things? **(Infer)**

_____

_____

_____

_____

3. Describe a dappled thing that you find beautiful. **(Connect)**

_____

_____

_____

_____

SPRING
and FALL:

To a Young Child

GERARD MANLEY HOPKINS

FOCUS

Margaret, a young child, is upset over the falling leaves. The speaker, an adult, realizes a truth about life from Margaret's sorrow. Read to learn about this truth.

Margaret, are you grieving
Over Goldengrove unleaving?
Leaves, like the things of man, you
With your fresh thoughts care for, can you?
5 Ah! as the heart grows older
It will come to such sights colder
By and by, nor spare a sigh
Though worlds of wanwood leafmeal lie;
And yet you *will* weep and know why.
10 Now no matter, child, the name:
Sorrow's springs are the same.
Nor mouth had, no nor mind, expressed
What heart heard of, ghost guessed:
It is the blight man was born for,
15 It is Margaret you mourn for.

Pause & *Reflect*

1–2 **Margaret . . . unleaving:** Are you sad because the trees are losing their leaves?

3–4 **Leaves . . . can you?:** Do you in your innocence care about falling leaves as though they were human?

5–7 **Ah! as the heart . . . By and by:** As you get older, you will not be so sensitive. The falling leaves will not upset you.

8 **wanwood:** faded woodland; **leafmeal:** dry, ground-up leaves.

9 **And yet . . . and know why:** When you are older, other sorrows will make you weep. You will also know why you weep.

11 **Sorrows springs . . . same:** All sorrows come from the same source.

12–13 The speaker realizes that Margaret has sensed an important truth, which she is too young to talk about or even understand.

12 **Nor:** neither.

13 **ghost:** spirit; soul.

14 **blight:** a condition that leads to withering and death.

As the poem begins . . .

- Margaret, a little girl, is sad to see the leaves falling.
- The speaker explains Margaret's *real* sadness.

English Learner Support
LANGUAGE

Alliteration *Alliteration* is the repetition of consonant sounds at the beginnings of words. Hopkins uses this device to create a musical effect. In lines 6–8, note the alliteration in the phrases "such sights," "By and by," "spare a sigh," "worlds of wanwood," and "leafmeal lie."

✔ Reading Check
In line 14, what is "the blight man was born for"?

Pause & Reflect
How will Margaret change as she gets older? Check two phrases below. **(Infer)**

will care more about the falling leaves

will not weep over the falling leaves

will experience great sorrows

CHALLENGE
Style is the way in which a piece of literature is written. One element that contributes to style is **diction**—a writer's choice of words and their order or arrangement. Mark examples of unusual words and word order in these poems.

Active Reading SkillBuilder

Recognizing Coined Words

Hopkins often coined, or invented, words to say things in new ways. In some cases, the **coined word** is made by joining two familiar words in an unfamiliar arrangement, as in "couple-color." Use the chart below to list the coined words you find in Hopkins's poems. Describe the image or feeling that each word conveys. An example is shown.

Coined Words	Images or Feelings
rose-moles	pink specks on a rainbow trout's skin

Literary Analysis SkillBuilder

Sprung Rhythm

To reflect the rhythms of natural speech in his poetry, Hopkins used what he called **sprung rhythm.** The lines have the same number of stressed syllables but varying numbers of unstressed syllables. Read the poems aloud. Then choose three lines from each poem. Write them in the charts below, and mark the stressed (′) and unstressed (˘) syllables. An example is shown.

"Pied Beauty"

For skíes of couplĕ colŏr aś ă brindĕd ców

_____

_____

_____

"Spring and Fall: To a Young Child"

_____

_____

_____

William Butler Yeats

THE SECOND COMING

SAILING TO BYZANTIUM

Before You Read

Connect to Your Life

What are your hopes and fears about the future? Write your responses in
the chart below.

HOPES	FEARS

Key to the Poems

WHAT YOU NEED TO KNOW Yeats often used **symbols** in his poems. Symbols
are people, places, objects, or actions that represent other things. In the
following two poems, Yeats's symbols include a beast, fire, and gold. As
you read, think about what these symbols might represent.

As the poem begins...

- The poet describes a scene of chaos and horror.

English Learner Support
VOCABULARY

Loosed The verb *loosed* is the past tense of *loose,* meaning "to set loose," or "to release."

What Does It Mean?

Here, *conviction* means "strong belief."

THE SECOND COMING

William Butler Yeats

PREVIEW "The Second Coming" was written in 1919, not long after the Russian Revolution and the end of World War I. This period was marked by chaos and violence. Familiar traditions and ideas were disappearing, and people had to deal with rapid change. Many feared that worse things were yet to come. Yeats portrays this troubled time in the first stanza of the poem. Then, in the second stanza, he describes his vision of the future.

The phrase "Second Coming" usually refers to the Christian belief that Jesus Christ will one day return to earth. According to the New Testament, the time just before Christ's return will be filled with terror and confusion. In the poem, Yeats uses the phrase to describe a terrible change that he sees coming.

FOCUS ON
In the first stanza, the speaker describes the disorder and violence he sees in the world.

MARK IT UP Underline details that describe the speaker's world. An example is highlighted.

Turning and turning in the widening gyre
The falcon cannot hear the falconer;
Things fall apart; the center cannot hold;
Mere anarchy is loosed upon the world,
5   The blood-dimmed tide is loosed, and everywhere
The ceremony of innocence is drowned;
The best lack all conviction, while the worst
Are full of passionate intensity.

Pause & Reflect

Use this guide for help with unfamiliar words and difficult passages.

1–2 gyre (jīr): spiral. (Yeats, however, pronounced this word with a hard g.); **falcon:** a hawklike bird of prey; **falconer:** a person who uses trained falcons to hunt small game. The image in these lines is of a falcon flying in wider and wider circles. The bird flies so far away that it can no longer hear the falconer when he calls to it.

3–8 These lines describe a time of disorder and confusion.

4 anarchy (ăn'ər-kē): lack of all order; chaos.

5 blood-dimmed tide: ocean water discolored by blood.

6 ceremony of innocence: the rituals (such as the rites of baptism and marriage) that give order to life.

7–8 According to Yeats, these lines refer to the Russian Revolution of 1917. The lines suggest that no one is committed to preserving an orderly society. People either don't want to be involved **(lack all conviction)** or are wildly fanatic **(full of passionate intensity).**

Reading Tip

Use the semicolons in the poem to help you find places to pause after a complete thought. The entire first stanza of the poem is a single sentence. However, if you read each part between semicolons as a separate sentence, you can break it down easily.

Pause & Reflect

1. Look back at the details that you underlined as you read. Circle the three sentences below that describe the speaker's world. **(Infer)**

Disorder is everywhere.

Violence is widespread.

Leaders are taking too much control.

Leaders have no control.

MARK IT UP **2.** Lines 1–6 contain images that picture a situation getting out of control. Circle the detail that you find most interesting. Explain what you think it means. **(Clarify Meaning in Poetry)**

_____

_____

_____

_____

READ ALOUD **3.** Read aloud the boxed passage on page 268. Then review the note for those lines on page 269. What do you think it would be like to live in such a world? **(Connect)**

_____

_____

_____

_____

FOCUS ON

In this stanza, the speaker describes his personal vision of the future. This vision is like a nightmare. The speaker imagines a mysterious beast about to appear in the world.

MARK IT UP As you read, underline details that describe the strange beast.

Surely some (revelation) is at hand;

10 Surely the Second Coming is at hand.

The Second Coming! Hardly are those words out

When a vast image out of *Spiritus Mundi*

Troubles my sight: somewhere in sands of the desert

A shape with lion body and the head of a man,

15 A gaze blank and pitiless as the sun,

Is moving its slow thighs, while all about it

Reel shadows of the indignant desert birds.

The darkness drops again; but now I know

That twenty centuries of stony sleep

20 Were vexed to nightmare by a rocking cradle,

And what rough beast, its hour come round at last,

Slouches towards Bethlehem to be born?

Pause **&** *Reflect*

10 **Second Coming:** For the speaker, the Second Coming signals something unknown, something never seen yet in human history.

12 ***Spiritus Mundi*** (spĭr'ĭ-tōōs mōōn'dē). *Latin:* Spirit of the World. This spirit, or soul, contains all the memories of human history. This storehouse of images lies in the deepest part of the human mind.

14 This image suggests the Great Sphinx in Egypt, built more than 40 centuries ago.

17 **Reel:** to whirl in circles; **indignant:** angry because of being disturbed.

19–22 **That . . . born:** The "twenty centuries of stony sleep" may refer to the 2,000 years since the birth of Christ **(rocking cradle).** That period has now reached a time of revolutions and wars **(vexed to nightmare).** A new era is about to begin. This new era is pictured as a frightening creature **(what rough beast)** getting ready to enter the world **(slouches towards Bethlehem to be born).**

As the poem ends . . .

• The poet foresees the birth of a new and world-threatening period of history.

More About . . .

THE BOOK OF **REVELATION** The Book of Revelation is the last book in the New Testament. Among other things, this book includes a vision of Jesus' return to Earth and the end of time. In one part of the vision, Satan, who has been imprisoned for 1,000 years, also returns to Earth, and may be the "rough beast" Yeats refers to in the poem. Once back on Earth, Satan convinces some humans to join him in a huge battle against God—which God wins.

✔ **Reading Check**

Jesus Christ was born in the town of Bethlehem. Why do you think the poet says a beast is coming "towards Bethlehem to be born"?

Pause & *Reflect*

1. Look back at the details that you underlined as you read. Circle two phrases below that describe the beast. **(Clarify Meaning in Poetry)**

   a kind of monster

   peaceful and childlike

   delicate and beautiful

   powerful and threatening

2. The speaker uses the "vast image" (line 12) of the beast to describe his view of the future. What kind of future does the speaker foresee? Circle the answer below. **(Infer)**

   The future will be uncertain, frightening, and full of change.

   The future will bring new order and meaning.

SAILING TO BYZANTIUM

William Butler Yeats

PREVIEW "Sailing to Byzantium" was written in 1926. Byzantium (bĭ-zăn'tē-əm) was an ancient city in southeastern Europe (now Istanbul, Turkey). In the Middle Ages, it was a center of civilization, especially art and religion. For Yeats, Byzantium symbolized the life of the imagination. It represented a creative eternal life rather than a life limited by time and death. The speaker in the poem is an aging poet searching for meaning and permanence. In his mind he leaves the natural world and sails to Byzantium. There, he hopes to find timelessness and unchanging beauty.

FOCUS

In the first stanza, the speaker describes the physical world, which seems to have no place for him. In the second stanza, he introduces the possibility of escaping the physical world and even death itself.

 MARK IT UP As you read, circle phrases that tell how the speaker sees himself. An example is highlighted.

I

That is no country for old men. The young
In one another's arms, birds in the trees
—Those dying generations—at their song,
The salmon-falls, the mackerel-crowded seas,
Fish, flesh, or fowl, commend all summer long
Whatever is begotten, born, and dies.
Caught in that sensual music all neglect
Monuments of unaging intellect.

II

An aged man is but a paltry thing,
A tattered coat upon a stick, unless
Soul clap its hands and sing, and louder sing
For every tatter in its mortal dress,
Nor is there singing school but studying
Monuments of its own magnificence;
And therefore I have sailed the seas and come
To the holy city of Byzantium.

Pause & *Reflect*

272

Use this guide for help with unfamiliar words and difficult passages.

1–6 These lines describe a world ruled by time. All creatures—lovers, birds, and fish—belong to the cycle of birth and death.

1 That: the physical world, or the world governed by time.

4 salmon-falls: the rapids in rivers where salmon go to lay their eggs.

7–8 Caught . . . intellect: A reference to those creatures who are completely involved in the cycle of physical life **(sensual music).** They pay no attention to the life of the mind.

9–14 An aged man . . . magnificence: An old man is as unimportant **(paltry)** as a scarecrow unless his soul—his mind and spirit—expresses itself in ideas and art **(clap its hands and sing).** These expressions **(Monuments of its own magnificence)** go beyond the limtis of physical life. They enrich the human spirit.

13 but: except for.

15–16 The speaker pictures himself sailing to Byzantium, where the life of art and the mind can be carried on.

As the poem begins . . .

- The speaker describes the physical world as a world for young people.

- The speaker, an older man, imagines his mind and art will be more alive in Byzantium, the historic land he dreams about.

What Does It Mean?

Salmon-falls refers to salmon swimming up rapids to spawn. After the salmon have laid or fertilized their eggs, they die, an image that symbolizes the world of life and death.

✔ Reading Check

What do the people of the speaker's country value most?

Pause & Reflect

1. The speaker imagines himself sailing away from the world he lives in. Circle two phrases below that describe this world. **(Visualize/Infer)**

   limited by time and death

   values works of the mind

   makes old people feel wanted

   brings forth new life

   MARK IT UP 2. The speaker says that the soul must "clap its hands and sing" (line 11). What might cause the soul to do this? Underline the phrase in the second stanza that tells the answer. **(Compare and Contrast)**

FOCUS

In these stanzas, the speaker describes what he seeks in the world of art. Read to find out what Byzantium offers the aging poet.

III

O sages standing in God's holy fire
As in the gold mosaic of a wall,
Come from the holy fire, perne in a gyre,
20 And be the singing-masters of my soul.
Consume my heart away; sick with desire
And fastened to a dying animal
It knows not what it is; and gather me
Into the artifice of eternity.

IV

25 Once out of nature I shall never take
My bodily form from any natural thing,
But such a form as Grecian goldsmiths make
Of hammered gold and gold enameling
To keep a drowsy Emperor awake;
30 Or set upon a golden bough to sing
To lords and ladies of Byzantium
Of what is past, or passing, or to come.

Pause & Reflect

17–18 The speaker addresses saints **(sages)** pictured in the artwork of an ancient church **(gold mosaic of a wall).** In the painting, the saints are surrounded by purifying fire.

19–24 The speaker asks the saints to be his teachers. He wants them to help him to get beyond physical decay and to enter the eternal world of art and ideas.

19 perne (pûrn) in a **gyre:** whirl in a spiral.

22 dying animal: the speaker's own body.

23 It: the speaker's heart.

24 artifice: work of art.

25–26 Once . . . thing: After the speaker has entered the eternal world of art, thought, and beauty, he does not want to return to a physical life.

27–32 The speaker wants to exist as a work of art does, timeless and outside the cycle of birth and death.

29 Emperor: the ninth-century Byzantine emperor Theophilus. According to legend he possessed a golden sculpture of a tree with mechanical singing birds on its branches.

As the poem ends . . .

- The speaker asks the sages of Byzantium to help him achieve immortality, or eternal life, in art.

English Learner Support
LANGUAGE

Repetition Notice the poet's use of the word *gold* in stanzas 3 and 4. The repetition of the word shows how important this mineral is to the speaker as a symbol for something beautiful and lasting.

Pause **&** Reflect

MARK IT UP **1.** Whom does the speaker ask to be the "singing-masters of my soul" (line 20)? Circle the line in stanza 3 that tells you. **(Clarify)**

2. In the country that the speaker left, there were lovers, birds in trees, and seas full of fish. How are the golden birds and tree of Byzantium different from living birds and trees? **(Clarify Meaning in Poetry)**

_____

_____

_____

_____

CHALLENGE

In both poems, Yeats uses sensory imagery, or images that appeal to the senses. Make a list of the images you can "see," and explain why these images are important to the poems' meanings. For example, a visual image in "The Second Coming" is the "blood-dimmed tide." This image expresses the idea that many lives have been lost in war and that the world is a violent place. **(Analyze)**

Active Reading SkillBuilder

Clarifying Meaning in Poetry

A complex poem may include unfamiliar ideas and images. Reading it several times may help to **clarify** its **meaning**.

- During a first reading, look at the explanations in the notes and think about the poem's subject.
- During a second reading, note any images that stand out in your mind.
- During following readings, be aware of any lines that you find difficult.

Use these strategies to clarify the meaning of "The Second Coming" and "Sailing to Byzantium." In the charts below, briefly describe the general subject of each poem. Then write down images and lines that you want to focus on. Two examples are given.

Title: "The Second Coming"	
Subject:	
Images That Stand Out	**Difficult Lines**
falcon flying out of falconer's control	

Title: "Sailing to Byzantium"	
Subject:	
Images That Stand Out	**Difficult Lines**
	"Caught in that sensual music all neglect Monuments of unaging intellect." (lines 7–8)

Literary Analysis SkillBuilder

Symbols

Symbols—persons, places, objects, or actions that stand for things beyond themselves—are an important part of Yeats's poetry. Yeats uses symbols to convey major ideas and themes. In the chart, list symbolic details in "The Second Coming" and "Sailing to Byzantium." Note what each symbol might represent. Two examples are given.

"The Second Coming"		"Sailing to Byzantium"	
Symbol	**What It Represents**	**Symbol**	**What It Represents**
gyre, or spiral	repetition in life; life repeats itself even as it moves forward	fish, flesh, fowl	cycle of life and death

The Rocking-Horse WINNER

D. H. Lawrence

Before You Read

Connect to Your Life

The young boy in this story develops a friendship with his uncle. Think of
a relative or family friend with whom you are close. How would you
describe him or her? What do you have in common? Write the person's
name in the center oval below. Then fill in the other ovals with examples
of things you share with this person.

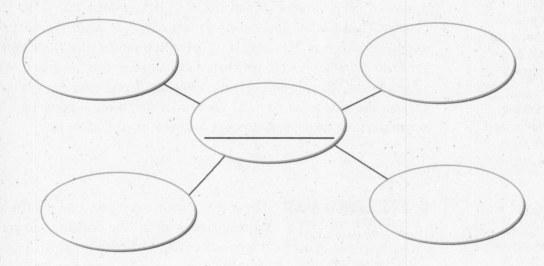

Key to the Story

WHAT'S THE BIG IDEA? In "The Rocking-Horse Winner," luck, or the lack
of it, plays an important role. Think about what having good luck or bad
luck means to you. Do you believe in luck at all? Then read the story to
find out what luck means to the main character and his family.

Reading Tips

This **short story** is like a fairy tale in that it has an element of magic about it. The characters' problems and **conflicts,** though, are realistic.

- Much of the story is told through **dialogue,** or written conversation. The author usually doesn't tell you why the characters act as they do. You must read between the lines, using what they say to infer their **motives.**

- As you read, think about how the events in the plot are connected. Ask yourself which events cause—or bring about—other events in the story.

As the story begins . . .

- The mother of the family realizes that she does not love her children.

- The family lives in style, but they are always in debt.

MARK IT UP **KEEP TRACK**

As you read, you can use these marks to keep track of your understanding.

✔ ..... I understand.

? ..... I don't understand this.

! ..... Interesting or surprising idea

English Learner Support
VOCABULARY

Idiom To read something in someone's eyes means to "see" or understand someone's thoughts.

The Rocking-Horse WINNER

D. H. Lawrence

PREVIEW In his novels and short stories, D. H. Lawrence (1885–1930) often attacked what he believed were the false values of society—such as the love of money. This story is set in England shortly after World War I. The main character is a boy who bets on horseraces. The amount of money that can be won on a horserace depends on the odds. For example, suppose the odds against a horse are 4 to 1. If that horse wins the race, then everyone who bet on it receives 4 dollars for each dollar bet.

FOCUS
The narrator describes the mother of a family living beyond its means. Her children sense the tension in the household.

MARK IT UP As you read, circle details that help you form impressions of the mother. An example is highlighted.

There was a woman who was beautiful, who started with all the advantages, yet she had no luck. She married for love, and the love turned to dust. She had bonny[1] children, yet she felt they had been thrust upon her, and she could not love them. They looked at her coldly, as if they were finding fault with her. And hurriedly she felt she must cover up some fault in herself. Yet what it was that she must cover up she never knew. Nevertheless, when her children were present, she always felt the center of her heart go hard. This troubled her, and in her manner she was all the more gentle and anxious for her children, as if she loved them very much. Only she herself knew that at the center of her heart was a hard little place that could not feel love, no, not for anybody. Everybody else said of her: "She is such a good mother. She adores her children." Only she herself, and her children themselves, knew it was not so. They read it in each other's eyes.

There were a boy and two little girls. They lived in a pleasant house, with a garden, and they had discreet servants, and felt themselves superior to anyone in the neighborhood.

---

1. **bonny:** pretty.

Although they lived in style, they felt always an anxiety in the house. There was never enough money. The mother had a small income, and the father had a small income, but not nearly enough for the social position which they had to keep up. The father went into town to some office. But though he had good prospects, these prospects never materialized. There was always the grinding sense of the shortage of money, though the style was always kept up.

At last the mother said: "I will see if *I* can't make something." But she did not know where to begin. She racked[2] her brains, and tried this thing and the other, but could not find anything successful. The failure made deep lines come into her face. Her children were growing up, they would have to go to school. There must be more money, there must be more money. The father, who was always very handsome and expensive in his tastes, seemed as if he never *would* be able to do anything worth doing. And the mother, who had a great belief in herself, did not succeed any better, and her tastes were just as expensive.

And so the house came to be haunted by the unspoken phrase: *There must be more money! There must be more money!* The children could hear it all the time, though nobody said it aloud. They heard it at Christmas, when the expensive and splendid toys filled the nursery. Behind the shining modern rocking-horse, behind the smart[3] doll's house, a voice would start whispering: "There *must* be more money! There *must* be more money!" And the children would stop playing, to listen for a moment. They would look into each other's eyes, to see if they had all heard. And each one saw in the eyes of the other two that they too had heard. "There *must* be more money! There *must* be more money!"

It came whispering from the springs of the still-swaying rocking-horse, and even the horse, bending his wooden, champing head, heard it. The big doll, sitting so pink and smirking in her new pram,[4] could hear it quite plainly, and seemed to be smirking all the more self-consciously because of it. The foolish puppy, too, that took the place of the teddy bear, he was looking so extraordinarily foolish for no other reason but that he heard the secret whisper all over the house: "There *must* be more money!"

---

2. **racked:** strained; tortured.

3. **smart:** elegant.

4. **pram:** baby carriage (a shortened form of *perambulator*).

Why is the family always in debt? **(Draw Conclusions)**

_____

_____

_____

_____

Reading Tip

Several factors contribute to the tension in this household. This tension is the **effect**. Highlight each **cause** of the tension that you see on pages 280–281. The first cause is that the woman realizes she cannot love her children.

Reading Tip

Writers use italic type to alert readers to words and phrases that they want to emphasize. Find the examples of italic type on this page and think about the reason these words are emphasized.

English Learner Support
LANGUAGE

Metaphor The house that speaks and whispers is a metaphor for the extreme tension in this family. The house is compared to a person who stands in the shadows and whispers unpleasant and frightening things.

Review the details you circled
as you read. Which phrase
below is true of the mother?
Circle or check it. **(Clarify)**

is not pretty

grew up poor

married for money

doesn't love her children

As the story continues . . .

- The son, Paul, asks his mother why the family seems to have little money.

- Paul and his mother discuss luck.

Reading Tip

Highlight Paul's and the mother's dialogue on pages 282–283 in different colors. Work with a partner to read the dialogue aloud. Look for adverbs such as *bitterly* and *timidly* to help you decide how to read different lines of dialogue.

Reading Check

What does the mother value most in life?

Yet nobody ever said it aloud. The whisper was everywhere, and therefore no one spoke it. Just as no one ever says: "We are breathing!" in spite of the fact that breath is coming and going all the time.

Pause & Reflect

FOCUS

The mother and her young son, Paul, have a serious talk about money and luck. Read to find out what the mother values most in life.

70

"Mother," said the boy Paul one day, "why don't we keep a car of our own? Why do we always use uncle's, or else a taxi?"

"Because we're the poor members of the family," said the mother.

"But why *are* we, mother?"

"Well—I suppose," she said slowly and bitterly, "it's because your father has no luck."

The boy was silent for some time.

"Is luck money, mother?" he asked, rather timidly.

"No, Paul. Not quite. It's what causes you to have money."

"Oh!" said Paul vaguely. "I thought when Uncle Oscar said *filthy lucker*, it meant money."

80

"*Filthy lucre*[5] does mean money," said the mother. "But it's lucre, not luck."

"Oh!" said the boy. "Then what *is* luck, mother?"

"It's what causes you to have money. If you're lucky you have money. That's why it's better to be born lucky than rich. If you're rich, you may lose your money. But if you're lucky, you will always get more money."

"Oh! Will you? And is father not lucky?"

"Very unlucky, I should say," she said bitterly.

The boy watched her with unsure eyes.

90

"Why?" he asked.

"I don't know. Nobody ever knows why one person is lucky and another unlucky."

"Don't they? Nobody at all? Does *nobody* know?"

"Perhaps God. But He never tells."

"He ought to, then. And aren't you lucky either, mother?"

"I can't be, if I married an unlucky husband."

"But by yourself, aren't you?"

"I used to think I was, before I married. Now I think I am very unlucky indeed."

5. *Filthy lucre* (lōō′kər): money or profits.

100 "Why?"

"Well—never mind! Perhaps I'm not really," she said.

The child looked at her to see if she meant it. But he saw, by the lines of her mouth, that she was only trying to hide something from him.

"Well, anyhow," he said stoutly,[6] "I'm a lucky person."

"Why?" said his mother, with a sudden laugh.

He stared at her. He didn't even know why he had said it.

"God told me," he asserted, brazening it out.[7]

"I hope He did, dear!" she said, again with a laugh, but
110 rather bitter.

"He did, mother!"

"Excellent!" said the mother, using one of her husband's exclamations.

The boy saw she did not believe him; or rather, that she paid no attention to his assertion. This angered him somewhere, and made him want to compel her attention.

Pause & Reflect

FOCUS

Paul withdraws from the other members of his family. He lives in
120 his own little world, riding his rocking horse. **MARK IT UP** As you read, circle details that help you visualize Paul on his rocking horse.

He went off by himself, vaguely, in a childish way, seeking for the clue to "luck." Absorbed, taking no heed of other people, he went about with a sort of stealth, seeking inwardly for luck. He wanted luck, he wanted it, he wanted it. When the two girls were playing dolls in the nursery, he would sit on his big rocking-horse, charging madly into space, with a frenzy that made the little girls peer at him uneasily. Wildly the horse <u>careered</u>, the waving dark hair of the boy tossed, his eyes had a strange glare in them. The little girls dared not speak to him.

When he had ridden to the end of his mad little journey, he
130 climbed down and stood in front of his rocking-horse, staring fixedly into its lowered face. Its red mouth was slightly open, its big eye was wide and glassy-bright.

---

6. **stoutly:** bravely; firmly.

7. **brazening it out:** facing something boldly.

WORDS
TO
KNOW

career (kə-rîr´) v. to move at full speed; rush

Pause & Reflect

📖 **READ ALOUD** 1. Read aloud the boxed passage on page 282. Why does Paul at first confuse luck with money? **(Draw Conclusions)**

_____

_____

_____

2. Paul's mother pays "no attention" to his statement that God has told him he is lucky. What do you think Paul might do to force his mother to notice him? **(Predict)**

_____

_____

_____

_____

As the story continues…

• Paul goes in search of luck.

• He begins to spend more and more time with his rocking horse.

Reading Tip

List some words and phrases that help you see that Paul's focus on luck and money is not healthy.

What Does It Mean?

I wish he'd leave off means "I wish he'd stop."

English Learner Support
VOCABULARY

Idiom The highlighted sentence means that the nurse could not understand him.

Reading Tip

In lines 143 and 151, notice the references to Paul's eyes. Highlight the words and phrases used to describe them. Descriptions of Paul's eyes are used throughout the story to show his emotional state. Highlight each example as you come to it.

More About...

(HORSE RACES) Horse racing is a very important sport in England. There are many famous races, such the Ascot, the Derby, and others, named in this story. Many people follow the progress of the horses from race to race and bet on them as a serious pastime.

"Now!" he would silently command the snorting steed. "Now, take me to where there is luck! Now take me!"

And he would slash the horse on the neck with the little whip he had asked Uncle Oscar for. He *knew* the horse could take him to where there was luck, if only he forced it. So he would mount again and start on his furious ride, hoping at last to get there. He knew he could get there.

140 "You'll break your horse, Paul!" said the nurse.

"He's always riding like that! I wish he'd leave off!" said his elder sister Joan.

But he only glared down on them in silence. Nurse gave him up. She could make nothing of him. Anyhow, he was growing beyond her.

One day his mother and his Uncle Oscar came in when he was on one of his furious rides. He did not speak to them.

"Hallo, you young jockey! Riding a winner?" said his uncle.

"Aren't you growing too big for a rocking-horse? You're

150 not a very little boy any longer, you know," said his mother.

But Paul only gave a blue glare from his big, rather close-set eyes. He would speak to nobody when he was in full tilt.[8] His mother watched him with an anxious expression on her face.

At last he suddenly stopped forcing his horse into the mechanical gallop and slid down.

"Well, I got there!" he announced fiercely, his blue eyes still flaring, and his sturdy long legs straddling apart.

"Where did you get to?" asked his mother.

"Where I wanted to go," he flared back at her.

160 "That's right, son!" said Uncle Oscar. "Don't you stop till you get there. What's the horse's name?"

"He doesn't have a name," said the boy.

"Gets on without all right?" asked the uncle.

"Well, he has different names. He was called Sansovino last week."

"Sansovino, eh? Won the Ascot.[9] How did you know his name?"

"He always talks about (horse races) with Bassett," said Joan.

The uncle was delighted to find that his small nephew was

170 posted with all the racing news. Bassett, the young gardener,

---

8. **in full tilt:** moving at full speed.

9. **Ascot:** the Ascot Gold Cup, an important English horserace. Other horseraces mentioned in the story include the Lincolnshire, the St. Leger Stakes, the Grand National, and the Derby.

who had been wounded in the left foot in the war[10] and had got his present job through Oscar Cresswell, whose batman[11] he had been, was a perfect blade of the "turf."[12] He lived in the racing events, and the small boy lived with him.

Oscar Cresswell got it all from Bassett.

Pause & Reflect

FOCUS

Oscar Cresswell, Paul's uncle, learns that his nephew has been betting on horseraces. Read to find out how Paul's uncle reacts to Paul's betting.

180

"Master Paul comes and asks me, so I can't do more than tell him, sir," said Bassett, his face terribly serious, as if he were speaking of religious matters.

"And does he ever put anything on a horse he fancies?"

"Well—I don't want to give him away—he's a young sport[13] a fine sport, sir. Would you mind asking him himself? He sort of takes a pleasure in it, and perhaps he'd feel I was giving him away, sir, if you don't mind."

Bassett was serious as a church.

The uncle went back to his nephew and took him off for a ride in the car.

"Say, Paul, old man, do you ever put anything on a horse?"
190 the uncle asked.

The boy watched the handsome man closely.

"Why, do you think I oughtn't to?" he parried.

"Not a bit of it! I thought perhaps you might give me a tip for the Lincoln."

The car sped on into the country, going down to Uncle Oscar's place in Hampshire.

"Honor bright?"[14] said the nephew.

"Honor bright, son!" said the uncle.

"Well, then, Daffodil."
200 "Daffodil! I doubt it, sonny. What about Mirza?"

---

10. **the war:** World War I (1914–1918).

11. **batman:** in Britain, a soldier who acts as an officer's servant.

12. **blade of the "turf":** one who knows much about horseracing.

13. **sport:** good fellow.

14. **honor bright:** an expression meaning "on your (or my) honor."

WORDS
TO
KNOW

parry (păr'ē) *v.* to respond by turning aside or evading (a question or argument)

Pause & Reflect

Review the details you circled as you read. How would you describe the way Paul rides his rocking horse? **(Summarize)**

_____

_____

_____

_____

As the story continues...

• Paul's uncle learns that Paul has become interested in horse races.

• Uncle Oscar asks Paul about his betting on particular horses.

What Does It Mean?

Fancies means "likes" in British English.

English Learner Support

LANGUAGE

Simile *Bassett was serious as a church* is a simile. A simile compares two unlike things using the words *like* or *as*. What two things are compared in this simile?

✔ **Reading Check**

How does Uncle Oscar feel about Paul's betting?

"I only know the winner," said the boy. "That's Daffodil."

"Daffodil, eh?"

There was a pause. Daffodil was an <u>obscure</u> horse comparatively.

"Uncle!"

"Yes, son?"

"You won't let it go any further, will you? I promised Bassett."

"Bassett be damned, old man! What's he got to do with it?"

"We're partners. We've been partners from the first. Uncle,
210 he lent me my first five shillings,[15] which I lost. I promised him, honor bright, it was only between me and him; only you gave me that ten-shilling note I started winning with, so I thought you were lucky. You won't let it go any further, will you?"

The boy gazed at his uncle from those big, hot, blue eyes, set rather close together. The uncle stirred and laughed uneasily.

"Right you are, son! I'll keep your tip private. Daffodil, eh? How much are you putting on him?"

"All except twenty pounds,"[16] said the boy. "I keep that in reserve."[17]

220 The uncle thought it a good joke.

"You keep twenty pounds in reserve, do you, you young romancer? What are you betting, then?"

"I'm betting three hundred," said the boy gravely. "But it's between you and me, Uncle Oscar! Honor bright?"

The uncle burst into a roar of laughter.

"It's between you and me all right, you young Nat Gould,"[18] he said, laughing. "But where's your three hundred?"

"Bassett keeps it for me. We're partners."

"You are, are you! And what is Bassett putting on Daffodil?"

230 "He won't go quite as high as I do, I expect. Perhaps he'll go a hundred and fifty."

"What, pennies?" laughed the uncle.

"Pounds," said the child, with a surprised look at his uncle. "Bassett keeps a bigger reserve than I do."

---

15. **shillings:** coins formerly used in Britain. (There were 20 shillings in a pound.)

16. **twenty pounds:** a sum worth about $1,000 in today's dollars. In the mid-1920s, a pound was worth about $5, and the purchasing power of a dollar was about 10 times what it is now.

17. **in reserve:** money saved rather than risked on bets.

18. **Nat Gould:** a British authority on horseracing.

What Does It Mean?

The repetition of *Honor bright* contrasts with the boy's adult concern about horse racing. The phrase suggests the purity of Paul's motives in trying to get money.

WORDS TO KNOW

obscure (ŏb-skyŏŏr') *adj.* not well-known; undistinguished

Between wonder and amusement Uncle Oscar was silent. He pursued the matter no further, but he determined to take his nephew with him to the Lincoln races.

Pause & Reflect

FOCUS
Uncle Oscar takes Paul to the Lincoln races. Read to find out what happens there.

240

"Now, son," he said, "I'm putting twenty on Mirza, and I'll put five on for you on any horse you fancy. What's your pick?"

"Daffodil, uncle."

"No, not the fiver on Daffodil!"

"I should if it was my own fiver," said the child.

"Good! Good! Right you are! A fiver for me and a fiver for you on Daffodil."

The child had never been to a race-meeting before, and his eyes were blue fire. He pursed his mouth tight and watched. A Frenchman just in front had put his money on Lancelot. Wild

250 with excitement, he flayed his arms up and down, yelling *"Lancelot! Lancelot!"* in his French accent.

Daffodil came in first, Lancelot second, Mirza third. The child, flushed and with eyes blazing, was curiously serene.[19] His uncle brought him four five-pound notes, four to one.

"What am I to do with these?" he cried, waving them before the boy's eyes.

"I suppose we'll talk to Bassett," said the boy. "I expect I have fifteen hundred now; and twenty in reserve; and this twenty."

260 His uncle studied him for some moments.

"Look here, son!" he said. "You're not serious about Bassett and that fifteen hundred, are you?"

"Yes, I am. But it's between you and me, uncle. Honor bright?"

"Honor bright all right, son! But I must talk to Bassett."

"If you'd like to be a partner, uncle, with Bassett and me, we could all be partners. Only, you'd have to promise, honor bright, uncle, not to let it go beyond us three. Bassett and I are lucky, and you must be lucky, because it was your ten

270 shillings I started winning with. . . ."

---

19. serene: calm.

Pause & Reflect
Paul doesn't want his uncle to tell anyone else about the tip on Daffodil. Why not? **(Infer)**

_____
_____
_____
_____

As the story continues . . .
• Paul and his uncle Oscar attend a horse race.
• Uncle Oscar continues to be amazed at Paul's knowledge of the sport.

What Does It Mean?
Race-meeting is a British term for "horse race."

Reading Tip
Remember that in dialogue it is acceptable to use incomplete sentences. See Uncle Oscar's dialogue in lines 290 and 298, for example.

✔ **Reading Check**
What do you think Paul plans to do with all the money he is winning at the races?

Uncle Oscar took both Bassett and Paul into Richmond Park for an afternoon, and there they talked.

"It's like this, you see, sir," Bassett said. "Master Paul would get me talking about racing events, spinning yarns,[20] you know, sir. And he was always keen on knowing if I'd made or if I'd lost. It's about a year since, now, that I put five shillings on Blush of Dawn for him: and we lost. Then the luck turned, with that ten shillings he had from you: that we put on Singhalese. And since that time, it's been pretty steady, 280 all things considering. What do you say, Master Paul?"

"We're all right when we're sure," said Paul. "It's when we're not quite sure that we go down."

"Oh, but we're careful then," said Bassett.

"But when are you *sure?*" smiled Uncle Oscar.

"It's Master Paul, sir," said Bassett in a secret, religious voice. "It's as if he had it from heaven. Like Daffodil, now, for the Lincoln. That was as sure as eggs."[21]

"Did you put anything on Daffodil?" asked Oscar Cresswell.

"Yes, sir. I made my bit."

290 "And my nephew?"

Bassett was obstinately[22] silent, looking at Paul.

"I made twelve hundred, didn't I, Bassett? I told uncle I was putting three hundred on Daffodil."

"That's right," said Bassett, nodding.

"But where's the money?" asked the uncle.

"I keep it safe locked up, sir. Master Paul he can have it any minute he likes to ask for it."

"What, fifteen hundred pounds?"

"And twenty! And *forty*, that is, with the twenty he made 300 on the course."

"It's amazing!" said the uncle.

"If Master Paul offers you to be partners, sir, I would, if I were you: if you'll excuse me," said Bassett.

Oscar Cresswell thought about it.

"I'll see the money," he said.

They drove home again, and, sure enough, Bassett came round to the garden-house with fifteen hundred pounds in notes. The twenty pounds reserve was left with Joe Glee, in the Turf Commission deposit.[23]

---

20. **spinning yarns:** telling stories.

21. **as sure as eggs:** absolutely certain.

22. **obstinately:** with great stubbornness.

23. **Turf Commission deposit:** a bank where bettors keep money for future bets.

310 "You see, it's all right, uncle, when I'm *sure!* Then we go strong, for all we're worth. Don't we, Bassett?"

"We do that, Master Paul."

"And when are you sure?" said the uncle, laughing.

"Oh, well, sometimes I'm *absolutely* sure, like about Daffodil," said the boy; "and sometimes I have an idea; and sometimes I haven't even an idea, have I, Bassett? Then we're careful, because we mostly go down."

"You do, do you! And when you're sure, like about Daffodil, what makes you sure, sonny?"

320 "Oh, well, I don't know," said the boy uneasily. "I'm sure, you know, uncle; that's all."

"It's as if he had it from heaven, sir," Bassett reiterated.

"I should say so!" said the uncle.

Pause & Reflect

Pause & Reflect

✏ **MARK IT UP** 1. Paul picks Daffodil to win the Lincoln race. Where does Daffodil finish in this race? Circle the sentence on page 287 that tells the answer. **(Clarify)**

2. How did Paul get started betting? **(Summarize)**

_____

_____

_____

_____

FOCUS
Paul continues to bet on horseraces. Read to find out why he started betting and what he plans to give his mother for her birthday.

But he became a partner. And when the Leger was coming on Paul was "sure" about Lively Spark, which was a quite <u>inconsiderable</u> horse. The boy insisted on putting a thousand on the horse, Bassett went for five hundred, and Oscar

330 Cresswell two hundred. Lively Spark came in first, and the betting had been ten to one against him. Paul had made ten thousand.

"You see," he said, "I was absolutely sure of him."

Even Oscar Cresswell had cleared two thousand.

"Look here, son," he said, "this sort of thing makes me nervous."

"It needn't, uncle! Perhaps I shan't be sure again for a long time."

"But what are you going to do with your money?" asked 340 the uncle.

"Of course," said the boy, "I started it for mother. She said she had no luck, because father is unlucky, so I thought if I was lucky, it might stop whispering."

"What might stop whispering?"

"Our house. I *hate* our house for whispering."

As the story continues...
• Paul and his uncle bet and win at the races.
• Paul's obsession with betting begins to worry his Uncle Oscar.

 Reading Check
Why does Paul's betting make Oscar nervous?

WORDS TO KNOW

inconsiderable (ĭn′kən-sĭd′ər-ə-bəl) *adj.* not worth consideration; insignificant

Reading Tip

Line 365 begins a very long sentence. You can read it more easily if you pause after each comma to see what has just taken place. Write a list of events that occur in the sentence, starting with *1. Paul hands over five thousand pounds to his uncle; 2. Paul's uncle deposits the money with the family lawyer,* and so on.

Pause & Reflect

1. Why did Paul start betting on horseraces? Circle the phrase below that tells the answer. **(Clarify)**

   to win Uncle Oscar's respect

   to earn extra money for toys

   to help Bassett support his family

   to stop the whispering in the house

2. Do you think Uncle Oscar should keep Paul's gambling a secret from his mother? *Yes/No,* because _____

   _____

   _____

   _____

   (Evaluate)

As the story continues...

• Paul hears the house "whispering" more and more.

• Paul plans to give the 5,000 pounds to his mother over five years, but she has a different idea.

"What does it whisper?"

"Why—why"—the boy fidgeted—"why, I don't know. But it's always short of money, you know, uncle."

"I know it, son, I know it."

350 "You know people send mother writs,[24] don't you, uncle?"

"I'm afraid I do," said the uncle.

"And then the house whispers, like people laughing at you behind your back. It's awful, that is! I thought if I was lucky—"

"You might stop it," added the uncle.

The boy watched him with big blue eyes, that had an uncanny cold fire in them, and he said never a word.

"Well, then!" said the uncle. "What are we doing?"

"I shouldn't like mother to know I was lucky," said the boy.

"Why not, son?"

360 "She'd stop me."

"I don't think she would."

"Oh!"—and the boy writhed[25] in an odd way—"I *don't* want her to know, uncle."

"All right, son! We'll manage it without her knowing."

They managed it very easily. Paul, at the other's suggestion, handed over five thousand pounds to his uncle, who deposited it with the family lawyer, who was then to inform Paul's mother that a relative had put five thousand pounds into his hands, which sum was to be paid out a thousand pounds at a

370 time, on the mother's birthday, for the next five years.

"So she'll have a birthday present of a thousand pounds for five successive years," said Uncle Oscar. "I hope it won't make it all the harder for her later."

Pause & Reflect

FOCUS

Read to find out how Paul's mother reacts to her present and what happens to Paul as he bets heavily.

MARK IT UP As you read, circle any details that help you understand the mother's reaction.

380 Paul's mother had her birthday in November. The house had been "whispering" worse than ever lately, and, even in spite of his luck, Paul could not bear up against it. He was very anxious to see the effect of the birthday letter, telling his mother about the thousand pounds.

---

24. **writs:** legal documents (in this case, demands for the payment of debts).
25. **writhed** (rĭ*th*d): twisted.

When there were no visitors, Paul now took his meals with his parents, as he was beyond the nursery control. His mother went into town nearly every day. She had discovered that she had an odd knack of sketching furs and dress materials, so she worked secretly in the studio of a friend who was the chief "artist" for the leading drapers.[26] She drew the figures of ladies in furs and ladies in silk and sequins for the newspaper advertisements. This young woman artist earned several thousand pounds a year, but Paul's mother only made several hundreds, and she was again dissatisfied. She so wanted to be first in something, and she did not succeed, even in making sketches for drapery advertisements.

She was down to breakfast on the morning of her birthday. Paul watched her face as she read her letters. He knew the lawyer's letter. As his mother read it, her face hardened and became more expressionless. Then a cold, determined look came on her mouth. She hid the letter under the pile of others, and said not a word about it.

"Didn't you have anything nice in the post for your birthday, mother?" said Paul.

"Quite moderately nice," she said, her voice cold and absent.

She went away to town without saying more.

But in the afternoon Uncle Oscar appeared. He said Paul's mother had had a long interview with the lawyer, asking if the whole five thousand could not be advanced at once, as she was in debt.

"What do you think, uncle?" said the boy.

"I leave it to you, son."

"Oh, let her have it, then! We can get some more with the other," said the boy.

"A bird in the hand is worth two in the bush, laddie!" said Uncle Oscar.

"But I'm sure to *know* for the Grand National; or the Lincolnshire; or else the Derby. I'm sure to know for *one* of them," said Paul.

So Uncle Oscar signed the agreement, and Paul's mother touched[27] the whole five thousand. Then something very curious happened. The voices in the house suddenly went mad, like a chorus of frogs on a spring evening. There were certain new furnishings, and Paul had a tutor. He was *really* going to Eton, his father's school, in the following autumn.

---

26. **drapers:** in Britain, dealers in cloth and dry goods.
27. **touched:** received.

English Learner Support
CULTURE

British Education Children in upper-class British families often studied Greek, Latin, and other subjects with a private tutor, or teacher, before they began regular schooling. Then they attended costly private schools. This is just one more reason for Paul's mother to worry about money.

Reading Tip

Highlight the occurrences that cause the "whispering" of the house to increase. Find examples starting with *new furnishings* in line 421 of page 291 and continue on this page.

English Learner Support
LANGUAGE

Symbolism The screaming house in this story symbolizes Paul's mental breakdown. At the beginning of the story, all the children are described as hearing the house whisper, but their experiences are mild compared to those of Paul, who is now approaching a full breakdown.

Pause & *Reflect*

1. Review the details you circled as you read. Why doesn't Paul's mother tell him or anyone else in the family about her birthday present? **(Infer)**

_____

_____

_____

MARK IT UP **2.** As Paul continues to bet on races, he gets more and more nervous. Underline any details on this page that help you visualize him. **(Locate Details)**

As the story continues...

• Paul becomes more and more distressed by the approaching Derby race.

• His mother is worried when Paul says he doesn't want to go to the seaside to rest.

There were flowers in the winter, and a blossoming of the luxury Paul's mother had been used to. And yet the voices in the house, behind the sprays of mimosa and almond-blossom, and from under the piles of iridescent[28] cushions, simply trilled and screamed in a sort of ecstasy: "There *must* be more money! Oh-h-h; there *must* be more money. Oh, now, now-w! Now-w-w—there *must* be more money!—more than ever!
430 More than ever!"

It frightened Paul terribly. He studied away at his Latin and Greek with his tutor. But his intense hours were spent with Bassett. The Grand National had gone by: he had not "known," and had lost a hundred pounds. Summer was at hand. He was in agony for the Lincoln. But even for the Lincoln he didn't "know," and he lost fifty pounds. He became wild-eyed and strange, as if something were going to explode in him.

"Let it alone, son! Don't you bother about it!" urged Uncle Oscar. But it was as if the boy couldn't really hear what his 440 uncle was saying.

"I've got to know for the Derby! I've got to know for the Derby!" the child reiterated, his big blue eyes blazing with a sort of madness.

Pause & *Reflect*

FOCUS
Paul's mother notices his poor condition. She suggests that he visit the seaside. Read to find out how Paul reacts to her idea.

His mother noticed how overwrought[29] he was.

"You'd better go to the seaside. Wouldn't you like to go now to the seaside, instead of waiting? I think you'd better," she said, looking down at him anxiously, her heart 450 curiously heavy because of him.

But the child lifted his uncanny blue eyes.

"I couldn't possibly go before the Derby, mother!" he said. "I couldn't possibly!"

"Why not?" she said, her voice becoming heavy when she was opposed. "Why not? You can still go from the seaside to see the Derby with your Uncle Oscar, if that's what you wish. No need for you to wait here. Besides, I think you care too much about these races. It's a bad sign. My family has been a

---

28. **iridescent** (ĭr´ĭ-dĕs´ənt): shining with rainbowlike colors.

29. **overwrought:** very nervous or excited.

gambling family, and you won't know till you grow up how
much damage it has done. But it has done damage. I shall
have to send Bassett away, and ask Uncle Oscar not to talk
racing to you, unless you promise to be reasonable about it:
go away to the seaside and forget it. You're all nerves!"

"I'll do what you like, mother, so long as you don't send
me away till after the Derby," the boy said.

"Send you away from where? Just from this house?"

"Yes," he said, gazing at her.

"Why, you curious child, what makes you care about this
house so much, suddenly? I never knew you loved it."

He gazed at her without speaking. He had a secret within a
secret, something he had not divulged, even to Bassett or to
his Uncle Oscar.

But his mother, after standing undecided and a little bit
sullen for some moments, said:

"Very well, then! Don't go to the seaside till after the
Derby, if you don't wish it. But promise me you won't let your
nerves go to pieces. Promise you won't think so much about
horse-racing and *events,* as you call them!"

"Oh no," said the boy casually. "I won't think much about
them, mother. You needn't worry. I wouldn't worry, mother, if
I were you."

"If you were me and I were you," said his mother, "I
wonder what we *should* do!"

"But you know you needn't worry, mother, don't you?" the
boy repeated.

"I should be awfully glad to know it," she said wearily.

"Oh, well, you *can,* you know. I mean, you *ought* to know
you needn't worry," he insisted.

"Ought I? Then I'll see about it," she said.

Paul's secret of secrets was his wooden horse, that which
had no name. Since he was emancipated[30] from a nurse and a
nursery-governess, he had had his rocking-horse removed to
his own bedroom at the top of the house.

"Surely you're too big for a rocking-horse!" his mother
had <u>remonstrated</u>.

"Well, you see, mother, till I can have a *real* horse, I like to
have *some* sort of animal about," had been his quaint answer.

---

30. **emancipated:** freed.

WORDS
TO
KNOW

remonstrate (rĭ-mŏn′strāt′) *v.* to protest or object

Can you predict Paul's secret,
the reason he does not want
to leave the house before the
Derby?

Reading Tip

Star some of the places on
pages 292–293 that show
Paul's increasing madness.
For example, what do his eyes
look like? Where does he
show how stubborn he can
be? Where does he repeat
himself several times to his
mother?

As the story ends...

• The tension in Paul and his mother increases as the Derby approaches.

• Paul rides his rocking horse to guess the winner of the Derby.

• Paul develops a fever.

English Learner Support
VOCABULARY

Idioms To be *rung up* means "to be called on the telephone." *Don't sit up* means "don't wait for us."

"Do you feel he keeps you company?" she laughed.

"Oh yes! He's very good, he always keeps me company, 500 when I'm there," said Paul.

So the horse, rather shabby, stood in an arrested prance in the boy's bedroom.

Pause **&** Reflect

FOCUS
As the time for the Derby draws near, Paul's mother worries more and more about her son. Read to find out what happens to Paul and his mother after the race.

510 The Derby was drawing near, and the boy grew more and more tense. He hardly heard what was spoken to him, he was very frail, and his eyes were really uncanny. His mother had sudden strange seizures of uneasiness about him. Sometimes, for half an hour, she would feel a sudden anxiety about him that was almost anguish. She wanted to rush to him at once, and know he was safe.

Two nights before the Derby, she was at a big party in town, when one of her rushes of anxiety about her boy, her first-born, gripped her heart till she could hardly speak. She fought with the feeling, might and main,[31] for she believed in common sense. But it was too strong. She had to leave the dance and go downstairs to telephone to the country. The children's nursery-governess was terribly surprised and startled 520 at being rung up in the night.

"Are the children all right, Miss Wilmot?"

"Oh yes, they are quite all right."

"Master Paul? Is he all right?"

"He went to bed as right as a trivet.[32] Shall I run up and look at him?"

"No," said Paul's mother reluctantly. "No! Don't trouble. It's all right. Don't sit up. We shall be home fairly soon." She did not want her son's privacy intruded upon.

"Very good," said the governess.

530 It was about one o'clock when Paul's mother and father drove up to their house. All was still. Paul's mother went to her room and slipped off her white fur cloak. She had told

---

31. **might and main:** with all her strength.

32. **as right as a trivet:** in perfect condition.

her maid not to wait up for her. She heard her husband downstairs, mixing a whisky and soda.

And then, because of the strange anxiety at her heart, she stole upstairs to her son's room. Noiselessly she went along the upper corridor. Was there a faint noise? What was it?

She stood, with arrested muscles, outside his door, listening. There was a strange, heavy, and yet not loud noise. Her heart 540 stood still. It was a soundless noise, yet rushing and powerful. Something huge, in violent, hushed motion. What was it? What in God's name was it? She ought to know. She felt that she knew the noise. She knew what it was.

Yet she could not place it. She couldn't say what it was. And on and on it went, like a madness.

Softly, frozen with anxiety and fear, she turned the door handle.

> The room was dark. Yet in the space near the window, she heard and saw something plunging to and fro. She gazed in 550 fear and amazement.
>
> Then suddenly she switched on the light, and saw her son, in his green pajamas, madly surging on the rocking-horse. The blaze of light suddenly lit him up, as he urged the wooden horse, and lit her up, as she stood, blonde, in her dress of pale green and crystal, in the doorway.
>
> "Paul!" she cried. "Whatever are you doing?"
>
> "It's Malabar!" he screamed in a powerful, strange voice. "It's Malabar!"
>
> His eyes blazed at her for one strange and senseless second, 560 as he ceased urging his wooden horse. Then he fell with a crash to the ground, and she, all her tormented motherhood flooding upon her, rushed to gather him up.

But he was unconscious, and unconscious he remained, with some brain-fever. He talked and tossed, and his mother sat stonily by his side.

"Malabar! It's Malabar! Bassett, Bassett, I *know!* It's Malabar!"

So the child cried, trying to get up and urge the rocking-horse that gave him his inspiration.

570 "What does he mean by Malabar?" asked the heart-frozen mother.

"I don't know," said the father stonily.

"What does he mean by Malabar?" she asked her brother Oscar.

More About...

FEVERS In the days before antibiotics, high fevers were believed either to break (go down), or to get worse after the third day. Therefore, people caring for someone with a fever would be particularly observant on the third day.

✔ Reading Check

Which of the adult characters do you think cares most about Paul? Why?

Pause & Reflect

READ ALOUD Read aloud the boxed passage on this page. Oscar Cresswell says that Paul is better off dead. Do you think he's right? *Yes/No,* because

_____

_____

_____

_____ .

(Connect)

✎ CHALLENGE

The values of a society are those qualities or principles that a particular society considers to be most important. What social values does the author criticize in this story? What message does he want to convey to readers? In thinking about this question, consider the values of the adults who influence young Paul—his mother, his uncle, and Bassett. Mark passages in the story to support your opinion. **(Analyze)**

The InterActive Reader PLUS
296 For English Learners

"It's one of the horses running for the Derby," was the answer.

And, in spite of himself, Oscar Cresswell spoke to Bassett, and himself put a thousand on Malabar: at fourteen to one.

The third day of the illness was critical: they were waiting
580 for a change. The boy, with his rather long, curly hair, was tossing ceaselessly on the pillow. He neither slept nor regained consciousness, and his eyes were like blue stones. His mother sat, feeling her heart had gone, turned actually into a stone.

In the evening, Oscar Cresswell did not come, but Bassett sent a message, saying could he come up for one moment, just one moment? Paul's mother was very angry at the intrusion, but on second thoughts she agreed. The boy was the same. Perhaps Bassett might bring him to consciousness.

The gardener, a shortish fellow with a little brown mustache
590 and sharp little brown eyes, tiptoed into the room, touched his imaginary cap to Paul's mother, and stole to the bedside, staring with glittering, smallish eyes at the tossing, dying child.

"Master Paul!" he whispered. "Master Paul! Malabar came in first all right, a clean win. I did as you told me. You've made over seventy thousand pounds, you have; you've got over eighty thousand.³³ Malabar came in all right, Master Paul."

"Malabar! Malabar! Did I say Malabar, mother? Did I say Malabar? Do you think I'm lucky, mother? I knew Malabar, didn't I? Over eighty thousand pounds! I call that lucky, don't
600 you, mother? Over eighty thousand pounds! I knew, didn't I know I knew? Malabar came in all right. If I ride my horse till I'm sure, then I tell you, Bassett, you can go as high as you like. Did you go for all you were worth, Bassett?"

"I went a thousand on it, Master Paul."

"I never told you, mother, that if I can ride my horse, and *get there,* then I'm absolutely sure—oh, absolutely! Mother, did I ever tell you? I *am* lucky!"

"No, you never did," said his mother.

But the boy died in the night.
610 And even as he lay dead, his mother heard her brother's voice saying to her: "My God, Hester, you're eighty-odd thousand to the good, and a poor devil of a son to the bad. But, poor devil, poor devil, he's best gone out of a life where he rides his rocking-horse to find a winner."

Pause & Reflect

---

33. **eighty thousand:** the equivalent of about $4 million in today's dollars.

Active Reading SkillBuilder

Drawing Conclusions

In "The Rocking-Horse Winner," luck plays a role in the characters' lives, though Lawrence does not always state that role. To **draw conclusions** about the role of luck in the story, combine the facts that are stated in the text, the facts that you can infer, and your own prior knowledge. Use the chart below to note both the stated facts and the inferred facts about each character's experiences with luck. Examples are shown.

Characters	Stated Facts	Inferred Facts
Paul	*Paul rides his rocking horse furiously.*	*Paul wants to find out which horse will win the upcoming race.*
Paul's mother		
Oscar		

Literary Analysis SkillBuilder

Foreshadowing in Fiction

In a short story, a writer may use hints or clues to suggest events that will occur later. This technique, called **foreshadowing,** creates suspense and prepares readers for what is to come. The use of foreshadowing points readers to important events later in the story. On the chart below, list examples of foreshadowing in "The Rocking-Horse Winner." Note how each one prepares you for the tragic ending.

Example of Foreshadowing	How It Suggests the Ending
Paul charges madly on his rocking horse while his sisters watch.	foreshadows final mad ride

Words to Know SkillBuilder

Words to Know

career   inconsiderable   obscure   parry   remonstrate

A. Circle familiar words in the puzzle. Then use five words from the puzzle to fill in the blanks in the sentences below. Don't use the same word more than once.

```
S   Y   T   A   L   E   N   T
H   N   E   B   W   E   L   L
I   O   G   A   L   L   O   P
F   S   R   D   T   R   O   T
T   Y   E   L   A   E   G   O
Y   V   A   Y   F   A   M   E
L   I   T   T   L   E   G   S
```

1. Someone with an *inconsiderable* fortune has _____ wealth.

2. When horses *career,* they move at a _____.

3. A parent is likely to *remonstrate* with a child for behaving _____.

4. People who frequently *parry* questions could be called _____.

5. An *obscure* novelist is a writer without _____.

B. For each phrase in the first column, find the phrase in the second column that is closest in meaning. Write the letter of that phrase in the blank.

_____ 1. oddly obscure   A. minor matter

_____ 2. powerlessly parry   B. dash disastrously

_____ 3. inconsiderable incident   C. strangely unsung

_____ 4. career catastrophically   D. frequently find fault

_____ 5. repeatedly remonstrate   E. weakly ward off

C. Write a dialogue between Uncle Oscar and Paul's mother in which Oscar confronts his sister about her attitude toward money, her spending habits, and their effect on the family. Use at least **three** of the Words to Know.

ARABY

JAMES
JOYCE

Before You Read

Connect to Your Life

Think about the first time you had a crush on someone. How did you feel?
Did you do anything foolish or embarrassing? Write about your experience
on the lines below.

_____

_____

_____

_____

_____

_____

_____

_____

_____

Key to the Story

WHAT YOU NEED TO KNOW This story is one of a series collected in Joyce's
book *Dubliners*. The events in each story lead up to what Joyce called an
epiphany—an ordinary moment or situation in which an important truth
about a character is suddenly revealed.

A R A B Y

J A M E S

J O Y C E

PREVIEW This story is set in a poor part of Dublin, Ireland, in the early 20th century. The narrator is remembering an incident from his childhood. At the time of the story, he has a crush on his friend's sister and thinks about her constantly. When he finally gets a chance to speak to her, she asks him if he is going to Araby (ăr′ə-bē). Araby is a special charity bazaar, or market, that is coming to Dublin for just a few days. Getting the girl a present from the fair becomes the main focus of his thoughts.

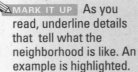
North Richmond Street, being blind, was a quiet street except at the hour when the Christian Brothers' School set the boys free. An uninhabited house of two stories stood at the blind end, detached from its neighbors in a square ground.

The other houses of the street, conscious of decent lives within them, gazed at one another with brown <u>imperturbable</u> faces.

The former tenant of our house, a priest, had died in the back drawing-room. Air, musty from having been long enclosed, hung in all the rooms, and the waste room behind the kitchen was littered with old useless papers. Among these I found a few paper-covered books, the pages of which were curled and damp: *The Abbot,* by Walter Scott, *The Devout Communicant* and *The Memoirs of Vidocq.* I liked the last best because its leaves were yellow. The wild garden behind the house contained a

WORDS
TO
KNOW

imperturbable (ĭm′pər-tûr′bə-bəl) *adj.* not easily disturbed; calm

Use this guide for help with unfamiliar words and difficult passages.

1 blind: dead-end.

4 uninhabited (ŭn'ĭn-hăb'ĭ-tĭd): not lived in; empty.

13 musty (mŭs'tē): smelling stale and moldy.

17–18 *The Abbot . . . Vidocq* (vē-dôk'): These are three 19th-century works. The first is a novel, and the second is a book of religious instruction. The third is an auto-biography of a French police detective.

English Learner Support
VOCABULARY

Homonym Here, *leaves* means pages of a book.

20 central apple-tree and a few straggling bushes under one of which I found the late tenant's rusty bicycle-pump. He had been a very charitable priest; in his will he had left all his money to institutions and the furniture of his house to his sister.

When the short days of winter came dusk fell before we had well eaten our dinners. When we met in the street the houses had grown somber. The space of sky above us was the color of ever-changing violet and towards it the lamps of the street lifted their feeble lanterns. The cold air stung us and we played till our bodies glowed. Our shouts echoed in the silent street.

30 The career of our play brought us through the dark muddy lanes behind the houses where we ran the gantlet of the rough tribes from the cottages, to the back doors of the dark dripping gardens where odors arose from the ashpits, to the dark odorous stables where a coachman smoothed and combed the horse or shook music from the buckled harness. When we returned to the street, light from the kitchen windows had filled the areas. If my uncle was seen turning the corner we hid in the shadow until we had seen him safely housed. Or if Mangan's sister came out on the doorstep to call her brother in 40 to his   we watched her from our shadow peer up and down the street. We waited to see whether she would remain or go in and, if she remained, we left our shadow and walked up to Mangan's steps resignedly. She was waiting for us, her figure defined by the light from the half-opened door. Her brother always teased her before he obeyed and I stood by the railings looking at her. Her dress swung as she moved her body and the soft rope of her hair tossed from side to side.

Pause & *Reflect*

FOCUS

As the story continues, the boy thinks constantly about the girl. When she asks him about going to Araby, he immediately decides to go.

✏ MARK IT UP As you read, circle passages that show how much the boy is thinking about the girl.

50 **Every morning I lay** on the floor in the front parlor watching her door. The blind was pulled down to within an inch of the sash so that I could not be seen. When she came out on the doorstep my heart leaped. I ran to the hall, seized my books and followed her. I kept her brown figure always in my eye and, when we came near the point at which our ways diverged, I quickened my pace

26 somber (sŏm'bər): dark and gloomy.

30 career . . . play: the direction we took as we played.

31–32 ran the gantlet . . . cottages: A gantlet is an area of attack. The boys had to make their way down the alley **(lane)** past the wild children from the poorer section of the neighborhood **(the rough tribes from the cottages).**

33 ashpits: places where ashes from fireplaces and stoves were dumped.

57 diverged (dĭ-vûrjd'): separated.

English Learner Support
CULTURE

Tea In the British Isles, *tea* as it is used here is not just a drink. It refers to the late-afternoon or early-evening meal, which did include tea, as well as sandwiches and other foods.

Pause & Reflect

1. Review the details that you underlined as you read. What kind of neighborhood does the boy live in? **(Visualize/Infer)**

   _____

   _____

   _____

   _____

2. What was the narrator like at the time the story takes place? **(Infer)**

   _____

   _____

   _____

   _____

As the story continues . . .

• The narrator tries to find ways to catch sight of Mangan's sister.

• She finally speaks to him and asks him if he is going to a special bazaar.

and passed her. This happened morning after morning. I had never spoken to her, except for a few casual words, and yet her name was like a summons to all my foolish blood.

Her image accompanied me even in places the most hostile to romance. On Saturday evenings when my aunt went marketing I had to go to carry some of the parcels. We walked through the flaring streets, jostled by drunken men and bargaining women, amid the curses of laborers, the shrill litanies of shopboys who stood on guard by the barrels of pigs' cheeks, the nasal chanting of street-singers, who sang a *come-all-you* about O'Donovan Rossa, or a ballad about the troubles in our native land. These noises converged in a single sensation of life for me: I imagined that I bore my chalice safely through a throng of foes. Her name sprang to my lips at moments in strange prayers and praises which I myself did not understand. My eyes were often full of tears (I could not tell why) and at times a flood from my heart seemed to pour itself out into my bosom. I thought little of the future. I did not know whether I would ever speak to her or not or, if I spoke to her, how I could tell her of my confused adoration. But my body was like a harp and her words and gestures were like fingers running upon the wires.

One evening I went into the back drawing-room in which the priest had died. It was a dark rainy evening and there was no sound in the house. Through one of the broken panes I heard the rain impinge upon the earth, the fine incessant needles of water playing in the sodden beds. Some distant lamp or lighted window gleamed below me. I was thankful that I could see so little. All my senses seemed to desire to veil themselves and, feeling that I was about to slip from them, I pressed the palms of my hands together until they trembled, murmuring: *O love! O love!* many times.

At last she spoke to me. When she addressed the first words to me I was so confused that I did not know what to answer. She asked me was I going to *Araby.* I forgot whether I answered yes or no. It would be a splendid (bazaar,) she said; she would love to go.

—And why can't you? I asked.

While she spoke she turned a silver bracelet round and round her wrist. She could not go, she said, because there

WORDS
TO
KNOW

litany (lĭt'n-ē) *n.* a repetitive chant or recital

61 hostile: unfavorable.

64 flaring streets: referring to the flames of the gas lamps lighting the streets at night.

67–68 *come-all-you . . . native land:* The phrase *come-all-you* refers to a popular type of ballad that began, "Come, all you Irishmen." The "troubles" in this passage refer to the Irish fight for independence from Great Britain. Jeremiah O'Donovan (1831–1915) was known as Dynamite Rossa for urging the use of violence against the British.

70 chalice (chăl'ĭs)**:** cup used to hold communion wine in a religious service. The boy thinks of his love for the girl as holy and superior to everything else around him.

78 fingers . . . wires: fingers playing music on the strings of a harp.

82 impinge (ĭm-pĭnj')**:** hit; strike; **incessant** (ĭn-sĕs'ənt)**:** constant.

85–88 All my senses. . . many times: The boy's feelings for the girl are so powerful that he is almost numb. He presses his hands together and repeats "O love!" because he wants to keep feeling his emotions as strongly as possible.

What Does It Mean?

The narrator's use of religious terminology in this paragraph—*chalice, prayers, adoration*—suggests that his feelings for Mangan's sister are like a religious experience.

English Learner Support
`LANGUAGE`

Simile The simile in lines 77–78 compares the narrator's body to a harp, on which Mangan's sister plays music. This suggests that the boy is very sensitive to everything the girl says and does.

☑ Reading Check

Summarize the narrator's feelings about Mangan's sister.

More About . . .

(BAZAARS) The term *bazaar* comes from a Persian word that refers to open-air markets. These markets were common in the Middle East, where Arabic is one of the main languages. By Joyce's time, the word *bazaar* had come to mean any fair or sale at which a variety of items are sold, often with the profits going to charity.

would be a retreat that week in her convent. Her brother and two other boys were fighting for their caps and I was alone at the railings. She held one of the spikes, bowing her head 100 towards me. The light from the lamp opposite our door caught the white curve of her neck, lit up her hair that rested there and, falling, lit up the hand upon the railing. It fell over one side of her dress and caught the white border of a petticoat, just visible as she stood at ease.

—It's well for you, she said.

—If I go, I said, I will bring you something.

What innumerable follies laid waste my waking and sleeping thoughts after that evening! I wished to annihilate the tedious intervening days. I chafed against the work of school. At night 110 in my bedroom and by day in the classroom her image came between me and the page I strove to read. The syllables of the word *Araby* were called to me through the silence in which my soul luxuriated, and cast an Eastern enchantment over me. I asked for leave to go to the bazaar on Saturday night. My aunt was surprised and hoped it was not some Freemason affair. I answered few questions in class. I watched my master's face pass from amiability to sternness; he hoped I was not beginning to idle. I could not call my wandering thoughts together. I had hardly any patience with the serious work of 120 life which, now that it stood between me and my desire, seemed to me child's play, ugly monotonous child's play.

Pause & Reflect

FOCUS

This section describes the day that the boy will go to Araby. As you read, notice what the boy is feeling as he waits for the moment to finally come.

On Saturday morning I reminded my uncle that I wished to go to the bazaar in the evening. He was fussing at the hallstand, looking for the hat-brush, and answered me curtly:

—Yes, boy, I know.

As he was in the hall I could not go into the front parlor and lie at the 130 window. I left the house in bad humor and walked slowly

WORDS
TO
KNOW

luxuriate (lŭg-zhoŏr′ē-āt′) *v.* to take great delight

97 a retreat . . . convent: a time set apart from normal activities to devote to religious instruction and prayer; *convent* refers to a Catholic school for girls.

108–109 I wished . . . days: The boy wished he could get rid of **(annihilate)** all the boring **(tedious)** days between the time he spoke with the girl and the day he could go to Araby.

109 chafed (chāfd)**:** reacted with irritation.

113 Eastern enchantment: Araby is supposed to be like an Arabian market. Arabia was viewed as an exciting and mysterious land.

115 Freemason: having to do with the Free and Accepted Masons, a social organization. Religious groups have often disapproved its use of secret rituals and signs.

117 amiability (ā'mē-ə-bĭl'ə-tē)**:** friendliness; cheerfulness.

126 curtly: rudely and bluntly.

English Learner Support
VOCABULARY

Strove *Strove* is the past tense of the verb *to strive,* meaning "to try."

What Does It Mean?
I asked for leave means "I asked for permission."

Pause & *Reflect*
MARK IT UP   What promise does the boy make to Mangan's sister? Underline the passage on page 308 that tells you. **(Clarify)**

As the story continues . . .

- The boy tells his uncle he wants to attend the bazaar.
- He grows impatient because it is late and his uncle still hasn't returned.

towards the school. The air was pitilessly raw and already my heart misgave me.

When I came home to dinner my uncle had not yet been home. Still it was early. I sat staring at the clock for some time and, when its ticking began to irritate me, I left the room. I mounted the staircase and gained the upper part of the house. The high cold empty gloomy rooms liberated me and I went from room to room singing. From the front window I saw my companions playing below in the street. Their cries reached me weakened and indistinct and, leaning my forehead against the cool glass, I looked over at the dark house where she lived. I may have stood there for an hour, seeing nothing but the brown-clad figure cast by my imagination, touched discreetly by the lamplight at the curved neck, at the hand upon the railings and at the border below the dress.

When I came downstairs again I found Mrs. Mercer sitting at the fire. She was an old garrulous woman, a pawnbroker's widow, who collected used stamps for some pious purpose. I had to endure the gossip of the tea table. The meal was prolonged beyond an hour and still my uncle did not come. Mrs. Mercer stood up to go: she was sorry she couldn't wait any longer, but it was after eight o'clock and she did not like to be out late, as the night air was bad for her. When she had gone I began to walk up and down the room, clenching my fists. My aunt said:

—I'm afraid you may put off your bazaar for this night of Our Lord.

At nine o'clock I heard my uncle's latchkey in the hall-door. I heard him talking to himself and heard the hall-stand rocking when it had received the weight of his overcoat. I could interpret these signs. When he was midway through his dinner I asked him to give me the money to go to the bazaar. He had forgotten.

—The people are in bed and after their first sleep now, he said.

I did not smile. My aunt said to him energetically:

—Can't you give him the money and let him go? You've kept him late enough as it is.

WORDS TO KNOW

garrulous (gărʹə-ləs) *adj.* rambling in speech; tiresomely talkative

132 misgave: caused to feel doubt or anxiety.

What Does It Mean?

In this context, *gained* means "reached," or "arrived at."

143 discreetly: delicately; in a way that is not showy.

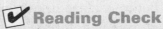
READ ALOUD Lines 146–154

What is the boy's opinion of Mrs. Mercer? (Infer)

_____

_____

_____

147 pawnbroker: a person who lends money to people in exchange for personal possessions they leave as a deposit.

148 collected . . . purpose: Mrs. Mercer saved used postage stamps that were sold to raise money for church activities or organizations **(some pious purpose).**

What Does It Mean?

Families often keep secrets about behavior that embarrasses them. In the highlighted sentence, the narrator refers to the fact that his uncle is drunk. His statement implies that this happens often. However, it is unlikely that the narrator and his aunt ever mention this fact to each other.

161 these signs: The boy can tell by his uncle's behavior that he has been drinking too much.

✔ Reading Check

Why does the boy have to wait for his uncle to return before he can go to the bazaar?

My uncle said he was very sorry he had forgotten. He said he believed in the old saying: *All work and no play makes Jack a dull boy.* He asked me where I was going and, when I had told him a second time he asked me did I know *The Arab's Farewell to His Steed.* When I left the kitchen he was about to recite the opening lines of the piece to my aunt.

Pause & Reflect

FOCUS

Read on to see what happens when the boy goes to Araby.

I held a florin tightly in my hand as I strode down Buckingham Street towards the station. The sight of the streets thronged with buyers and glaring with gas recalled to me the purpose of my journey. I took my seat in a third-class carriage of a deserted train. After an intolerable delay the train moved out of the station slowly. It crept onward among ruinous houses and over the twinkling river. At Westland Row Station a crowd of people pressed to the carriage doors; but the porters moved them back, saying that it was a special train for the bazaar. I remained alone in the bare carriage. In a few minutes the train drew up beside an improvised wooden platform. I passed out on to the road and saw by the lighted dial of a clock that it was ten minutes to ten. In front of me was a large building which displayed the magical name.

I could not find any sixpenny entrance and, fearing that the bazaar would be closed, I passed in quickly through a turnstile, handing a shilling to a weary-looking man. I found myself in a big hall girdled at half its height by a gallery. Nearly all the stalls were closed and the greater part of the hall was in darkness. I recognized a silence like that which <u>pervades</u> a church after a service. I walked into the center of the bazaar timidly. A few people were gathered about the stalls which were still open. Before a curtain, over which the words *Café Chantant* were written in colored lamps, two men were counting money on a salver. I listened to the fall of the coins.

Remembering with difficulty why I had come I went over to one of the stalls and examined porcelain vases and flowered

WORDS
TO
KNOW

pervade (pər-vād´) *v.* to spread throughout; completely fill

169–174 My uncle . . . my aunt: The boy's uncle finally gives him the money to go to Araby. The uncle is easily side-tracked, though. He asks again where the boy is going. When he hears the word *Araby,* he is reminded of a poem. He starts to quote it as the boy leaves the house.

175 florin: a former British coin worth 2 shillings (24 pence). A florin would be worth about ten dollars in today's money.

179 gas: gaslight.

180 third-class carriage: a passenger train car with the cheapest seats.

191–193 sixpenny entrance . . . shilling: A shilling is worth 12 pence. The boy has to pay twice as much as he expected to get into the fair.

199 *Café Chantant* (kä-fä′ shäɴ-täɴ′): a café providing musical entertainment.
201 salver: serving tray.

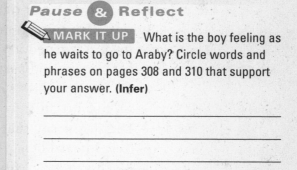

Pause & Reflect

MARK IT UP What is the boy feeling as he waits to go to Araby? Circle words and phrases on pages 308 and 310 that support your answer. **(Infer)**

_____

_____

_____

_____

As the story ends . . .

• The boy sets off for the bazaar.

• When he arrives, it is almost ten o'clock. Many of the bazaar stalls are already closed.

• The boy faces his disappointment.

✔ Reading Check

What is the bazaar like when the boy gets there?

tea-sets. At the door of the stall a young lady was talking and laughing with two young gentlemen. I remarked their English accents and listened vaguely to their conversation.

—O, I never said such a thing!

—O, but you did!

—O, but I didn't!

—Didn't she say that?

—Yes. I heard her.

—O, there's a . . . fib!

Observing me the young lady came over and asked me did I wish to buy anything. The tone of her voice was not encouraging; she seemed to have spoken to me out of a sense of duty. I looked humbly at the great jars that stood like eastern guards at either side of the dark entrance to the stall and murmured:

—No, thank you.

The young lady changed the position of one of the vases and went back to the two young men. They began to talk of the same subject. Once or twice the young lady glanced at me over her shoulder.

I lingered before her stall, though I knew my stay was useless, to make my interest in her wares seem the more real. Then I turned away slowly and walked down the middle of the bazaar. I allowed the two pennies to fall against the sixpence in my pocket. I heard a voice call from one end of the gallery that the light was out. The upper part of the hall was now completely dark.

Gazing up into the darkness I saw myself as a creature driven and derided by vanity; and my eyes burned with anguish and anger.

Pause & Reflect

207–212 O, I never said . . . fib: The woman is flirting with the two men.

215–216 spoken . . . duty: The boy feels that the woman doesn't really want to be bothered selling anything to him.

232 vanity: desires and dreams that turn out to be useless and worthless.

✔ Reading Check

Is the boy able to keep his promise to the girl about bringing her something from the bazaar? Why or why not?

Pause & Reflect

1. Is the boy able to keep his promise? *Yes/No*, because _____

_____

_____.

(Clarify)

MARK IT UP   2. How do you think the boy is feeling as he leaves the fair? Circle phrases that reveal his emotions. **(Infer)**

CHALLENGE

To identify the **theme** of a story, it is often helpful to focus on what the main character learns. Make a chart to record your thoughts about what the boy finds out about himself and the world.

Active Reading SkillBuilder

Making Inferences

Making inferences about characters involves using clues in the text and "reading between the lines" to understand why characters think and act as they do. While reading "Araby," try to infer how the narrator feels during the various events and situations he recalls. Record your inferences on the chart. Examples are given.

Narrator's Situation	Narrator's Feelings
before talking to Mangan's sister	longing, amazement
during conversation with Mangan's sister	
at school	

Literary Analysis SkillBuilder

Point of View

Point of view refers to the method used to tell a story. "Araby" is told from the **first-person point of view**—the narrator is a character in the story and takes part in the story's action. Readers usually feel some sense of connection to a first-person narrator. Choose two passages from "Araby" that reveal something about the narrator. In the first column of the chart below, write down each passage. In the second column, analyze what each passage reveals about the narrator. In the third column, jot down your own reactions to the narrator at that stage in the story. An example is shown.

Passage	Analysis	Your Response
"At last she spoke to me. When she addressed the first words to me I was so confused that I did not know what to answer." (lines 89–90)	The narrator has such strong feelings for the girl that he is tongue-tied. He must feel foolish.	I felt embarrassed and sorry for him.

Follow Up: Why do you think Joyce wrote the story from the first-person point of view?

Words to Know SkillBuilder

Words to Know

garrulous   imperturbable   litany   luxuriate   pervade

A. Decide which word from the word list belongs in each numbered blank. Then
write the word on the blank line on the right.

I love to dust, to mop, to scrub, which flabbergasts my spouse.   _____
Yes, it is true, I do (1) in cleaning house.   (1)

She never gets upset or worried,
Never rushes or is hurried.
You may search from A to Z,
But there is no one you will see
As (2) as she.   _____
                                                                                                              (2)

He talked all through his life
And talked upon his deathbed,
Talking, talking on and on
Until no more was said.
Yes, he was (3) up to the end.   _____
                                                                                                              (3)

If you have mice, the smell of mouse
May very soon (4) your house.   _____
                                                                                                              (4)

"Are we there yet? Are we there?"
They keep asking in my ear,
"Are we there?" But, no, we're *here*.
The (5) just will not cease   _____
Until we're there, and then there's peace.   (5)

B. For each phrase in the first column, find the phrase in the second column that is
closest in meaning. Write the letter of that phrase in the blank.

_____ 1. dangerously talkative   A. to pervade the glade

_____ 2. a repetitive recital in London   B. an imperturbable gerbil

_____ 3. a continually calm rodent   C. to luxuriate in curry

_____ 4. to spread through the clearing   D. perilously garrulous

_____ 5. to thoroughly enjoy a spice   E. a litany in Britain

C. Write a note that the narrator might write to Mangan's sister if he had the courage
to share his thoughts. Use at least **two** of the Words to Know.

The Duchess and the Jeweller

Virginia
Woolf

Before You Read

Connect to Your Life

How have you changed since you were younger? Enter some examples below.

When I was a child, I felt _____

Now I feel _____

When I was a child, my favorite activity was _____

_____

Now my favorite activity is _____

Key to the Story

WHAT'S THE BIG IDEA? The narrator of this story enters into a bargain that might not be so wise. Have you ever agreed to do something you didn't want to do? Why did you agree to do it? Did you make the right decision? Write about the experience below.

_____

_____

_____

_____

_____

_____

_____

_____

_____

Reading Tips

In this **short story**, the author uses a technique called **stream-of-consciousness**. It presents the flow of thoughts, feelings, and memories in a character's mind. Some sentences are long, and the vocabulary is challenging.

- Read the story one paragraph at a time and try to see the overall meaning. Use the Guide for Reading to help you understand unfamiliar words and difficult passages.

- Look for shifts in time. The main character often thinks about past events in his life.

- Be aware of social class. The duchess is from the highest class; the jeweller, though rich, comes from the lowest class.

The Duchess and the Jeweller

Virginia Woolf

PREVIEW Virginia Woolf (1882–1941) was a brilliant and original writer. She was fascinated with the ways that the mind connects present and past events. The story you are about to read is set in London, England, in the early 20th century. The main character is a jeweller. He has overcome great odds in his rise from poverty to wealth. Famous people now come to his door, seeking his help.

As the story begins . . .

- The narrator describes in detail the location and the interior of Oliver's apartment.

- Oliver is a very successful jeweller, but he was poor as a boy.

FOCUS

The narrator describes the apartment of Oliver Bacon, a rich jeweller. It looks beautifully furnished. As Oliver goes through his morning routine, he recalls his rise from rags to riches.

MARK IT UP As you read, circle details that help you get to know Oliver Bacon. An example is highlighted on page 324.

Oliver Bacon lived at the top of a house overlooking the Green Park. He had a flat; chairs jutted out at the right angles—chairs covered in hide. Sofas filled the bays of the windows—sofas covered in tapestry. The windows, the three long windows, had the proper allowance of (discreet) net and figured satin. The mahogany sideboard bulged discreetly with the right brandies, whiskeys and liqueurs. And from the middle window he looked down upon the glossy roofs of fashionable cars packed in the narrow straits of Piccadilly. A more central position could not be imagined. And at eight in the morning he would have his breakfast

Use this guide for help with unfamiliar words and difficult passages.

MARK IT UP KEEP TRACK

As you read, you can use these marks to keep track of your understanding.

✔ ..... I understand.

? ..... I don't understand this.

! ..... Interesting or surprising idea

2–6 He had a flat . . . sofas covered in tapestry: Oliver Bacon's apartment **(flat)** has chairs covered in leather **(hide)** and sofas covered in heavy cloth, woven with rich designs **(tapestry)**.

8–9 discreet net and figured satin: curtains made of lace and satin with a design woven into it.

10 discreetly: in a quiet way.

MARK IT UP WORD POWER

Mark words that you'd like to add to your **Personal Word List.** After reading, you can record the words and their meanings beginning on page 508.

More About...

DISCREET FURNISHINGS Oliver has furnished his apartment discreetly—that is "with discretion," or "tastefully." It was considered vulgar to have furnishings that showed one's wealth too obviously.

Reading Tip

Reread the description of Oliver's flat. Highlight details that give information about his character.

15 Piccadilly (pĭk′ə-dĭl′ē): one of London's main business streets.

brought in on a tray by a manservant; the manservant would unfold his crimson dressing gown; he would rip his letters open with his long pointed nails and would extract thick white cards of invitation upon which the engraving stood up roughly from duchesses, countesses, viscountesses and Honorable Ladies. Then he would wash; then he would eat his toast; then he would read his paper by the bright burning fire of electric coals.

"Behold Oliver," he would say, addressing himself. "You who began life in a filthy little alley, you who . . ." and he would look down at his legs, so shapely in their perfect trousers; at his boots; at his spats. They were all shapely, shining; cut from the best cloth by the best scissors in Savile Row. But he dismantled himself often and became again a little boy in a dark alley. He had once thought that the height of his ambition—selling stolen dogs to fashionable women in Whitechapel. And once he had been done. "Oh, Oliver," his mother had wailed. "Oh, Oliver! When will you have sense, my son?" . . . Then he had gone behind a counter; had sold cheap watches; then he had taken a wallet to Amsterdam. . . . At that memory he would chuckle—the old Oliver remembering the young. Yes, he had done well with the three diamonds; also there was the commission on the emerald.

After that he went into the private room behind the shop in Hatton Garden; the room with the scales, the safe, the thick magnifying glasses. And then . . . and then . . . He chuckled. When he passed through the knots of jewellers in the hot evening who were discussing prices, gold mines, diamonds, reports from South Africa, one of them would lay a finger to the side of his nose and murmur, "Hum–m–m," as he passed. It was no more than a murmur; no more than a nudge on the shoulder, a finger on the nose, a buzz that ran through the cluster of jewellers in Hatton Garden on a hot afternoon—oh, many years ago now! But still Oliver felt it purring down his spine, the nudge, the murmur that meant, "Look at him—young Oliver, the young jeweller—there he goes." Young he was then. And he dressed better and better; and had, first a hansom cab; then a car; and first he went up to the dress circle, then down into the stalls. And he had a villa at Richmond, overlooking the river, with trellises of red roses; and Mademoiselle used to pick one every morning and stick it in his buttonhole.

GUIDE FOR READING

21 viscountesses (vī'koun'tĭs-ĭz): noblewomen ranking below duchesses and countesses.

28 spats: cloth covering the ankle and the upper part of the shoe.

29–30 Savile (săv'ĭl) **Row:** a London street in which many stylish men's clothing stores are located.

30 dismantled himself: took himself apart. Oliver often recalls what he was like as a poor youth.

31 that: The word is used as a pronoun here. It refers to the selling of stolen dogs mentioned later in the sentence.

33 Whitechapel: a poor area in eastern London.

33 done: British slang meaning "arrested and charged with a crime."

41 Hatton Garden: the center of London's jewelry trade.

54 hansom cab: a two-wheeled horse-drawn carriage.

55 dress circle . . . stalls: The dress circle is a section of seats above the main floor in a theater or concert hall. These seats are expensive but available to all. The stalls are seats near the stage that are usually reserved for people of high rank.

57 Mademoiselle (măd'ə-mə-zĕl'): a form of polite address for a young woman in a French-speaking area.

English Learner Support
LANGUAGE

Punctuation Notice the use of dashes (—) and ellipses (…). A dash is used to set off an idea, as in, *he would chuckle— the old Oliver remembering the young*. An ellipsis is generally used to suggest missing words or thoughts. In this story, each form of punctuation breaks up the flow of description and memory.

Reading Tip

Look at the descriptions of the young Oliver and the descriptions of the adult Oliver. What differences do you see? What similarities do you see? Fill in the following Venn diagram.

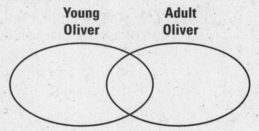

MARK IT UP Reread Lines 43–53

Oliver recalls how the other jewellers reacted to him when he was an up-and-coming young jeweller. Underline the details that describe their reactions. **(Clarify)**

More About . . .

SOUTH AFRICA Diamonds were discovered in South Africa in 1886. This discovery caused British colonists to flock there to make their fortunes. The result was the Boer War (1899–1902), which the British won.

"So," said Oliver Bacon, rising and stretching his legs.
60 "So . . ."

And he stood beneath the picture of an old lady on the mantelpiece and raised his hands. "I have kept my word," he said, laying his hands together, palm to palm, as if he were doing homage to her. "I have won my bet." That was so; he was the richest jeweller in England; but his nose, which was long and flexible, like an elephant's trunk, seemed to say by its curious quiver at the nostrils (but it seemed as if the whole nose quivered, not only the nostrils) that he was not satisfied yet; still smelt something under the ground a little further off.
70 Imagine a giant hog in a pasture rich with truffles; after unearthing this truffle and that, still it smells a bigger, a blacker truffle under the ground further off. So Oliver snuffed always in the rich earth of Mayfair another truffle, a blacker, a bigger further off.

Now then he straightened the pearl in his tie, cased himself in his smart blue overcoat; took his yellow gloves and his cane; and swayed as he descended the stairs and half snuffed, half sighed through his long sharp nose as he passed out into Piccadilly. For was he not still a sad man, a dissatisfied man, a man who seeks
80 something that is hidden, though he had won his bet?

Pause & Reflect

FOCUS

Oliver walks to his "dark little shop." Upon arriving, he goes directly to his private room. He unlocks his safes and looks at his jewels. Read to find out how he reacts to his jewels.

He swayed slightly as he walked, as the camel at the zoo sways from side to side when it walks along the asphalt paths laden with grocers and their wives eating from paper bags and throwing little bits of silver paper crumpled up on to the path. The camel despises the grocers; the camel is dissatisfied with its lot; the camel sees the blue lake and the
90 fringe of palm trees in front of it. So the great jeweller, the greatest jeweller in the whole world, swung down Piccadilly, perfectly dressed, with his gloves, with his cane; but dissatisfied still, till he reached the dark little shop, that was famous in France, in Germany, in Austria, in Italy, and all over America—the dark little shop in the street off Bond Street.

64 **homage** (hŏm′ĭj): special honor or respect.

70 **truffles:** edible organisms, such as yeasts and molds, that grow underground. They are considered a delicacy. Hogs are often used to sniff them out.

73 **Mayfair:** a stylish residential section of London.

95 **Bond Street:** a main business street passing through the jewellers' district in London.

English Learner Support
LANGUAGE

Style In the highlighted sentence, the author has dropped some words to condense her writing. You can understand the lines more easily if you read them this way: "So Oliver snuffed always in the rich earth of Mayfair another truffle, a blacker *one,* a bigger *one* further off.

Pause & Reflect

READ ALOUD **1.** Read aloud the boxed passage on page 326. In this passage, Oliver talks to his mother's picture and says he kept his word. What promise do you think he kept to his mother? **(Draw Conclusions)**

_____
_____
_____
_____

2. Despite his wealth and success, Oliver is "still a sad man" (line 79). Why do you think he is sad? **(Infer)**

_____
_____
_____
_____

As the story continues . . .
- Oliver walks through Mayfair to his shop.
- He continues to be dissatisfied with his life.

English Learner Support
CULTURE

Zoo Rides At some zoos, people can ride on a camel, which is led on a path. Here, the narrator describes the ride from the camel's point of view. Like this camel, the jeweller sees the world beyond and is unhappy with his life.

As usual he strode through the shop without speaking, though the four men, the two old men, Marshall and Spencer, and the two young men, Hammond and Wicks, stood straight behind the counter as he passed and looked at him, envying him. It was only with one finger of the amber-colored glove, waggling, that he acknowledged their presence. And he went in and shut the door of his private room behind him.

Then he unlocked the grating that barred the window. The cries of Bond Street came in; the purr of the distant traffic. The light from reflectors at the back of the shop struck upwards. One tree waved six green leaves, for it was June. But Mademoiselle had married Mr. Pedder of the local brewery—no one stuck roses in his buttonhole now.

"So," he half sighed, half snorted, "so . . ."

Then he touched a spring in the wall and slowly the paneling slid open, and behind it were the steel safes, five, no, six of them, all of burnished steel. He twisted a key; unlocked one; then another. Each was lined with a pad of deep crimson velvet; in each lay jewels—bracelets, necklaces, rings, tiaras, ducal coronets; loose stones in glass shells; rubies, emeralds, pearls, diamonds. All safe, shining, cool, yet burning, eternally, with their own compressed light.

> "Tears!" said Oliver, looking at the pearls.
>
> "Heart's blood!" he said, looking at the rubies.
>
> "Gunpowder!" he continued, rattling the diamonds so that they flashed and blazed.
>
> "Gunpowder enough to blow up Mayfair—sky high, high, high!" He threw his head back and made a sound like a horse neighing as he said it.

Pause **&** *Reflect*

The phone rings, and Oliver is told that the Duchess is in the outer office. He makes her wait ten minutes before allowing her to enter his private room.

MARK IT UP As you read, circle details that help you visualize the Duchess.

The telephone buzzed obsequiously in a low muted voice on his table. He shut the safe.

"In ten minutes," he said. "Not before." And he sat down at his desk and looked at the heads of the Roman emperors that were graved on his sleeve links. And again he dismantled himself and became once more the little boy

WORDS
TO
KNOW

obsequiously (ŏb-sē'kwē-əs-lē) *adv.* in a subservient or fawning manner

112 burnished: shining.

115 ducal (dōō′kəl) **coronets:** small crowns worn by dukes and duchesses.

131 graved: engraved.
131–132 sleeve links: buttons for a shirt cuff.

Pause & Reflect

READ ALOUD Read aloud the boxed passage on page 328. Oliver reacts to his jewels in a surprising way. Which jewel does he associate with violence? Circle the answer below. **(Draw Conclusions)**

pearls

rubies

diamonds

English Learner Support
LANGUAGE

Metaphors *Tears, heart's blood,* and *gunpowder* are all metaphors for gems. These comparisons show the jeweller's bitterness and anger about his life. He feels that he has sacrificed part of himself to become wealthy.

As the story continues . . .

- A phone call demands Oliver's attention.
- He tells his employee to keep the customer waiting.

playing marbles in the alley where they sell stolen dogs on
Sunday. He became that wily astute little boy, with lips like
wet cherries. He dabbled his fingers in ropes of tripe; he
dipped them in pans of frying fish; he dodged in and out
among the crowds. He was slim, lissome, with eyes like licked
stones. And now—now—the hands of the clock ticked on.

140 One, two, three, four . . . The Duchess of Lambourne waited
his pleasure; the Duchess of Lambourne, daughter of a
hundred Earls. She would wait for ten minutes on a chair at
the counter. She would wait his pleasure. She would wait till
he was ready to see her. He watched the clock in its shagreen
case. The hand moved on. With each tick the clock handed
him—so it seemed—pâté de foie gras; a glass of champagne;
another of fine brandy; a cigar costing one guinea. The clock
laid them on the table beside him, as the ten minutes passed.
Then he heard soft slow footsteps approaching; a rustle in the
150 corridor. The door opened. Mr. Hammond flattened himself
against the wall.

"Her Grace!" he announced.

And he waited there, flattened against the wall.

And Oliver, rising, could hear the rustle of the dress of the
Duchess as she came down the passage. Then she loomed up,
filling the door, filling the room with the aroma, the prestige,
the arrogance, the pomp, the pride of all the Dukes and
Duchesses swollen in one wave. And as a wave breaks, she
broke, as she sat down, spreading and splashing and falling
160 over Oliver Bacon the great jeweller, covering him with
sparkling bright colors, green, rose, violet; and odors; and
iridescences; and rays shooting from fingers, nodding from
plumes, flashing from silk; for she was very large, very fat,
tightly girt in pink taffeta, and past her prime. As a parasol
with many flounces, as a peacock with many feathers, shuts
its flounces, folds its feathers, so she subsided and shut herself
as she sank down in the leather armchair.

Pause **&** **Reflect**

WORDS
TO
KNOW

astute (ə-stōōt′) *adj.* clever; shrewd
lissome (lĭs′əm) *adj.* easy and graceful in movement
arrogance (ăr′ə-gəns) *n.* overbearing pride; exaggerated
self-importance

330

136 tripe: the stomach lining of a cow or calf, used as a food.

144 shagreen (shə-grēn'): untanned leather, often dyed green.

146 pâté de foie gras (pä-tā' də fwä grä'): a delicacy made from goose liver.

162 iridescences (ĭr'ĭ-dĕs'ən-sĭz): brilliant displays of changing, rainbowlike colors.

164 girt: wrapped; encircled.

164 taffeta (tăf'ĭ-tə): a crisp fabric made of silk, rayon, or nylon.

164–165 parasol with many flounces: umbrella with many ruffles.

✔ Reading Check

Why does Oliver remember several events from his childhood as he keeps the Duchess waiting?

More About . . .

BRITISH SOCIAL CLASS In the British class system, people such as the jeweller may rise out of poverty and earn their wealth through business. But no matter how wealthy they become, these people are never considered the social equals of aristocrats. An aristocrat such as the (Duchess of Lambourne) belongs to a class of people who are born into families with titles of nobility.

English Learner Support
LANGUAGE

Personification In lines 145–148, the writer personifies the clock. She gives the clock human qualities. The description suggests that the clock lays objects on the table for Oliver as a person might do. This figurative language is meant to show the reader that each minute Oliver keeps the duchess waiting is as enjoyable to him as a fine rich thing.

English Learner Support
LANGUAGE

Metaphor The Duchess is compared to a wave of the ocean. This shows that she, like a wave, had a surging and overwhelming presence.

Pause & Reflect

Why does Oliver make the Duchess wait? Check the sentence below that tells the answer. **(Infer)**

He needs time to get things ready for her visit.

He gets a sense of power from keeping her waiting.

He needs time to calm his nerves.

FOCUS

The Duchess has come to sell Oliver pearls. He must decide whether they are real and worth the money she is asking.

170

"Good morning, Mr. Bacon," said the Duchess. And she held out her hand which came through the slit of her white glove. And Oliver bent low as he shook it. And as their hands touched the link was <u>forged</u> between them once more. They were friends, yet enemies; he was master, she was mistress; each cheated the other, each needed the other, each feared the other, each felt this and knew this every time they touched hands thus in the little back room with the white light outside, and the tree with its six leaves, and the sound of the street in the distance and behind

180 them the safes.

"And today, Duchess—what can I do for you today?" said Oliver, very softly.

The Duchess opened; her heart, her private heart, gaped wide. And with a sigh, but no words, she took from her bag a long wash-leather pouch—it looked like a lean yellow ferret. And from a slit in the ferret's belly she dropped pearls—ten pearls. They rolled from the slit in the ferret's belly—one, two, three, four—like the eggs of some heavenly bird.

"All that's left me, dear Mr. Bacon," she moaned. Five, six,

190 seven—down they rolled, down the slopes of the vast mountainsides that fell between her knees into one narrow valley—the eighth, the ninth, and the tenth. There they lay in the glow of the peach-blossom taffeta. Ten pearls.

"From the Appleby cincture," she mourned. "The last . . . the last of them all."

Oliver stretched out and took one of the pearls between finger and thumb. It was round, it was lustrous. But real was it, or false? Was she lying again? Did she dare?

She laid her plump padded finger across her lips. "If the

200 Duke knew . . ." she whispered. "Dear Mr. Bacon, a bit of bad luck . . ."

Been gambling again, had she?

"That villain! That sharper!" she hissed.

The man with the chipped cheek bone? A bad 'un. And the Duke was straight as a poker; with side whiskers; would cut her off, shut her up down there if he knew—what I know, thought Oliver, and glanced at the safe.

WORDS
TO
KNOW

forge (fôrj) *v.* to form, shape, or produce

As the story continues . . .

• The Duchess and Oliver greet one another.

• Neither one completely trusts the other.

185 ferret: a small weasel-like mammal.

194 cincture (sĭngk′chər): an ornamental belt.

 Reading Check

Why has the Duchess come to see Oliver?

203 sharper: a cheating gambler.

205 poker: a metal rod used to stir a fire.

"Araminta, Daphne, Diana," she moaned. "It's for *them*."

The Ladies Araminta, Daphne, Diana—her daughters. He knew them; adored them. But it was Diana he loved.

"You have all my secrets," she leered. Tears slid; tears fell; tears, like diamonds, collecting powder in the ruts of her cherry-blossom cheeks.

"Old friend," she murmured, "old friend."

"Old friend," he repeated, "old friend," as if he licked the words.

"How much?" he queried.

She covered the pearls with her hand.

"Twenty thousand," she whispered.

But was it real or false, the one he held in his hand? The Appleby cincture—hadn't she sold it already? He would ring for Spencer or Hammond. "Take it and test it," he would say. He stretched to the bell.

"You will come down tomorrow?" she urged, she interrupted. "The Prime Minister—His Royal Highness . . ." She stopped. "And Diana," she added.

Oliver took his hand off the bell.

Pause & **Reflect**

FOCUS

Oliver must decide whether to have the pearls tested or buy them on the spot from the Duchess. Read to find out what he decides and why.

He looked past her, at the backs of the houses in Bond Street. But he saw, not the houses in Bond Street, but a dimpling river; and trout rising and salmon; and the Prime Minister; and himself too; in white waistcoats; and then, Diana. He looked down at the pearl in his hand. But how could he test it, in the light of the river, in the light of the eyes of Diana? But the eyes of the Duchess were on him.

"Twenty thousand," she moaned. "My honor!"

The honor of the mother of Diana! He drew his checkbook towards him; he took out his pen.

"Twenty," he wrote. Then he stopped writing. The eyes of the old woman in the picture were on him—of the old woman, his mother.

"Oliver!" she warned him. "Have sense! Don't be a fool!"

"Oliver!" the Duchess entreated—it was "Oliver" now, not

219 Twenty thousand: The Duchess is asking for 20,000 pounds, a huge sum of money, well over $100,000. In the mid-1920s, a pound was worth about $5, and the purchasing power of a dollar was about 10 times what it is now.

229–234 But he saw . . . Diana: Oliver's imagination pictures the estate where the Duchess lives—with its river, the fish, leaders of state in vests **(waistcoats)**, and the Duchess's daughter Diana.

238 My honor: If the duchess fails to get money from Oliver, her husband will find out about her gambling debts. Her reputation will be ruined forever.

Reading Tip

In lines 214–215, the Duchess and Oliver call each other "old friend." What do you imagine they are really thinking? Write a short description of how each one judges the other in his or her unspoken thoughts.

Pause Reflect

1. What does the Duchess want to keep hidden from her husband? Circle the phrase below that tells the answer. **(Clarify)**

   her drinking

   her love affairs

   her gambling

   her stealing

2. Oliver is about to call an employee to test the Duchess's pearls. Why does he change his mind? **(Cause and Effect)**

   _____

   _____

   _____

   _____

As the story ends . . .

• Oliver has to decide whether to buy the Duchess's pearls.

• If he accepts the Duchess's offer, he will see her daughter Diana, whom he loves.

"Mr. Bacon." "You'll come for a long weekend?"

Alone in the woods with Diana! Riding alone in the woods with Diana!

"Thousand," he wrote, and signed it.

250 "Here you are," he said.

And there opened all the flounces of the parasol, all the plumes of the peacock, the radiance of the wave, the swords and spears of (Agincourt,) as she rose from her chair. And the two old men and the two young men, Spencer and Marshall, Wicks and Hammond, flattened themselves behind the counter envying him as he led her through the shop to the door. And he waggled his yellow glove in their faces, and she held her honor—a check for twenty thousand pounds with his signature—quite firmly in her hands.

260 "Are they false or are they real?" asked Oliver, shutting his private door. There they were, ten pearls on the blotting paper on the table. He took them to the window. He held them under his lens to the light. . . . This, then, was the truffle he had routed out of the earth! Rotten at the center—rotten at the core!

"Forgive me, oh my mother!" he sighed, raising his hands as if he asked pardon of the old woman in the picture. And again he was a little boy in the alley where they sold dogs on Sunday.

270 "For," he murmured, laying the palms of his hands together, "it is to be a long weekend."

Pause & *Reflect*

253 Agincourt (ăj′ĭn-kôrt′)**:** a French village where, in 1415, Henry V's English forces defeated a much larger French army. This battle is considered one of England's most glorious victories.

More About . . .

(AGINCOURT) By referring to Agincourt, the author implies that the Duchess has won a great battle over the jeweller.

English Learner Support
LANGUAGE

Metaphor The truffle is a metaphor for the pearls—which were fake.

Pause & Reflect

1. Why does Oliver buy the pearls without having them tested? Write the answer below. Then underline any details on pages 334 and 336 that led you to your answer. **(Infer)**

_____

_____

_____

 READ ALOUD **2.** Read aloud the boxed passage on page 336.
What does Oliver ask his mother to forgive him for?
(Draw Conclusions)

CHALLENGE

Description is writing that helps readers picture scenes, events, and characters. To create description, writers often use **figurative language,** or language that communicates meaning beyond the literal meaning of words. Mark passages in which the author compares the jeweller to various animals. What does each comparison suggest about his character? **(Analyze)**

Active Reading SkillBuilder

Making Inferences

Understanding what motivates a character is often the key to understanding an entire story. Sometimes, the character's motivation—the driving force behind his or her thoughts, feelings, and actions—is obvious; other times, you must **infer** it from clues in the story. Record the actions and the motivations of the duchess and the jeweller on the diagrams below. Examples are given.

Character: Jeweller	
Action	**Motivation**
often recalls that he sold stolen dogs as a boy	likes to contrast his former poverty with his present wealth

Character: Duchess	
Action	**Motivation**
comes to sell pearls to the jeweller	

Literary Analysis SkillBuilder

Style

An important element of Woolf's **style** is her use of stream of consciousness. It presents the flow of thoughts, feelings, and sensations in a character's mind. On the chart below, write down a passage in "The Duchess and the Jeweller" that records Oliver Bacon's thoughts or feelings. Then write down what the passage tells about his character. An example is shown.

What Bacon Is Thinking or Feeling:	What the Passage Tells About Bacon's Character:
"One tree waved six green leaves, for it was June. But Mademoiselle had married Mr. Pedder of the local brewery—no one stuck roses in his buttonhole now." (page 288, lines 106–108)	Oliver still regrets his lost love.

Words to Know SkillBuilder

Words to Know

arrogance   astute   forge   lissome   obsequiously

A. Decide which word from the word list belongs in each numbered blank.
Then write the word on the blank line on the right.

He's haughty and scornful, conceited and proud,
And his attitude has all laughing out loud.
Yes, his (1) has us collapsing in stitches.
He's more than a little too big for his britches.

_____
(1)

I'd happily watch dolphins any day,
Gliding in their lovely, (2) way.

_____
(2)

"Your Highness is a clever chap!"
"Your Highness, what a stunning cap!"
"Your Highness, if you'd be so kind . . ."
"Of course, your Highness, I don't mind."
Their subjects often say such things
(3) to their kings.

_____
(3)

She's studied them in fields and streams.
Now salamanders fill her dreams.
She can predict what they will do
In habitats both old and new.
She really has become (4)
About the habits of the newt.

_____
(4)

Our sharing of our goals and joys and fears
Helped (5) a friendship that survived the years.

_____
(5)

B. For each phrase in the first column, find the phrase in the second column
that is closest in meaning. Write the letter of that phrase in the blank.

_____ 1. a lissome lass   A. a clever counselor

_____ 2. flawlessly forge   B. pretend pride

_____ 3. an astute advisor   C. a graceful girl

_____ 4. obsequiously offered   D. perfectly produce

_____ 5. artificial arrogance   E. submissively submitted

C. Write a marriage proposal that the jeweller might offer to Diana. Use at least
three of the Words to Know.

PRELUDES

T. S. ELIOT

Before You Read

Connect to Your Life

What are some images that come to mind when you think of a city?
Record your thoughts in the web below.

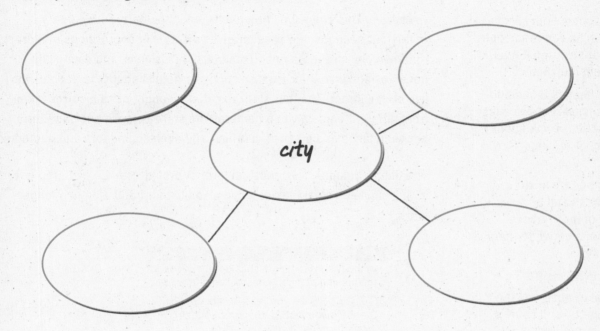

Key to the Poem

WHAT YOU NEED TO KNOW "Preludes" was written during World War I.
At the time, many readers disliked the poem because it focused on images
that were considered ordinary and even ugly. Such images were unusual in
the poetry of the early twentieth century. Like many other artists of the
time, Eliot was upset by the horrors of the war. This poem shows how he
thinks society was changing as a result of the pressures of modern times.

Reading Tips

This poem, like much of **modern poetry,** requires you to work to understand it. The poet presents **images** of city life, but the reader has to figure out their meaning.

- Read the poem both silently and aloud. As you read each section, answer the Pause and Reflect questions.

- Note the images that stand out, and visualize the scenes they describe. Think about the **mood,** or feelings, they create.

- Note the poem's mixture of sentences and phrases. You may or may not see connections between them right away.

As the poem begins . . .

- The speaker observes the smells, sights, and sounds of a city street at nightfall.

- This street scene is in a poor neighborhood.

More About . . .

ELIOT'S STYLE T. S. Eliot's unique style marks the beginning of modern poetry. Key aspects of Eliot's style include

- a use of everyday language, including slang and references to popular culture

- a focus on ordinary, often unpleasant experiences

- the use of free verse, in which the rhythms don't follow a fixed pattern

- a patchwork of images, symbols, and allusions, in which the reader must supply connections

P R E L U D E S

T. S. ELIOT

PREVIEW This poem was first published in the early 20th century. In the four sections, the speaker gives a series of impressions of a dreary, rundown city street. He describes the sights, smells, and sounds he observes and imagines. He also suggests details about the people who live on the street. The four stanzas can be thought of as pictures taken from different angles with a camera. The stanzas move back and forth between times and places—morning and evening, indoors and outdoors.

The title, "Preludes," is a musical term. A prelude can be a short piece with a single musical theme. It can also be an introduction to a longer work.

> **FOCUS**
> In the first section, the speaker describes the coming of night to a city street in winter.
> **MARK IT UP** As you read, circle details that help you picture the street scene. An example is highlighted.

I

The winter evening settles down
With smell of steaks in passageways.
Six o'clock.
The burnt-out ends of smoky days.
And now a gusty shower wraps
The grimy scraps
Of withered leaves about your feet
And newspapers from vacant lots;
The showers beat
On broken blinds and chimney-pots,
And at the corner of the street
A lonely cab-horse steams and stamps.
And then the lighting of the lamps.

Pause & Reflect

Use this guide for help with unfamiliar words
and difficult passages.

2 steaks: In the early 20th century, steaks
were usually cheap cuts from low-grade
beef; **passageways:** the hallways in a slum
apartment building.

4 An image comparing the end of a dirty,
gray day to a cigarette butt.

10 blinds: wooden window shutters;
chimney-pots: short pipes on top of
chimneys to carry away smoke. They are
usually found on older buildings.

12 cab-horse: A horse that drew a cab,
a small carriage that carried passengers
for a fee.

13 lighting of the lamps: Before there was
electricity, gas streetlights were lit by hand
every night.

English Learner Support
LANGUAGE

Alliteration In poetry, *alliteration* is the
repetition of consonant sounds, especially at the beginnings of words. An
example is the repetition of the consonant *s* in *settles down / With smell of
steaks in passageways. / Six o'clock.*

What Does It Mean?

When the poet says the horse *steams and
stamps,* he is describing the steam formed
when the horse's breath hits the cold
winter air, and how the horse is stamping
its feet to keep warm.

Pause & Reflect

1. Look at the details you circled as you read.
What picture do you have of the street?
(Visualize)

_____

_____

_____

_____

2. Do you find this street scene appealing or
inviting? *Yes/No*, because _____

_____

_____

_____

_____.

(Connect)

FOCUS

This section of the poem describes the city
street coming to life in the early morning.

✎ MARK IT UP As you read, underline phrases
that refer to people.

II

The morning comes to consciousness

15 Of faint stale smells of beer
From the sawdust-trampled street
With all its muddy feet that press
To early coffee-stands.
With the other masquerades

20 That time resumes,
One thinks of all the hands
That are raising dingy shades
In a thousand furnished rooms.

Pause **&** *Reflect*

As the poem continues...
* The speaker describes the following morning.
* The morning is presented as a person, observing men and women going to work.

14 morning . . . consciousness: Morning is personified, or given human qualities, in this line. It is pictured as a person waking up.

18 early coffee-stands: street stands of venders who sell to early-morning customers.

19–20 With . . . resumes: referring to daily activities, such as stopping for morning coffee. Everyday routines **(masquerades)** can cover up problems, such as boredom or lack of purpose in life.

22 dingy (dĭn'jē)**:** faded and dirty.

23 furnished rooms: one-room apartments with furniture included, usually cheap and rundown.

English Learner Support
VOCABULARY

Compound Words Eliot uses several hyphenated compound words in this poem. He creates both adjectives (*sawdust-trampled* to modify *streets*) and nouns (*coffee-stands*). Understanding each word individually will help you figure out the meaning of the compound words.

✔ **Reading Check**
What kind of neighborhood is the speaker describing?

Pause **&** *Reflect*

1. Look at the phrases you underlined as you read. How much does the speaker tell you about the people in the street? (**Read Modern Verse**)

_____

_____

_____

_____

READ ALOUD 2. Read aloud the boxed passage on page 346. What mental picture do you form of the people living in these rooms? (**Visualize**)

_____

_____

_____

_____

The speaker now makes a shift from the
street outside to an indoor scene. He
focuses on a woman who is slowly waking
up inside one of the apartments. He
imagines speaking to her directly. As you
read, pay attention to what she sees as she
slips between waking and sleeping.

III

You tossed a blanket from the bed,

25 You lay upon your back, and waited;
You dozed, and watched the night revealing
The thousand sordid images
Of which your soul was constituted;
They flickered against the ceiling.

30 And when all the world came back
And the light crept up between the shutters
And you heard the sparrows in the gutters,
You had such a vision of the street
As the street hardly understands;

35 Sitting along the bed's edge, where
You curled the papers from your hair,
Or clasped the yellow soles of feet
In the palms of both soiled hands.

Pause & *Reflect*

26–28 **You dozed . . . constituted:** You fell back asleep. In your dreams you saw **(watched the night revealing)** the many ugly details **(thousand sordid images)** that made up **(constituted)** your life.

29 **flickered:** moved quickly on and off.

30 **when . . . back:** when morning came.

33–34 **You had . . . understands:** The woman lives in her own world. Her experience of life in the street **(vision of the street)** would not be recognized or shared by others.

36 **papers from your hair:** At this time, women curled their hair by wrapping it around pieces of special curling paper at night.

As the poem continues . . .

• The speaker looks inside the apartment of a woman whose morning is just beginning and describes her.

English Learner Support
LANGUAGE

Extended Metaphor In the highlighted lines, the poet suggests that the woman is watching a film of her life. The words and phrases *watched, images,* and *flickered against the ceiling* help you see the comparison between her life and a film.

 READ ALOUD **Lines 30–34**

Read these lines slowly, as if you were about to discover something important. Pay attention to the rhythms you hear, and emphasize the rhyme of "shutters" and "gutters." **(Read Modern Verse)**

 Reading Check

What does the speaker suggest about this woman's life?

Pause & Reflect

MARK IT UP **1.** After first waking up, the woman falls asleep and dreams. Are her dreams pleasant or unpleasant? Star the line that tells you. **(Clarify)**

2. The speaker addresses the woman as "you." Does he seem to feel concern for her? Explain the reasons for your answer. **(Read Modern Verse)**

_____

_____

_____

_____

FOCUS

In this section the speaker moves back to describing the street at the end of a day. He also tells how the images he has seen have affected him. As you read, look for the speaker's varied reactions to the street.

IV

His soul stretched tight across the skies
40 That fade behind a city block,
Or trampled by insistent feet
At four and five and six o'clock;
And short square fingers stuffing pipes,
And evening newspapers, and eyes
45 Assured of certain certainties,
The conscience of a blackened street
Impatient to assume the world.

I am moved by fancies that are curled
Around these images, and cling:
50 The notion of some infinitely gentle
Infinitely suffering thing.

Wipe your hand across your mouth, and laugh;
The worlds revolve like ancient women
Gathering fuel in vacant lots.

Pause & *Reflect*

39–42 The street is personified in these lines, as if it were a man **(his)**. The "soul" of the street is pictured as the sky fading at the end of the day. The street is "trampled" by the people hurrying home from work.

43–47 And short . . . world: These lines describe the street at the end of the day. People arrive at home to carry on with their habits **(pipes, evening newspapers)** and usual routines **(eyes assured of certain certainties)**. The street is dark **(blackened)** with the coming of night and with dirt and grime. It waits for the lamps to be lit **(impatient to assume the world)**.

48–51 I am moved . . . thing: The speaker finally shares his own feelings. The street scenes have made him imagine **(moved by fancies)** another possibility. He thinks of something—or someone—gentle and full of suffering.

52 This line is in contrast to the quiet and peace of the two previous lines. The speaker here describes a rough, mocking gesture.

53–54 The worlds . . . lots: Life goes on **(the worlds revolve)** like old women collecting firewood every day from abandoned lots. Such a life is full of endless repetition and hopelessness.

As the poem ends . . .

- The street is now personified as a man at the end of the day.
- The speaker finally makes his own observations about the images he has presented in the poem.

What Does It Mean?

Infinitely means "in a manner without limits." In lines 50–51, the poet imagines a creature whose gentleness and suffering are without limits.

Pause & Reflect

READ ALOUD **1.** Read aloud the boxed passage on page 350. How does the speaker view the street at this point? Circle the answer below. **(Infer)**

The street is confusing and ugly, and the speaker feels impatient with it.

The speaker feels pity and sympathy toward the street and its people.

2. In the last three lines, the speaker's reactions toward the street seem to change. Circle two phrases below that reflect the speaker's final responses. **(Analyze)**

thinks everything will be fine

is disappointed and bitter

doesn't see much hope

CHALLENGE

Throughout the poem, people are referred to by parts of their body—feet, heads, fingers, eyes, mouth. The speaker never describes a complete person. Why do you think Eliot does this? What do you think he means to say about modern life by referring to people only in this way?

Active Reading SkillBuilder

Strategies for Reading Modern Verse

Modern poetry can be hard to understand. Follow these guidelines while reading Eliot's "Preludes."

- Read each section of the poem aloud.
- Pay attention to images that make an impression on you.
- Use the notes in the Guide for Reading to understand difficult passages and unfamiliar allusions, or references.
- Paraphrase passages that you find puzzling.

In the chart below, list some of the images that impress you. Write down your reactions to each image. Then record any lines that puzzle you. Try to paraphrase them to get at their meaning. Examples are given.

Images That Make a Strong Impression	Your Reaction
"burnt-out ends of smoky days" (line 4)	creates the empty feeling a person has at the end of a long, dull day

Puzzling Lines	Your Paraphrase
"The morning comes to consciousness" (line 14)	Morning dawns in the street.

Literary Analysis SkillBuilder

Rhythm in Modern Verse

Rhythm is the pattern of stressed and unstressed syllables in a line of poetry. In the early 20th century, many poets stopped using regular rhythms. Instead they wrote **free verse**—poetry with no fixed, or set, rhythm. In " Preludes," Eliot combines traditional rhythms and free verse. For example, lines 1 and 2 have a regular rhythm. There are eight syllables with four accented syllables in each line. Line 3, however, has only three syllables with two accents. This break in the pattern makes the reader pay attention and signals a possible change.

> The winter evening settles down
> With smell of steaks in passageways.
> Six o'clock.

Choose two additional passages that combine lines with regular rhythm and lines with varying rhythm. Mark the accented syllables. Then put a check next to the lines that do not have a regular rhythm. At the bottom of the page, briefly explain some of the effects of mixing traditional rhythms and free verse.

Lines: _____

Lines: _____

Effects: _____

_____

Musée des

Beaux Arts

W. H. AUDEN

Before You Read

Connect to Your Life

Each of us has experienced some form of personal loss and the heartfelt emotional impact of such a loss. In contrast, when we read about a human tragedy in the newspaper we may not experience a strong emotional reaction. Why do you think some tragedies affect us deeply while others only evoke momentary feelings or none at all? Write your ideas on the lines below.

_____

_____

_____

_____

_____

Key to the Poem

WHAT YOU NEED TO KNOW W. H. Auden was born and educated in England and he moved to the United States in 1939. His collection of poems *The Age of Anxiety* won the Pulitzer Prize in 1948. Auden had a passionate moral sense and responded to the social and political crises of his time. The quest for spiritual and social justice, sin and redemption, and human imperfection are all common themes explored in his poetry.

Reading Tips

This poem falls into two parts. In the first part, the **speaker** states his or her views on human suffering. In the second part, the speaker describes a painting that supports those views.

- Imagine that you and the speaker are walking together through an art museum. You stop to look closely at certain paintings. The speaker then turns to you and comments on them.

- Use the Guide for Reading to help you understand unfamiliar words and difficult lines.

As the poem begins . . .

- The speaker is viewing several famous paintings.

- He describes how the characters in the paintings react to scenes of suffering.

Reading Tip

If possible, use the Internet or art history books to view the paintings the speaker discusses in this poem. *Landscape with the Fall of Icarus* is on page 1077 of **The Language of Literature**.

Musée des Beaux Arts

W. H. AUDEN

PREVIEW W. H. Auden (1907–1973) is regarded as one of the great poets of the 20th century. The title of the poem "Musée des Beaux Arts" (mū-zā dā bō zär) is French for the Museum of Fine Arts in Brussels, the capital city of Belgium. Auden visited this city several times. In its art museum, he saw paintings by the painter Pieter Breughel (pē′tər broi′gəl) the Elder (1520?–1569). This poem includes descriptions of three Breughel paintings.

> **FOCUS**
> The speaker tells why he admires a group of painters known as the Old Masters. Their paintings teach the truth about human suffering—namely, that while someone is suffering, other people are going about their daily activities.
>
> MARK IT UP As you read, circle details that describe these activities. An example is highlighted.

About suffering they were never wrong,
The Old Masters: how well they understood
Its human position; how it takes place
While someone else is eating or opening a window or just
    walking dully along;
5 How, when the aged are reverently, passionately waiting
For the miraculous birth, there always must be
Children who did not specially want it to happen, skating
On a pond at the edge of the wood:
They never forgot
10 That even the dreadful martyrdom must run its course
Anyhow in a corner, some untidy spot
Where the dogs go on with their doggy life and the
    torturer's horse
Scratches its innocent behind on a tree.

Pause & Reflect

Use this guide for help with unfamiliar words and difficult passages.

2 Old Masters: the great European painters of the 16th, 17th, and 18th centuries.

3 *Its* and *it* refer to the word *suffering* in line 1.

5–8 How, when the aged . . . edge of the wood: a reference to Breughel's painting, *The Numbering at Bethlehem*. A village scene portrays the biblical story of Joseph and Mary's arrival in Bethlehem just before the baby Jesus is born. The village is filled with adults and children. They seem unconcerned about the event soon to happen.

7 *It* refers to the miraculous birth of Jesus.

9 *They* refers to the Old Masters mentioned in line 2.

10–13 These lines refer to Breughel's painting *The Massacre of the Innocents*. The painting portrays the biblical story of King Herod's soldiers. They are shown killing baby boys in an attempt to destroy the Christ child. The parents look horrified, but the soldiers and animals seem unconcerned.

10–11 The terrible suffering **(dreadful martyrdom)** occurs off to the side of the painting.

12 Where the dogs . . . doggy life: The dogs go about their daily activities.

Reading Tip

This poem talks about three different paintings. Use three different-colored markers to highlight images from each painting.

English Learner Support
LANGUAGE

Diction In the phrase *about suffering they were never wrong,* the subject and object are reversed. In regular speech, one might say, "they were never wrong about suffering."

What Does It Mean?

Reverently means "done with great respect or awe."

Pause & Reflect

Review the details you circled as you read. How would you describe the activities that the speaker mentions? Check one word below. **(Evaluate)**

ordinary   unusual

amazing   amusing

The speaker next describes a particular painting. It portrays a drowning boy named Icarus. He has fallen from the sky into the sea. Read to find out how the onlookers respond to his suffering.

In Breughel's *Icarus,* for instance: how everything turns
    away

15 Quite leisurely from the disaster; the ploughman may
Have heard the splash, the forsaken cry,
But for him it was not an important failure; the sun shone
As it had to on the white legs disappearing into the green
Water; and the expensive delicate ship that must have seen
20 Something amazing, a boy falling out of the sky,
Had somewhere to get to and sailed calmly on.

Pause & Reflect

14 Breughel's Icarus (ĭk'ər-əs)**:** a reference to Breughel's painting *Landscape with the Fall of Icarus*. In Greek mythology, Icarus was the son of the craftsman Daedalus (dĕd'l-əs). Both father and son were held in prison. To fly away from prison, the father invented wings made of feathers and wax. Icarus, however, flew too close to the sun. Its heat melted the wax that held together his wings. Icarus then fell into the sea and drowned. The painting portrays his death as being ignored by the bystanders. A ship passes by, and a man plows his field. Only the legs of the drowning boy are shown disappearing into the sea.

15 ploughman: a farmer plowing his fields before planting seeds.

16 Icarus screams **(the forsaken cry)** as he falls into the sea **(the splash).**

As the poem ends . . .

- The speaker describes a painting of the story of Icarus, a character from Greek mythology.
- The speaker makes a comment on human suffering.

 Reading Check

How do the bystanders react to Icarus' fall?

More About . . .

IRONY Here, Auden uses irony to depict people's self-centeredness and indifference to others' suffering. The ship sails calmly even though the people on it see a boy drowning.

Pause & Reflect

1. To the ploughman in the painting, the boy's drowning is not an "important failure" (line 17). What kind of failure would the ploughman probably regard as important? Check one phrase below. **(Infer)**

a fire in the next village

the death of his horse

a disaster in a far-off land

 READ ALOUD **2.** Read aloud the boxed passage on page 358. Why doesn't the ship's captain simply turn his ship around and try to rescue the drowning boy? **(Cause and Effect)**

_____

_____

_____

✎ CHALLENGE

Tone is the author's attitude toward a subject. The subject of this poem is the way people respond to the suffering of strangers. How would you describe the author's attitude toward this subject? Mark words and phrases in the poem that support your answer. **(Analyze)**

Active Reading SkillBuilder

Drawing Conclusions

A work's **theme** is a central idea or message about life or human nature. To **draw conclusions** about a poem's theme, you combine what is implied or stated in the poem with your own prior knowledge. After reading "Musée des Beaux Arts," write down key phrases, images, and lines in the first column of the chart below. Then, in the second column, state your conclusions about them. An example is shown.

Phrases, Images, Lines	Conclusions
"how it [suffering] takes place/While someone else is eating ..." (lines 3–4)	While some people suffer, others go on about their daily activities.

Follow Up: Review your conclusions. State a central idea of the poem in your own words.

_____

_____

Literary Analysis SkillBuilder

Irony in Modern Poetry

In "Musée des Beaux Arts," the poet uses a technique called **situational irony.** This type of irony involves a contrast between what readers expect and what actually happens. Use the chart below to record examples of situational irony. In the first column, write down lines from the poem that you find ironic. In the second column, explain the irony. An example is shown.

Lines	Irony
"... even the dreadful martyrdom must run its course/Anyhow in a corner, some untidy spot/Where the dogs go on with their doggy life ... (lines 10–12)	I expected the dreadful martyrdom to occur in a special place, not in a place where animals run free.

Do Not Go Gentle into That Good Night

Dylan Thomas

Before You Read

Connect to Your Life

Dylan Thomas wrote poems about the things that were closest to his heart.
If you were a poet, what topics would you be inspired to write about?
What personal events would motivate you to begin writing? Jot down
your ideas in the space below.

_____

_____

_____

_____

Key to the Poem

WHAT YOU NEED TO KNOW In this poem, Thomas refers to light to
represent life and to the dark to represent death. As you read the poem,
look for examples of light that are contrasted with darkness or night.

Reading Tips

This poem is a **lyric poem**. It expresses deep feelings by using emotional language.

- Read the poem first silently and then aloud to get a sense of the speaker's feelings.

- Don't worry if you can't pin down the exact meaning of certain words and phrases. Instead, try to get a general idea of what the speaker means.

- The speaker describes various types of people. As you read, think of examples of people who fit each type.

- Use the Guide for Reading to help you understand unfamiliar words and difficult lines.

As the poem begins . . .

- The speaker tells how he thinks people should deal with their own deaths.

MARK IT UP **KEEP TRACK**

As you read, you can use these marks to keep track of your understanding.

✔ ..... I understand.

? ..... I don't understand this.

! ..... Interesting or surprising idea

Do Not Go Gentle into That Good Night

Dylan Thomas

PREVIEW Dylan Thomas (1914–1953) was a gifted poet who grew up in South Wales. Sadly, he died young—at the age of 39. Still, the poems he left behind seem fresh, alive, and new. He wrote of the things closest to his heart. He described his poetry as "the record of my individual struggle from darkness toward some measure of light."

One of his finest poems is "Do Not Go Gentle into That Good Night." Thomas wrote this poem as his father, a schoolteacher, was dying. The phrase "that good night" refers to death itself.

FOCUS

The speaker gives his dying father advice about how to face death. Read to find out what the speaker wants his father to do.

Do not go gentle into that good night,
Old age should burn and rave at close of day;
Rage, rage against the dying of the light.

Though wise men at their end know dark is right,
Because their words had forked no lightning they
Do not go gentle into that good night.

Good men, the last wave by, crying how bright
Their frail deeds might have danced in a green bay,
Rage, rage against the dying of the light.

Use this guide for help with unfamiliar words and difficult passages.

2 Old age should burn and rave at close of day: Old people should be hot-tempered and shout wildly as they near the end of life.

4 dark is right: death is a fitting end.

5 forked no lightning: This phrase may mean that the wise men's words could not produce lightning. That is, their words had no great effect.

7–8 how bright / Their frail deeds might have danced in a green bay: These lines suggest that good people realize that their acts, though weak **(frail),** might have worked wonders **(might have danced)** under different conditions **(in a green bay).**

English Learner Support
LANGUAGE

Metaphor Here, *close of day* means that life is like a single day. Just like night signals the end of a day, *that good night* signals the end of life, or death.

JOT IT DOWN **Reread Lines 1–3**

What does the speaker want his father to do? Check *one* phrase below. **(Infer)**

to die in peace

to draw up his will

to fight to stay alive

to trust in a higher power

10 Wild men who caught and sang the sun in flight,
And learn, too late, they grieved it on its way,
Do not go gentle into that good night.

Grave men, near death, who see with blinding sight
Blind eyes could blaze like meteors and be gay,
15 Rage, rage against the dying of the light.

And you, my (father,) there on the sad height,
Curse, bless, me now with your fierce tears, I pray.
Do not go gentle into that good night.
Rage, rage against the dying of the light.

Pause & *Reflect*

10 Wild men who caught and sang the sun in flight: This line may refer to poets—like Thomas himself—who live for the moment. They experience the present moment so strongly that time itself seems to stop.

13 Grave: serious.

14 Blind eyes could blaze like meteors and be gay: Thomas's father was blind; **meteors:** falling stars, or bright streaks that appear in the sky; **gay:** happy.

16 the sad height: This phrase may suggest that the father's bed is raised or that he is propped up in some way.

 Reading Check

What four kinds of people does the speaker mention? What do they all have in common?

More About . . .

DYLAN THOMAS'S FATHER David John Thomas was treated for tongue cancer in the 1930s, but he never fully recovered. By the time of his father's death in 1952, his son felt his father had lost his pride and his will to fight.

Pause & Reflect

 MARK IT UP Read aloud lines 16–19. How does the speaker feel about his father? Write your answer below. Then circle any words or phrases that led you to your answer. **(Draw Conclusions)**

_____

_____

_____

_____

CHALLENGE

Diction is a writer's choice of words. In this poem, strong verbs—such as *rage*—express powerful emotions. Mark at least four other examples of strong verbs in the poem. What emotions do they express? How do they contrast with the words used to describe death, such as "that good night"? **(Analyze)**

Active Reading SkillBuilder

Visualizing Setting in Poetry

"Do Not Go Gentle into That Good Night" is not a narrative poem. Still, the poem's subject implies a **setting.** After reading the poem, try to visualize a time and place for the speaker. On the chart below, write down words and phrases that suggest the setting. Then tell what the setting adds to the poem's meaning.

Time and Place	*by the father's bed as he lies ill and dying*
Words and Phrases That Suggest the Setting	
What the Setting Adds to the Meaning	

Literary Analysis SkillBuilder

Consonance and Assonance

Thomas's love of the sound of words is reflected in his use of **consonance** (a repetition of consonant sounds within and at the ends of words) and **assonance** (a repetition of vowel sounds in words). He uses both assonance and consonance to emphasize particular words, to create mood, and to add a musical quality to his poems. In the chart, record examples of consonance and assonance in "Do Not Go Gentle into That Good Night." Then describe the mood these examples help to create. An example is shown.

"Do Not Go Gentle into That Good Night"	
Assonance	**Consonance**
"Old age should burn and rave at close of day." (line 2) The long "o" and the long "a" vowel sounds are repeated.	
Mood	

from

The SPEECHES

May 19, 1940

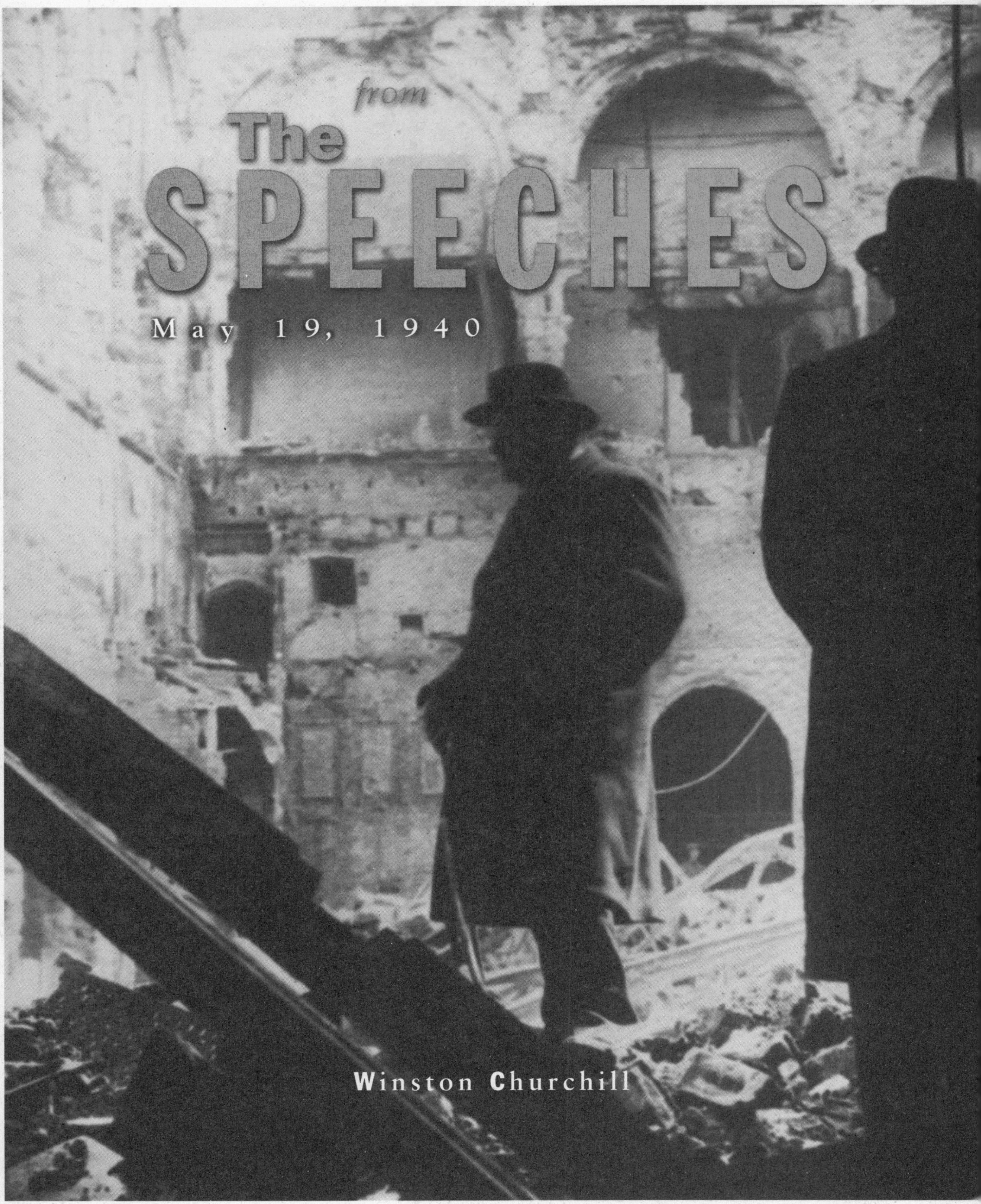

Winston Churchill

Before You Read

Connect to Your Life

The speeches you are about to read were delivered in a time of war. What kinds of thoughts and ideas would you like to hear from your leaders during a war? What kinds of words or behavior would make you feel confident during such a national crisis? Use the lines below to list some of your ideas.

_____

_____

_____

_____

Key to the Speech

WHAT YOU NEED TO KNOW Winston Churchill was one of the great leaders—and public speakers—of the 20th century. During World War II, he gave many radio speeches designed to keep up the spirits of the British people by instilling in them pride and a will to fight. For example, when talking about the need for all Britons to contribute to the war effort, he ended with the following:

> **The interests of property, the hours of labor, are nothing**
>
> **compared with the struggle for life and honor, for right**
>
> **and freedom, to which we have vowed ourselves.**

As you read Churchill's speeches, watch for particularly stirring passages that seem designed to instill in the British people pride, passion, and a will to win the war.

Reading Tips

Imagine yourself in England in the early years of World War II. The enemy is advancing, and you're worried about your country. You turn on the radio and hear Winston Churchill, your new prime minister, make his first **speech** to the nation.

- As you read this speech, remember that the words were written to be spoken. Try reading passages aloud.
- Watch for **loaded language**—words and phrases with strong emotional content.
- Use the Guide for Reading to help you understand unfamiliar words and difficult passages.

As the speech begins . . .

- Churchill describes how the French are fighting against the Germans.
- He explains that he is confident that together with the French, the British can defeat the Germans.

from

The SPEECHES

May 19, 1940

Winston Churchill

PREVIEW World War II began in Europe in 1939. By May of 1940, Nazi Germany had already taken control of Austria and Czechoslovakia and conquered Poland, Denmark, and Norway. On May 10, Hitler's forces invaded Holland and Belgium. Within days, the German forces began sweeping across France. British troops fighting in France were ready to retreat to England. The British people were worried about the fate of their nation and of the free world. Hoping to boost morale, Prime Minister Winston Churchill made the following radio speech to the British people.

FOCUS

Churchill explains how the war against the Germans is going. Read to find out about the military situation in May of 1940.

MARK IT UP As you read, circle details that describe the movement of the German forces across Europe. An example is highlighted.

I speak to you for the first time as Prime Minister in a solemn hour for the life of our country, of our Empire, of our Allies, and, above all, of the cause of Freedom. A tremendous battle is raging in France and Flanders. The Germans, by a remarkable combination of air bombing and heavily armored tanks, have broken through the French defenses north of the Maginot Line, and strong columns of their armored vehicles are ravaging the open country, which for the first day or two was without defenders. They have penetrated deeply and spread alarm and confusion in their track. Behind them there are now appearing infantry in lorries, and behind them, again, the large masses are moving forward. The regroupment of the French armies to make head against, and also to strike at, this intruding wedge has been proceeding for several days, largely assisted by the magnificent efforts of the Royal Air Force.

GUIDE FOR READING

Use this guide for help with unfamiliar words and difficult passages.

4 Allies: in World War II, the nations, such as England and France, that joined together to fight Germany, Italy, and Japan.

6 Flanders: western Belgium.

10 Maginot (măzh′ə-nō′) **Line:** a military fortification system built in the 1930s to guard the eastern border of France. It extended from Switzerland up to the Belgian border. The Germans bypassed the Maginot Line by entering France through Belgium.

16 lorries: the British term for motor trucks.

Reading Tip

Some of the sentences in this speech are long. Try to break the long sentences into shorter ones. Use the Guide for Reading, the side notes, and a dictionary for help with difficult words.

More About . . .

THE (PRIME MINISTER) England is a constitutional monarchy. In a constitutional monarchy, the monarch (queen or king) is the symbolic head of the nation. However, the prime minister is the real head of the government, just as the president is in the United States.

What Does It Mean?

Here, *columns* means "lines or formations of soldiers or war machines"—in this case, "lines of armored vehicles or tanks."

English Learner Support
VOCABULARY

Idiom *To make head against* means "to make progress against."

We must not allow ourselves to be intimidated by the presence of these armored vehicles in unexpected places behind our lines. If they are behind our Front, the French are also at many points fighting actively behind theirs. Both sides are therefore in an extremely dangerous position. And if the French Army, and our own Army, are well handled, as I believe they will be; if the French retain that genius for recovery and counterattack for which they have so long been famous; and if the British Army shows the <u>dogged</u> endurance and solid fighting power of which there have been so many examples in the past—then a sudden transformation of the scene might spring into being.

It would be foolish, however, to disguise the <u>gravity</u> of the hour. It would be still more foolish to lose heart and courage or to suppose that well-trained, well-equipped armies numbering three or four millions of men can be overcome in the space of a few weeks, or even months, by a scoop, or raid of mechanized vehicles, however formidable. We may look with confidence to the stabilization of the Front in France, and to the general engagement of the masses, which will enable the qualities of the French and British soldiers to be matched squarely against those of their adversaries. For myself, I have invincible confidence in the French Army and its leaders. Only a very small part of that splendid army has yet been heavily engaged; and only a very small part of France has yet been invaded. There is good evidence to show that practically the whole of the specialized and mechanized forces of the enemy have been already thrown into the battle; and we know that very heavy losses have been inflicted upon them. No officer or man, no brigade or division, which grapples at close quarters with the enemy, wherever encountered, can fail to make a worthy contribution to the general result. The Armies must cast away the idea of resisting behind concrete lines or natural obstacles, and must realize that mastery can only be regained by furious and unrelenting assault. And this spirit must not only <u>animate</u> the High Command, but must inspire every fighting man.

WORDS
TO
KNOW

dogged (dô′gĭd) *adj.* persistent; stubborn
gravity (grăv′ĭ-tē) *n.* seriousness; importance
animate (ăn′ə-māt′) *v.* to encourage; motivate

23 Front: the area where major fighting is taking place.

47–48 specialized and mechanical forces . . . into the battle: After World War I, the Germans rebuilt their armed forces, using the newest, most powerful tanks, aircraft, and weapons available.

53–55 The Armies must cast away . . . unrelenting assault: In World War II, the Germans launched swift and sudden attacks, using air and land forces. This type of warfare was known as a *blitzkrieg* (blĭts′krēg), or "lightning war." Churchill says that the Allies must launch a "furious and unrelenting" counterattack to win the war.

What Does It Mean?

Here, *front* means "the place where two armies meet and fight." When enemy soldiers get "behind the Front," it means that they have gotten into the defender's territory.

English Learner Support
LANGUAGE

Usage The highlighted phrase in lines 31–32 is complicated. However, it simply means" then things might suddenly change."

English Learner Support
LANGUAGE

Expression *Of the hour* means "of this time right now."

What Does It Mean?

Invincible means "unbeatable." Churchill means that nothing can make him lose confidence in the French Army and its leaders.

 **Reading Check**
Which countries are at war?

In the air—often at serious odds—often at odds hitherto thought overwhelming—we have been clawing down three or four to one of our enemies; and the relative balance of the British and German Air Forces is now considerably more favorable to us than at the beginning of the battle. In cutting down the German bombers, we are fighting our own battle as well as that of France. My confidence in our ability to fight it out to the finish with the German Air Force has been strengthened by the fierce encounters which have taken place and are taking place. At the same time, our heavy bombers are striking nightly at the taproot of German mechanized power, and have already inflicted serious damage upon the oil refineries on which the Nazi effort to dominate the world directly depends.

Pause & Reflect

FOCUS

Now Churchill prepares the British for the possibility of a German attack. He warns his fellow citizens that they must increase their efforts to win the war.

MARK IT UP As you read, underline passages that describe what the British public can do to help fight the war.

We must expect that as soon as stability is reached on the Western Front, the bulk of that hideous apparatus of aggression which gashed Holland into ruin and slavery in a few days, will be turned upon us. I am sure I speak for all when I say we are ready to face it; to endure it; and to <u>retaliate</u> against it—to any extent that the unwritten laws of war permit. There will be many men, and many women, in this island who when the ordeal comes upon them, as come it will, will feel comfort, and even a pride—that they are sharing the perils of our lads at the Front—soldiers, sailors and airmen, God bless them—and are drawing away from them a part at least of the onslaught they have to bear. Is not this the appointed time for all to make the utmost exertions in their power? If the battle is to be won, we must provide our men with ever-increasing quantities of the weapons and ammunition they need. We must have, and have quickly, more

WORDS TO KNOW

retaliate (rĭ-tăl′ē-āt′) v. to take revenge; pay back in kind

68 taproot: the main root, from which smaller roots spread out. In this case, the main source of power.

87 onslaught: violent attack.

English Learner Support

LANGUAGE

Metaphor In lines 59–60, Churchill is comparing his country's air force to eagles fighting with their sharp claws.

 Reading Check

How are British bombers hurting Germany?

Pause & *Reflect*

1. Review the details that you circled as you read. What gave Germany the advantage at this stage of the war? **(Draw Conclusions)**

_____

_____

 MARK IT UP **2.** Underline passages on pages 374 and 376 that explain why Churchill believes that the Allies can still turn back the Germans. **(Cause and Effect)**

As the speech continues ...

• Churchill warns civilians about what they should expect to happen.

• He explains what the British can to do help in the war effort.

What Does It Mean?

Hideous apparatus of aggression means "ugly machinery of war."

English Learner Support

LANGUAGE

Usage In lines 87–89, Churchill is using a rhetorical question to encourage people to prepare for war. A rhetorical question is a question that does not require a verbal answer. The sentence could be restated in this way: "It is now time for all of us to do as much as we can to help."

airplanes, more tanks, more shells, more guns. There is imperious need for these vital munitions. They increase our strength against the powerfully armed enemy. They replace the wastage of the obstinate struggle; and the knowledge that wastage will speedily be replaced enables us to draw more readily upon our reserves and throw them in now that everything counts so much.

Our task is not only to win the battle—but to win the War. After this battle in France abates its force, there will come the battle for our island—for all that Britain is, and all that Britain means. That will be the struggle. In that supreme emergency we shall not hesitate to take every step, even the most drastic, to call forth from our people the last ounce and the last inch of effort of which they are capable. The interests of property, the hours of labor, are nothing compared with the struggle for life and honor, for right and freedom, to which we have vowed ourselves.

Pause **&** *Reflect*

FOCUS

Read to find out why Churchill feels unity is so important and which groups he wants to unite.

I have received from the Chiefs of the French Republic, and in particular from its <u>indomitable</u> Prime Minister, M. Reynaud, the most sacred pledges that whatever happens they will fight to the end, be it bitter or be it glorious. Nay, if we fight to the end, it can only be glorious.

Having received His Majesty's commission, I have found an administration of men and women of every party and of almost every point of view. We have differed and quarreled in the past; but now one bond unites us all—to wage war until victory is won, and never to surrender ourselves to servitude and shame, whatever the cost and the agony may be. This is one of the most awe-striking periods in the long history of France and Britain. It is also beyond doubt the most sublime. Side by side, unaided except by their kith and kin in the great Dominions and by the wide Empires which rest beneath their

WORDS
TO
KNOW

indomitable (ĭn-dŏm′ĭ-tə-bəl) *adj.* not easily discouraged or defeated; unconquerable

GUIDE FOR READING

93 imperious (ĭm-pîr'ē-əs): urgent; pressing.

95 obstinate: difficult.

100 abates: lessens, weakens.

111–112 M. Reynaud: Paul Reynaud, who had long argued, like Churchill, for firmness toward Germany and for a close British-French alliance. (M. is an abbreviation of *Monsieur,* "Mister.")

116 commission: the authority to carry out particular duties. Churchill had just been appointed Prime Minister, the leader of Britain's parliamentary democracy.

120 servitude: lack of freedom.

124 kith and kin: friends and relatives.

125 Dominions: self-governing nations within the British Commonwealth. The British Commonwealth of Nations consists of the United Kingdom and former colonies that are now independent countries.

What Does It Mean?

Vital munitions means "the very important weaponry needed to fight the war."

English Learner Support
LANGUAGE

Figure of Speech When Churchill asks for "the last ounce and the last inch of effort," he means that the British must give all of their effort to help in the war.

Pause & Reflect

Review the passages that you underlined as you read. Then complete the following sentence:

In order to beat the German army, British civilians must _____

_____

_____

_____ .

(Clarify)

As the speech ends . . .

• Churchill declares that Britain and France will support each other in the war.

✔ Reading Check

What have the French leaders promised Churchill?

English Learner Support
VOCABULARY

Nay The word *nay* means "no."

shield—side by side, the British and French peoples have advanced to rescue not only Europe but mankind from the foulest and most soul-destroying tyranny which has ever darkened and stained the pages of history. Behind them—

130 behind us—behind the armies and fleets of Britain and France—gather a group of shattered States and bludgeoned races: the Czechs, the Poles, the Norwegians, the Danes, the Dutch, the Belgians—upon all of whom the long night of barbarism will descend, unbroken even by a star of hope, unless we conquer, as conquer we must; as conquer we shall.

Today is Trinity Sunday. Centuries ago words were written to be a call and a spur to the faithful servants of Truth and Justice: "Arm yourselves, and be ye men of valor, and be in readiness for the conflict; for it is better for us to perish in

140 battle than to look upon the outrage of our nation and our altar. As the Will of God is in Heaven, even so let it be."

Pause & Reflect

131 **bludgeoned:** beaten down.

136 **Trinity Sunday:** in Christianity, the eighth Sunday after Easter, dedicated to the Trinity (Father, Son, and Holy Spirit).

138 **"Arm yourselves . . . let it be":** a quotation from the Bible (1 Maccabees 3:58–60). This book of the Old Testament tells of the heroism of the Maccabees (măk′a-beez′). This brave Jewish family helped free the Jews from Syrian (sîr′ē-ən) rule during the second century B.C.

English Learner Support
LANGUAGE

Metaphor In this phrase, Churchill is referring to the countries that belong to the French and British Empires. He is equating the Empires to a shield that protects the subject countries.

What Does It Mean?
A *spur* is something that encourages action.

Pause & Reflect

READ ALOUD **1.** Read aloud the boxed passage on page 380. Why do you think Churchill repeats the words *behind* and *conquer?* **(Persuasive Language)**

_____

_____

MARK IT UP **2.** Circle the passage in this speech that you find most memorable. Explain why it sticks in your mind. **(Connect)**

_____

_____

CHALLENGE

Churchill's speeches had a great impact on the British people. How does Churchill appeal to the emotions of his audience? In your response, consider his use of words with strong emotional force. Mark words and phrases in the speech that support your answer. **(Style)**

Active Reading SkillBuilder

Evaluating Persuasive Language

In making emotional appeals to an audience, a speaker or writer may use **loaded language**—words and phrases with strong emotional content. Loaded language may be used to reinforce arguments. It may also be used to control the feelings of the audience. On the chart, note examples of loaded language in Winston Churchill's speech. Record the information the examples convey, the ideas they suggest, and the emotions they inspire. Examples are shown.

Loaded Word or Phrase	Information Provided	Ideas Suggested	Emotions Inspired
"the bulk of that hideous apparatus of aggression which gashed Holland into ruin and slavery . . . will be turned upon us" (lines 73–77)	The German army conquered Holland and will attack England.	The German army comes across as cruel and ferocious. It will destroy anything in its path.	fear, anger

Literary Analysis SkillBuilder

Persuasion

Persuasion is the technique of convincing an audience to adopt an opinion, perform an action, or both. It appeals to the mind by putting forward reasons and evidence to support opinions. It appeals to the emotions by stirring strong feelings within the audience. Find examples of these types of appeals in Churchill's speech. Two examples are shown.

Appeals to Reason	Appeals to Emotion
"If the battle is to be won, we must provide our men with ever-increasing quantities of the weapons and ammunition they need." (lines 89–91)	"There will be many ... who ... will feel comfort, and even a pride—that they are sharing the perils of our lads at the Front ..." (lines 81–85)

Words to Know SkillBuilder

Words to Know

| animate | dogged | gravity | indomitable | retaliate |

A. On each blank line, write the word from the word list that seems to go with each set of clues.

1. This is what people do by settling a score, getting even, and giving other people a dose of their own medicine.

_____

2. This describes those who stick with it, follow through, and keep their noses to the grindstone.

_____

3. This is more the purpose of the carrot than the stick. It's what "a shot in the arm" does. It helps people take heart.

_____

4. You are this if it's nigh unto impossible to get you to bite the dust or go down for the count. You just can't be beaten.

_____

5. This is what you want people to understand, all kidding aside, when something is no laughing matter.

_____

B. Decide which word from the word list belongs in each numbered blank. Then write the word on the blank line on the right.

We yelled and whooped; we tried and tried to (1) the team,
But there was little we could do, for they were out of steam.
So at the end, we taunted our opponents with the cheer,
"We'll mop the floor with you when we (2) next year!"

_____
(1)

_____
(2)

The mountain went straight up, it seemed,
But, (3), we kept climbing on,
Determined that, by afternoon,
The top is what we'd stand upon.
We reached the summit. Out I leaned,
So that the valley I could see.
My father said, "Please bear in mind
The (4) of gravity."

_____
(3)

_____
(4)

The foe that I face is almighty and strong.
I must use every weapon I've got.
My foe is the fear I must face to know if
It's (5) or not.

_____
(5)

C. Imagine that you are directing a scene from a play about Churchill in which an actor is to deliver the speech in the selection. Write notes to the actor about how the speech should be delivered. Use at least **three** of the Words to Know.

A SUNRISE ON THE VELD

DORIS LESSING

Before You Read

Connect to Your Life

Have you ever had an experience that changed the way you thought about yourself or the world? Use the chart to jot down your thoughts about this experience.

Experience: _____

HOW YOU VIEWED YOURSELF/ THE WORLD BEFORE	HOW YOU VIEWED YOURSELF/ THE WORLD AFTER

Key to the Story

WHAT'S THE BIG IDEA? The boy in the story is growing up, going through both physical and emotional changes. Use the concept web below to describe some of the changes that happen when people begin to reach adulthood.

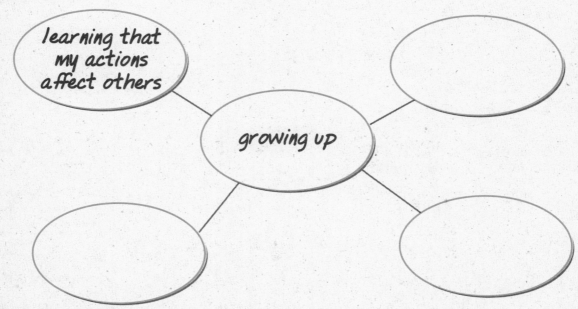

learning that my actions affect others

growing up

A SUNRISE ON THE VELD

DORIS LESSING

PREVIEW The veld (fĕlt) region of southern Africa is a beautiful, grassy land having only a few bushes and almost no trees. It is rich with wildlife. This story is about a 15-year-old boy living on the veld. On this particular morning, he feels completely in control of his life. While the boy is celebrating his happiness, he hears a strange cry. When the boy finally discovers the reasons for the sound, his beliefs about his place in the world are threatened. Will he ever be the same?

Reading Tips

This story may be difficult to read, especially in the beginning, because it has a great deal of **description** and not much action. The following strategies may help.

- Be patient and keep reading at a steady pace.

- Don't skip over the details because they will often provide you with important information about the **setting** and **main character.**

- As you read, try to put yourself in the position of the main character. Try to see, hear, and feel all the things that he does.

- Pay attention to how the main character changes and why this change takes place.

FOCUS

In this part of the story, you will get to know the main character. You will also learn about his morning routine of getting up before dawn and going out onto the veld to hunt.

MARK IT UP As you read, circle passages that tell you about his thoughts and what is important to him. An example is highlighted on page 388.

Every night that winter he said aloud into the dark of the pillow: Half-past four! Half-past four! till he felt his brain had gripped the words and held them fast. Then he fell asleep at once, as if a shutter had fallen; and lay with his face turned to the clock so that he could see it first thing when he woke.

It was half-past four to the minute, every morning. Triumphantly pressing down the alarm-knob of the clock, which the dark half of his mind had outwitted, remaining <u>vigilant</u> all night and counting the hours as he lay relaxed in sleep, he huddled down for a last warm moment under the clothes, playing with

As the story begins . . .

- The main character begins his morning activities.

MARK IT UP **KEEP TRACK**

As you read, you can use these marks to keep track of your understanding.

✔ ..... I understand.

? ..... I don't understand this.

! ..... Interesting or surprising idea

WORDS
TO
KNOW   **vigilant** (vĭj′ə-lənt) *adj.* ever watchful and alert

English Learner Support

VOCABULARY

Similarly Spelled Words The word *lightening* is sometimes confused with the word *lightning*. The word *lightening* means "an increase in light." *Lightning* refers to electrical discharges during a storm.

What Does It Mean?

The window is dangerous because it is the boy's parents' bedroom window and he doesn't want to wake them.

the idea of lying abed for this once only. But he played with it for the fun of knowing that it was a weakness he could defeat without effort; just as he set the alarm each night for the delight of the moment when he woke and stretched his limbs, feeling the muscles tighten, and thought: Even my brain—even that! I can control every part of myself.

Luxury of warm rested body, with the arms and legs and fingers waiting like soldiers for a word of command! Joy of knowing that the precious hours were given to sleep voluntarily!—for he had once stayed awake three nights running, to prove that he could, and then worked all day, refusing even to admit that he was tired; and now sleep seemed to him a servant to be commanded and refused.

The boy stretched his frame full-length, touching the wall at his head with his hands, and the bedfoot with his toes; then he sprung out, like a fish leaping from water. And it was cold, cold.

He always dressed rapidly, so as to try and conserve his night-warmth till the sun rose two hours later; but by the time he had on his clothes his hands were numbed and he could scarcely hold his shoes. These he could not put on for fear of waking his parents, who never came to know how early he rose.

As soon as he stepped over the lintel,[1] the flesh of his soles contracted on the chilled earth, and his legs began to ache with cold. It was night: the stars were glittering, the trees standing black and still. He looked for signs of day, for the greying of the edge of a stone, or a lightening in the sky where the sun would rise, but there was nothing yet. Alert as an animal he crept past the dangerous window, standing poised with his hand on the sill for one proudly <u>fastidious</u> moment, looking in at the stuffy blackness of the room where his parents lay.

Feeling for the grass-edge of the path with his toes, he reached inside another window further along the wall, where his gun had been set in readiness the night before. The steel was icy, and numbed fingers slipped along it, so that he had to hold it in the crook of his arm for safety. Then he tiptoed to the room where the dogs slept, and was fearful that they might

---

1. **lintel:** a piece of wood or stone beneath a doorway.

WORDS
TO
KNOW

fastidious (fă-stĭd′ē-əs) *adj.* displaying meticulous attention to detail

have been tempted to go before him; but they were waiting, their haunches crouched in reluctance at the cold, but ears and swinging tails greeting the gun ecstatically. His warning undertone kept them secret and silent till the house was a hundred yards back: then they bolted off into the bush, yelping excitedly. The boy imagined his parents turning in their beds and muttering: Those dogs again! before they were dragged back in sleep; and he smiled scornfully. He always looked back over his shoulder at the house before he passed a wall of trees that shut it from sight. It looked so low and small, crouching there under a tall and brilliant sky. Then he turned his back on it, and on the frowsting[2] sleepers, and forgot them.

He would have to hurry. Before the light grew strong he must be four miles away; and already a tint of green stood in the hollow of a leaf, and the air smelled of morning and the stars were dimming.

He slung the shoes over his shoulder, veld *skoen*[3] that were crinkled and hard with the dews of a hundred mornings. They would be necessary when the ground became too hot to bear. Now he felt the chilled dust push up between his toes, and he let the muscles of his feet spread and settle into the shapes of the earth; and he thought: I could walk a hundred miles on feet like these! I could walk all day, and never tire!

He was walking swiftly through the dark tunnel of foliage that in day-time was a road. The dogs were invisibly ranging the lower travelways of the bush, and he heard them panting. Sometimes he felt a cold muzzle on his leg before they were off again, scouting for a trail to follow. They were not trained, but free-running companions of the hunt, who often tired of the long stalk before the final shots, and went off on their own pleasure. Soon he could see them, small and wild-looking in a wild strange light, now that the bush stood trembling on the verge of color, waiting for the sun to paint earth and grass afresh.

The grass stood to his shoulders; and the trees were showering a faint silvery rain. He was soaked; his whole body was clenched in a steady shiver.

Once he bent to the road that was newly scored with animal trails, and regretfully straightened, reminding himself that the pleasure of tracking must wait till another day.

---

2. **frowsting** (frou′stĭng): a British term for lounging about.

3. *skoen* (skōōn) *Afrikaans*: shoes.

English Learner Support
VOCABULARY

Ecstatically *Ecstatically* means "in an extremely happy way."

More About...

THE BUSH is another name for the veld. This area of South Africa is nearly treeless and gets its name from the low, bushy plants that cover it.

English Learner Support
CULTURE

Skoen *Skoen* is a word in the Afrikaans language. Afrikaans developed from the native language of the Dutch settlers who moved to South Africa more than 300 years ago. The language, which is spoken in South Africa and Namibia, also contains elements of English, German, French, and some African languages.

What Does It Mean?

With the dews of a hundred mornings means that when the boy went out in the early mornings, his shoes got wet in the dew and then dried out over and over. A hundred mornings means "many mornings"—not necessarily one hundred.

Pause & Reflect

Circle the four words or phrases below that best describe the boy at this point in the story. **(Draw Conclusions)**

adventurous	fearful
practical	confident
disorganized	in control

As the story continues . . .

- The boy goes out to the landscape of the veld.
- The boy expresses great happiness.

English Learner Support
LANGUAGE

Metaphor *Diamond drops sparkled on each frond* is a metaphor that compares the dew on the leaves to diamonds.

He began to run along the edge of a field, noting jerkily how it was filmed over with fresh spiderweb, so that the long reaches of great black clods seemed netted in glistening grey. He was using the steady lope he had learned by watching the natives, the run that is a dropping of the weight of the body from one foot to the next in a slow balancing movement that never tires, nor shortens the breath; and he felt the blood 100 pulsing down his legs and along his arms, and the exultation and pride of body mounted in him till he was shutting his teeth hard against a violent desire to shout his triumph.

Pause & Reflect

FOCUS
Now the boy and his dogs leave the farm and go out onto the veld. Soon the boy is overcome with joy. Read to learn more about why he feels so happy this particular morning.

110

Soon he had left the cultivated part of the farm. Behind him the bush was low and black. In front was a long vlei,[4] acres of long pale grass that sent back a hollowing gleam of light to a satiny sky. Near him thick swathes of grass were bent with the weight of water, and diamond drops sparkled on each frond.

The first bird woke at his feet and at once a flock of them sprang into the air calling shrilly that day had come; and suddenly, behind him, the bush woke into song, and he could hear the guinea fowl[5] calling far ahead of him. That meant they would now be sailing down from their trees into thick grass, and it was for them he had come: he was too late. But he did not mind. He forgot he had come to shoot. He set his legs wide, and balanced from foot to foot, and swung his gun up and down in both hands horizontally, 120 in a kind of improvised exercise, and let his head sink back till it was pillowed in his neck muscles, and watched how above him small rosy clouds floated in a lake of gold.

---

4. **vlei** (flā): low, swampy land.

5. **guinea fowl:** pheasantlike birds that have dark gray bodies flecked with white.

Suddenly it all rose in him: it was unbearable. He leapt up into the air, shouting and yelling wild, unrecognizable noises. Then he began to run, not carefully, as he had before, but madly, like a wild thing. He was clean crazy, yelling mad with the joy of living and a superfluity of youth. He rushed down the vlei under a tumult of crimson and gold, while all the birds of the world sang about him. He ran in great leaping strides, and shouted as

130 he ran, feeling his body rise into the crisp rushing air and fall back surely on to sure feet; and thought briefly, not believing that such a thing could happen to him, that he could break his ankle any moment, in this thick tangled grass. He cleared bushes like a duiker,[6] leapt over rocks; and finally came to a dead stop at a place where the ground fell abruptly away below him to the river. It had been a two-mile-long dash through waist-high growth, and he was breathing hoarsely and could no longer sing. But he poised on a rock and looked down at stretches of water that gleamed through stooping trees, and thought suddenly, I am

140 fifteen! Fifteen! The words came new to him; so that he kept repeating them wonderingly, with swelling excitement; and he felt the years of his life with his hands, as if he were counting marbles, each one hard and separate and compact, each one a wonderful shining thing. That was what he was: fifteen years of this rich soil, and this slow-moving water, and air that smelt like a challenge whether it was warm and sultry at noon, or as brisk as cold water, like it was now.

There was nothing he couldn't do, nothing! A vision came to him, as he stood there, like when a child hears the word

150 "eternity" and tries to understand it, and time takes possession of the mind. He felt his life ahead of him as a great and wonderful thing, something that was his; and he said aloud, with the blood rising to his head: all the great men of the world have been as I am now, and there is nothing I can't become, nothing I can't do; there is no country in the world I cannot make part of myself, if I choose. I contain the world. I can make of it what I want. If I choose, I can change everything that is going to happen: it depends on me, and what I decide now.

Pause & Reflect

---

6. **duiker** (dī′kər): small African antelope.

superfluity (soo′pər-floo′ĭ-tē) *n.* excess; overabundance; oversupply

Clean In this context, *clean* means "completely."

Pause & Reflect

MARK IT UP 1. Why does the boy go so far out onto the veld each morning? Star the passage on page 390 that tells what he usually does there. (**Clarify**)

READ ALOUD 2. Read aloud the boxed passage. What do the boy's words reveal about his attitude toward life? (**Draw Conclusions**)

_____

_____

_____

_____

3. As the veld comes to life, the boy begins to leap, shout, yell, and run. From the list below, circle two reasons that help explain why. (**Infer**)

The boy is proud of his hunting skills.

The boy is happy to be alive.

The boy feels that he can do anything.

The boy has achieved victory.

As the story continues . . .

- The boy's happy mood changes after he hears a terrible noise.

- The boy sees a wounded animal.

English Learner Support

VOCABULARY

Idiom *He came to himself* means that the boy began to pay attention to his surroundings again.

FOCUS

As the boy continues to sing, he hears another voice—the voice of an animal crying out in agony. Read to find out what is causing the animal's pain.

The urgency, and the truth and the courage of what his voice was saying exulted him so that he began to sing again, at the top of his voice, and the sound went echoing down the river gorge. He stopped for the echo, and sang again: stopped and shouted. That was what he was!—he sang, if he chose; and the world had to answer him.

And for minutes he stood there, shouting and singing and waiting for the lovely eddying[7] sound of the echo; so that his own new strong thoughts came back and washed round his head, as if someone were answering him and encouraging him; till the gorge was full of soft voices clashing back and forth from rock to rock over the river. And then it seemed as if there was a new voice. He listened, puzzled, for it was not his own. Soon he was leaning forward, all his nerves alert, quite still: somewhere close to him there was a noise that was no joyful bird, nor tinkle of falling water, nor ponderous[8] movement of cattle.

There it was again. In the deep morning hush that held his future and his past, was a sound of pain, and repeated over and over: it was a kind of shortened scream, as if someone, something, had no breath to scream. He came to himself, looked about him, and called for the dogs. They did not appear: they had gone off on their own business, and he was alone. Now he was clean sober, all the madness gone. His heart beating fast, because of that frightened screaming, he stepped carefully off the rock and went towards a belt of trees. He was moving cautiously, for not so long ago he had seen a leopard in just this spot.

At the edge of the trees he stopped and peered, holding his gun ready; he advanced, looking steadily about him, his eyes narrowed. Then, all at once, in the middle of a step, he faltered, and his face was puzzled. He shook his head impatiently, as if he doubted his own sight.

There, between two trees, against a background of gaunt black rocks, was a figure from a dream, a strange beast that was horned and drunken-legged, but like something he had never even imagined. It seemed to be ragged. It looked like a

---

7. **eddying** (ĕd'ē-ĭng): moving contrary to the main current; circling.

8. **ponderous:** clumsy because of heaviness and size.

small buck that had black ragged tufts of fur standing up
200 irregularly all over it, with patches of raw flesh beneath . . .
but the patches of rawness were disappearing under moving
black and came again elsewhere; and all the time the creature
screamed, in small gasping screams, and leaped drunkenly
from side to side, as if it were blind.

Then the boy understood: it *was* a buck. He ran closer, and
again stood still, stopped by a new fear. Around him the grass
was whispering and alive. He looked wildly about, and then
down. The ground was black with (ants,) great energetic ants
that took no notice of him, but hurried and scurried towards
210 the fighting shape, like glistening black water flowing through
the grass.

And, as he drew in his breath and pity and terror seized
him, the beast fell and the screaming stopped. Now he could
hear nothing but one bird singing, and the sound of the
rustling, whispering ants.

He peered over at the writhing blackness that jerked
convulsively with the jerking nerves. It grew quieter. There
were small twitches from the mass that still looked vaguely
like the shape of a small animal.

Pause & *Reflect*

FOCUS
220
The buck is dying a
slow, painful death. The
boy wonders if he
should shoot the buck
to end its pain or let it
die naturally. Read to
find out what the boy
decides to do.

It came into his mind that he should
shoot it and end its pain; and he raised
the gun. Then he lowered it again. The
buck could no longer feel; its fighting
was a mechanical protest of the nerves.
But it was not that which made him put
down the gun. It was a swelling feeling
of rage and misery and protest that
expressed itself in the thought: if I had not come it would
have died like this: so why should I interfere? All over the
230 bush things like this happen; they happen all the time; this is
how life goes on, by living things dying in anguish. He
gripped the gun between his knees and felt in his own limbs
the myriad swarming pain of the twitching animal that could
no longer feel, and set his teeth, and said over and over again

✔ Reading Check
What is happening to the buck?

More About . . .
ANTS The driver ants of Africa
swarm over the ground looking
for food. They live in colonies of
over one million ants. These
colonies can kill lizards, birds,
snakes, and sometimes animals
as large as horses. A single
colony can eat 100,000 insects
in one day.

Pause & Reflect
How do the buck's screams
affect the boy? (Cause and
Effect)

_____
_____
_____
_____

As the story
continues . . .
• As he watches the buck,
the boy learns an important
lesson about life.

WORDS
TO
KNOW
myriad (mĭr´ē-əd) *adj.* made up of many different
elements or parts

MARK IT UP **1.** The boy
thinks about shooting the buck
but changes his mind. Why?
Circle details on page 393 that
support your answer. **(Evaluate)**

_____

_____

_____

_____

2. A change is beginning to take
place in the boy's feelings about
himself. Circle two phrases
below that correctly complete
the following sentence:
The boy begins to realize that

_____.

everything must die

he is unsafe

there are things in life he
  cannot control
(Analyze)

As the story continues . . .

• The boy watches the ants and
becomes angry.

• He tries to figure out how the
buck could have been killed
so easily.

English Learner Support

Swear Here, *swear* means
"to curse." It can also mean
"to make a promise."

under his breath: I can't stop it. I can't stop it. There is
nothing I can do.

He was glad that the buck was unconscious and had gone
past suffering so that he did not have to make a decision to
kill it even when he was feeling with his whole body: this is
240 what happens, this is how things work.

It was right—that was what he was feeling. *It was right
and nothing could alter it.*

The knowledge of fatality, of what has to be, had gripped
him and for the first time in his life; and he was left unable to
make any movement of brain or body, except to say: "Yes,
yes. That is what living is." It had entered his flesh and his
bones and grown in to the furthest corners of his brain and
would never leave him. And at that moment he could not
have performed the smallest action of mercy, knowing as he
250 did, having lived on it all his life, the vast unalterable, cruel
veld, where at any moment one might stumble over a skull or
crush the skeleton of some small creature.

FOCUS
Read on to learn why
the buck's death
angers the boy.

Suffering, sick, and angry, but also
grimly satisfied with his new stoicism,[9]
he stood there leaning on his rifle, and
watched the seething black mound grow
smaller. At his feet, now, were ants
trickling back with pink fragments in their mouths, and there
was a fresh acid smell in his nostrils. He sternly controlled the
260 uselessly convulsing muscles of his empty stomach, and
reminded himself: the ants must eat too! At the same time he
found that the tears were streaming down his face, and his
clothes were soaked with the sweat of that other creature's pain.

The shape had grown small. Now it looked like nothing
recognizable. He did not know how long it was before he saw
the blackness thin, and bits of white showed through, shining
in the sun—yes, there was the sun, just up, glowing over the
rocks. Why, the whole thing could not have taken longer than
a few minutes.

270 He began to swear, as if the shortness of the time was in
itself unbearable, using the words he had heard his father say.

---

9. **stoicism** (stō′ĭ-sĭz′əm): calm acceptance of events, whether good or bad.

He strode forward, crushing ants with each step, and brushing them off his clothes, till he stood above the skeleton, which lay sprawled under a small bush. It was clean-picked. It might have been lying there years, save that on the white bone were pink fragments of gristle. About the bones ants were ebbing away, their pincers full of meat.

The boy looked at them, big black ugly insects. A few were standing and gazing up at him with small glittering eyes.

280 "Go away!" he said to the ants, very coldly. "I am not for you—not just yet, at any rate. Go away." And he fancied that the ants turned and went away.

He bent over the bones and touched the sockets in the skull; that was where the eyes were, he thought underlinedly incredulously, remembering the liquid dark eyes of a buck. And then he bent the slim foreleg bone, swinging it horizontally in his palm.

That morning, perhaps an hour ago, this small creature had been stepping proud and free through the bush, feeling the chill on its hide even as he himself had done, exhilarated by it.
290 Proudly stepping the earth, tossing its horns, frisking a pretty white tail, it had sniffed the cold morning air. Walking like kings and conquerors it had moved through this free-held bush, where each blade of grass grew for it alone, and where the river ran pure sparkling water for its slaking.[10]

And then—what had happened? Such a swift surefooted thing could surely not be trapped by a swarm of ants?

Pause & Reflect

FOCUS

Read the rest of the story to learn what circumstances may 300 have caused the buck to be trapped by the ants.

MARK IT UP As you read, note in the margins any changes you see in the boy's behavior and feelings.

The boy bent curiously to the skeleton. Then he saw that the back leg that lay uppermost and strained out in the tension of death, was snapped midway in the thigh, so that broken bones jutted over each other uselessly. So that was it! Limping into the ant-masses it could not escape, once it had sensed the danger. Yes, but how had the leg

10. **slaking:** quenching of thirst.

WORDS
TO
KNOW

incredulously (mĭr'ē-əd) *adj.* in a manner showing disbelief.

What Does It Mean?

Here, *fancied* means "imagined" or "wanted to believe it to be true."

Pause & Reflect

1. What is left of the buck after the ants have finished their attack? Circle details on pages 394–395 that support your answer. **(Visualize)**

_____

_____

2. The boy accepts the knowledge that death comes to all, yet he can't keep from crying and getting angry. Why? **(Infer)**

_____

_____

3. What questions does the boy begin to ask about the buck's fate? **(Clarify)**

_____

_____

As the story ends . . .

• The boy guesses why the buck became trapped.

• He returns to the farm in a very different mood from when he left it.

Idiom *Knitting his brows* means that the boy is thinking so hard that he is frowning, causing his forehead to wrinkle.

Pause & Reflect

1. The boy imagines two possible causes that may have led to the buck's injury. **Summarize** each of these possibilities.

_____

_____

_____

MARK IT UP 2. How does the boy feel as he returns home? Underline passages in the story that support your answer. (**Draw Conclusions**)

_____

_____

_____

3. Review the notes you made as you read. How has the boy changed since the beginning of the story? (**Analyze**)

_____

_____

_____

_____

CHALLENGE
What is the main message, or **theme,** of this story? Think about how the main character changed after seeing the buck. What did he learn from the experience? Mark the passages that you think show the theme.

been broken? Had it fallen, perhaps? Impossible, a buck was too light and graceful. Had some jealous rival horned it?

What could possibly have happened? Perhaps some Africans had thrown stones at it, as they do, trying to kill it
310 for meat, and had broken its leg. Yes, that must be it.

Even as he imagined the crowd of running, shouting natives, and the flying stones, and the leaping buck, another picture came into his mind. He saw himself, on any one of these bright ringing mornings, drunk with excitement, taking a snap shot at some half-seen buck. He saw himself with the gun lowered, wondering whether he had missed or not; and thinking at last that it was late, and he wanted his breakfast, and it was not worth while to track miles after an animal that would very likely get away from him in any case.

320 For a moment he would not face it. He was a small boy again, kicking sulkily at the skeleton, hanging his head, refusing to accept the responsibility.

Then he straightened up, and looked down at the bones with an odd expression of dismay, all the anger gone out of him. His mind went quite empty: all around him he could see trickles of ants disappearing into the grass. The whispering noise was faint and dry, like the rustling of a cast snakeskin.

At last he picked up his gun and walked homewards. He was telling himself half defiantly that he wanted his breakfast.
330 He was telling himself that it was getting very hot, much too hot to be out roaming the bush.

Really, he was tired. He walked heavily, not looking where he put his feet. When he came within sight of his home he stopped, knitting his brows. There was something he had to think out. The death of that small animal was a thing that concerned him, and he was by no means finished with it. It lay at the back of his mind uncomfortably.

Soon, the very next morning, he would get clear of everybody and go to the bush and think about it.

340

Pause & Reflect

Active Reading SkillBuilder

Analyzing Character Development

Characters frequently change over the course of a story. A key event often
causes this change. Being aware of a character's thoughts and actions can help
readers figure out what event causes a character to change and how the
character develops as a result. Fill in the chart, listing the thoughts and actions of the
boy in "A Sunrise on the Veld." Choose examples that you think are important for
understanding his character. The chart is started for you.

Thoughts	Actions
"I can control every part of myself." (line 21)	The boy programs himself to wake up at exactly 4:30 every morning.

Literary Analysis SkillBuilder

Kinesthetic Imagery

Imagery that describes the tension and movement of muscles, tendons, and joints is called **kinesthetic** (kĭn´ĭs-thĕt´ĭc) **imagery.** In "A Sunrise on the Veld," Lessing uses this type of imagery to describe the boy, his dogs, and the veld wildlife. Find examples of kinesthetic imagery in the story and record them on the chart. Examples are provided.

Kinesthetic Imagery Describing . . .		
The Boy	**His Dogs**	**Veld Wildlife**
"stretched his limbs, feeling the muscles tighten" (lines 19–20)	"their haunches crouched in reluctance at the cold" (line 54)	"sailing down from their trees into thick grass" (lines 115–116)

Words to Know SkillBuilder

Words to Know

fastidious   incredulously   myriad   superfluity   vigilant

A. Decide which word from the word list belongs in each numbered blank.
Then write the word on the blank line on the right.

His shirt's not stained by pumpkin pie.
There are no wrinkles in his tie.
Why is he such a tidy guy?
He's quite (1), that's why.

_____
(1)

Hors d'oeuvres, then soup, then fish, then meat,
Then salad, cheese, and something sweet . . .
I'm glad I didn't have to miss
A feast as (2) as this!

_____
(2)

The owl will catch and eat you—it's his habit—
If you're not (3), my little rabbit.

_____
(3)

I said, "There's no such thing as too much cake."
I never thought that you would go and bake
Four cakes for me
And, for you, three.
Yes, I give up. You're right. This makes
A (4) of cakes.

_____
(4)

"Let me buy you a large sundae, any flavor,"
My brother said. "I do not need a favor.
My motives are quite innocent and pure."
(5), I said, "Oh, I'm sure."

_____
(5)

B. Fill in each blank with the correct word from the word list.

1. During a _____ of rain, flooding may occur.

2. She is too _____ to make careless errors.

3. It is a sentry's job to be _____ .

4. Imagine how _____ Europeans must have
   reacted upon seeing a
   giraffe for the first time.

5. I am fascinated by the _____ opportunities in
   the city.

C. Write a diary entry the boy in "A Sunrise on the Veld" might have written as part of his
planned effort to "think out" the event he witnessed. Use at least **two** of the Words to Know.

Chinua Achebe

CIVIL PEACE

Before You Read

Connect to Your Life

War has been described as the great equalizer—wealth, social position, and material possessions do not insure survival and therefore have less value. How do you think survivors of war might view life differently than they did before the war? What aspects of life would be valued more? What would seem less important? Describe your ideas on the lines below.

_____

_____

_____

_____

_____

Key to the Story

WHAT YOU NEED TO KNOW Chinua Achebe is considered one of the founders of a new literature that draws inspiration from the African oral tradition and culture. Achebe, who writes in English, conveys the perspective and experience of the Nigerian people. He uses imagery, proverbs, folktales, and religious beliefs to express the wisdom and beauty of traditional Africa.

CIVIL PEACE

Chinua Achebe

PREVIEW Chinua Achebe (chĭn'wä ä-chä'bä) was born in Nigeria. He first learned to speak in his native Ibo (ē'bō) and then, at the age of eight, began to study English. He often writes about conflicts in his native country, which is on the western coast of Africa. In 1967, the Ibo people in the eastern part set up their own republic, called Biafra (bē-äf'rə). A civil war began, which lasted until 1970. More than 1.5 million people in Biafra starved to death before their leaders surrendered.

This story is about a family struggling to survive in the first days of peace. Times are dangerous, and money is scarce. Many people are without food and housing.

FOCUS
In this part, you meet the main character, Jonathan Iwegbu (ē-wĕg'boo). He is trying to put his family's life back together after the terrible war.

🖉 **MARK IT UP** As you read, underline details that help you get to know this character. An example is highlighted.

Jonathan Iwegbu counted himself extraordinarily lucky. "Happy survival!" meant so much more to him than just a current fashion of greeting old friends in the first hazy days of peace. It went deep to his heart. He had come out of the war with five inestimable[1] blessings—his head, his wife Maria's head and the heads of three out of their four children. As a bonus he also had his old bicycle—a miracle too but naturally not to be compared to the safety of five human heads.

---

1. **inestimable** (ĭn-ĕs'tə-mə-bəl): of great value.

The bicycle had a little history of its own. One day at the height of the war it was commandeered[2] "for urgent military action." Hard as its loss would have been to him he would still have let it go without a thought had he not had some doubts about the genuineness of the officer. It wasn't his disreputable[3] rags, nor the toes peeping out of one blue and one brown
20 canvas shoes, nor yet the two stars of his rank done obviously in a hurry in biro,[4] that troubled Jonathan; many good and heroic soldiers looked the same or worse. It was rather a certain lack of grip and firmness in his manner. So Jonathan, suspecting he might be amenable[5] to influence, rummaged in his raffia[6] bag and produced the two pounds with which he had been going to buy firewood which his wife, Maria, retailed[7] to camp officials for extra stock-fish and corn meal, and got his bicycle back. That night he buried it in the little clearing in the bush where the dead of the camp, including his
30 own youngest son, were buried. When he dug it up again a year later after the surrender all it needed was a little palm-oil greasing. "Nothing puzzles God," he said in wonder.

He put it to immediate use as a taxi and accumulated a small pile of Biafran money ferrying camp officials and their families across the four-mile stretch to the nearest tarred road. His standard charge per trip was six pounds and those who had the money were only glad to be rid of some of it in this way. At the end of a fortnight[8] he had made a small fortune of one hundred and fifteen pounds.

40 Then he made the journey to Enugu[9] and found another miracle waiting for him. It was unbelievable. He rubbed his eyes and looked again and it was still standing there before him. But, needless to say, even that monumental[10] blessing must be accounted also totally inferior to the five heads in the family.

---

2. **commandeered** (kŏm'ən-dîrd'): taken for military use.

3. **disreputable** (dĭs-rĕp'yə-tə-bəl): shameful.

4. **biro** (bîr'ō): a British term for a ballpoint pen. The officer's insignia, that is, had been drawn in ink.

5. **amenable** (ə-mē'nə-bəl): responsive; open.

6. **raffia**: a palm fiber used for weaving mats, baskets, and hats.

7. **retailed**: sold.

8. **fortnight**: 14 days or two weeks.

9. **Enugu** (ā-nōō'gōō): a city in southeastern Nigeria.

10. **monumental**: great.

What Does It Mean?

Of the camp refers to the fact that Jonathan and his family have been living in a refugee camp. A refugee camp is a temporary living place for people who have lost their homes, often during war.

✔ Reading Check

Which member of Jonathan's family died during the war?

Reading Tip

The sentence "Nothing puzzles God" is repeated in this story. Highlight the sentence each time it appears. Then, in a chart like this one, jot down words and phrases to describe what is happening in the story each time that sentence appears.

Nothing puzzles God.	
p. 403	Jonathan finds his bicycle again; he can't believe it.

This newest miracle was his little house in Ogui Overside. Indeed nothing puzzles God! Only two houses away a huge concrete edifice some wealthy contractor had put up just before the war was a mountain of rubble. And here was Jonathan's little zinc house[11] of no regrets built with mud blocks quite intact!

50 Of course the doors and windows were missing and five sheets off the roof. But what was that? And anyhow he had returned to Enugu early enough to pick up bits of old zinc and wood and soggy sheets of cardboard lying around the neighborhood before thousands more came out of their forest holes looking for the same things. He got a destitute[12] carpenter with one old hammer, a blunt plane and a few bent and rusty nails in his tool bag to turn this assortment of wood, paper and metal into door and window shutters for five Nigerian shillings or fifty Biafran pounds.[13] He paid the pounds, and moved in with his overjoyed

60 family carrying five heads on their shoulders.

Pause & *Reflect*

His children picked mangoes near the military cemetery and sold them to soldiers' wives for a few pennies—real pennies this time—and his wife started making breakfast akara[14] balls for neighbors in a hurry to start life again. With his family earnings he took his bicycle to the villages around and bought fresh palm-wine which he mixed generously in his rooms with the water which had recently started running

70 again in the public tap down the road, and opened up a bar for soldiers and other lucky people with good money.

At first he went daily, then every other day and finally once a week, to the offices of the Coal Corporation where he used to be a miner, to find out what was what. The only thing he did find out in the end was that that little house of his was even a greater blessing than he had thought. Some of his fellow examiners who had nowhere to return at the end of the

---

11. **zinc house:** a house roofed with sheets of metal.

12. **destitute:** poor.

13. **five Nigerian shillings or fifty Biafran pounds:** There are two types of money in Biafra after the civil war: Nigerian money and Biafran money. Nigerian money is worth much more.

14. **akara** (ä-kä′rä) **balls:** bean cakes.

day's waiting just slept outside the doors of the offices and cooked what meal they could scrounge together in Bournvita tins. As the weeks lengthened and still nobody could say what was what Jonathan discontinued his weekly visits altogether and faced his palm-wine bar.

But nothing puzzles God. Came the day of the windfall[15] when after five days of endless scuffles in queues[16] and counter-queues in the sun outside the Treasury he had twenty pounds counted into his palms as ex-gratia[17] award for the rebel money he had turned in. It was like Christmas for him and for many others like him when the payments began. They called it (since few could manage its proper official name) *egg-rasher*.

As soon as the pound notes were placed in his palm Jonathan simply closed it tight over them and buried fist and money inside his trouser pocket. He had to be extra careful because he had seen a man a couple of days earlier collapse into near-madness in an instant before that oceanic crowd[18] because no sooner had he got his twenty pounds than some heartless ruffian[19] picked it off him. Though it was not right that a man in such an extremity of agony should be blamed yet many in the queues that day were able to remark quietly on the victim's carelessness, especially after he pulled out the innards of his pocket and revealed a hole in it big enough to pass a thief's head. But of course he had insisted that the money had been in the other pocket, pulling it out too to show its comparative wholeness. So one had to be careful.

Jonathan soon transferred the money to his left hand and pocket so as to leave his right free for shaking hands should the need arise, though by fixing his gaze at such an elevation as to miss all approaching human faces he made sure that the need did not arise, until he got home.

He was normally a heavy sleeper but that night he heard all the neighborhood noises die down one after another. Even the night watchman who knocked the hour on some metal somewhere in the distance had fallen silent after knocking one o'clock. That must have been the last thought in Jonathan's mind

---

15. **windfall:** a sudden bit of good luck.

16. **queues** (kyo͞oz): lines of waiting people.

17. **ex-gratia** (ĕks′grā′shə): given as a favor.

18. **that oceanic crowd:** a crowd of great size and force.

19. **ruffian** (rŭf′ē-ən): a tough fellow.

Do you think Jonathan will be able to keep the 20 pounds? *Yes/No*, because _____

_____

_____

_____ .

(Predict)

As the story ends . . .

• Jonathan's family is threatened by a group of thieves.

• Jonathan handles the thieves and goes on with his life.

English Learner Support
VOCABULARY

Dialect The thieves in the story speak a dialect of English that is found in Nigeria. The spelling and pronunciation of this dialect are different from standard English. Use context clues, the footnotes, and the following glossary to help you read the lines of dialect.

  na means "it is"

  soja means "soldiers"

  commot means "leave"

  am means "it"

  wetin means "what"

  katakata means "trouble"

before he was finally carried away himself. He couldn't have been gone for long, though, when he was violently awakened again.

"Who is knocking?" whispered his wife lying beside him on the floor.

"I don't know," he whispered back breathlessly.

Pause **&** **Reflect**

FOCUS

A thief and his followers pound on Jonathan's door. They try to force him to give up his money. Read to find out how Jonathan reacts to this threat.

The second time the knocking came it was so loud and imperious[20] that the rickety old door could have fallen down.

"Who is knocking?" he asked then, his voice parched and trembling.

"Na tief-man and him people,"[21] came the cool reply. "Make you hopen de door." This was followed by the heaviest knocking of all.

Maria was the first to raise the alarm, then he followed and all their children.

"Police-o! Thieves-o! Neighbors-o! Police-o! We are lost! We are dead! Neighbors, are you asleep? Wake up! Police-o!"

This went on for a long time and then stopped suddenly. Perhaps they had scared the thief away. There was total silence. But only for a short while.

"You done finish?" asked the voice outside. "Make we help you small. Oya, everybody!"

"Police-o! Tief-man-o! Neighbors-o! we done loss-o! Police-o! . . ."

There were at least five other voices besides the leader's.

Jonathan and his family were now completely paralyzed by terror. Maria and the children sobbed inaudibly like lost souls. Jonathan groaned continuously.

The silence that followed the thieves' alarm vibrated horribly. Jonathan all but begged their leader to speak again and be done with it.

"My frien," said he at long last, "we don try our best for call dem but I tink say dem all done sleep-o. . . . So wetin we go do now? Sometaim you wan call soja?[22] Or you wan make we call dem for you? Soja better pass police. No be so?"

---

20. **imperious** (ĭm-pîr′ē-əs): demanding.

21. **"Na tief man and him people"**: "It is the thief and his people."

22. **"So wetin we go do now? Sometaim you wan call soja?"**: "So what are we going to do now? Sometime do you want to call the soldiers?"

"Na so!"[23] replied his men. Jonathan thought he heard even more voices now than before and groaned heavily. His legs were sagging under him and his throat felt like sand-paper.

"My frien, why you no de talk again. I de ask you say you wan make we call soja?"

"No."

"Awrighto. Now make we talk business. We no be bad tief. We no like for make trouble. Trouble done finish. War done finish and all the katakata wey de for inside.[24] No Civil War again. This time na[25] Civil Peace. No be so?"

"Na so!" answered the horrible chorus.

"What do you want from me? I am a poor man. Everything I had went with this war. Why do you come to me? You know people who have money. We . . ."

"Awright! We know say you no get plenty money. But we sef no get even anini.[26] So derefore make you open dis window and give us one hundred pound and we go commot.[27] Orderwise we de come for inside now to show you guitar-boy[28] like dis . . ."

A volley of automatic fire rang through the sky. Maria and the children began to weep aloud again.

"Ah, missisi[29] de cry again. No need for dat. We done talk say we na good tief.[30] We just take our small money and go nwayorly. No molest. Abi we de molest?"

"At all!" sang the chorus.

"My friends," began Jonathan hoarsely. "I hear what you say and I thank you. If I had one hundred pounds . . ."

"Lookia my frien, no be play we come play for your house. If we make mistake and step for inside you no go like am-o. So derefore . . ."

"To God who made me; if you come inside and find one hundred pounds, take it and shoot me and shoot my wife and children. I swear to God. The only money I have in this life is this twenty-pounds *egg-rasher* they gave me today . . ."

---

23. **"Na so!"**: "It is so."

24. **"all the katakata wey de for inside"**: "all the trouble that went with it."

25. **na:** it is.

26. **anini** (ă-nē′nē): a small coin worth less than a penny.

27. **"and we go commot"**: "and we will leave."

28. **guitar-boy:** automatic gun.

29. **missisi:** woman or wife.

30. **"we na good tief"**: "we are good thieves."

More About . . .

CIVIL WAR A *civil war* is a war that takes place between different regions or groups in the same country. The Nigerian Civil War started because of a military takeover of the government (a coup d'etat) on January 15, 1966.

✔ **Reading Check**

What do the thieves want from Jonathan?

What Does It Mean?

Volley of automatic fire means that someone fired an automatic rifle, which lets off many shots in a short amount of time.

Reading Tip

Complete the web with phrases and words that describe Jonathan's character.

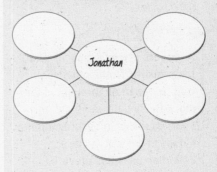

Jonathan

Reading Check

How much money does
Jonathan give the thieves?

Pause & Reflect

1. How would you describe the
thief who threatens Jonathan?
Circle two phrases below.
**(Make Judgments About
Characters)**

seems willing to bargain

wants to harm Jonathan's
family

can control his followers

MARK IT UP **2.** How does
Jonathan react to the loss of
the 20 pounds? Write the
answer below. Then circle
details in the last two paragraphs of this story that led
you to the answer. **(Draw
Conclusions)**

_____

_____

_____

_____

CHALLENGE

A **proverb** is a wise saying. The
Ibo proverb "Nothing puzzles
God" is repeated throughout this
story. Review the story and the
chart you filled in describing the
places in the story where
Jonathan uses this proverb.
Why does Jonathan say it each
time? What **theme,** or message
about life, does this proverb
suggest?

"OK. Time de go. Make you open dis window and bring
the twenty pound. We go manage am like dat."[31]

There were now loud murmurs of dissent[32] among the
chorus: "Na lie de man de lie; e get plenty money. . . . Make
we go inside and search properly well. . . . Wetin be twenty
pound?[33] . . ."

"Shurrup!" rang the leader's voice like a lone shot in the
190 sky and silenced the murmuring at once. "Are you dere? Bring
the money quick!"

"I am coming," said Jonathan fumbling in the darkness
with the key of the small wooden box he kept by his side on
the mat.

At the first sign of light as neighbors and others assembled
to commiserate with[34] him he was already strapping his five-
gallon demijohn[35] to his bicycle carrier and his wife, sweating
in the open fire, was turning over akara balls in a wide clay
bowl of boiling oil. In the corner his eldest son was rinsing
200 out dregs[36] of yesterday's palm wine from old beer bottles.

"I count it as nothing," he told his sympathizers, his eyes
on the rope he was tying. "What is *egg-rasher*? Did I depend
on it last week? Or is it greater than other things that went
with the war? I say, let *egg-rasher* perish in the flames! Let it
go where everything else has gone. Nothing puzzles God."

Pause & Reflect

---

31. **"We go manage am like dat":** "We will go manage it like that."
32. **dissent:** disagreement.
33. **"Wetin be twenty pound?":** "What are twenty pounds?"
34. **commiserate with:** show sympathy toward.
35. **demijohn** (děm′ē-jŏn′): a large bottle with a narrow neck.
36. **dregs:** liquid left at the bottom.

Active Reading SkillBuilder

Making Judgments About Characters

When reading a story, readers make **judgments** about the characters based on their speech, thoughts, feelings, and reactions to events. In "Civil Peace," Jonathan Iwegbu considers himself very lucky. Think about whether you agree with this judgment. Use the chart below to record what you consider to be his losses and his blessings. An example is shown.

Jonathan's Luck	
Losses	**Blessings**
His youngest son is killed in the war.	

Literary Analysis SkillBuilder

Dialect

A **dialect** is a form of a language that is spoken in one place by a certain group of people. Dialect reflects the pronunciations, vocabulary, and grammatical rules that are typical of a region. In "Civil Peace," Chinua Achebe uses two dialects of English: the Nigerian dialect of the thieves and the dialect of Jonathan and his family. Read aloud passages that contain dialect. In the chart below, jot down any words or phrases you have trouble understanding. Then explain what you think the use of dialect adds to the story. An example is shown.

Difficult Words or Phrases
Katakata: "trouble"

What Dialect Adds to the Story:

_____

_____

_____

_____

Six Feet of the Country

Nadine Gordimer

Before You Read

Connect to Your Life

What words or phrases do you think of when you hear the word *racism*?
Record your thoughts in the web below.

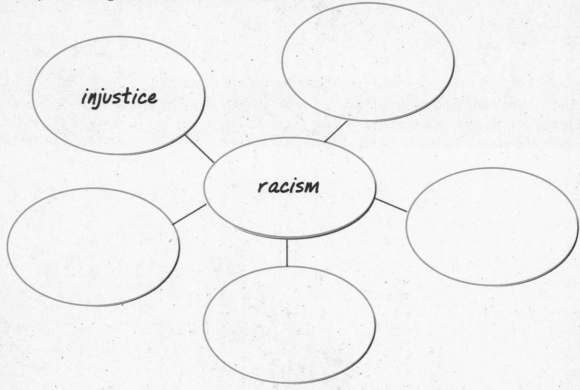

injustice

racism

Key to the Story

WHAT DO YOU THINK? This story takes place during a period in South
African history when black people lived under a system called *apartheid*.
It was a legal system of segregation and discrimination. For a period of
time in the United States, Jim Crow laws existed in the South. These laws
also forced segregation between the races as *apartheid* did in South Africa.

Six Feet of the Country

Nadine Gordimer

SHORT STORY

Reading Tips
This story is told from the **point of view** of the story's main character. He is a wealthy white businessman who lives on a farm in South Africa. The workers on his farm are black and poor.

- To understand this story, read between the lines. Judge the narrator at key spots, and try to see through him. Look for clues that reveal his attitude toward his workers. Ask yourself how his attitude makes you feel about him.

- Think about the author's view of the society in South Africa. What are its faults? What injustices exist?

- Read at your usual pace, even when you come upon long sentences or difficult passages. Keep in mind that you don't have to understand every word to get at the overall meaning of a sentence or a passage.

As the story begins . . .

- The narrator and his wife, who live on a farm in South Africa, are introduced.

- They moved to the farm to get away from the racial problems in the city.

PREVIEW In 1991, Nadine Gordimer was awarded the Nobel Prize in literature. Much of her writing is set in South Africa, where she grew up. In that country, a system of racial separation—known as apartheid (ə-pärt′hīt′)—was in place from 1948 to 1991. The word *apartheid* means "separateness." This system separated blacks, who made up most of the population, from whites, who made up a minority. Blacks suffered discrimination in housing, education, health care, and employment. Only after years of protest and violence did this system finally end.

In her novels and stories, Gordimer shows the effects of apartheid upon personal relationships. Her story "Six Feet of the Country" is set on a farm ten miles from Johannesburg (jō-hăn′ĭs-bûrg′), the largest city in South Africa. The main character and his wife, Lerice (lä-rēs′), have chosen to live away from the city.

FOCUS
The narrator and his wife live on a farm. They hope that life in the country will improve their marriage.

MARK IT UP As you read, circle details that help you get to know the narrator. An example is highlighted on page 414.

My wife and I are not real farmers—not even Lerice, really. We bought our place, ten miles out of Johannesburg on one of the main roads, to change something in ourselves, I suppose; you seem to rattle about so much within a marriage like ours. You long to hear nothing but a deep, satisfying silence when you sound a marriage. The farm hasn't managed that for us, of course, but it has done other things, unexpected, illogical. Lerice, who I thought would retire there in Chekhovian[1] sadness for a month or two, and then leave the place to the servants while she tried yet again to get a part she wanted and become the actress she would like to be, has sunk into the business of running the farm with all the serious intensity with which she once <u>imbued</u> the shadows in a

---

1. **Chekhovian** (chĕ-kō′vē-ən): like a character in a play by Anton Chekhov (chĕk′ôf), who lived from 1860 to 1904. His characters often talk about their troubles but do little to improve their lives.

WORDS
TO
KNOW

imbue (ĭm-byōō′) *v.* to fill with a quality; saturate

English Learner Support

Flourishing *Flourishing* means "doing very well."

Reading Tip

Make a character chart to record your ideas and thoughts about each character in the story.

Character	Character Traits
Narrator	
Lerice	

MARK IT UP WORD POWER

Mark words that you'd like to add to your **Personal Word List**. After reading, you can record the words and their meanings beginning on page 508.

playwright's mind. I should have given it up long ago if it had not been for her. Her hands, once small and plain and well-kept—she was not the sort of actress who wears red paint and
20 diamond rings—are hard as a dog's pads.[2]

I, of course, am there only in the evenings and at week-ends. I am a partner in a luxury-travel agency, which is flourishing—needs to be, as I tell Lerice, in order to carry on the farm. Still, though I know we can't afford it, and though the sweetish smell of the fowls Lerice breeds sickens me, so that I avoid going past their runs, the farm is beautiful in a way I had almost forgotten—especially on a Sunday morning when I get up and go out into the paddock[3] and see not the palm trees and fish pond and imitation-stone bird-bath of the suburbs but
30 white ducks on the dam, the lucerne[4] field brilliant as window-dresser's grass, and the little, stocky, mean-eyed bull, lustful but bored, having his face tenderly licked by one of his ladies. Lerice comes out with her hair uncombed, in her hand a stick dripping with cattle-dip.[5] She will stand and look dreamily for a moment, the way she would pretend to look sometimes in those plays. "They'll mate tomorrow," she will say. "This is their second day. Look how she loves him, my little Napoleon." So that when people come out to see us on Sunday afternoon, I am likely to hear myself saying, as I pour out the
40 drinks, "When I drive back home from the city every day, past those rows of suburban houses, I wonder how the devil we ever did stand it. . . . Would you care to look around?" And there I am, taking some pretty girl and her young husband stumbling down to our river-bank, the girl catching her stockings on the mealie-stooks[6] and stepping over cow-turds humming with jewel-green flies while she says, ". . . the *tensions* of the damned city. And you're near enough to get into town to a show, too! I think it's wonderful. Why, you've got it both ways!"[7]
50 And for a moment I accept the triumph as if I *had* managed it—the impossibility that I've been trying for all my life—just as if the truth was that you could get it "both ways," instead

---

2. **a dog's pads:** thin flesh on the underpart of a dog's foot.

3. **paddock:** a fenced area, used chiefly for grazing horses.

4. **lucerne** (loo-sûrn′): a British term for alfalfa, used as a pasture crop.

5. **cattle dip:** a liquid for killing germs in cattle.

6. **mealie-stooks:** a South African term for cornstalks.

7. **"Why, you've got it both ways":** You have the advantages of both the city and the country.

of finding yourself with not even one way or the other but a third, one you had not provided for at all.

But even in our saner moments, when I find Lerice's earthy enthusiasms just as irritating as I once found her histrionical[8] ones, and she finds what she calls my "jealousy" of her capacity for enthusiasm as big a proof of my inadequacy for her as a mate as ever it was, we do believe that we have at
60 least honestly escaped those tensions peculiar to the city about which our visitors speak. When Johannesburg people speak of "tension" they don't mean hurrying people in crowded streets, the struggle for money, or the general competitive character of city life. They mean the guns under the white men's pillows and the burglar bars on the white men's windows. They mean those strange moments on city pavements when a black man won't stand aside for a white man.

Pause & Reflect

FOCUS
One of the boys on the
70 farm knocks on the window late at night. The narrator goes with him to the workers' huts. Read to find out what he discovers in one of the huts.

Out in the country, even ten miles out, life is better than that. In the country, there is a lingering remnant of the pretransitional stage; our relationship with the blacks is almost feudal.[9] Wrong, I suppose, obsolete, but more comfortable all round. We have no burglar bars, no gun. Lerice's farm-boys have their wives and their piccanins living with them on the land.[10] They brew their sour beer without the fear of police raids. In fact, we've always rather prided ourselves that the poor devils have nothing much to fear, being with us; Lerice even keeps an eye on their children, with all
80 the competence of a woman who has never had a child of her own, and she certainly doctors them all—children and adults— like babies whenever they happen to be sick.

---

8. **histrionical** (hĭs′trē-ŏn′ĭ-kəl): theatrical; dramatic.

9. **feudal** (fyōōd′l): characteristic of feudalism—the economic system of Europe in the Middle Ages. Farm workers labored for a lord who owned the land. In return for their labors, the workers were given protection.

10. **Lerice's farm boys . . . on the land:** Under apartheid, black men who left their homelands to work on white-owned farms were not allowed to bring their families; **piccanins** (pĭk′ə-nĭnz′): in South Africa, a negative term for native African children.

What Does It Mean?
Enthusiasms refers to Lerice's hobbies and interests.

Pause & Reflect

MARK IT UP **1.** Who seems more personally involved with life on the farm, the narrator or Lerice? Write the answer below. Then underline details on pages 413–415 that support your answer. **(Compare and Contrast)**

_____

READ ALOUD **2.** Read aloud the boxed passage on this page. What are the white people in Johannesburg afraid of? **(Clarify)**

_____

_____

As the story continues...
• A worker wakes the narrator and his wife to ask for help.

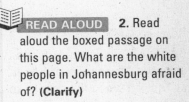

English Learner Support
VOCABULARY

Idiom The narrator refers to his workers as *poor devils,* or "unfortunate beings." The idiom shows that the narrator views them as inferior to himself.

✔ **Reading Check**

What is Lerice's reaction to being awakened so late at night?

More About...

(BAAS) Native South Africans used the Afrikaans word *baas,* or "boss," when they spoke to their white employers. The term *baas* shows the unequal relationship between blacks and whites in South Africa.

What Does It Mean?

He had given me the path means that Albert had let the narrator go ahead of him on the path.

English Learner Support
LANGUAGE

Dialect The native African's speech in this story is a dialect that includes Afrikaans words. The dialect also includes word orders and verb tenses that are not ordinarily used in Standard English. *"Petrus he send me"* means "Petrus sent me."

It was because of this that we were not particularly startled one night last winter when the boy Albert came knocking at our window long after we had gone to bed. I wasn't in our bed but sleeping in the little dressing-room-cum-linen room next door, because Lerice had annoyed me, and I didn't want to find myself softening toward her simply because of the sweet smell of the talcum powder on her flesh after her bath.

90 She came and woke me up. "Albert says one of the boys is very sick," she said. "I think you'd better go down and see. He wouldn't get us up at this hour for nothing."

"What time is it?"

"What does it matter?" Lerice is maddeningly logical.

I got up awkwardly as she watched me—how is it I always feel a fool when I have deserted her bed? After all, I know from the way she never looks at me when she talks to me at breakfast the next day that she is hurt and humiliated at my not wanting her—and I went out, clumsy with sleep.

100 "Which of the boys is it?" I asked Albert as we followed the dance of my torch.[11]

"He's too sick. Very sick, (Baas,)"[12] he said.

"But who? Franz?" I remembered Franz had had a bad cough for the past week.

Albert did not answer; he had given me the path, and was walking along beside me in the tall dead grass. When the light of the torch caught his face, I saw that he looked acutely embarrassed. "What's this all about?" I said.

He lowered his head under the glance of the light. "It's not

110 me, *Baas.* I don't know. Petrus he send me."

Irritated, I hurried him along to the huts. And there, on Petrus's iron bedstead, with its brick stilts, was a young man, dead. On his forehead there was still a light, cold sweat; his body was warm. The boys stood around as they do in the kitchen when it is discovered that someone has broken a dish—uncooperative, silent. Somebody's wife hung about in the shadows, her hands wrung together under her apron.

I had not seen a dead man since the war. This was very different. I felt like the others—<u>extraneous</u>, useless.

---

11. **torch:** flashlight.

12. *Baas* (bäs) *Afrikaans:* master; boss (formerly used as a term of address by black South Africans when speaking to a white man).

WORDS
TO
KNOW

extraneous (ĭk-strā′nē-əs) *adj.* not relevant; not essential

120 "What was the matter?" I asked.

The woman patted at her chest and shook her head to indicate the painful impossibility of breathing.

He must have died of pneumonia.

I turned to Petrus. "Who was this boy? What was he doing here?" The light of a candle on the floor showed that Petrus was weeping. He followed me out the door.

When we were outside, in the dark, I waited for him to speak. But he didn't. "Now come on, Petrus, you must tell me who this boy was. Was he a friend of yours?"

130 "He's my brother, *Baas*. He come from (Rhodesia) to look for work."

Pause & Reflect

FOCUS
The narrator and his wife, Lerice, react differently to the death of Petrus's brother.

MARK IT UP As you read, circle words and phrases that help you understand each character's reaction.

The story startled Lerice and me a little. The young boy had walked down from Rhodesia to look for work in Johannesburg, had caught a chill from sleeping out along the way, and had lain ill in his brother Petrus's hut since his arrival three days before. Our boys had been frightened to ask us for help for him because we had not been intended

140 ever to know of his presence. Rhodesian natives are barred from entering the Union[13] unless they have a permit; the young man was an illegal immigrant. No doubt our boys had managed the whole thing successfully several times before; a number of relatives must have walked the seven or eight hundred miles from poverty to the paradise of zoot suits,[14] police raids, and black slum townships that is their *Egoli*, City of Gold—the Bantu[15] name for Johannesburg. It was merely a matter of getting such a man to lie low on our farm until a

150 job could be found with someone who would be glad to take

---

13. **Union:** Union of South Africa. The name of the country before it became the Republic of South Africa in 1961.

14. **zoot suits:** flashy men's suits with broad padded shoulders and baggy trousers.

15. *Egoli* (ā-gō′lē) . . . **Bantu** (băn′tōō): *Bantu* refers to a group of African languages spoken throughout southern Africa.

More About . . .
(RHODESIA) Rhodesia is the former name of the Republic of Zimbabwe, a country that borders South Africa to the north.

Pause & Reflect

MARK IT UP 1. What does the narrator find in one of the huts? Circle the sentence on page 416 that tells the answer. (Clarify)

2. How is Petrus related to the dead person? (Clarify)

_____

_____

As the story continues . . .
• The relationship between the narrator and his wife becomes more tense.
• The narrator decides what to do concerning the dead boy.

✔ **Reading Check**
Why didn't the workers ask the narrator for help when they first saw that Petrus's brother was ill?

English Learner Support
VOCABULARY

Idiom *To lie low* means "to hide."

the risk of prosecution for employing an illegal immigrant in exchange for the services of someone as yet <u>untainted</u> by the city.

Well, this was one who would never get up again.

"You would think they would have felt they could tell *us*," said Lerice next morning. "Once the man was ill. You would have thought at least—" When she is getting intense over something, she has a way of standing in the middle of a room as people do when they are shortly to leave 160 on a journey, looking searchingly about her at the most familiar objects as if she had never seen them before. I had noticed that in Petrus's presence in the kitchen, earlier, she had the air of being almost offended with him, almost hurt.

In any case, I really haven't the time or inclination any more to go into everything in our life that I know Lerice, from those alarmed and pressing eyes of hers, would like us to go into. She is the kind of woman who doesn't mind if she looks plain, or odd; I don't suppose she 170 would even care if she knew how strange she looks when her whole face is out of proportion with urgent uncertainty.

I said, "Now, I'm the one who'll have to do all the dirty work, I suppose."

She was still staring at me, trying me out with those eyes—wasting her time, if she only knew.

"I'll have to notify the health authorities," I said calmly. "They can't just cart him off and bury him. After all, we don't really know what he died of."

She simply stood there, as if she had given up—simply 180 ceased to see me at all.

I don't know when I've been so irritated. "It might have been something contagious," I said. "God knows?" There was no answer.

I am not <u>enamored</u> of holding conversations with myself. I went out to shout to one of the boys to open the garage and get the car ready for my morning drive to town.

Pause **&** *Reflect*

Sidebar

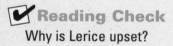

Reading Check

Why is Lerice upset?

Pause **&** *Reflect*

1. Instead of letting Petrus bury his brother, the narrator decides to tell the authorities about the dead boy. Do you think he is making the right decision? *Yes/No,* because _____

_____

_____

_____ .

(Evaluate)

READ ALOUD   **2.** Review the boxed passage on this page. What can you conclude about the narrator and Lerice? Circle one sentence below. **(Draw Conclusions)**

They have a close relationship.

They do not share deep feelings.

WORDS
TO
KNOW

untainted (ŭn-tān′tĭd) *adj.* not contaminated; unspoiled
enamor (ĭ-năm′ər) *v.* to inspire with love; fascinate

FOCUS

The narrator tells the authorities about the dead boy. Read to find out what happens later to the body.

190

As I had expected, it turned out to be quite a business. I had to notify the police as well as the health authorities, and answer a lot of tedious questions: How was it I was ignorant of the boy's presence? If I did not supervise my native quarters, how did I know that that sort of thing didn't go on all the time? Et cetera, et cetera. And when I flared up and told them that so long as my natives did their work, I didn't think it my right or concern to poke my nose into their private lives, I got from the coarse, dull-witted police sergeant one of those looks that come not from any thinking process going on in the brain but from that faculty common to all

200

who are possessed by the master-race theory[16]—a look of insanely <u>inane</u> certainty. He grinned at me with a mixture of scorn and delight at my stupidity.

Then I had to explain to Petrus why the health authorities had to take away the body for a post-mortem[17]—and, in fact, what a post-mortem was. When I telephoned the health department some days later to find out the result, I was told the cause of death was, as we had thought, pneumonia, and that the body had been suitably disposed of. I went out to where Petrus was mixing a mash for the fowls and told him

210

that it was all right, there would be no trouble; his brother had died from that pain in his chest. Petrus put down the paraffin tin and said, "When can we go to fetch him, *Baas?*"

"To fetch him?"

"Will the *Baas* please ask them when we must come?"

I went back inside and called Lerice, all over the house. She came down the stairs from the spare bedrooms, and I said, "*Now* what am I going to do? When I told Petrus, he just asked calmly when they could go and fetch the body. They think they're going to bury him themselves."

220

"Well, go back and tell him," said Lerice. "You must tell him. Why didn't you tell him then?"

As the story continues . . .

- Health authorities take the body of Petrus's brother.

- Petrus asks the narrator to help get the body back.

English Learner Support

LANGUAGE

Latin Words *Et cetera* is Latin for "and so on." It is often abbreviated as *etc.*

English Learner Support

VOCABULARY

Idiom *Poke my nose into* means "get involved in situations where I am not wanted."

---

16. **master-race theory:** the belief that one race is better than another race.

17. **post-mortem:** an examination of a corpse to find out the cause of death.

WORDS
TO
KNOW   **inane** (ĭn-ān′) *adj.* foolish; senseless

Pause & Reflect

MARK IT UP **1.** How does Petrus feel about his dead brother? Circle details on pages 419 and 420 that show his feelings. **(Infer)**

2. Review the boxed passage on this page. Petrus asks the narrator for help. How do you think the narrator should respond? **(Evaluate)**

_____

_____

_____

_____

3. Do you think the narrator will be able to get the body back? *Yes/No*, because _____

_____

_____

_____ .

(Predict)

When I found Petrus again, he looked up politely. "Look, Petrus," I said. "You can't go to fetch your brother. They've done it already—they've *buried* him, you understand?"

"Where?" he said, slowly, dully, as if he thought that perhaps he was getting this wrong.

"You see, he was a stranger. They knew he wasn't from here, and they didn't know he had some of his people here, so they thought they must bury him." It was difficult to make a pauper's grave[18] sound like a privilege.

"Please, *Baas*, the *Baas* must ask them?" But he did not mean that he wanted to know the burial-place. He simply ignored the incomprehensible machinery[19] I told him had set to work on his dead brother; he wanted the brother back.

"But Petrus," I said, "how can I? Your brother is buried already. I can't ask them now."

"Oh *Baas*!" he said. He stood with his bran-smeared hands uncurled at his sides, one corner of his mouth twitching.

"Good God, Petrus, they won't listen to me! They can't, anyway. I'm sorry, but I can't do it. You understand?"

He just kept on looking at me, out of his knowledge that white men have everything, can do anything; if they don't, it is because they won't.

And then, at dinner Lerice started. "You could at least phone," she said.

"*Christ*, what d'you think I am? Am I supposed to bring the dead back to life?"

But I could not exaggerate my way out of this ridiculous responsibility that had been thrust on me. "Phone them up," she went on. "And at least you'll be able to tell him you've done it and they've explained that it's impossible."

She disappeared somewhere into the kitchen quarters after coffee. A little later she came back to tell me, "The old father's coming down from Rhodesia to be at the funeral. He's got a permit and he's already on his way."

Pause & Reflect

18. **a pauper's grave:** a common burial place for the poor and unknown.

19. **incomprehensible machinery:** government rules that are impossible to understand.

FOCUS

The narrator can get the body back—but at the high cost of 20 pounds. Read to find out how Petrus raises the money.

260

Unfortunately, it was not impossible to get the body back. The authorities said that it was somewhat irregular, but that since the hygiene conditions had been fulfilled, they could not refuse permission for exhumation.[20] I found out that, with the undertaker's charges, it would cost twenty pounds. Ah, I thought, that settles it. On five pounds a month, Petrus won't have twenty pounds—and just as well, since it couldn't do the dead any good. Certainly I should not offer it to him myself. Twenty pounds—or anything else within reason, for that matter—I would have

270 spent without grudging it on doctors or medicines that might have helped the boy when he was alive. Once he was dead, I had no intention of encouraging Petrus to throw away, on a gesture, more than he spent to clothe his whole family in a year.

When I told him, in the kitchen that night, he said, "Twenty pounds?"

I said, "Yes, that's right, twenty pounds."

For a moment, I had the feeling, from the look on his face, that he was calculating. But when he spoke again I

280 thought I must have imagined it. "We must pay twenty pounds!" he said in the far-away voice in which a person speaks of something so unattainable that it does not bear thinking about.

"All right, Petrus," I said in dismissal, and went back to the living-room.

The next morning before I went to town, Petrus asked to see me. "Please *Baas*," he said, awkwardly handing me a bundle of notes. They're so seldom on the giving rather than the receiving side, poor devils, that they don't really know

290 how to hand money to a white man. There it was, the twenty pounds, in ones and halves, some creased and folded until they were soft as dirty rags, others smooth and fairly new— Franz's money, I suppose, and Albert's, and Dora the cook's, and Jacob the gardener's, and God knows who else's besides, from all the farms and small holdings round about. I took it in irritation more than in astonishment, really—irritation at the waste, the uselessness of this sacrifice by people so poor.

---

20. **exhumation** (ĕg´zyo͞o-mā´shən): the digging up of a corpse from a grave.

As the story continues...

• Petrus makes a decision about his brother's body.

• The narrator cannot understand Petrus's decision.

English Learner Support
VOCABULARY

Usage *Besides* is an adverb that means "in addition to" or "also." Be careful not to confuse it with *beside*, a preposition that means "next to."

 Reading Check

Why does the narrator think that spending money on a burial is a bad idea?

Pause & Reflect

Insert the words *narrator* and *farm workers* in the correct slots in the following sentences:

To the _____, it is important to honor the dead.

To the _____, it is foolish to do so.

(Compare and Contrast)

As the story continues...

• The narrator watches the funeral procession.

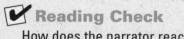 **Reading Check**

How does the narrator react to Lerice's project?

Just like the poor everywhere, I thought, who <u>stint</u> themselves the decencies of life in order to insure themselves the decencies of death. So incomprehensible to people like Lerice and me, who regard life as something to be spent extravagantly and, if we think about death at all, regard it as the final bankruptcy.[21]

Pause & Reflect

FOCUS

The narrator forgets about the funeral of Petrus's brother. Still, he finds himself looking on as the funeral procession passes. Read to find out about his thoughts and feelings.

The servants don't work on Saturday afternoon anyway, so it was a good day for the funeral. Petrus and his father had borrowed our donkey-cart to fetch the coffin from the city, where, Petrus told Lerice on their return, everything was "nice"—the coffin waiting for them, already sealed up to save them from what must have been a rather unpleasant sight after two weeks' interment.[22] (It had taken all that time for the authorities and the undertaker to make the final arrangements for moving the body.) All morning, the coffin lay in Petrus's hut, awaiting the trip to the little old burial-ground, just outside the eastern boundary of our farm, that was a relic of the days when this was a real farming district rather than a fashionable rural estate. It was pure chance that I happened to be down there near the fence when the procession came past; once again Lerice had forgotten her promise to me and had made the house uninhabitable on a Saturday afternoon. I had come home and been infuriated to find her in a pair of filthy old slacks and with her hair uncombed since the night before, having all the varnish scraped off the living-room floor, if you please. So I had taken my No. 8 iron[23] and gone off to practice my approach shots. In my annoyance I had forgotten about the funeral, and was reminded only when I saw the procession coming up the path along the outside of the fence toward me; from where I was standing, you can see the graves quite

---

21. **bankruptcy:** total loss of money and resources.

22. **interment:** burial in the ground.

23. **No. 8 iron:** a type of golf club.

WORDS
TO
KNOW

stint (stĭnt) *v.* to limit to a small amount; give sparingly

330 clearly, and that day the sun glinted on bits of broken pottery, a lopsided homemade cross, and jam-jars brown with rain-water and dead flowers.

I felt a little awkward, and did not know whether to go on hitting my golf ball or stop at least until the whole gathering was decently past. The donkey-cart creaks and screeches with every revolution of the wheels and it came along in a slow, halting fashion somehow peculiarly suited to the two donkeys who drew it, their little potbellies rubbed and rough, their heads sunk between the shafts, and their ears flattened back

340 with an air <u>submissive</u> and downcast; peculiarly suited, too, to the group of men and women who came along slowly behind. The patient ass. Watching, I thought, you can see now why the creature became a Biblical symbol.[24] Then the procession drew level with me and stopped, so I had to put down my club. The coffin was taken down off the cart—it was a shiny, yellow-varnished wood, like cheap furniture—and the donkeys twitched their ears against the flies. Petrus, Franz, Albert and the old father from Rhodesia hoisted it on their shoulders and the procession moved on, on foot. It was really a very

350 awkward moment. I stood there rather foolishly at the fence, quite still, and slowly they filed past, not looking up, the four men bent beneath the shiny wooden box, and the straggling troop of mourners. All of them were servants or neighbors' servants whom I knew as casual, easygoing gossipers about our lands or kitchen. I heard the old man's breathing.

Pause & Reflect

FOCUS
Read to find out about the surprising event that halts the funeral.

I had just bent to pick up my club again when there was a sort of jar in the flowing solemnity of their processional mood; I felt it at once, like a wave of heat along the air, or one of those

360 sudden currents of cold catching at your legs in a placid stream.

---

24. **a Biblical symbol:** In the Bible, the donkey, or ass, is a beast of burden and is viewed as a lowly animal. It sometimes symbolizes humility or meekness.

WORDS
TO
KNOW

submissive (səb-mĭs′ĭv) *adj.* yielding to the control of another

Pause & Reflect

1. What can you conclude about the narrator from the fact that he forgets about the funeral of Petrus's brother? **(Draw Conclusions)**

_____

_____

2. How would you contrast the narrator and the people attending the funeral? **(Compare and Contrast)**

_____

_____

As the story continues...
• The dead boy's father notices something unusual and stops the funeral.

The old man's voice was muttering something, and they bumped into one another, some pressing to go on, others hissing at them to be still. I could see that they were embarrassed, but they could not ignore the voice; it was much the way that the mumblings of a prophet,[25] though not clear at first, arrest the mind. The corner of the coffin the old man carried was sagging at an angle; he seemed to be trying to get out from under the weight of it. Now Petrus <u>expostulated</u> with him.

370   The little boy who had been left to watch the donkeys dropped the reins and ran to see. I don't know why—unless it was for the same reason people crowd round someone who has fainted in a cinema[26]—but I parted the wires of the fence and went through, after him.

   Petrus lifted his eyes to me—to anybody—with distress and horror. The old man from Rhodesia had let go of the coffin entirely, and the three others, unable to support it on their own, had laid it on the ground, in the pathway. Already there was a film of dust lightly wavering up its shiny sides. I did not

380 understand what the old man was saying; I hesitated to interfere. But now the whole seething group turned on my silence. The old man himself came over to me, with his hands outspread and shaking, and spoke directly to me, saying something that I could tell from the tone, without understanding the words, was shocking and extraordinary.

   "What is it, Petrus? What's wrong?" I appealed.

   Petrus threw up his hands, bowed his head in a series of hysterical shakes, then thrust his face up at me suddenly.

   "He says, 'My son was not so heavy.'"

390   Silence. I could hear the old man breathing; he kept his mouth a little open as old people do.

   "My son was young and thin," he said, at last, in English.

   Again silence. Then babble broke out. The old man thundered against everybody; his teeth were yellowed and few, and he had one of those fine, grizzled, sweeping moustaches that one doesn't often see nowadays, which must have been grown in emulation of early Empire

---

25. **prophet:** in the Bible, a messenger of God who spoke the truth and warned the people.

26. **cinema:** movie theater.

WORDS TO KNOW   **expostulate** (ĭk-spŏs'chə-lāt') *v.* to reason earnestly in an effort to correct or dissuade

builders.[27] It seemed to frame all his utterances with a special validity, perhaps merely because it was the symbol of the traditional wisdom of age—an idea so fearfully rooted that it carries still something awesome beyond reason. He shocked them; they thought he was mad, but they had to listen to him. With his own hands he began to prise the lid off the coffin and three of the men came forward to help him. Then he sat down on the ground; very old, very weak, and unable to speak, he merely lifted a trembling hand toward what was there. He abdicated, he handed it over to them; he was no good any more.

They crowded round to look (and so did I), and now they forgot the nature of this surprise and the occasion of grief to which it belonged, and for a few minutes were carried up in the astonishment of the surprise itself. They gasped and flared noisily with excitement. I even noticed the little boy who had held the donkeys jumping up and down, almost weeping with rage because the backs of the grown-ups crowded him out of his view.

In the coffin was someone no one had ever seen before: a heavily built, rather light-skinned native with a neatly stitched scar on his forehead—perhaps from a blow in a brawl that had also dealt him some other, slower-working injury which had killed him.

Pause & Reflect

FOCUS
Again, the narrator tries to get the body of Petrus's brother from the authorities. Read to find out what happens.

I wrangled with the authorities for a week over that body. I had the feeling that they were shocked, in a laconic fashion, by their own mistake, but that in the confusion of their anonymous dead[28] they were helpless to put it right. They said to me, "We are trying to find out," and "We are still

---

27. **in emulation of early Empire builders:** in imitation of the British settlers who became powerful people in the African colonies.

28. **anonymous dead:** bodies that have not been identified.

WORDS
TO
KNOW
laconic (lə-kŏn′ĭk) *adj.* making use of few words

 What Does It Mean?
Prise is the British usage of the verb "to pry open."

 Reading Check
What do the people attending the funeral find in the coffin?

Pause & Reflect

1. How does the old man know that his son's body is not in the coffin? **(Infer)**

_____

_____

_____

_____

MARK IT UP 2. The old man is filled with wild emotions. What details on pages 424 and 425 express the force of his emotions? Circle these details. **(Evaluate)**

 **As the story ends...**

• The narrator seems to try to fix the problem.

• The narrator's attitudes toward his wife and his workers become clear.

making enquiries." It was as if at any moment they might
430 conduct me into their mortuary and say, "There! Lift up the
sheets; look for him—your poultry boy's brother. There are so
many black faces—surely one will do?"

And every evening when I got home Petrus was waiting in
the kitchen. "Well, they're trying. They're still looking. The
Baas is seeing to it for you, Petrus," I would tell him. "God,
half the time I should be in the office I'm driving around the
back end of town chasing after this affair," I added aside, to
Lerice, one night.

She and Petrus both kept their eyes turned on me as I
440 spoke, and, oddly, for those moments they looked exactly
alike, though it sounds impossible: my wife, with her high,
white forehead and her <u>attenuated</u> Englishwoman's body, and
the poultry boy, with his horny[29] bare feet below khaki
trousers tied at the knee with string and the peculiar rankness
of his nervous sweat coming from his skin.

"What makes you so indignant,[30] so determined about this
now?" said Lerice suddenly.

I stared at her. "It's a matter of principle. Why should they
get away with a swindle? It's time these officials had a jolt
450 from someone who'll bother to take the trouble."

She said, "Oh." And as Petrus slowly opened the kitchen
door to leave, sensing that the talk had gone beyond him, she
turned away too.

I continued to pass on assurances to Petrus every evening,
but although what I said was the same, and the voice in
which I said it was the same, every evening it sounded
weaker. At last, it became clear that we would never get
Petrus's brother back, because nobody really knew where he
was. Somewhere in a graveyard as uniform as a housing
460 scheme, somewhere under a number that didn't belong to
him, or in the medical school, perhaps, laboriously reduced
to layers of muscles and strings of nerves? Goodness knows.
He had no identity in this world anyway.

It was only then, and in a voice of shame, that Petrus asked
me to try and get the money back.

---

29. **horny:** tough and calloused.

30. **indignant:** angry for a good reason.

What Does It Mean?

A *swindle* is "a cheat," or "an act that unfairly takes a person's money or property."

English Learner Support
LANGUAGE

Usage *Housing scheme* is the British term for a housing development—a planned neighborhood of single-family homes.

More About . . .

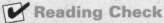 MEDICAL SCHOOL Unclaimed bodies may be sent to medical schools to help train student doctors. Students use the bodies to see what human anatomy really looks like or to practice medical activities such as surgery.

✔ **Reading Check**

What does Petrus want from the narrator?

"From the way he asks, you'd think he was robbing his dead brother," I said to Lerice later. But as I've said, Lerice had got so intense about this business that she couldn't even appreciate a little ironic smile.

470   I tried to get the money; Lerice tried. We both telephoned and wrote and argued, but nothing came of it. It appeared that the main expense had been the undertaker, and, after all, he had done his job. So the whole thing was a complete waste, even more of a waste for the poor devils than I had thought it would be.

The old man from Rhodesia was about Lerice's father's size, so she gave him one of her father's old suits and he went back home rather better off, for the winter, than he had come.

Pause & *Reflect*

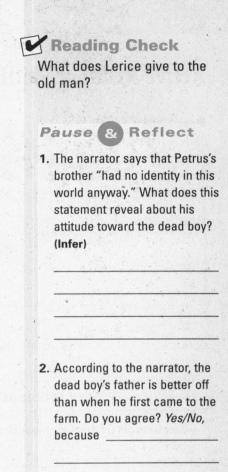

☑ **Reading Check**
What does Lerice give to the old man?

Pause & Reflect

1. The narrator says that Petrus's brother "had no identity in this world anyway." What does this statement reveal about his attitude toward the dead boy? **(Infer)**

_____

_____

_____

_____

2. According to the narrator, the dead boy's father is better off than when he first came to the farm. Do you agree? *Yes/No,* because _____

_____

_____

_____ .

(Evaluate)

✏ CHALLENGE

The title of a work of literature often gives clues about its **theme,** or main message. The title of this story refers to the size of a grave—usually six feet long and six feet deep. What connection do you see between the title and the message about South African society in this story? **(Analyze)**

Active Reading SkillBuilder

Predicting

To make a **prediction,** try to figure out what will happen next. What you know about a narrator's subject and even the story's title can help you make predictions. Use background information in the Preview on page 413 and the title "Six Feet of the Country" to predict what the story will be about. Write your prediction here:

Prediction

At key moments in the story, continue to record predictions in the chart below about what will happen next. An example is shown.

Key Moment	Prediction
Albert knocks at the window late at night.	Something is wrong—maybe someone is hurt.

Literary Analysis SkillBuilder

Point of View

"Six Feet of the Country" is told from the **point of view** of the story's main character. What you know about the characters and the story's events is based on his observations and thoughts. Choose a passage that has a strong effect on you. Rewrite the passage in the chart below, telling the events from the third-person point of view. Then consider why Gordimer chose to use the first-person point of view.

Passage: page _____ **lines** _____

Rewrite in third-person point of view:

Why Gordimer chose first-person point of view:

_____

_____

_____

_____

Words to Know SkillBuilder

Words to Know

attenuated	expostulate	imbue	laconic	submissive
enamor	extraneous	inane	stint	untainted

A. Fill in each set of blanks with the correct word from the word list. The boxed letters, when unscrambled, will spell out what *apartheid* means in English.

1. This could describe well-trained dogs, horses, and employees.

   ☐ _ _ _ _ _ ☐ ☐ _ _ _

2. You might do this with a child who misbehaves, but not with a puppy.

   ☐ _ ☐ _ _ _ _ _ _ ☐ _ _

3. This would describe words and ideas that you edit out of your writing.

   _ _ _ ☐ ☐ _ _ _ _ _

4. Long-distance runners tend to be this; so do long-distance phone lines.

   _ _ ☐ _ _ _ _ _ _ ☐ _

5. This is another way of saying "pure as the driven snow."

   _ _ _ _ _ ☐ _ ☐ _

What *apartheid* means in English: _____

B. Fill in each blank with the correct word from the word list.

Q. How did the man who hated to talk on the phone describe himself?
A. "I'm telephonically _____."
                  (1)

Q. What did the makeup artist say to the very pale actor?
A. "I need to _____ you with hue."
          (2)

Q. What does the man who noisily serenades a woman believe?
A. "My clamor will _____ her."
             (3)

Q. What was the caveman's advice to his friends on building fires?
A. "Don't _____ on the flint."
         (4)

Q. What do stubborn chuckleheads say when you tell them not to be silly?
A. "I fully intend to remain _____."
           (5)

C. Write a dramatic monologue in which either Petrus or Lerice reveals how the incident has affected his or her life. Use at least **five** of the Words to Know.

Academic and Informational Reading

In this section, you will find strategies to help you read all kinds of informational materials. The examples here range from magazines you read for fun to textbooks and maps you read for information. Applying these simple and effective techniques will help you be a successful reader of the many texts you encounter every day.

Reading a Magazine Article

A magazine article is designed to catch and hold your interest. Learning how to recognize the items on a magazine page will help you read even the most complicated articles. Look at the sample magazine article as you read each strategy below.

A Read the **title** and any other **headings** to get an idea of what the article is about. Frequently, the title presents the article's main topic. Smaller headings may introduce subtopics related to the main topic.

B Note text that is set off in some way, such as an **indented paragraph** or a passage in a **different typeface.** This text often summarizes the article.

C Study **visuals**—photos, pictures, or maps. Read their captions and make sure you know how they relate to the main text.

D Look for **special features,** such as charts, tables, or graphs, that provide more detailed information on the topic or on a subtopic.

∥ MARK IT UP ⬧ Use the sample magazine page at right and the tips above to help you answer the following questions.

1. What is the article's main topic? _____

_____

2. Underline the sentence that states the main idea of the article.

3. Do you think the use of a contract will ensure student compliance with school rules for behavior? Why or why not? _____

_____

4. How does the visual help you understand the article? _____

_____

5. What information appears in the box? _____

_____

A Graduate Manners

Are graduations marred by bad behavior?

by Jennifer Tinnin

Jessica M., a recent high school graduate, says she does not have fond memories of her graduation. "I was really looking forward to graduation, but during the ceremony, kids were shouting and dancing on the stage," she recalls. "I was so embarrassed by my peers' behavior."

B "I was so embarrassed by my peers' behavior."

Jessica's experience is not unique. Graduation ceremonies across the country are being disrupted by the graduates' behavior. Middle school students in Illinois acted like they had just scored a touchdown as they strutted across the stage, pumping their fists into the air. A student in Minnesota took a pratfall and then had a loud confrontation with police who attempted to escort him from the building. Students in Illinois were not invited back to the site where their graduation was held last year after thousands of dollars of damage was done to the site's restrooms.

These students are not all troublemakers. One student who performed a prank was president of his school's student body, and another student was the valedictorian of his class. Nor are students the sole disruption at graduations. Friends and family in the audience often cheer on students' antics or create additional noise by blowing air horns or screaming when their graduate's name is called.

Many school officials and audience members believe that the dignity of graduation is being sacrificed for a few laughs. Ellen, a high school student from California, remarks, "Kids yell and dance because they're happy. It's no big deal. We should be allowed to celebrate our accomplishments and success." Dr. Amos White, principal of a high school in Houston, Texas, disagrees: "These students are graduating into the adult world. They should mark the transition with good manners and courtesy toward their peers, parents, and school officials. We will do whatever we can to keep graduation dignified."

Some schools have started to require students to sign a contract ensuring their compliance with school rules for behavior during the graduation ceremony before they will allow students to attend the ceremony. Is a legal contract necessary to deter students and audiences alike from ruining graduation? Or are graduates and their friends and families simply showing exuberance for a job well done?

GRADUATION BEHAVIOR SURVEY D

Do you think there should be stricter enforcement of rules and conduct at graduation ceremonies?

Parents		High School Students	
Yes	77%	Yes	48%
No	20%	No	46%
Not Sure	3%	Not Sure	6%

Do you think students should be required to sign a contract dictating rules of behavior in order to participate in the graduation ceremony?

Parents		High School Students	
Yes	54%	Yes	21%
No	29%	No	68%
Not Sure	17%	Not Sure	11%

Reading a Textbook

The first page of a textbook lesson introduces you to a particular topic. The page also provides important information that will guide you through the rest of the lesson. Look at the sample textbook page as you read each strategy below.

A Preview the **title** and other **headings** to find out the lesson's main topic and related subtopics.

B Look for a list of terms or **vocabulary words.** These words will be identified and defined throughout the lesson. They are often set in special type, such as **italics** or **boldface.**

C Read the **main idea, objectives, or focus.** These items summarize the lesson and establish a purpose for your reading.

D Many math textbooks have an **activity box** that supplements each lesson. These activities will give you more practice and help you further understand each concept.

E Examine **visuals,** such as graphs, photos, and drawings, and their captions. Visuals can help the topic come alive.

MARK IT UP Use the sample textbook page and the tips above to help you answer the following questions.

1. What does this lesson focus on? _____

_____

2. Circle the vocabulary terms defined in the lesson.

3. What does Figure 1.14 illustrate? _____

_____

4. Where is the activity box in this lesson? _____

_____

5. Give an example of how graphing linear equations in two variables can be used to solve a real-life problem. _____

_____

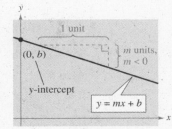

A 1.2   # Linear Equations in Two Variables

C ▶ **What you should learn**

- How to use slope to graph linear equations in two variables
- How to find slopes of lines
- How to write linear equations in two variables
- How to use slope to identify parallel and perpendicular lines
- How to use linear equations in two variables to model and solve real-life problems

▶ **Why you should learn it**

Linear equations in two variables can be used to model and solve real-life problems. For instance, Exercise 112 on page 123 shows how to use a linear equation to model the average annual salaries of major league baseball players from 1988 to 1998.

Walter Schmid/The Stock Market

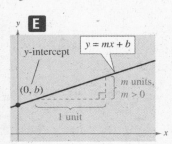

A computer simulation of this concept appears in the *Interactive* CD-ROM and *Internet* versions of this text.

Using Slope

The simplest mathematical model for relating two variables is the **linear equation in two variables** $y = mx + b$. The equation is called *linear* because its graph is a line. (In mathematics, the term *line* means *straight line*.) By letting $x = 0$, you can see that the line crosses the y-axis at $y = b$, as shown in Figure 1.14. In other words, the y-intercept is $(0, b)$. The steepness or slope of the line is m.

$$y = mx + b$$

Slope ———⌐   ⌐——— y-Intercept

B The **slope** of a nonvertical line is the number of units the line rises (or falls) vertically for each unit of horizontal change from left to right, as shown in Figure 1.14.

E

Positive slope, line rises.   *Negative slope, line falls.*
FIGURE 1.14

A linear equation that is written in the form $y = mx + b$ is said to be written in **slope-intercept form.**

> **The Slope-Intercept Form of the Equation of a Line**
>
> The graph of the equation
>
> $$y = mx + b$$
>
> is a line whose slope is m and whose y-intercept is $(0, b)$.

D ◀ **Exploration** ▶

Use a graphing utility to compare the slopes of the lines $y = mx$ where $m = 0.5, 1, 2,$ and 4. Which line rises most quickly? Now, let $m = -0.5, -1, -2,$ and -4. Which line falls most quickly? Use a square setting to obtain a true geometric perspective. What can you conclude about the slope and the "rate" at which the line rises or falls?

Reading a Graph

Graphs arrange data so that you can see the relationships among numbers at a glance. Line graphs connect each point on a graph, which makes it easy to see trends over time. Use these strategies to read the line graph below.

A Read the **title** to find out what the graph illustrates.

B Read the **labels** for each line on the graph to find out what is being compared.

C Look at the **relationship** among different elements on the graph. Try to express it in a sentence. For example, this graph shows how levels of pollutants released into the air from 1970 to 1998 compare to pollutant levels in 1970.

D Look at the **heading** of each row and column. To find specific information, find the place where a row and column intersect.

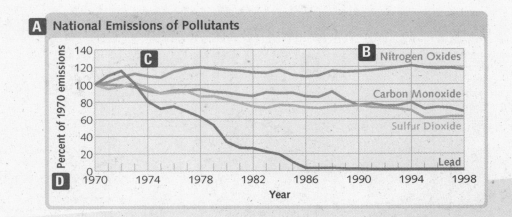

A National Emissions of Pollutants

MARK IT UP Answer the following questions using the graph of pollutant emissions.

1. What are emissions levels after 1970 being compared to? _____

_____

2. What period of time is covered by the graph? _____

_____

3. Circle the pollutant that was emitted at higher levels in 1994 than it was in 1970.

4. What conclusion(s) can you draw from the direction of the lines on the graph? _____

_____

Reading a Map

To read a map correctly, you have to identify and understand its elements. Look at the example below as you read each strategy in this list.

A Scan the **title** to understand the context of the map.

B Study the **legend,** or **key,** to find out what the symbols and colors on the map stand for.

C Study **geographic labels** to understand specific places on the map.

D Look at the **compass rose,** or **pointer,** to determine direction.

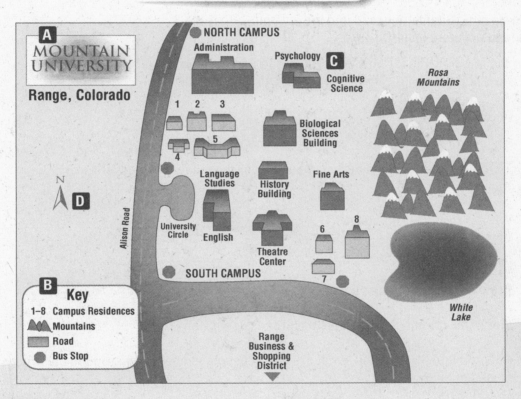

A
MOUNTAIN UNIVERSITY
Range, Colorado

NORTH CAMPUS
Administration
Psychology
C Cognitive Science
Rosa Mountains
1 2 3
Biological Sciences Building
4 5
Language Studies
History Building
Fine Arts
N **D**
Alison Road
University Circle
English
Theatre Center
6 8
7
SOUTH CAMPUS
White Lake

B Key
1–8 Campus Residences
Mountains
Road
Bus Stop

Range Business & Shopping District

MARK IT UP ▷ Use the map to answer the following questions.

1. What is the purpose of this map? _____

2. Circle the Administration building.

3. What mountains are located near the campus? _____

4. What buildings are directly south of the Fine Arts building? _____

5. What road is west of the Mountain University campus? _____

_____

Reading a Diagram

Diagrams combine pictures with a few words to provide a lot of information. Look at the example on the opposite page as you read each of the following strategies.

A Look at the **title** to get a sense of what the diagram is about.

B Carefully examine the **images** to understand each part of the diagram.

C Read the **captions** written beneath the pictures.

D Study the **labels** to understand what different parts are named.

E Look for **arrows** or other markers that show relationships between different parts of the diagram.

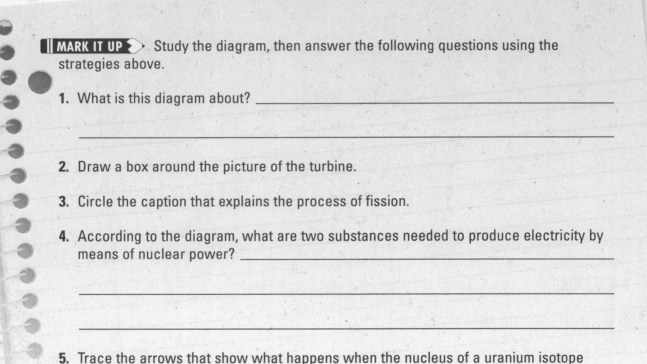

MARK IT UP Study the diagram, then answer the following questions using the strategies above.

1. What is this diagram about? _____

_____

2. Draw a box around the picture of the turbine.

3. Circle the caption that explains the process of fission.

4. According to the diagram, what are two substances needed to produce electricity by means of nuclear power? _____

_____

_____

5. Trace the arrows that show what happens when the nucleus of a uranium isotope absorbs a neutron.

A Nuclear Power

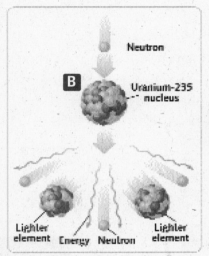

B Neutron

Uranium-235 nucleus

Lighter element   Energy   Neutron   Lighter element

C

1 Fission occurs when the nucleus of a uranium isotope absorbs a neutron. Lighter elements form and much energy is released.

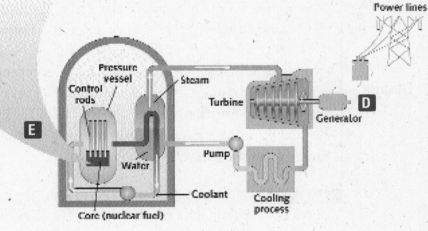

Power lines

Pressure vessel

Control rods

Steam

Turbine

Generator **D**

E

Pump

Water

Coolant

Cooling process

Core (nuclear fuel)

2 The energy produced by fission heats the nuclear reactor's coolant.

3 The hot coolant converts water to steam. The steam is used to generate electricity.

Main Idea and Supporting Details

The *main idea* in a paragraph is its most important point. *Details* in the paragraph support the main idea. Identifying the main idea will help you focus on the main message the writer wants to communicate. Use the following strategies to help you identify a paragraph's main idea and supporting details.

- Look for the **main idea,** which is often the first or last sentence in a paragraph.

- Use the main idea to help you **summarize** what the paragraph is about.

- Identify specific **details,** including facts and examples, that **support** the main idea.

Problems Faced by James I

Main idea —— King James I of England inherited the unsettled issues of Queen Elizabeth's reign. Elizabeth left a huge debt. This debt, combined with James's foreign wars and expensive court, caused constant struggles between the king and Parliament about money. Another issue was **Details** —— how much power Parliament should have. James I also clashed with the Puritans over remaining Catholic practices in the Church of England.

■ MARK IT UP ▷ Read the following paragraph. Circle its main idea. Then underline three of the paragraph's supporting details, numbering each one.

The Restoration, which began in 1660 when Charles II assumed the throne, is known as a period when the arts thrived. Charles II restored many aspects of English cultural and political life. Charles restored the theater, sporting events, and dancing, all of which the Puritans had banned. Theater, especially comedy, and other arts flourished during the Restoration.

Problem and Solution

Does the proposed solution to a problem make sense? In order to decide, you need to look at each part of the text. Use the following strategies to read the text below.

- Look at the beginning or middle of a paragraph to find the **statement of the problem.**

- Find **details** that explain the problem and tell why it is important.

- Look for the **proposed solution.**

- Identify the **supporting details** for the proposed solution.

- Think about whether the solution is a good one.

An Untapped Resource *by Iris Goldfarb*

Energy supplies are decreasing, and the cost of electricity in the western United States has been extremely high in the past few years. Blackouts and brownouts have forced residents of California to come face-to-face with the energy problem. If new sources of energy aren't found soon, we may be headed for a new Dark Age.

Statement of problem ⎡ face-to-face with the energy problem. If new sources of energy aren't found soon, we may be headed for a new Dark Age. ⎤

The good news is that the earth has an abundant source of energy just waiting to be tapped: geothermal energy, or "earth heat." This energy, stored in the rocks and water of the earth's crust, can be used to generate electricity and provide heat.

Explanation of the solution ⎡ Underground streams of magma, or molten rock, are found throughout the Northwest. Some scientists believe that the geothermal energy in Oregon alone could produce as much electricity as two nuclear power plants. Geothermal heat pumps installed in homes could reduce electricity costs by as much as 75 percent. ⎤

What are we waiting for?

MARK IT UP ▷ Read the text above. Then answer these questions.

1. Underline the proposed solution.

2. Circle at least one detail that supports the solution.

3. Do you think the solution is a good one? Explain why or why not. _____

_____

Sequence

It's important to understand the *sequence,* or order of events, in what you read. It helps you know what happens and why. Read the tips below to make sure a sequence is clear to you. Then look at the example on the opposite page.

- Read through the passage and think about what its **main steps,** or stages, are.

- Look for **words and phrases that signal time,** such as *in a year, three hours earlier, 202 B.C.,* or *later.*

- Look for **words and phrases that signal order,** such as *first, second, now, after that,* or *finally.*

∥ MARK IT UP ❖ Read the article on the next page, which describes Henry VIII's efforts to secure a male heir to the English throne. Use the information from the article and the tips above to answer the questions.

1. Circle words or phrases that signal time.

2. Underline the phrases in the article that signal order.

3. A time line can help you understand a sequence of events. Use the information from the article to complete this time line.

Events in the Life of Henry VIII

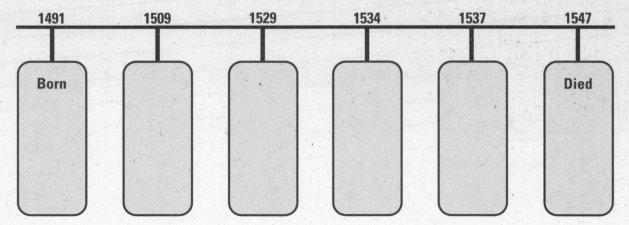

1491	1509	1529	1534	1537	1547
Born					Died

Henry VIII and His Six Wives

Born in 1491, Henry VIII was crowned king of England when he was 18 years old. He was a devout Catholic, but his politics soon clashed with his religion.

Henry's father had become king after a long civil war. Henry was afraid that a similar war might start if he died without a son to take over the throne. The history of England during his reign became the bloody story of his need for a son.

Henry and his wife, Catherine of Aragon, had one living child—a daughter, Mary, born in 1516. However, a woman had never successfully claimed the English throne. By 1529, Catherine was 42 years

old, and Henry was convinced that she would have no more children. He wanted to divorce her and marry a younger woman, but Church law did not permit divorce. Henry asked the pope to annul the marriage—in other words, declare that it had never existed. The pope refused.

Henry then decided to take matters into his own hands. Later in 1529, he asked Parliament to pass laws to end the pope's power in England. Four years later, he secretly married Anne Boleyn, and Parliament voted to make his divorce from his first wife legal. But Henry was not satisfied and wanted to break completely with the pope. In 1534, Parliament passed the Act of Supremacy, which made the king the official head of the Church of England.

Although Henry had turned the country inside out in his attempt to have a son, Anne Boleyn gave birth to a daughter. Following the birth, Henry had her imprisoned in the Tower of London. In 1536, he had her beheaded.

Henry did not get his wish for a son until his third wife, Jane Seymour, gave birth to Edward in 1537. Jane died in childbirth. In 1540, Henry married Anne of Cleves, but the marriage was quickly annulled. Later that same year, he married his fifth wife, Catherine Howard. However, the king soon learned of Catherine's affairs before their marriage and had her beheaded in 1543. Henry was survived by his sixth wife, Katherine Parr. He died in 1547 at the age of 56.

Cause and Effect

A *cause* is an event that brings about another event. An *effect* is something that happens as a result of the first event. Identifying causes and effects helps you understand how events are related. The tips below can help you find causes and effects in any reading.

- Look for an action or event that answers the question "What happened?" This is the **effect.**

- Look for an action or event that answers the question "Why did it happen?" This is the **cause.**

- Identify words or phrases that **signal** causes and effects, such as *because, as a result, therefore, thus, consequently, since,* and *led to.*

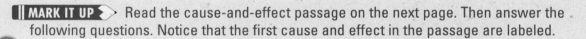 **MARK IT UP** Read the cause-and-effect passage on the next page. Then answer the following questions. Notice that the first cause and effect in the passage are labeled.

1. Identify the main effect the writer describes. Write it in the diagram below.

2. Circle words in the passage that signal causes and effects. The first one is done for you.

3. Sometimes an effect has more than one cause. Use information from the article to complete the following diagram.

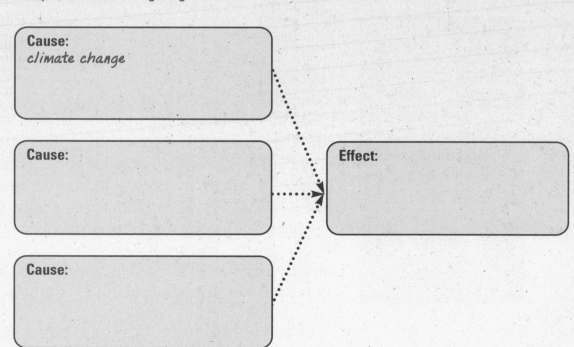

Cause:
climate change

Cause:

Cause:

Effect:

Mass Extinction: A Scientific Mystery

At the peak of the last Ice Age, about 20,000 years ago, herds of giant animals —megafauna—lumbered through the forests and plains of North America. There were beavers the size of modern bears, hairy mastodons and mammoths with massive curved tusks, and bison with horns measuring six feet across. These awesome animals were hunted by jaguars, saber-toothed tigers, and bears that weighed twice as much as today's grizzlies. But by about 13,000 years ago—not long after the first humans appeared on the scene—almost all of these huge beasts had disappeared.

Effect

No one knows for sure what caused this mass extinction, but there are several competing theories. One possible cause might have been a change in climate.

Cause

Increasing temperatures resulted in a retreat of the glaciers that had covered the land during the Ice Age. Consequently, the forests and grasslands that thrived in the cold climate and provided food for the animals grew smaller. Without a source of food, the animals eventually died off.

Signal word

According to another theory, the disappearance of the giant animals was caused by an epidemic outbreak of disease. Some scientists think that prehistoric humans may have brought disease-causing organisms with them when they crossed the land bridge connecting Asia and North America. Since the animals living in North America had no immunity to these diseases, great numbers of them may have died.

A third theory points a finger straight at human hunters. If hunters had killed only a few more animals than were born each year, the populations of megafauna would have decreased steadily. As a result, nearly all the species could have become extinct within a thousand years or so.

Scientists are now using new techniques to solve this mystery. They are looking at fossils and rocks for evidence, analyzing frozen tissues and bone marrow from mammoths, and using new ways of dating ancient remains. Scientists hope to identify the cause of this mass extinction soon.

Comparison and Contrast

Comparing two things means showing how they are the same. *Contrasting* two things means showing how they are different. Comparisons and contrasts are often used in science and history books to make a subject clearer. Use these tips to help you understand comparison and contrast in reading assignments, such as the article on the opposite page.

- Look for **direct statements** of comparison and contrast: "These things are similar because . . . " or "One major difference is. . . ."

- Pay attention to **words and phrases that signal comparisons,** such as *also, both, is the same as,* and *in the same way.*

- Notice **words and phrases that signal contrasts.** Some of these are *however, still, but,* and *on the other hand.*

MARK IT UP Read the essay on the opposite page. Then use the information from the article and the tips above to answer the questions.

1. Circle the words and phrases that signal comparisons. A sample has been done for you.

2. Underline the words and phrases that signal contrasts. A sample has been done for you.

3. A Venn diagram shows how two subjects are similar and how they are different. Complete this diagram, which uses information from the essay to compare and contrast jazz music with classical music. Add at least one similarity to the middle part of the diagram. Add at least one difference to each outer circle.

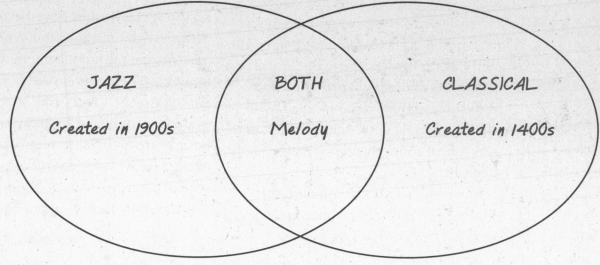

JAZZ

Created in 1900s

BOTH

Melody

CLASSICAL

Created in 1400s

Jazz: Music in Motion

As the piano player's hands bounce off the keys, the bassist slaps his strings, the drummer drives the beat forward, and the trumpet player splits the air with rapid-fire notes. At this moment, jazz is created.

For a newcomer to this music, jazz is perhaps easiest to understand when it is compared with the music of the Western classical tradition. The melody and harmony in traditional classical music are based on the seven-note major scale that most of us have sung in school—do-re-mi-fa-sol-la-ti-do (*do* is repeated at a higher pitch). European in origin, classical music developed in the 1400s during the Renaissance. Until the twentieth century, the rhythms used in classical music were very regularly accented on the beat. Also, the classical composer strictly controls a musical performance by writing exactly what each musician will play. The written music is followed closely.

Contrast

In contrast, jazz is still in its infancy, having originated in the southern United States in the early 1900s. Both the European and African traditions contributed to its development. **Comparison** Like classical music, jazz is composed of melody, harmony, and rhythm. However, because jazz is a direct descendent of the blues, the melody and harmony are based on the blues scale, which has a flatted third and a flatted seventh scale note. Also, jazz rhythms are syncopated. This means that the accents come on the off-beats. The rhythms produce a bouncing or swinging feeling.

What most distinguishes jazz from classical music is the art of improvisation. The word *improvise* means "to compose without preparation." A jazz trumpeter, for example, improvises when he or she replaces the melody of a song with a new melody played over the chords, or the harmony of the song. The improviser composes in the moment while the band provides rhythmic and harmonic support. As a result, new musical ideas are expressed each time a jazz musician takes a solo. Louis Armstrong summed it up when he said, "Jazz is music that's never played the same way once."

Argument

An *argument* is an opinion backed up with reasons and facts.
Examining an opinion and the reasons and facts that back it up will
help you decide if the opinion makes sense. Look at the argument on
the right as you read each of these tips.

- Look for words that **signal an opinion:** *I believe; I think; in my view; they claim, argue,* or *disagree.*

- Look for reasons, facts, or expert opinions that **support** the argument.

- Ask yourself if the argument and reasons **make sense.**

- Look for overgeneralizations or other **errors in reasoning** that might affect the argument.

MARK IT UP Read the argument on the next page, and then answer the questions below.

1. Circle any words that signal an opinion.

2. Underline the words or phrases that give the writer's opinion.

3. The writer presents both sides of the argument. Fill in the chart below to show the two sides. One reason has been provided for you.

Reasons to Ban Soft Drinks	Reasons Not to Ban Soft Drinks
1. lack of nutritional value	

Should Soft Drinks Be Banned from Schools?

by J. T. Fox

A new substance has joined the list of those banned on school grounds: soft drinks. As the number of obese teenagers rises, a movement to limit the empty calories available in school vending machines is growing. Los Angeles has banned the sale of soft drinks on the district's high school and elementary campuses. Other districts are debating whether to implement similar policies. Activists who favor the soda ban say schools must make a choice between student health and vending machine revenues.

Advocates of banning sodas point out that a typical can of soda has at least 10 teaspoons of sugar. Its 140 calories contain no vitamins, minerals, fiber, or other nutritional value. Poor eating habits contribute to teenage obesity. Dr. Jonathan E. Fielding, director of Public Health for Los Angeles County, describes obesity as a fast-growing, chronic disease that is "entirely preventable."

However, not everyone agrees that carbonated soft drinks are a hazard to students' health. A Georgetown University study found no link between 12- to 16-year-olds' soda consumption and obesity. Surgeon General David Hatcher, while concerned about unhealthy eating habits, considers lack of physical activity another important cause of excess weight.

Some schools are responding to the problem by expanding instead of restricting students' choices. A pilot program that offered Metro Detroit students a choice of pop or flavored milk was so successful that the district installed 80 more milk machines. In Hemingford, Nebraska, students organized an effort to purchase a machine that sells seven flavors of milk. Other schools offer students a selection of juice-based drinks.

Stakes on both sides of the question are high: student health versus the $750 million students put into school vending machines each year. The evidence currently available does not prove that having soda pop available in school vending machines causes obesity. Until that evidence is provided, I believe banning pop is an extreme solution. Instead, schools should keep both students and the budget healthy by offering both soft drinks and healthier alternatives.

Social Studies

Social studies class becomes easier when you understand how your textbook's words, pictures, and maps work together to give you information. Following these tips can make you a better reader of social studies lessons. As you read the tips, look at the sample lesson on the right-hand page.

A First, look at any **headlines** or **subheads** on the page. These give you an idea of what each section covers.

B Make sure you know the meaning of any boldfaced or underlined **vocabulary terms.** These terms often appear on tests.

C Carefully read the text and think about **ways the information is organized.** Social studies books are full of sequence, comparison and contrast, and organization by geographic location.

D Look closely at **graphics,** such as tables, maps, and illustrations. Think about how the graphic and the text are related.

E Read any **study tips** in the margins or at the bottom of the page. These let you check your understanding as you read.

|| MARK IT UP ▷ Carefully read the textbook page at right. Use the information from the page and from the tips above to answer these questions.

1. What is the main subject covered on this page? _____

2. What secondary subject is covered? _____

3. Circle the part of the text that gives background information about what will be presented in the chapter.

4. What role did Zhou Enlai play in Chinese politics? _____

_____

_____

5. What is the relationship between the table of "Mao's Attempts to Change China" and the subject of this chapter? _____

_____

_____

China Follows Its Own Path

B TERMS & NAMES
- Zhou Enlai
- Deng Xiaoping
- Four Modernizations
- Tiananmen Square
- Hong Kong

MAIN IDEA	WHY IT MATTERS NOW
In recent years, China's government has experimented with capitalism but has rejected calls for democracy.	After the 1997 death of Chinese leader Deng Xiaoping, President Jiang Zemin seemed to be continuing those policies.

C **SETTING THE STAGE** The trend toward democracy around the world also affected China to a limited degree. A political reform movement arose in the late 1980s. It built on economic reforms begun earlier in the decade. China's Communist government clamped down on the reformers, however, and maintained a firm grip on power.

Mao's Unexpected Legacy

After the Communists came to power in China in 1949, Mao Zedong set out to transform China. Mao believed that peasant equality, revolutionary spirit, and hard work were all that was needed to improve the Chinese economy. For example, intensive labor could make up for the lack of tractors on the huge agricultural cooperatives that the government had created.

However, lack of modern technology damaged Chinese efforts to increase agricultural and industrial output. In addition, Mao's policies stifled economic growth. He eliminated incentives for higher production. He tried to replace family life with life in the communes. These policies took away the peasants' motive to work for the good of themselves and their families.

Facing economic disaster, some Chinese Communists talked of modernizing the economy. Accusing them of "taking the capitalist road," Mao began the Cultural Revolution to cleanse China of anti-revolutionary influences. The movement proved so destructive, however, that it caused many Chinese to distrust party leadership. Instead of saving radical communism, the Cultural Revolution turned many people against it. In the early 1970s, China entered another moderate period under **Zhou Enlai** (joh ehn·ly). Zhou had been premiere since 1949. During the Cultural Revolution, he had tried to restrain the radicals.

D

Mao's Attempts to Change China

Mao's Programs	Program's Results
First Five-Year Plan 1953–1957	• Industry grew 15 percent a year. • Agricultural output grew very slowly.
Great Leap Forward 1958–1962	• China suffered economic disaster—industrial declines and food shortages. • Mao lost influence.
Cultural Revolution 1966–1976	• Mao regained influence by backing radicals. • Purges and conflicts among leaders created economic, social, and political chaos. • Moderates increasingly opposed radicals in Communist Party.

SKILLBUILDER: Interpreting Charts
1. *Which had more successful results, the first five-year plan or the Great Leap Forward? Explain.*
2. *Did conditions improve or grow worse during the Cultural Revolution? Explain.*

E

THINK THROUGH HISTORY
A. Recognizing Effects What was the ultimate result of Mao's radical Communist policies? Why?
A. Answer The destructiveness of the Cultural Revolution turned many Chinese people away from radical communism.

China and the West

Throughout the Cultural Revolution, China played almost no role in world affairs. In the early 1960s, China had split with the Soviet Union over the leadership of world communism. In addition, China displayed hostility toward the United States because of U.S. support for the government on Taiwan and memories of the Korean War.

China Opened Its Doors China's isolation worried Zhou. He began to send out signals that he was willing to form ties to the West. In 1971, Zhou startled the world by

Science

Reading a science textbook becomes easier when you understand how the explanations, drawings, and special terms work together. Use the strategies below to help you better understand your science textbook. Look at the examples on the opposite page as you read each strategy in this list.

A Preview the **title** and **headings** on the page to see what scientific concepts will be covered.

B Read the **key idea, objectives,** or **focus.** These items summarize the lesson and establish a purpose for your reading.

C Look for **boldfaced** and **italicized** words that appear in the text and for **definitions** of those words.

D Carefully examine any **pictures** or **diagrams.** Read the **captions** and evaluate how the graphics help to illustrate and explain the text.

E Many science textbooks discuss **scientific concepts** in terms of **everyday events** or **experiences.** Look for these places and consider how they improve your understanding.

∥ MARK IT UP Use the sample science page and the tips above to help you answer the following questions.

1. Underline the objective of this lesson.

2. Circle the key term *energy* and underline its definition.

3. What are the two types of energy? _____

_____

4. What law states that the energy of the universe is constant? _____

_____

5. What does Figure 10.1 illustrate? _____

_____

_____

Energy is the essence of our very existence as individuals and as a society. The food that we eat furnishes the energy to live, work, and play, just as the coal and oil consumed by manufacturing and transportation systems power our modern industrialized civilization.

Huge quantities of carbon-based fossil fuels have been available for the taking. This abundance of fuels has led to a world society with a voracious appetite for energy, consuming millions of barrels of petroleum every day. We are now dangerously dependent on the dwindling supplies of oil, and this dependence is an important source of tension among nations in today's world. In an incredibly short time we have moved from a period of ample and cheap supplies of petroleum to one of high prices and uncertain supplies. If our present standard of living is to be maintained, we must find alternatives to petroleum. To do this, we need to know the relationship between chemistry and energy, which we explore in this chapter.

10.1 The Nature of Energy

Objective: *To understand the general properties of energy.*

Although energy is a familiar concept, it is difficult to define precisely. For our purposes we will define **energy** as *the ability to do work or produce heat*. We will define these terms below.

Energy can be classified as either potential or kinetic energy. **Potential energy** is energy due to position or composition. For example, water behind a dam has potential energy that can be converted to work when the water flows down through turbines, thereby creating electricity. Attractive and repulsive forces also lead to potential energy. The energy released when gasoline is burned results from differences in attractive forces between the nuclei and electrons in the reactants and products. The **kinetic energy** of an object is energy due to the motion of the object and depends on the mass of the object m and its velocity v: $KE = \frac{1}{2}mv^2$.

One of the most important characteristics of energy is that it is conserved. The **law of conservation of energy** states *that energy can be converted from one form to another but can be neither created nor destroyed*. That is, the energy of the universe is constant.

Although the energy of the universe is constant, it can be converted from one form to another. Consider the two balls in **Figure 10.1a.** Ball A, because of its initially higher position, has more potential energy than ball B.

When ball A is released, it moves down the hill and strikes ball B. Eventually, the arrangement shown in **Figure 10.1b** is achieved. What has happened in going from the initial to the final arrangement? The potential energy of A has decreased because its position was lowered. However, this energy cannot disappear. Where is the energy lost by A?

WHAT IF?

What if energy were not conserved? How would it affect our lives?

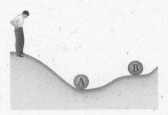

Held in place

(a) Initial

(b) Final

Figure 10.1
(a) In the initial positions, ball A has a higher potential energy than ball B. (b) After A has rolled down the hill, the potential energy lost by A has been converted to random motions of the components of the hill (frictional heating) and to an increase in the potential energy of B.

Mathematics

Reading in mathematics is different from reading in history, literature, or science. Use the strategies below to help you better understand your mathematics textbook. Look at the example on the opposite page as you read each strategy in the list.

A Preview the **title** and **headings** on the page to see what math concepts will be covered.

B Find and read the **goals** or **objectives** for the lesson. These will tell you the most important points to know.

C Read **explanations** carefully. Sometimes a concept is explained in more than one way to make sure you understand it.

D Look for **special features,** such as study or vocabulary tips. They provide more help or information.

E Study any **worked-out solutions** to sample problems. These are the key to understanding how to do the homework assignment.

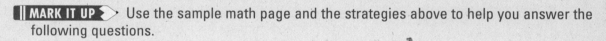 **MARK IT UP** Use the sample math page and the strategies above to help you answer the following questions.

1. Circle the learning goal for this lesson.

2. Underline the definition of the vocabulary word *intersection.*

3. What do the illustrations under the heading "Modeling Intersections" demonstrate?

_____

_____

4. Place a check mark by the example of how to sketch intersections.

5. Draw a box around the text and diagram that show how to draw the intersection of two planes.

A

C Two or more geometric figures **intersect** if they have one or more points in common. The **intersection** of the figures is the set of points the figures have in common.

▶ **ACTIVITY**

Developing Concepts

Modeling Intersections

Use two index cards. Label them as shown and cut slots halfway along each card.

1. What is the intersection of $\overline{AB}$ and $\overline{CD}$? of $\overline{AB}$ and $\overline{EF}$? **point G, point G**

2. Slide the cards together. What is the intersection of $\overline{CD}$ and $\overline{EF}$? **point G**

3. What is the intersection of planes M and N? $\overleftrightarrow{AB}$

4. Are $\overleftrightarrow{CD}$ and $\overleftrightarrow{EF}$ coplanar? Explain.
   Yes; *Sample answer:* **They are in plane** *CEG.*

EXAMPLE 4 *Sketching Intersections*

D STUDENT HELP

INTERNET HOMEWORK HELP
Visit our Web site
www.mcdougallittell.com
for extra examples.

Sketch the figure described.

a. a line that intersects a plane in one point

b. two planes that intersect in a line

E **SOLUTION**

a.

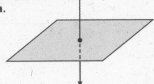

b.

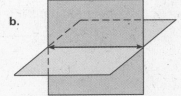

Draw a plane and a line.

Emphasize the point where they meet.

Dashes indicate where the line is hidden by the plane.

Draw two planes.

Emphasize the line where they meet.

Dashes indicate where one plane is hidden by the other plane.

Reading an Application

Reading and understanding an application will help you fill it out correctly and avoid mistakes. Use the following strategies to help you understand any application. Look at the example on the next page as you read each strategy.

A **Begin at the top.** Scan the application to understand the different sections.

B Look for special **instructions for filling out** the application.

C Note any **request for materials** that must be attached to the application.

D Look for difficult or confusing words or abbreviations.

‖ MARK IT UP Imagine that you are applying to Mountain University. Read the application on the next page. Then answer the following questions.

1. Can a student wishing to enter Mountain University in the spring use this application? Explain. _____

_____

2. What other materials are required besides the application? _____

_____

_____

3. What information should be included in the personal essay? _____

_____

4. What happens if the university discovers an applicant submitted false information on the application? _____

_____

5. **ASSESSMENT PRACTICE** Circle the letter of the correct answer.
   How many references do you need to provide?
   A. one personal reference
   B. one reference from an employer
   C. two letters of recommendation
   D. two business and two personal references

A APPLICATION FOR UNDERGRADUATE ADMISSION

APPLICATION INSTRUCTIONS This application is for students who will enter Mountain University in <u>the fall of the current year</u>. Send completed applications by regular or overnight mail to:

**Mountain University, Office of Undergraduate Admissions, 511 University Circle, Range, CO 80695
or apply online at www.mountainu.edu.**

PLEASE NOTE: Your admissions application *must be completed by April 1* if you wish to apply for the Mountain University merit scholarships. A separate scholarship application is also required.

Complete the Mountain University admissions application form (including your essay).
There is a *$25 nonrefundable application fee.* Please make checks payable to Mountain University.

C **Arrange to have official transcripts sent to the Undergraduate Office.** Your most recent high school transcript and your ACT or SAT test results are required.

If applicable, submit TOEFL results. **The TOEFL is required for international students for proof of English proficiency.** The minimum score required is 550 on the written test or 213 on the computer-based test.

Submit two letters of recommendation from an instructor or other individual who is qualified to comment on your college potential.

B **Please type the application or complete it in blue or black ink.**

Autobiographical Information

Social security number _____ - _____ - _____

Last name _____ First name _____

Mailing address _____ City _____ State _____ Zip _____

Phone number (_____) _____

Date of birth: Month _____ Day _____ Year _____

If you are not a U.S. citizen, please complete the following (check one):

❏ Immigrant   ❏ Visa; Type of visa (e.g., F-1 Student, J-2 Dependent, etc.): _____   ❏ Permanent resident in the U.S.

❏ I plan to enter Mountain University as a   ❏ full-time student (12 credit hours or more)   ❏ part-time student

Residency Information (answer both questions)

❏ Yes ❏ No   I will have lived in Colorado one full year before becoming a student at Mountain.

❏ Yes ❏ No   I will be claimed as a tax dependent by at least one parent who resides in Colorado.

Please provide the name of the high school from which you will graduate:

High School	City, State	GPA	(Expected) Graduation Date

Intended Major _____

Personal Statement

Please submit an original personal statement of 1,500 words or fewer describing what your goals are in the coming year, the next five years, and the next ten years.

D I understand that providing false information may make me ineligible for admission to Mountain University. I agree to abide by the regulations of Mountain as set forth in its current catalog and other official publications. I attest that all information I have supplied in this application and accompanying documentation is true and valid.

Applicant's Signature _____ Date Submitted _____

Reading a Public Notice

Public notices can tell you about events in your community and give you valuable information about safety. When you read a public notice, follow these tips. Each tip relates to a specific part of the notice on the opposite page.

A Read the notice's **title,** if it has one. The title often gives the main idea or purpose of the notice.

B See if there is a logo, credit, or other way of telling **who created the notice.**

C Ask yourself, **"Who should read this notice?"** If the information in it might be important to you or someone you know, then you should pay attention to it.

D Look for **instructions**—things the notice is asking or telling you to do.

E See if there are details that tell you how you can **find out more** about the topic.

‖ MARK IT UP ⟩ The notice on the opposite page is from a town government's bylaws. Read it carefully and answer the questions below.

1. Who is the notice from? _____

2. Who is the notice for? _____

3. What is the purpose of the notice? _____

4. How much must the owner pay each day that a dog is in the custody of the animal control officer? _____

_____

5. Put a star next to the portion of the notice that explains where people can get more information.

6. **ASSESSMENT PRACTICE** Circle the letter of the correct answer.
   According to the notice, a dog owner would pay a fine of $75.00
   A. for the first offense.
   B. for the second offense.
   C. for the third offense.
   D. when the dog is declared a neighborhood nuisance.

PUBLIC NOTICE
B Arlan Heights Town Bylaws: Title VIII

A *PUBLIC HEALTH AND SAFETY: ARTICLE 2: CANINE CONTROL*

Section 1. Dogs
No person shall own or keep any dog which by biting, barking, howling, or in any other manner disturbs the peace and quiet of any neighborhood, or endangers the safety of any person.

Section 2. Leashing of Dogs
C A. **Leash Required** No person owning or keeping a dog in the Town of Arlan Heights shall permit such dog to be at large in the Town of Arlan Heights elsewhere than on the premises of the owner or keeper, except if it be on the premises of another person with the knowledge and permission of such other person. Such owner or keeper of a dog in the Town of Arlan Heights, which is not on the premises of the owner or upon the premises of another person with the knowledge and permission of such person, shall restrain such dog by a chain or leash not exceeding six feet in length.

D B. **Enforcement** Any dog found to be at large in violation of this Bylaw shall be caught and confined by the dog officer who shall notify forthwith the licensed owner or keeper of said dog, giving the owner or keeper a period of ten days within which to recover the dog. The dog officer shall enter and prosecute a complaint against the owner or keeper of any dog taken into his custody under this section. A dog officer having custody of a dog confined under this Bylaw shall be allowed the sum of five dollars per day for each day of confinement for the care of such dog, payable by the owner or keeper thereof.

C. **Fines** Violations of Sections 2 of this Article shall be punishable as follows:
First offense: Warning
Second offense: By a fine of $50.00
Third offense: By a fine of $75.00
Fourth and each subsequent offense: By a fine of $100.00

E D. **Reporting Offenses** Residents who wish to report problems with a dog, or who have questions about this ordinance, can contact Animal Control at 321-3380.

Reading a Web Page

If you need information for a report, project, or hobby, the World Wide Web can probably help you. The tips below will help you understand the Web pages you read. As you look at the tips, notice where they match up to the sample Web page on the right.

A Notice the page's **Web address,** or URL. You may want to write it down in case you need to access the same page at another time.

B Look for **menu bars** along the top, bottom, or side of the page. These guide you to other parts of the site that may be useful.

C Look for **links** to other parts of the site or to related pages. Links are often shown as underlined words.

D Use a **search** feature to quickly find out whether information about a specific topic can be found anywhere on the site.

E Many sites have a link that allows you to **contact** the creators with questions or feedback.

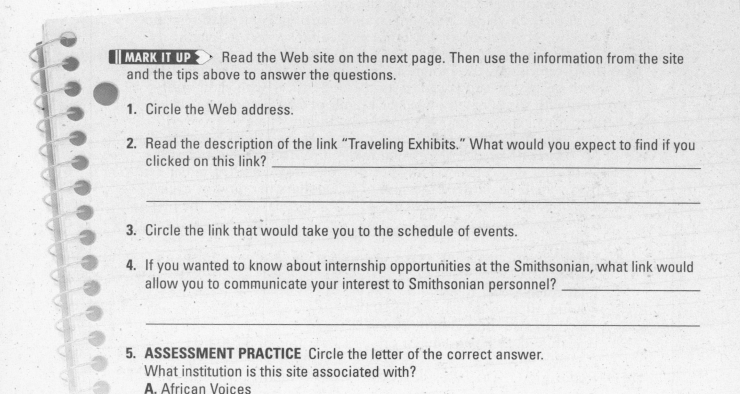

MARK IT UP Read the Web site on the next page. Then use the information from the site and the tips above to answer the questions.

1. Circle the Web address.

2. Read the description of the link "Traveling Exhibits." What would you expect to find if you clicked on this link? _____

_____

3. Circle the link that would take you to the schedule of events.

4. If you wanted to know about internship opportunities at the Smithsonian, what link would allow you to communicate your interest to Smithsonian personnel? _____

_____

5. **ASSESSMENT PRACTICE** Circle the letter of the correct answer.
   What institution is this site associated with?
   A. African Voices
   B. National Geographic
   C. Public Broadcasting Service (PBS)
   D. The Smithsonian Institution

Back   Forward   Reload   Home   Images   Print   Security   Stop   **B**

A Location: http://www.mnh.si.edu

Smithsonian Institution

NATIONAL MUSEUM OF NATURAL HISTORY

C Information Desk
Calendar of Events
Exhibits
Educational Resources

Johnson
IMAX® Theater

What's New ?
D Search the NMNH Web
Research & Collections
Search the NMNH Web

Natural History Highlight

Parataxonomy

NMNH scientists are part of a growing trend - training of and reliance upon parataxonomists.

CATCH THE BUZZ!
INSECT SAFARI
www.insectsafari.com

The National Museum of Natural History is dedicated to understanding the natural world and our place in it.

 Smithsonian
National Museum of Natural History

New Exhibits

HATCHER

Triceratops - A new mount of *Triceratops* has been unveiled. Also, as the first digital dinosaur, it can be shared with researchers as easily as e-mail. This new approach will tell us many more things about how this three-horned dinosaur lived and moved over 65 million years ago.

African Voices - examines the diversity, dynamism, and global influence of Africa's peoples and cultures over time in the realms of family, work, community, and the natural environment.

AFRICAN VOICES

Traveling Exhibits

Vikings: The North Atlantic Saga - Opening July 13, 2001, at the Houston Museum of Natural Science in Houston, Texas.

Smithsonian Store.com
Naturally...

Reading Technical Directions

Reading technical directions will help you understand how to use the products you buy. Use the following tips to help you read a variety of technical directions.

A Look carefully at any **diagrams** or **other images** of the product.

B **Read all the directions** carefully at least once before using the product.

C Notice **headings** or **rules** that separate one section from another.

D Watch for **warnings** or **notes** with more information.

MARK IT UP Use the tips above and the technical directions on the next page to help you answer the following questions.

1. What does this page explain how to do? _____

_____

2. Which control would you use to increase or decrease the amount of bass you hear?

_____

3. According to the instructions, how do you reduce tape hiss? _____

_____

4. Under what heading would you find directions about how to adjust the left and right output levels? _____

_____

5. **ASSESSMENT PRACTICE** Circle the letter of the correct answer.
   Where is the balance control found on this system?
   A. near the handle
   B. near the graphic equalizer controls
   C. next to the RECORD button
   D. on the bass speaker

Adjusting the Sound

B When playing CDs, tapes, or radio programs, use the MEGA BASS/GRAPHIC EQUALIZER controls to equalize the reproduced sound. You can also adjust the balance of the left and right output levels.

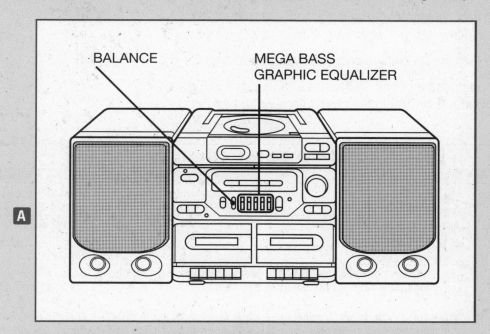

BALANCE   MEGA BASS
GRAPHIC EQUALIZER

A

C **To equalize the reproduced sound** Adjust the MEGA BASS/GRAPHIC EQUALIZER controls

Frequency coverage	Slide the control toward +10	Slide the control toward -10
MEGA BASS 100 Hz	**D** to increase heavy bass sounds	**D** to decrease heavy bass sounds
400 Hz	to emphasize speaking voice, middle frequencies of instrumental music	to de-emphasize speaking voice, middle frequencies of instrumental music
1 kHz	to provide more presence of vocals	to provide less presence of vocals
4 kHz	to heighten overall brightness of sound	to lessen overall brightness of sound
10 kHz	to increase high treble sounds	to decrease high treble sounds or reduce high frequencey noise/tape hiss

Product Information: Safety Guidelines

Safety guidelines are facts and recommendations provided by government agencies or product manufacturers offering instructions and warnings about safe use of these products. Look at the sample guidelines as you read each strategy below.

A The **title** identifies what product the safety guidelines focus on.

B This section lists **recommendations** that product owners and users should follow in order to ensure safe usage of the product.

C This section lists the **hazards** associated with the product.

D This section includes a phone number and e-mail address where dangerous products or product-related injuries can be reported.

A Proper Child Safety Seat Use Chart

	Infants	Toddlers	Young Children
Weight	Birth to 1 year At least 20–22 lbs.	Over 1 year and Over 20–40 lbs.	Over 40 lbs. Ages 4–8, unless 4' 9"
Type of Seat	Infant only or rear-facing convertible	Convertible/Forward-facing	Belt-positioning booster seat
Seat Position	Rear-facing only	Forward-facing	Forward-facing
Always Make Sure: **B**	Children to one year and at least 20 lbs. are in rear-facing seats. **C** Harness straps are at or below shoulder level (to avoid abdominal injury).	Harness straps are at or above shoulders. Most seats require top slot for forward-facing seats.	Belt-positioning booster seats are used with both lap and shoulder belt. The shoulder belt crosses the chest and shoulder (to avoid abdominal injury).
Warning	All children age 12 and under should ride in the back seat.	All children age 12 and under should ride in the back seat.	All children age 12 and under should ride in the back seat.

D For more information, contact the National Highway Traffic Safety Administration at 1-888-327-4236 or send e-mail to webmaster@nhtsa.dot.gov.

‖ MARK IT UP ▷ Read the safety guidelines to help you answer these questions.

1. Which way should safety seats for infants face? _____

2. What are the two types of seats that can be used with toddlers? _____

   _____

3. Circle the e-mail address you can use to contact the agency that issued these guidelines.

4. **ASSESSMENT PRACTICE** These safety guidelines are from the
   A. California Highway Patrol.
   B. Center for Science in the Public Interest.
   C. Automobile Insurers' Product Testing Institute.
   D. National Highway Traffic Safety Administration.

Reading a Bus Schedule

Knowing how to read a transportation schedule accurately will help you figure out how to get where you want to go. Look at the example as you read each strategy on this list.

A Scan the **title** to know what the schedule covers.

B Look for **labels** or **explanations** that explain what **dates** or **days of the week** the service is available.

C Look for **expressions of time** to know what hours or minutes are listed on the schedule.

D Study the **labels** identifying the different stops on the schedule.

E Look for changes or **exceptions** to the regular schedule.

A SCHEDULE   SPRING/SUMMER 2002

		TO YOSEMITE	FROM YOSEMITE
Mammoth Lakes	Mammoth Mountain Inn	7:00AM	8:50PM
	Juniper Springs Summit	7:08AM	8:42PM
	Old Mammoth Road	7:13AM	8:37PM
	Highway 203- Shilo Inn	7:15AM	8:35PM
	Highway 203- Mammoth Mountain RV Park	7:17AM	8:33PM
June Lake	Scenic Byway Kiosk	7:30AM	8:20PM
	June Mountain Ski Area Parking Lot	7:40AM	8:10PM
	Silver Lake Parking Lot	7:55AM	7:55PM
Lee Vining	Best Western Motel	8:10AM	7:40PM
	Forest Svc Visitor Center	8:13AM	7:37PM
	Tioga Mobil Gas Mart	8:18AM	7:32PM
Tuolumne Meadows	Tuolumne Meadows Store	9:00AM	6:50PM
	Tuolumne Meadows Visitors' Center	9:05AM	6:45PM
	Cathedral Trailhead	9:10AM	6:40PM
	White Wolf Lodge	9:50AM	6:00PM
	Crane Flat Gas Station	10:20AM	5:30PM
	Yosemite Visitor Center	10:50AM	5:00PM

B Spring/Summer 2002 service runs on Saturday and Sunday only through June. Starting July 1, runs are available daily through September 2. Starting on September 7, weekend-only service returns running Saturday and Sunday until September 29.

Service is available on the following holidays: May 27, July 4 and September 2.

E Service dates are based upon the assumption that Tioga Pass will be open. Service dates will change if the status of the pass differs.

Multi-passenger vans may be used on this run. Those riders with children requiring a car child seat or those riders with bikes or large backpacks should inquire about availability when calling for tickets.

CONNECTIONS

Runs connect to/from many tours in the Park, including the Valley Tour starting as early as Noon. **For information on tours call Yosemite Concession Services at (209) 372-1240.**

MARK IT UP Answer the following questions using the bus schedule.

1. What time span is covered by this schedule? _____

2. Circle the paragraph that tells you whether the buses run on July 4.

3. What is the latest time you could catch a bus from Yosemite Visitor Center? _____

4. **ASSESSMENT PRACTICE** In Mammoth Lakes, you can catch the bus at
   A. White Wolf Lodge.
   B. Old Mammoth Road.
   C. Silver Lakes Parking Lot.
   D. Tuolumne Meadows Store.

Test Preparation Strategies

In this section, you'll find strategies and practice to help you with many different kinds of standardized tests. The strategies apply to questions based on long and short readings as well as questions about charts, graphs, and product labels. You'll also find examples and practice for revising-and-editing tests and writing tests. Applying the strategies to the practice materials and thinking through the answers will help you succeed in many formal testing situations.

Test Preparation Strategies

You can prepare for tests in several ways. First, study and understand the content that will be on the test. Second, learn as many test-taking techniques as you can. These techniques will help you better understand the questions and how to answer them. Following are some general suggestions for preparing for and taking tests. In the next parts, you'll find more detailed suggestions, together with test-taking practice.

Successful Test Taking

 Study Content Throughout the Year

1. **Master the content of your language arts class.** The best way to study for tests is to read, understand, and review the content of your language arts class. Read your daily assignments carefully. Study the notes that you have taken in class. Participate in class discussions. Work with classmates in small groups to help one another learn. You might trade writing assignments and comment on your classmates' work.

2. **Use your textbook for practice.** Your textbook includes many different types of questions. Some may ask you to talk about a story you just read. Others may ask you to figure out what's wrong with a sentence or how to make a paragraph sound better. Try answering these questions out loud and in writing. This type of practice can make taking a test much easier.

3. **Learn how to understand the information in charts, maps, and graphic organizers.** One type of test question may ask you to look at a graphic organizer, such as a spider map, and explain something about the information you see there. Another type of question may ask you to look at a map to find a particular place. You'll find charts, maps, and graphic organizers to study in your literature textbook. You'll also find charts, maps, and graphs in your science, mathematics, and social studies textbooks. When you look at these, ask yourself, What information is being presented and why is it important?

4. **Practice taking tests.** Use copies of tests you have taken in the past or in other classes for practice. Every test has a time limit, so set a timer for 15 or 20 minutes and then begin your practice. Try to finish the test in the time you've given yourself.

✔ **Reading Check**

In what practical way can your textbooks help you prepare for a test?

5. **Talk about test-taking experiences.** After you've taken a classroom test or quiz, talk about it with your teacher and classmates. Which types of questions were the hardest to understand? What made them difficult? Which questions seemed easiest, and why? When you share test-taking techniques with your classmates, everyone can become a successful test taker.

 ## Use Strategies During the Test

1. **Read the directions carefully.** You can't be a successful test taker unless you know exactly what you are expected to do. Look for key words and phrases, such as *circle the best answer, write a paragraph,* or *choose the word that best completes each sentence.*

2. **Learn how to read test questions.** Test questions can sometimes be difficult to figure out. They may include unfamiliar language or be written in an unfamiliar way. Try rephrasing the question in a simpler way using words you understand. Always ask yourself, What type of information does this question want me to provide?

3. **Pay special attention when using a separate answer sheet.** If you accidentally skip a line on an answer sheet, all the rest of your answers may be wrong! Try one or more of the following techniques:

   • Use a ruler on the answer sheet to make sure you are placing your answers on the correct line.

   • After every five answers, check to make sure you're on the right line.

   • Each time you turn a page of the test booklet, check to make sure the number of the question is the same as the number of the answer line on the answer sheet.

   • If the answer sheet has circles, fill them in neatly. A stray pencil mark might cause the scoring machine to count the answer as incorrect.

4. **If you're not sure of the answer, make your best guess.** Unless you've been told that there is a penalty for guessing, choose the answer that you think is likeliest to be correct.

5. **Keep track of the time.** Answering all the questions on a test usually results in a better score. That's why finishing the test is important. Keep track of the time you have left. At the beginning of the test, figure out how many questions you will have to answer by the halfway point in order to finish in the time given.

✔ **Reading Check**
What are at least two good ways to avoid skipping lines on an answer sheet?

Understand Types of Test Questions

Most tests include two types of questions: multiple choice and open-ended. Specific strategies will help you understand and correctly answer each type of question.

A multiple-choice question has two parts. The first part is the question itself, called the stem. The second part is a series of possible answers. Usually four possible answers are provided, and only one of them is correct. Your task is to choose the correct answer. Here are some strategies to help you do just that.

1. Read and think about each question carefully before looking at the possible answers.

2. Pay close attention to key words in the question. For example, look for the word *not,* as in "Which of the following is not a cause of the conflict in this story?"

3. Read and think about all of the possible answers before making your choice.

4. Reduce the number of choices by eliminating any answers you know are incorrect. Then, think about why some of the remaining choices might also be incorrect.

   - If two of the choices are pretty much the same, both are probably wrong.

   - Answers that contain any of the following words are usually incorrect: *always, never, none, all,* and *only.*

5. If you're still unsure about an answer, see if any of the following applies:

   - When one choice is longer and more detailed than the others, it is often the correct answer.

   - When a choice repeats a word that is in the question, it may be the correct answer.

   - When two choices are direct opposites, one of them is likely the correct answer.

   - When one choice includes one or more of the other choices, it is often the correct answer.

   - When a choice includes the word *some* or *often,* it may well be the correct answer.

✔ **Reading Check**

What words in a multiple-choice question probably signal a wrong answer?

- If one of the choices is *All of the above,* make sure that at least two of the other choices seem correct.

- If one of the choices is *None of the above,* make sure that none of the other choices seems correct.

An **open-ended test item** can take many forms. It might ask you to write a word or phrase to complete a sentence. You might be asked to create a chart, draw a map, or fill in a graphic organizer. Sometimes, you will be asked to write one or more paragraphs in response to a writing prompt. Use the following strategies when reading and answering open-ended items:

1. If the item includes directions, read them carefully. Take note of any steps required.

2. Look for key words and phrases in the item as you plan how you will respond. Does the item ask you to identify a cause-and-effect relationship or to compare and contrast two or more things? Are you supposed to provide a sequence of events or make a generalization? Does the item ask you to write an essay in which you state your point of view and then try to persuade others that your view is correct?

3. If you're going to be writing a paragraph or more, plan your answer. Jot down notes and a brief outline of what you want to say before you begin writing.

4. Focus your answer. Don't include everything you can think of, but be sure to include everything the item asks for.

5. If you're creating a chart or drawing a map, make sure your work is as clear as possible.

✔ **Reading Check**
What are at least three key strategies for answering an open-ended question?

Reading Test Model
LONG SELECTIONS

DIRECTIONS Here is a selection titled "Waiting for the A-Train, The Sophisticated Pigeon" by Randy Kennedy. The notes in the side columns will help you prepare for the kinds of questions that are likely to follow readings like this. You might want to preview the questions on pages 477 and 478 before you begin reading.

Waiting for the A-Train, The Sophisticated Pigeon
by Randy Kennedy

In the annals of strange subway stories—some pure urban legend, some alarmingly real—there has always been a menagerie of animals.

Stories of alligators roaming the tunnels, of pet snakes loose on trains, of rats tough enough to survive the third rail. There have been eyewitness accounts of live chickens, on their way from poultry market to soup pot, escaping from sacks and running amok through the cars. Recently, someone posted a story on the Internet about a man in the subway walking a dog that was being ridden by a cat, the dog and cat dressed in matching Uncle Sam hats. (The story was accompanied by a photograph to prove that it was not made up by Dr. Seuss.)

But one subway animal story has been so persistent and widespread that it simply cried out to be investigated: the case of the train-riding pigeons of Far Rockaway.

A little more than a year ago, a motorman and conductor on the A line, which terminates at the Far Rockaway station in Queens, swore to this reporter that it was true. They said it was common knowledge among long-time riders and those who worked on the line. Pigeons, they said, would board the trains at the outdoor terminal and step off casually at the next station down the line, Beach 25th Street, as if they were heading south but were too lazy, or too fat, to fly.

The inquiry began the other afternoon, when the question was put to a car cleaning supervisor at the terminal. He appeared suspiciously nervous about the subject. "Oh, no," he said. "Our trains have no pigeons."

But Andrew Rizzo, 44, a cleaner sweeping in a nearby train, looked around and smiled broadly as if he were finally going to get to reveal his secret.

The birds ride the trains all the time, he explained, motivated not by sloth but by simple hunger and ignorance: when the trains lay over at the terminal to be cleaned, for about twenty minutes, pigeons amble through the doors, looking for forgotten crumbs. But being pigeons, they do not listen for the announcement that the train is leaving, and the doors close on them. They ride generally for one stop, exiting as soon as the doors open again.

"If you don't know what's going on," said Mr. Rizzo, pushing his glasses up on his nose, "you'd think they knew what they were doing. It's a little freaky."

Mr. Rizzo has a soft spot in his heart for pigeons, who helped him make a living in Central Park in the late 1980s when he was less gainfully employed. He would wear straps with tiny cups of birdfeed on his arms and head and would soon be covered with pigeons, Hitchcockstyle. He would put out a donation box, and pull in $200 a weekend. "I still feed them sometimes," he said. "I feel bad for the little guys." But he also admitted: "I run them out of the train. I don't want them to make no mistakes, if you know what I mean." Despite his efforts, they make many little mistakes.

Mr. Rizzo and many of his fellow employees at the terminal have become amateur ornithologists. They said that pigeons—known vulgarly as air rats, more elegantly as rock doves—ride trains at several outdoor stations, such as the Stillwell Avenue station in Coney Island.

Francisco Peña, a conductor on the A, said he watched them step off his train and promptly fly back to the Far Rockaway terminal. Perhaps not quite as impressive as the blue homing pigeon reported to have flown 7,200 miles from France back home to Vietnam in the 1930s, but still, Mr. Peña said, not bad.

Frank Maynor, a car cleaner, noted how the sparrows and seagulls, also plentiful at the terminal, are never bold enough to venture into the cars.

NOTES

Look for cause-and-effect relationships. Circle the statement that explains why the pigeons ride the trains.

Make inferences. What "little mistakes" is Mr. Rizzo referring to?

Use context clues. What are ornithologists?

Notice details and comparisons. Circle details the author gives about sparrows and seagulls. What comparisons does he make with pigeons?

Evaluate the reliability of information. Do you think the subway cleaners are reliable sources of information about the pigeons? Why or why not?

Consider the author's purpose. Why do you think the author wrote this selection?

The sparrows can be seen hopping onto the threshold, looking longingly inside. The gulls loiter outside, like thugs, waiting to tear pizza crusts from the bills of unsuspecting pigeons as soon as they carry them out.

"They shove the pigeons around," said Mr. Maynor, disapprovingly. "But they're going to evolve and start going into the trains, too. They're giving up a lot of food to the pigeons."

On the subject of evolution, Sarah Canty, another cleaner, said she had noticed that the pigeons might be evolving into more alert straphangers. "When the bell goes off, you watch them," she said. "They know the bell like we do." And indeed, when the next bell rang, signaling that a train was about to depart, several pigeons could be seen high-stepping it out of the trains.

But there are those who have either not learned or are yearning to break free from the nest. And at 10:45 yesterday morning, it finally happened: a dark, plump bird with iridescent purple feathers around the neck took a ride. Alone with the bird in the car was Eduard Karlov, a retired procurement officer for the United Nations.

Mr. Karlov, originally from Moscow, glanced over at his fellow passenger and smiled. "He does not bother me, and, in fact, I find him rather amusing," he said, adding, "I cannot give you any more details with respect to pigeons, however."

Now answer questions 1 through 6. Base your answers on the selection "Waiting for the A-Train, The Sophisticated Pigeon." Then check yourself by reading through the side column notes.

Answer Strategies

Think about the title. This question asks you to relate the title to information in the selection. Avoid answers that include factual errors or are only partly correct.

1 In the title, why does the author call the pigeons "sophisticated"?

A. because the pigeons have learned to read subway signs

B. because the author doesn't understand their unusual behavior

C. because the pigeons prove that all urban legends are true

D. because the pigeons have developed resourceful ways of surviving

Look for relevant details. Remember that the supervisor was nervous when questioned about the pigeons. What does this fact tell you about his feelings?

2 How does the cleaning supervisor feel about the pigeons?

E. proud   G. angry

F. embarrassed   H. indifferent

Identify cause-and-effect relationships. Key words and phrases such as *because, as a result,* and *so* often signal cause-and-effect relationships. But for this example, the cause follows the effect in the passage.

3 Why do the pigeons board the train at Far Rockaway station?

A. They're too lazy to fly south.

B. They want to hide from the other birds.

C. They're searching for crumbs of food.

D. They've learned to beg from passengers.

Make inferences. Think about activities pigeons ordinarily perform. Eliminate answers that are not mentioned in the selection, are unlikely, or would not be called mistakes.

4 Based on these sentences, what *little mistakes* do the pigeons make?

> "I don't want them to make no mistakes, if you know what I mean." Despite his efforts, they make many little mistakes.

E. They board trains going the wrong direction.

F. They have food stolen from them by seagulls.

G. They leave droppings in the subway cars.

H. They get stepped on by passengers.

Evaluate primary-source materials. Consider how reliable the author's sources of information are. Eliminate choices that are incorrect or are not really convincing.

5 What convincing information does the author give to support the truth of this subway story?

A. comparison with other urban legends

B. testimony of reliable witnesses

C. interviews with ornithologists

D. statements by government officials

Plan your response. Look at what the question asks and plan how to proceed. For this question, you must state your opinion and identify the details that support your opinion. Then you will need to restate those details in your own words or quote from the selection.

Study the response. Notice how this response includes details and quotations from the selection.

6 How do you think the author feels about the train-riding pigeons of Far Rockaway? Include details and comparisons from the selection to support your answer.

Sample short response for question 6:

The author seems to have great respect for the pigeons. The first clue is his use of the positive adjective "sophisticated" to describe them in the title. He goes on to compare them favorably with sparrows and seagulls, which he says "are never bold enough to venture into the cars." In contrast to the sparrows' timid pacing and the gulls' acting "like thugs, waiting to tear pizza crusts from the bills of unsuspecting pigeons," he describes the pigeons as evolving into "more alert straphangers" who can recognize the subway bell like people do. And that's a lot to say for a bird!

Reading Test Practice
LONG SELECTIONS

NOTES

DIRECTIONS Now it's time to practice what you've learned about reading test items and choosing the best answers. Read the following selection, "My Fight with Jack Dempsey" by Paul Gallico. Use the side columns to make notes about important parts of this selection: main ideas, cause and effect, comparisons and contrasts, difficult vocabulary, supporting details, and so on.

My Fight with Jack Dempsey
by Paul Gallico

It was 1923 and I had been movie critic for the New York *Daily News* a scant six months when the publisher demanded that the smart aleck who kept denouncing the daily film fare be fired. This might have ended my newspaper career had not a friendly managing editor concealed me in the sports department, where I wrote articles without a by-line.

I was assigned to Jack Dempsey's training camp at Saratoga Springs to write some color pieces on his preparation for the defense of his title against the massive Argentinean, Luis Angel Firpo, "the Wild Bull of the Pampas."

There was lots of color at Uncle (Crying) Tom Luther's camp: the rough, tough Dempsey, still no great distance from the hobo jungles of his youth; the scented Beau Brummell; Jack Kearns, his manager; the bland Tex Rickard; famous sports writers; and all the rag, tag and bobtail of the prize-fight world.

But there was also mystery there, at least for me. It was boxing itself.

I had attended a number of prize fights and watched boys tagged on the chin go rubbery at the knees, eyes glazing over suddenly, or seen them fall down, struggling to rise. What worked this havoc with the human mechanism? What was it like to be on the floor from a punch with nine seconds to rise? What thoughts pass through a man's head when he has bees in his brain, sickness gnawing at his middle and molasses in his legs?

How could I write about these things graphically and understandingly without having experienced them? I felt that I had to find out or I would never be any good at my job.

It was foolhardy for a chap who had never boxed in his life to want to climb into the ring with the man-destroyer Dempsey, yet I did just that. If ever a man began a literary career from the reclining position it was myself.

I presented myself to Dempsey one August afternoon on the porch of his cottage at the camp and asked whether he would spar a round with me so that I might write a story on how it felt to be hit by an expert. Dempsey, clad in an old sweater, sat on the porch rail. He looked me up and down and then inquired in that curiously high-pitched voice of his, "What's the matter, son? Doesn't your editor like you any more?"

I explained that I expected to survive and said my only serious doubt was my ability to take it in the region of the stomach. I asked the great man if he might confine his attentions to a less unhappy target.

Dempsey reflected and then replied, "I think I understand, son. You just want a good punch in the nose." He agreed to stage the affair the following Sunday. We shook hands and I departed well pleased.

Kearns was aghast when he learned what Dempsey had promised. It must be remembered that I was an unknown newcomer to the sports world; I was just under six feet three, weighed 190 pounds and was still in superb condition after having captained the varsity crew at Columbia. When I removed my glasses and stripped down I looked as ugly and capable as any professional pug. Nobody would have guessed that within this menacing monster beat the heart of a rabbit.

Thoughts of the plots and machinations of his profession inflamed the brain of Kearns. I might be what I said I was, or I might be a ringer for the Firpo camp sent to butt, cut or otherwise injure Dempsey before the fight. His verdict to Dempsey was: "Don't take chances with this guy—nail him quick!"

Sunday was a gala day at the camp and some 3,000 spectators were on hand. Hype Igoe, one of the leading sports writers of his time, said to me, "I understand you're fighting the champ this afternoon."

"Oh, not fighting," I said. "We're just going to fool around. He's going to take it easy."

Hype gave me a pitying look and said, "Son, don't you know that man *can't* take it easy?"

I stood near the ring clad in swim trunks, boxing shoes and boxing gloves. Dempsey, wearing a brown leather headprotector, was boxing with a middleweight to develop speed. In a clinch he cuffed the spar mate absently on the back of the neck with the side of his fist.

"What's that tapping on the back of the neck for?" I asked one of Jack's sparring partners.

The fighter replied, "Shakes you up. Here, I'll show you." Thereupon he hit me on the back of the neck with his gloved hand. My eyes glazed, my knees began to give and I nearly collapsed. I came close to being the first man ever to be knocked out *before* climbing into the ring.

Next, Farmer Lodge, a huge heavyweight, entered the ring with Dempsey. He shuffled about for a few seconds; then there was a flurry and a hook accompanied by the sound as of a steer being pole-axed. The Farmer sank to the canvas and lay there. Four mates reverently removed him. Kearns came over to me and said, "O.K., Gallico. You're next."

Kearns did up the introductions in style. "In this corner, the heavyweight champion of the world, Jack Dempsey!" The hills echoed the cheers of the spectators. Next: "In the opposite corner, Paul Gallico of the *Daily News*." From the 3,000 came only a clammy silence, except for one voice from the crowd which inquired mockingly, "Who?"

The bell rang. Reluctantly I left my corner. Dempsey danced over and touched my gloves perfunctorily, then went into his crouching weave from which he could explode those lethal hooks. I felt lonely and assumed my own version of "Pose A" from the *Boxer's Manual,* the same being left arm extended fully and all the rest of me removed as far from Jack as possible.

Dempsey pursued, weaving and bobbing. Gone was the friendly smile with which he had lulled me on the porch. With the broad leather headband across his brow, baleful eyes and snarling lips, he resembled nothing so much as a tiger stalking his kill. I wasn't angry at him, but he seemed irritated at my presence. I established that there was some room behind me and retreated thither.

Someone in the crowd made a rude noise. Its result was to undo me by arousing the pride of the Gallicos. Tentatively, I stuck out my left. Dempsey ran into it with his nose. Wow! A point for Gallico. Overwhelmed by what I had done, I poked out another left, and another, landing them all for the simple reason that Dempsey didn't bother to defend himself.

Three jabs landed! Why this was fun. Fancy Dan Gallico, the Galloping Ghost of the Squared Circle. I'll just try another. I did.

"BOOOOOOOOOOOM!"

I can remember seeing Dempsey's berry-brown arm flash for one instant before my eyes. Then there was this awful explosion within the confines of my skull, followed by a bright light, a tearing sensation and then darkness.

Slowly it grew light again. I was sitting on the canvas with one leg folded under me, my mouth bleeding, grinning foolishly. The ring made a clockwise revolution, stopped and then returned with a counterclockwise movement.

I heard Kearns counting over me. "Six—seven—eight—"
And, like an idiot, I got up!

I didn't have to. I had proved my point. I had gained the precious secret I had sought. But the posture on the deck was humiliating before all those people. And so, with my head swimming and a roaring in my ears, I climbed to my feet on legs of soft rubber tubing.

Dempsey rushed over and pulled me into a clinch, dancing me around and at the same time holding me up. He had proved *his* point, namely, that I wasn't any ringer but just a bum fresh out of college who had never had a glove on. Even Kearns was laughing.

Dempsey whispered into my ear, "Hang on and wrestle around until your head clears, son."

Mercy from the killer! I clutched him like a lost brother. We wrestled around a bit. Absently, Dempsey hit me a half dozen of those affectionate taps on the back of my neck, and the next thing I remember was Kearns again counting over me. I would have been there yet except they needed the premises for further exercises. They told me the affair lasted just one minute 37 seconds.

I was assisted from the enclosure and taken some place else to lie down until my addled wits collected themselves sufficiently for me to get to my typewriter. I had a splitting headache and was grateful to be alive.

My story was printed under my first sports by-line. They say that the publisher of the *News* laughed his head off when he read it and saw the photograph of me stretched out colder than a mackerel. About a year later he made me sports editor.

I do not recommend methods quite so drastic to other writers aspiring to more realism and more understanding in their writing. I only know that, for me, it worked. It taught me that, painful as it may be to acquire it, there is no substitute for experience.

Now answer questions 1 through 7. Base your answers on the selection, "My Fight with Jack Dempsey."

1 Why did the author decide to fight Jack Dempsey?

    A. because he wanted to prove he was as good a boxer as Dempsey

    B. because Dempsey would only talk to him in the boxing ring

    C. because he thought firsthand experience would enhance his writing

    D. because he hated sports writing and wanted to change careers

2 What is the meaning of the following sentence?

    If ever a man began a literary career from the reclining position it was myself.

    E. The author's first important sports writing was about getting knocked out in the boxing ring by Dempsey.

    F. Writing was so easy for the author that he was able to do it lying down while watching Dempsey box.

    G. The author looked up to Jack Dempsey as a boxer and a writer and someone who could give him career advice.

    H. The author began writing notes to Dempsey because he was afraid to talk to him face to face.

3 Jack Dempsey's initial attitude toward the author can best be described as

    A. annoyed and hostile.

    B. alarmed and protective.

    C. bored and indifferent.

    D. amused and accepting.

4 Why did the author get up and continue fighting after being knocked out?

    E. He hadn't yet proved his point.

    F. He couldn't accept being humiliated.

    G. The referee forced him to finish the fight.

    H. The blow had confused his thinking.

5 Based on information in the selection, how long do most boxing matches usually last?

    A. under thirty seconds

    B. more than a minute and a half

    C. ten minutes

    D. ten rounds

6 What was the author's primary purpose in writing this selection?

    E. to persuade readers to attend boxing matches

    F. to explain how to become a sports writer

    G. to share a personal experience and its lessons

    H. to amuse readers by poking fun at himself

7 Read the following sentences.

> I had proved my point. I had gained the precious secret I had sought. What was the author's "precious secret"? Support your answer with details from the selection.

_____

_____

_____

_____

_____

_____

_____

_____

_____

_____

_____

_____

_____

_____

THINKING IT THROUGH

The notes in the side columns will help you think through your answers. See the key at the bottom of the page.

1 Why did the author decide to fight Jack Dempsey?

   A. because he wanted to prove he was as good a boxer as Dempsey

   B. because Dempsey would only talk to him in the boxing ring

   C. because he thought firsthand experience would enhance his writing

   D. because he hated sports writing and wanted to change careers

> Eliminate reasons that are not supported in the selection. Did the author want to prove himself as a boxer or change careers? Did Dempsey refuse to talk to him outside the boxing ring? The only answer that makes sense is to gain *firsthand experience*.

2 What is the meaning of the following sentence?

   If ever a man began a literary career from the reclining position it was myself.

   E. The author's first important sports writing was about getting knocked out in the boxing ring by Dempsey.

   F. Writing was so easy for the author that he was able to do it lying down while watching Dempsey box.

   G. The author looked up to Jack Dempsey as a boxer and a writer and someone who could give him career advice.

   H. The author began writing notes to Dempsey because he was afraid to talk to him face to face.

> The key phrases from the quotation are *literary career* and *reclining position*. What meanings do they have in the context of the selection?

3 Jack Dempsey's initial attitude toward the author can best be described as

   A. annoyed and hostile.

   B. alarmed and protective.

   C. bored and indifferent.

   D. amused and accepting.

> Notice that choices A and D are opposites. This suggests that one of them is probably the correct answer.

4 Why did the author get up and continue fighting after being knocked out?

   E. He hadn't yet proved his point.

   F. He couldn't accept being humiliated.

   G. The referee forced him to finish the fight.

   H. The blow had confused his thinking.

> Reread the author's description of being knocked out. Then eliminate incorrect choices. The author says "I had proved my point," which rules out choice E. Is there evidence to support action by the referee or the author's fuzzy thinking?

Answers: 1. C, 2. E, 3. D, 4. F

5 Based on information in the selection, how long do most boxing matches usually last?

   A. under thirty seconds

   B. more than a minute and a half

   C. ten minutes

   D. ten rounds

6 What was the author's primary purpose in writing this selection?

   E. to persuade readers to attend boxing matches

   F. to explain how to become a sports writer

   G. to share a personal experience and its lessons

   H. to amuse readers by poking fun at himself

7 Read the following sentences.

> I had proved my point. I had gained the precious secret I had sought. What was the author's "precious secret"? Support your answer with details from the selection.

   The author's precious secret was that he had what it took to become a good writer. He had decided to fight Dempsey so he could "write a story on how it felt to be hit by an expert." He was willing to risk humiliation and bodily harm to get the only material that would make a good story—firsthand experience. And that's exactly the experience he got. After feeling the humiliation of "a clammy silence, except for one voice from the crowd which inquired mockingly, 'Who?'" when his name was announced in the ring, he ending up "sitting on the canvas with one leg folded under me, my mouth bleeding, grinning foolishly." He survived, though, and his courage paid off in the lesson he learned: "painful as it may be to acquire it, there is no substitute for experience." And that experience was the beginning of his literary career.

Reading Test Model
SHORT SELECTIONS

DIRECTIONS This reading selection is just two paragraphs long. The strategies you have just used can also help you with this shorter selection. As you read the selection, respond to the notes in the side column.

When you've finished reading, you'll find two multiple-choice questions. Again, use the side column notes to help you understand what each question is asking for and why each answer is the correct one.

Harriet Tubman, Freedom Fighter

One of the most famous conductors on the Underground Railroad was Harriet Tubman. Born into slavery in Maryland, the thirteen-year-old Tubman once tried to save another slave from punishment. The angry overseer fractured Tubman's skull with a two-pound weight. She suffered fainting spells for the rest of her life but did not let that stop her from working for freedom. When she was twenty-five, Tubman learned that her owner was about to sell her. Instead of accepting that fate, she escaped.

After her escape, Harriet Tubman made nineteen dangerous journeys to free enslaved persons. The tiny woman carried a pistol to frighten off slave hunters, and medicine to quiet crying babies. Her enemies offered $40,000 for her capture, but no one caught her. "I never run my train off the track and I never lost a passenger," she proudly declared. Among the people she saved were her parents.

1 Which statement from the passage supports the idea that Harriet Tubman demonstrated courage and strength of character?

   A. *The thirteen-year-old Tubman once tried to save another slave from punishment.*

   B. *She suffered fainting spells for the rest of her life.*

   C. *The angry overseer fractured Tubman's skull with a two-pound weight.*

   D. *When she was twenty-five, Tubman learned that her owner was about to sell her.*

2 Why did Tubman carry medicine to quiet crying babies?

   E. because the sound reminded her of her painful childhood

   F. to prove her qualifications to enter medical school

   G. to protect her charges against detection by slave hunters

   H. because she thought slaves shouldn't have children

Reading Strategies for Assessment

Find the main idea and supporting details. Write the main idea of this passage in your own words. Then underline details in the passage that support this idea.

Make inferences. Why might Tubman have wanted to quiet crying babies?

Answer Strategies

Identify supporting details. This question asks you to look for a detail that supports the main idea of Tubman's strong character. Eliminate choices that relate to other ideas.

Analyze the context. A major concern of travelers on the Underground Railroad was to move quickly and quietly. The only answer choice that addresses this concern is G. There is no information in the passage to support the other choices.

Answers:
1 A, 2 G

DIRECTIONS Some test questions ask you to analyze a visual rather than read a passage. Analyze this pie chart and answer the questions that follow.

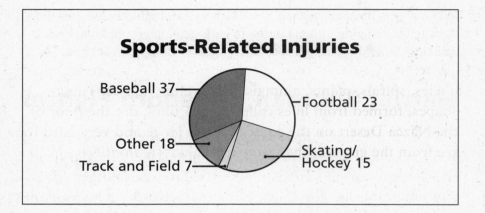

Read the title. Based on the title, what information does the chart provide?

Examine the body of the chart. Does it give exact numbers of injuries, percentages, or other information?

Analyze labels. What does the label *Other* mean?

Answer Strategies

Identify key words. The word to focus on in this question is *NOT*. Eliminate the three choices that give information that *is* found in the chart.

Analyze the question. The phrase *You'd be about as likely to be injured playing basketball* means that the answer will be a percentage about equal to the percentage of basketball injuries. Check each answer choice by doing the simple math.

Evaluate answer choices. You can eliminate A because the category *Other* is the sum of more than one unnamed sport. Look for the choice that is the smallest percentage.

3 What information would you NOT find in this chart?

A. the percentage of injuries for sports not named specifically

B. the percentage of injuries incurred in track and field events

C. the number of basketball injuries in the United States in 2001

D. the relative risks of injury when playing football and basketball

4 You'd be about as likely to be injured playing basketball as you would be

E. playing all other sports combined.

F. playing all the sports not named specifically.

G. participating in track and field and skating/hockey.

H. participating in skating/hockey and playing football.

5 According to this chart, in which sport are you LEAST likely to be injured?

A. a sport not named specifically

B. track and field

C. skating/hockey

D. football

Reading Test Practice
SHORT SELECTIONS

DIRECTIONS Use the following to practice your skills. Read "The Nazca Lines: A Big Question Mark" and circle the key ideas. Then answer the multiple-choice questions that follow.

NOTES

The Nazca Lines

There are thousands of shapes: long straight lines, triangles, circles, spirals, plants, animals, and human figures. These shapes, formed from lines called Nazca lines, dot the floor of the Nazca Desert on the coast of Peru. Huge and very hard to see from the ground, they were not discovered until the 1930s by pilots looking for water in the desert.

How did the lines get there? They were created by the Nazca people, who lived between 200 B.C. and A.D. 600 in Peru. No one knows for sure why the Nazca created the lines, but there are many different theories.

Because the complicated figures of lizards, hummingbirds, monkeys, and even a huge pelican can only be seen from the air, some people have proposed that the lines were created or directed by beings from another planet. Although this explanation has captured the imaginations of many people, there is no evidence to support it.

1 What was the author's purpose in writing this passage?

    A. to persuade readers that the Nazca lines are not real

    B. to inform readers about the mysterious Nazca lines

    C. to explain why the Nazca lines were created

    D. to explain theories of how the Nazca made the lines

2 Read the following sentence from the passage.

> **Although this explanation has captured the imaginations of many people, there is no evidence to support it.**

The words *this explanation has captured the imaginations of many people* means that

    E. many people understand why the Nazca lines were created.

    F. many people believe that aliens created the Nazca lines.

    G. many people imagine there are Nazca lines on other planets.

    H. people imagine many different explanations for the Nazca lines.

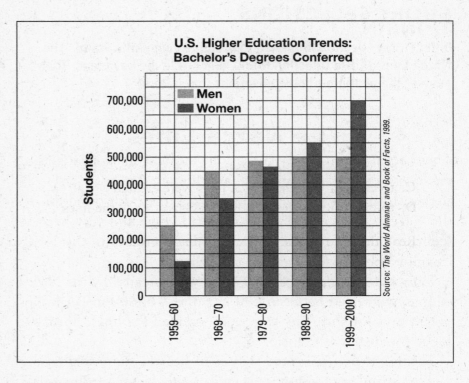

**U.S. Higher Education Trends:
Bachelor's Degrees Conferred**

Source: *The World Almanac and Book of Facts, 1999.*

DIRECTIONS Use the graph to answer questions 3, 4, and 5.

3 One conclusion you can draw from the chart is that between 1960 and 2000,

A. college women got increasingly better grades than men.

B. the number of men earning bachelor's degrees decreased.

C. the number of women earning bachelor's degrees almost tripled.

D. college men dropped out to serve in the armed forces.

4 In which year did the number of women earning bachelor's degrees first surpass the number of men?

E. 1970   G. 1990

F. 1980   H. 2000

5 If the trend for bachelor's degree earners presented in this chart continues, in 2010

A. the ratio of women to men will increase.

B. the numbers of women and men with bachelor's degrees will be equal.

C. the ratio of women to men will decrease.

D. the number of men will exceed the number of women.

THINKING IT THROUGH

The notes in the side columns will help you think through your answers. Check the key at the bottom of the page. How well did you do?

1 What was the author's purpose in writing this passage?

    A. to persuade readers that the Nazca lines are not real

    B. to inform readers about the mysterious Nazca lines

    C. to explain why the Nazca lines were created

    D. to explain theories of how the Nazca made the lines

> The key words are *author's purpose*. Which statement identifies the author's main reason for writing? Eliminate choices that are not addressed in the passage or are only partially true.

2 Read the following sentence from the passage.

> **Although this explanation has captured the imaginations of many people, there is no evidence to support it.**

The words *this explanation has captured the imaginations of many people* means that

    E. many people understand why the Nazca lines were created.

    F. many people believe that aliens created the Nazca lines.

    G. many people imagine there are Nazca lines on other planets.

    H. people imagine many different explanations for the Nazca lines.

> Find the quoted sentences in the passage and reread the entire paragraph. Note that the explanation referred to is *that the lines were created or directed by beings from another planet*.

3 One conclusion you can draw from the chart is that between 1960 and 2000,

    A. college women got increasingly better grades than men.

    B. the number of men earning bachelor's degrees decreased.

    C. the number of women earning bachelor's degrees almost tripled.

    D. college men dropped out to serve in the armed forces.

> The title of the chart indicates that it presents information only about bachelor's degrees conferred. Therefore, you can eliminate choices A and D, which deal with grades and service in the armed forces. Test the other choices against the evidence in the chart.

4 In which year did the number of women earning bachelor's degrees first surpass the number of men?

    E. 1970   **G.** 1990

    F. 1980   **H.** 2000

> The words *first surpass* tell you to examine the chart to find the earliest year in which the bar for women was taller than the bar for men.

5 If the trend for bachelor's degree earners presented in this chart continues, in 2010

    A. the ratio of women to men will increase.

    B. the numbers of women and men with bachelor's degrees will be equal.

    C. the ratio of women to men will decrease.

    D. the number of men will exceed the number of women.

> Identify the overall trend shown in the chart. Has the number of women earning bachelor's degrees been increasing faster than the number of men?

Answers:
1.B, 2.F, 3.C, 4.G, 5.A

Functional Reading Test Model

DIRECTIONS Study the warranty statement below. Then answer the questions that follow.

Littleton Electronics Full Five-Year Warranty

Coverage: For five years from the date of original consumer purchase of this product, we promise, without charge, to repair or replace, at our option, any defects in material or workmanship. Warranty coverage does not include defects due to lack of care (see accompanying instructions for guidance) or any other warranties made by any other person, including authorized distributors of our products.

ALL INCIDENTAL AND CONSEQUENTIAL DAMAGES ARE EXCLUDED FROM WARRANTY COVERAGE. SOME STATES DO NOT ALLOW THE EXCLUSION OR LIMITATION OF INCIDENTAL OR CONSEQUENTIAL DAMAGES, SO THE ABOVE EXCLUSION MAY NOT APPLY TO YOU. THIS WARRANTY GIVES YOU SPECIFIC LEGAL RIGHTS, AND YOU MAY ALSO HAVE OTHER RIGHTS THAT VARY FROM STATE TO STATE.

Warranty Service Procedure: When warranty service is needed, deliver or send the product, insured and properly packaged, freight prepaid, with a description of the apparent defect and the means to ascertain the date of original consumer purchase (such as copy of your receipt or canceled check) to the factory service center listed below. If at any time you are not satisfied with our warranty service, contact Vice President, Service and Distribution, 7777 Eastgate Rd., Wesley, OR 97777.

1 What promise does this warranty offer buyers of the company's product?

A. to replace the product if the buyer is not satisfied

B. to repair or replace a defective product

C. to repair the product for as long as the buyer owns it

D. to refund the buyer's money if the product is returned within five years

2 This warranty will not cover damages

E. due to mishandling or improper use of the product in certain states.

F. noticed after the product is purchased in every state.

G. due to defects in workmanship in certain states.

H. made by persons other than the buyers in every state.

3 How will a lifetime extended warranty offered by a store that sells Littleton Electronics products affect this warranty?

A. It will cancel out and replace this warranty.

B. It will take effect after this five-year warranty expires.

C. It will extend this warranty for the lifetime of the product.

D. It will have no effect under the terms of this warranty.

Functional Reading Test Practice

DIRECTIONS Study the following warning label from a can of insect spray. Circle the information you think is most important. Then answer the multiple-choice questions that follow.

PRECAUTIONARY STATEMENTS

Hazards to Humans and Domestic Animals

CAUTION: Harmful if swallowed or absorbed through the skin. Avoid breathing spray mist. Avoid contact with skin or clothing. Wash thoroughly with soap and water after using. Provide adequate ventilation of area being treated. Do not apply to humans, plants, or pets, or contaminate feed, foodstuffs, dishes, or utensils. Cover and avoid spraying fish aquariums. Cover or remove exposed food, dishes, utensils, and food-handling equipment. Keep out of reach of children.

Practical Treatment

If swallowed: Do not induce vomiting. Call a physician or Poison Control Center immediately. If in eyes: Flush with plenty of water.
If on skin: Wash promptly with soap and water. Get medical attention if irritation develops.

If inhaled: Remove victim to fresh air. Apply artificial respiration if indicated.

NOTE TO PHYSICIAN: Product contains petroleum distillate (aspiration hazard).

Physical or Chemical Hazards

FLAMMABLE. CONTENTS UNDER PRESSURE. Keep away from heat, sparks, open flame, or pilot lights. Do not puncture or incinerate container. Exposure to temperatures above 130° F may cause bursting.

Questions or comments: Call (888) BUG-SPRAY

---

1 What should you do if you accidentally touch an area that has just been sprayed with this product?

A. Call 911.
B. Call (888) BUG-SPRAY.
C. Get medical attention immediately.
D. Wash your hands with lots of soap and water.

2 Why does the warning label include a note to physicians?

E. so the manufacturer of the spray will not be legally responsible for injuries

F. because physicians use more insect sprays than other groups of people do

G. to give them information that will help them treat victims of inhalation

H. to reassure users that the label has been approved by physicians

3 What might cause the bug spray can to burst?

A. shaking it too hard

B. placing it near gardening tools

C. exposing it to high temperatures

D. dropping it

4 When using this product in the home, what are you advised to do?

E. Allow air to move through the area during and after treatment.

F. Drain fish tanks and then refill with fresh water.

G. Wash all dishes and utensils thoroughly after spraying.

H. Throw away all foodstuffs that were purchased before spraying the area.

THINKING IT THROUGH

The notes in the side columns will help you think through your answers. Check the key at the bottom of the page. How well did you do?

1 What should you do if you accidentally touch an area that has just been sprayed with this product?

A. Call 9ll.
B. Call (888) BUG-SPRAY.
C. Get medical attention immediately.
D. Wash your hands with lots of soap and water.

> If you have touched the product, the appropriate action would be found in the *Practical Treatment* section under "If on skin."

2 Why does the warning label include a note to physicians?

E. so the manufacturer of the spray will not be legally responsible for injuries
F. because physicians use more insect sprays than other groups of people do
G. to give them information that will help them treat victims of inhalation
H. to reassure users that the label has been approved by physicians

> Note that the section of the label referred to is called *NOTE TO PHYSICIAN*. You should then be able to eliminate choices that are not meant for physicians.

3 What might cause the bug spray can to burst?

A. shaking it too hard
B. placing it near gardening tools
C. exposing it to high temperatures
D. dropping it

> Scan the label for any statement about the can. Remember that spray cans are under pressure.

4 When using this product in the home, what are you advised to do?

E. Allow air to move through the area during and after treatment.
F. Drain fish tanks and then refill with fresh water.
G. Wash all dishes and utensils thoroughly after spraying.
H. Throw away all foodstuffs that were purchased before spraying the area.

> Reread important directions for use found in the *Caution* section. When using harmful sprays of any kind, what precautionary measures should be taken?

Revising-and-Editing Test Model

Reading Strategies for Assessment

Watch for common errors. Revising-and-editing test questions often focus on typical errors such as mistakes in punctuation, spelling, and capitalization; incomplete sentences; and missing or misplaced information.

DIRECTIONS Read the following paragraph carefully. Then answer the multiple-choice questions that follow. After answering the questions, read the material in the side column to check your answer strategies.

¹Tashi Wangchuk Tenzing an Austrian travel agent was a tired but happy man in May 1997, when he scaled Mount Everest. ²Much of his familys' history has involved mountain climbing. ³In fact, one of his grandfathers, Tenzing Norgay, have the honor of being among the first climbers to reach the top of Mount Everest. ⁴With this feat, he becomes the third generation of his family to successfully reach the summit. ⁵Statistics in the record books for his climb. ⁶Though many people have applauded this accomplishment, they're is a chance that his mountain-climbing days are over. ⁷He is not among the climbers who are planning to return to the peak. ⁸Does this surprise you? ⁹It should. ¹⁰More than 90 percent of the 700 people who have made it to the top of Everest try to scale the mighty mountain again.

Answer Strategies

Commas Use commas to set off appositives.
For help, see Pupil Edition, p. 1405* *Grammar, Usage, and Mechanics Book, p. 43*

1 Which of the following is the correct way to rewrite the first part of sentence 1?

  A. Tashi Wangchuk Tenzing an Austrian travel agent,
  B. Tashi Wangchuk Tenzing an Austrian, travel agent,
  C. Tashi Wangchuk Tenzing, an Austrian travel agent,
  D. Tashi Wangchuk Tenzing, an Austrian, travel agent

Possessive Nouns The phrase *familys' history* shows possession. Therefore, the correct spelling must include an apostrophe. Also note that *family* is a singular noun.
For help, see Pupil Edition, p. 1392 Grammar, Usage, and Mechanics Book, p. 115

2 What is the correct spelling of *familys'* in sentence 2?

  E. families'
  F. family's
  G. familys
  H. families

Complete Sentences A sentence must express a complete thought.
For help, see Pupil Edition, p. 1409 Grammar, Usage, and Mechanics Book, p. 73

3 Which sentence in the paragraph is a fragment?

  A. sentence 5
  B. sentence 8
  C. sentence 9
  D. sentence 10

Answers:
1.C,2.F,3.A

*Pages listed are for the Grammar Handbook in *The Language of Literature* Pupil Edition and the *Grammar, Usage, and Mechanics Book.*

4 What is the correct way to rewrite the main verb in sentence 3?

   E. has

   F. have had

   G. will have

   H. have been

Subject-Verb Agreement Note that the subject of the sentence is *one*. The verb must agree in person and number with this subject.
For help, see Pupil Edition, p. 1410 Grammar, Usage, and Mechanics Book, p. 97

5 Which phrase should replace *he* in sentence 4 to clarify its meaning?

   A. his grandfather

   B. Tashi Wangchuk Tenzing's grandfather

   C. Tenzing Norgay

   D. Tashi Wangchuk Tenzing

Vague Pronoun Reference In sentence 4, *he* is unclear because of the mention of Tenzing Norgay in sentence 3. To find the answer, reread the preceding sentences. Who is the central figure in this paragraph?
For help, see Grammar, Usage, and Mechanics Book, pp. 127-128

6 What is the best way to rewrite sentence 5?

   E. Statistics for his climb have been entered in the record books.

   F. Statistics have for his climb been entered in the record books.

   G. Statistics have been entered for his climb in the record books.

   H. Statistics have been for his climb entered in the record books.

Sentence Fragments A sentence fragment is only part of a sentence. In this case the sentence lacks a predicate.
For help, see Pupil Edition, p. 1409 Grammar, Usage, and Mechanics Book, p. 73

7 Which of the following changes should be made in sentence 6?

   A. Change *they're* to *there*.

   B. Change *they're* to *their*.

   C. Delete the hyphen in *mountain-climbing*.

   D. Change *Though* to *However*.

Commonly Confused Words *There* is often confused with *their* and the contraction *they're*. Choose the word that fits grammatically in the sentence.

8 Where in the paragraph would you add details about why Tenzing does not plan to climb Everest again?

   E. between sentences 1 and 2

   F. between sentences 6 and 7

   G. between sentences 7 and 8

   H. between sentences 8 and 9

Supporting Details Reread the paragraph, paying special attention to the sentences listed in the answer choices. Where would the additional information fit most logically?

Answers:
4.E, 5.D, 6.E, 7.A, 8.G

Revising-and-Editing Test Practice

DIRECTIONS Read the following paragraph carefully. As you read, circle each error you find and identify the error in the side column— for example, you might write *misspelled word* or *not a complete sentence.* When you have finished, circle the letter of the correct choice for each question that follows.

¹How good is your memory? ²Are you able to recall names, dates, and places effortlessly? ³If you can, you probably have a memory that is more sharper than average. ⁴Even so it is probably difficult for you to recall entire pages of text. ⁵That was not the case for the British author and adventurer T. E. Lawrence he accomplished an extraordinary act of memory. ⁶Toiling long and hard over his book *Seven Pillars of Wisdom,* an account of his Arabian adventures, he took the manuscript to his trusted adviser. ⁷Following their discussion, Lawrence put the manuscript in a briefcase and headed home. ⁸The briefcase had been given to him by his grandfather. ⁹While changing trains, the briefcase was lost. ¹⁰Lawrence didn't have no choice but to rewrite the manuscript from memory. ¹¹Yes, that's exactly what he did!

1 Which sentence in this paragraph should be deleted?

A. sentence 1

B. sentence 5

C. sentence 8

D. sentence 11

2 What is the correct form of the comparative adjective in sentence 3?

E. sharper

F. most sharp

G. most sharper

H. more sharpest

3 Which sentence in the paragraph is a run-on?

A. sentence 3

B. sentence 5

C. sentence 6

D. sentence 10

4 Which change should be made to sentence 4?

    E. Add a comma after *so*.
    F. Add a comma after *is*.
    G. Add commas after *even* and *so*.
    H. Add commas before and after *probably*.

5 Which transitional word or phrase should be inserted at the beginning of sentence 6?

    A. As a result of
    B. Meanwhile,
    C. After
    D. On the other hand,

6 Which of the following is the best way to rewrite sentence 9?

    E. While changing trains, Lawrence lost the briefcase.
    F. The briefcase was lost while changing trains.
    G. While changing trains, the briefcase was lost by Lawrence.
    H. While the briefcase was lost, Lawrence changed trains.

7 What change, if any, should be made in sentence 10?

    A. Change *didn't have* to *had*.
    B. Change *no* to *some*.
    C. Change *choice* to *choices*.
    D. No change is necessary.

8 In sentence 11, what is the antecedent of *that*?

    E. changing trains
    F. no choice
    G. the manuscript
    H. to rewrite the manuscript from memory

THINKING IT THROUGH

DIRECTIONS Use the notes in the side column to help you understand why some answers are correct and others are not. See the answer key on the next page. How well did you do?

Reread the paragraph, looking for information that is misplaced or does not belong. Focus on sentences that interrupt the flow of ideas.

1 Which sentence in this paragraph should be deleted?

   A. sentence 1

   B. sentence 5

   C. sentence 8

   D. sentence 11

Remember that the comparative form of most regular adjectives is formed by adding -er to the word. *For help, see Pupil Edition, p. 1399* Grammar, Usage, and Mechanics Book, p. 133*

2 What is the correct form of the comparative adjective in sentence 3?

   E. sharper

   F. most sharp

   G. most sharper

   H. more sharpest

Examine each answer choice, looking for a sentence that expresses more than one complete thought. *For help, see Pupil Edition, p. 1408 Grammar, Usage, and Mechanics Book, p. 73*

3 Which sentence in the paragraph is a run-on?

   A. sentence 3

   B. sentence 5

   C. sentence 6

   D. sentence 10

Introductory phrases are set off by commas. *For help, see Pupil Edition, p. 1413 Grammar, Usage, and Mechanics Book, p. 160*

4 Which change should be made to sentence 4?

   E. Add a comma after *so.*

   F. Add a comma after *is.*

   G. Add commas after *even* and *so.*

   H. Add commas before and after *probably.*

5 Which transitional word or phrase should be inserted at the beginning of sentence 6?

   A. As a result of
   B. Meanwhile,
   C. After
   D. On the other hand,

Transitional words and phrases clarify the relationship between ideas in a paragraph. Are sentences 5 and 6 related by cause and effect, comparison, chronology, or some other connection?

6 Which of the following is the best way to rewrite sentence 9?

   E. While changing trains, Lawrence lost the briefcase.
   F. The briefcase was lost while changing trains.
   G. While changing trains, the briefcase was lost by Lawrence.
   H. While the briefcase was lost, Lawrence changed trains.

Dangling modifiers are tricky. Ask yourself what the phrase *while changing trains* is modifying. Then make sure that the word being modified is the subject of the main part of the sentence.
For help, see Pupil Edition, p. 1406 Grammar, Usage, and Mechanics Book, p. 55

7 What change, if any, should be made in sentence 10?

   A. Change *didn't have* to *had*.
   B. Change *no* to *some*.
   C. Change *choice* to *choices*.
   D. No change is necessary.

Watch out for double negatives. Since the verb phrase includes the word *no*, the verb cannot include a negative element.
For help, see Pupil Edition, p. 1400 Grammar, Usage, and Mechanics Book, p. 139

8 In sentence 11, what is the antecedent of that?

   E. changing trains
   F. no choice
   G. the manuscript
   H. to rewrite the manuscript from memory

An antecedent is a word or phrase for which the pronoun stands. Substitute each choice to see which one makes sense in the sentence.
For help, see Pupil Edition, p. 1395 Grammar, Usage, and Mechanics Book, p. 121

Answers: 1.C, 2.E, 3.B, 4.E, 5.C, 6.E, 7.A, 8.H

Writing Test Model

DIRECTIONS Many tests ask you to write an essay in response to a writing prompt. A writing prompt is a brief statement that describes a writing situation. Some writing prompts ask you to explain what, why, or how. Others ask you to convince someone about something.

As you analyze the following writing prompts, read and respond to the notes in the side column. Then look at the response to each prompt. The notes in the side column will help you understand why each response is considered strong.

Prompt A

> Your school has a chance to receive free educational programs on a cable television network that also includes commercial advertising. Some people say that students shouldn't be watching advertisements during class time. Others think that the educational benefits are the most important consideration.
>
> What is your opinion about this issue? Write a letter to the members of the school board convincing them to accept or reject the plan to bring cable television into the classroom. Support your opinion with solid reasons and relevant details.

Strong Response

Educational programs offered on cable television are a great resource that could provide valuable information to both students and teachers. The benefits of making educational shows available in all classrooms far outweigh the drawbacks of the accompanying commercial advertising.

The main reason our school should take advantage of free educational television is the quantity of useful information it would provide. Much of this information is related to subjects taught in school and would be a good supplement to material provided in textbooks and by teachers. Color video and audio tracks would bring many subjects to life in a way not otherwise possible.

Analyzing the Prompt

Find the main idea. The first paragraph of the prompt clearly presents the writing situation. Restate the main idea in your own words.

Identify your writing task. What are you being asked to write about? What form should your writing take? Who is your audience?

Answer Strategies

State your opinion clearly in the first paragraph. This writer is in favor of educational programming in the school.

Present your argument logically, keeping your audience in mind. The writer begins her argument with the strongest reason. Notice that she uses vocabulary and sentence structure geared to the members of a school board.

Another reason to accept the educational programming is that it would make teachers' jobs easier. Teachers work very hard to stay informed about their subjects, and good educational programs would provide wonderful source material for them. This would both save them time and give them more professional material to share with their students.

A final reason to bring television programs in the classroom is that students have different learning styles. I happen to be an avid reader and a good listener; therefore, I do well with traditional teaching methods. But many students learn better when they can see a concept presented in three dimensions or when they do or make something.

I understand that some people will oppose the free programming because commercials are included with it. Those people may think it is not right to make students watch advertising, because it can create a desire for things people do not really want or need. That may be true, but students are sophisticated media consumers, and they know not to believe everything they see in ads.

In conclusion, the many potential benefits of free educational programming far outweigh the possible disadvantage of commercial advertising. Help students plug into education by not pulling the plug on this great opportunity.

Analyzing the Prompt

Find the main idea. Circle the main idea of this writing prompt.

Identify your writing task. What two issues must your essay address?

Answer Strategies

Clearly state the problem and your proposed solution. This writer identifies the problem of a rising drop-out rate and says a student-run tutoring program can help.

Address the prompt. Here, the writer addresses the first part of the prompt—the reasons students drop out of school.

Include opposing arguments. Notice how the writer describes the program and then addresses a possible objection to it.

Summarize your ideas in the conclusion. The writer sums up his ideas neatly, ending with a provocative, persuasive question.

Prompt B

Many students have trouble performing well in school, and the drop-out rate is increasing dramatically. Write an essay in which you describe the cause of the problem and a possible solution.

Strong Response

Too many students are leaving high school before they graduate. One of every five teens in our city does not earn a diploma. A tutoring program run by students can help turn this trend around.

In a recent survey of forty dropouts, more than half cited academic factors as a major reason for having left school. This lack of achievement may be due to poor study habits, reading problems, or learning disabilities. A student-run tutoring program would help teens with academic problems identify the source of their difficulty and work to overcome it. It would also show struggling students that their classmates care about. Students are the perfect people to staff a tutoring program because they can share helpful hints in a nonjudgmental, supportive atmosphere.

Some people might think that students would be embarrassed to take advantage of such a service, but those I have talked with were enthusiastic. One said, "Sure, I'd go. I know I need help, and maybe another student would understand my problem better than an adult or professional would."

In conclusion, we have a definite problem—dropouts. We also have a workable solution—a student-run tutoring program, and the means to make it work. So what are we waiting for?

Writing Test Practice

DIRECTIONS Read the following writing prompt. Using the strategies you've learned in this Test Preparation Guide, analyze the prompt, plan your response, and then write an essay explaining your position.

Prompt C

The school board is considering two ways to ease classroom overcrowding: (1) keeping schools open all year, with staggered vacation schedules, or (2) dividing the school day into two shifts, with some students attending the early shift and others attending the late shift.

Write an essay in which you discuss the issue, choose one of the options, and provide convincing reasons for your choice.

Scoring Rubrics

DIRECTIONS Use the following checklist to see whether you have written a strong persuasive essay. You will have succeeded if you can check nearly all of the items.

The Prompt

☐ My response meets all the requirements stated in the prompt. I have stated my position clearly and supported it with details. I raised and responded to opposing arguments.

☐ I addressed the audience appropriately.

☐ My essay fits the type of writing suggested in the prompt (letter to the editor, article for the school paper, and so on).

Reasons

☐ The reasons I offer really support my position.

☐ My audience will find the reasons convincing.

☐ I have stated my reasons clearly.

☐ I have given at least three reasons.

☐ I have supported my reasons with sufficient facts, examples, quotations, and other details.

☐ I have presented and responded to opposing arguments.

☐ My reasoning is sound. I have avoided faulty logic.

Order and Arrangement

☐ I have included a strong introduction.

☐ I have included a strong conclusion.

☐ The reasons are arranged in a logical order.

Word Choice

☐ The language of my essay is appropriate for my audience.

☐ I have used precise, vivid words and persuasive language.

Fluency

☐ I have used sentences of varying lengths and structures.

☐ I have connected ideas with transitions and other devices.

☐ I have used correct spelling, punctuation, and grammar.

Personal Word List

Use these pages to build your personal vocabulary. As you read the selections, take time to mark unfamiliar words. These should be words that seem interesting or important enough to add to your permanent vocabulary. After reading, look up the meanings of these words and record the information below. For each word, write a sentence that shows its correct use.

Review your list from time to time. Try to put these words into use in your writing and conversation.

Word: _____

Selection: _____

Page/Line: _____ / _____

Part of Speech: _____

Definition: _____

_____

_____

Sentence: _____

_____

Word: _____

Selection: _____

Page/Line: _____ / _____

Part of Speech: _____

Definition: _____

_____

_____

Sentence: _____

_____

Word: _____

Selection: _____

Page/Line: _____ / _____

Part of Speech: _____

Definition: _____

_____

_____

Sentence: _____

_____

Word: _____

Selection: _____

Page/Line: _____ / _____

Part of Speech: _____

Definition: _____

_____

_____

Sentence: _____

_____

Word: _____

Selection: _____

Page/Line: _____ / _____

Part of Speech: _____

Definition: _____

_____

_____

Sentence: _____

_____

Word: _____

Selection: _____

Page/Line: _____ / _____

Part of Speech: _____

Definition: _____

_____

_____

Sentence: _____

_____

Word:_____

Selection: _____

Page/Line: _____ / _____

Part of Speech: _____

Definition: _____

_____

_____

Sentence: _____

_____

Word:_____

Selection: _____

Page/Line: _____ / _____

Part of Speech: _____

Definition: _____

_____

_____

Sentence: _____

_____

Word:_____

Selection: _____

Page/Line: _____ / _____

Part of Speech: _____

Definition: _____

_____

_____

Sentence: _____

_____

Word:_____

Selection: _____

Page/Line: _____ / _____

Part of Speech: _____

Definition: _____

_____

_____

Sentence: _____

_____

Word:_____

Selection: _____

Page/Line: _____ / _____

Part of Speech: _____

Definition: _____

_____

_____

Sentence: _____

Word:_____

Selection: _____

Page/Line: _____ / _____

Part of Speech: _____

Definition: _____

_____

_____

Sentence: _____

Word:_____

Selection: _____

Page/Line: _____ / _____

Part of Speech: _____

Definition: _____

_____

_____

Sentence: _____

Word:_____

Selection: _____

Page/Line: _____ / _____

Part of Speech: _____

Definition: _____

_____

_____

Sentence: _____

Personal Word List (continued)

Word:_____

Selection: _____

Page/Line: _____ / _____

Part of Speech: _____

Definition: _____

_____

_____

Sentence: _____

_____

Word:_____

Selection: _____

Page/Line: _____ / _____

Part of Speech: _____

Definition: _____

_____

_____

Sentence: _____

_____

Word:_____

Selection: _____

Page/Line: _____ / _____

Part of Speech: _____

Definition: _____

_____

_____

Sentence: _____

_____

Word:_____

Selection: _____

Page/Line: _____ / _____

Part of Speech: _____

Definition: _____

_____

_____

Sentence: _____

Word:_____

Selection: _____

Page/Line: _____ / _____

Part of Speech: _____

Definition: _____

_____

_____

Sentence: _____

_____

Word:_____

Selection: _____

Page/Line: _____ / _____

Part of Speech: _____

Definition: _____

_____

_____

Sentence: _____

_____

Word:_____

Selection: _____

Page/Line: _____ / _____

Part of Speech: _____

Definition: _____

_____

_____

Sentence: _____

_____

Word:_____

Selection: _____

Page/Line: _____ / _____

Part of Speech: _____

Definition: _____

_____

_____

Sentence: _____

_____

Word:_____

Selection: _____

Page/Line: _____ / _____

Part of Speech: _____

Definition: _____

_____

_____

Sentence: _____

_____

Word:_____

Selection: _____

Page/Line: _____ / _____

Part of Speech: _____

Definition: _____

_____

_____

Sentence: _____

_____

Word:_____

Selection: _____

Page/Line: _____ / _____

Part of Speech: _____

Definition: _____

_____

_____

Sentence: _____

_____

Word:_____

Selection: _____

Page/Line: _____ / _____

Part of Speech: _____

Definition: _____

_____

_____

Sentence: _____

Word:_____

Selection: _____

Page/Line: _____ / _____

Part of Speech: _____

Definition: _____

_____

_____

Sentence: _____

_____

Word:_____

Selection: _____

Page/Line: _____ / _____

Part of Speech: _____

Definition: _____

_____

_____

Sentence: _____

_____

Word:_____

Selection: _____

Page/Line: _____ / _____

Part of Speech: _____

Definition: _____

_____

_____

Sentence: _____

_____

Word:_____

Selection: _____

Page/Line: _____ / _____

Part of Speech: _____

Definition: _____

_____

_____

Sentence: _____

Personal Word List (continued)

Word:_____

Selection: _____

Page/Line: _____ / _____

Part of Speech: _____

Definition: _____

_____

_____

Sentence: _____

_____

Word:_____

Selection: _____

Page/Line: _____ / _____

Part of Speech: _____

Definition: _____

_____

_____

Sentence: _____

_____

Word:_____

Selection: _____

Page/Line: _____ / _____

Part of Speech: _____

Definition: _____

_____

_____

Sentence: _____

_____

Word:_____

Selection: _____

Page/Line: _____ / _____

Part of Speech: _____

Definition: _____

_____

_____

Sentence: _____

_____

Word:_____

Selection: _____

Page/Line: _____ / _____

Part of Speech: _____

Definition: _____

_____

_____

Sentence: _____

_____

Word:_____

Selection: _____

Page/Line: _____ / _____

Part of Speech: _____

Definition: _____

_____

_____

Sentence: _____

_____

Word:_____

Selection: _____

Page/Line: _____ / _____

Part of Speech: _____

Definition: _____

_____

_____

Sentence: _____

_____

Word:_____

Selection: _____

Page/Line: _____ / _____

Part of Speech: _____

Definition: _____

_____

_____

Sentence: _____

_____

Word:_____

Selection: _____

Page/Line: _____ / _____

Part of Speech: _____

Definition: _____

_____

_____

Sentence: _____

_____

Word:_____

Selection: _____

Page/Line: _____ / _____

Part of Speech: _____

Definition: _____

_____

_____

Sentence: _____

_____

Word:_____

Selection: _____

Page/Line: _____ / _____

Part of Speech: _____

Definition: _____

_____

_____

Sentence: _____

_____

Word:_____

Selection: _____

Page/Line: _____ / _____

Part of Speech: _____

Definition: _____

_____

_____

Sentence: _____

Word:_____

Selection: _____

Page/Line: _____ / _____

Part of Speech: _____

Definition: _____

_____

_____

Sentence: _____

_____

Word:_____

Selection: _____

Page/Line: _____ / _____

Part of Speech: _____

Definition: _____

_____

_____

Sentence: _____

_____

Word:_____

Selection: _____

Page/Line: _____ / _____

Part of Speech: _____

Definition: _____

_____

_____

Sentence: _____

_____

Word:_____

Selection: _____

Page/Line: _____ / _____

Part of Speech: _____

Definition: _____

_____

_____

Sentence: _____

Personal Word List (continued)

Word:_____

Selection: _____

Page/Line: _____ / _____

Part of Speech: _____

Definition: _____

_____

_____

Sentence: _____

_____

Word:_____

Selection: _____

Page/Line: _____ / _____

Part of Speech: _____

Definition: _____

_____

_____

Sentence: _____

_____

Word:_____

Selection: _____

Page/Line: _____ / _____

Part of Speech: _____

Definition: _____

_____

_____

Sentence: _____

_____

Word:_____

Selection: _____

Page/Line: _____ / _____

Part of Speech: _____

Definition: _____

_____

_____

Sentence: _____

_____

Word:_____

Selection: _____

Page/Line: _____ / _____

Part of Speech: _____

Definition: _____

_____

_____

Sentence: _____

_____

Word:_____

Selection: _____

Page/Line: _____ / _____

Part of Speech: _____

Definition: _____

_____

_____

Sentence: _____

_____

Word:_____

Selection: _____

Page/Line: _____ / _____

Part of Speech: _____

Definition: _____

_____

_____

Sentence: _____

_____

Word:_____

Selection: _____

Page/Line: _____ / _____

Part of Speech: _____

Definition: _____

_____

_____

Sentence: _____

_____

Word:_____

Selection: _____

Page/Line: _____ / _____

Part of Speech: _____

Definition: _____

_____

_____

Sentence: _____

_____

Word:_____

Selection: _____

Page/Line: _____ / _____

Part of Speech: _____

Definition: _____

_____

_____

Sentence: _____

_____

Word:_____

Selection: _____

Page/Line: _____ / _____

Part of Speech: _____

Definition: _____

_____

_____

Sentence: _____

_____

Word:_____

Selection: _____

Page/Line: _____ / _____

Part of Speech: _____

Definition: _____

_____

_____

Sentence: _____

_____

Word:_____

Selection: _____

Page/Line: _____ / _____

Part of Speech: _____

Definition: _____

_____

_____

Sentence: _____

_____

Word:_____

Selection: _____

Page/Line: _____ / _____

Part of Speech: _____

Definition: _____

_____

_____

Sentence: _____

_____

Word:_____

Selection: _____

Page/Line: _____ / _____

Part of Speech: _____

Definition: _____

_____

_____

Sentence: _____

_____

Word:_____

Selection: _____

Page/Line: _____ / _____

Part of Speech: _____

Definition: _____

_____

_____

Sentence: _____

_____

Personal Word List (continued)

Word:_____

Selection: _____

Page/Line: _____ / _____

Part of Speech: _____

Definition: _____

_____

_____

Sentence: _____

_____

Word:_____

Selection: _____

Page/Line: _____ / _____

Part of Speech: _____

Definition: _____

_____

_____

Sentence: _____

_____

Word:_____

Selection: _____

Page/Line: _____ / _____

Part of Speech: _____

Definition: _____

_____

_____

Sentence: _____

_____

Word:_____

Selection: _____

Page/Line: _____ / _____

Part of Speech: _____

Definition: _____

_____

_____

Sentence: _____

Word:_____

Selection: _____

Page/Line: _____ / _____

Part of Speech: _____

Definition: _____

_____

_____

Sentence: _____

_____

Word:_____

Selection: _____

Page/Line: _____ / _____

Part of Speech: _____

Definition: _____

_____

_____

Sentence: _____

_____

Word:_____

Selection: _____

Page/Line: _____ / _____

Part of Speech: _____

Definition: _____

_____

_____

Sentence: _____

_____

Word:_____

Selection: _____

Page/Line: _____ / _____

Part of Speech: _____

Definition: _____

_____

_____

Sentence: _____

Word: _____
Selection: _____
Page/Line: _____ / _____
Part of Speech: _____
Definition: _____
_____
_____
Sentence: _____
_____

Word: _____
Selection: _____
Page/Line: _____ / _____
Part of Speech: _____
Definition: _____
_____
_____
Sentence: _____
_____

Word: _____
Selection: _____
Page/Line: _____ / _____
Part of Speech: _____
Definition: _____
_____
_____
Sentence: _____
_____

Word: _____
Selection: _____
Page/Line: _____ / _____
Part of Speech: _____
Definition: _____
_____
_____
Sentence: _____
_____

Word: _____
Selection: _____
Page/Line: _____ / _____
Part of Speech: _____
Definition: _____
_____
_____
Sentence: _____
_____

Word: _____
Selection: _____
Page/Line: _____ / _____
Part of Speech: _____
Definition: _____
_____
_____
Sentence: _____
_____

Word: _____
Selection: _____
Page/Line: _____ / _____
Part of Speech: _____
Definition: _____
_____
_____
Sentence: _____
_____

Word: _____
Selection: _____
Page/Line: _____ / _____
Part of Speech: _____
Definition: _____
_____
_____
Sentence: _____
_____

Personal Word List (continued)

Word:_____

Selection: _____

Page/Line: _____ / _____

Part of Speech: _____

Definition: _____

_____

Sentence: _____

_____

Word:_____

Selection: _____

Page/Line: _____ / _____

Part of Speech: _____

Definition: _____

_____

Sentence: _____

_____

Word:_____

Selection: _____

Page/Line: _____ / _____

Part of Speech: _____

Definition: _____

_____

Sentence: _____

_____

Word:_____

Selection: _____

Page/Line: _____ / _____

Part of Speech: _____

Definition: _____

_____

Sentence: _____

Word:_____

Selection: _____

Page/Line: _____ / _____

Part of Speech: _____

Definition: _____

_____

Sentence: _____

_____

Word:_____

Selection: _____

Page/Line: _____ / _____

Part of Speech: _____

Definition: _____

_____

Sentence: _____

_____

Word:_____

Selection: _____

Page/Line: _____ / _____

Part of Speech: _____

Definition: _____

_____

Sentence: _____

_____

Word:_____

Selection: _____

Page/Line: _____ / _____

Part of Speech: _____

Definition: _____

_____

Sentence: _____

Word:_____

Selection: _____

Page/Line: _____ / _____

Part of Speech: _____

Definition: _____

_____

_____

Sentence: _____

_____

Word:_____

Selection: _____

Page/Line: _____ / _____

Part of Speech: _____

Definition: _____

_____

_____

Sentence: _____

_____

Word:_____

Selection: _____

Page/Line: _____ / _____

Part of Speech: _____

Definition: _____

_____

_____

Sentence: _____

_____

Word:_____

Selection: _____

Page/Line: _____ / _____

Part of Speech: _____

Definition: _____

_____

_____

Sentence: _____

_____

Word:_____

Selection: _____

Page/Line: _____ / _____

Part of Speech: _____

Definition: _____

_____

_____

Sentence: _____

_____

Word:_____

Selection: _____

Page/Line: _____ / _____

Part of Speech: _____

Definition: _____

_____

_____

Sentence: _____

_____

Word:_____

Selection: _____

Page/Line: _____ / _____

Part of Speech: _____

Definition: _____

_____

_____

Sentence: _____

_____

Word:_____

Selection: _____

Page/Line: _____ / _____

Part of Speech: _____

Definition: _____

_____

_____

Sentence: _____

_____

Personal Word List (continued)

Word:_____

Selection: _____

Page/Line: _____ / _____

Part of Speech: _____

Definition: _____

_____

_____

Sentence: _____

_____

Word:_____

Selection: _____

Page/Line: _____ / _____

Part of Speech: _____

Definition: _____

_____

_____

Sentence: _____

_____

Word:_____

Selection: _____

Page/Line: _____ / _____

Part of Speech: _____

Definition: _____

_____

_____

Sentence: _____

_____

Word:_____

Selection: _____

Page/Line: _____ / _____

Part of Speech: _____

Definition: _____

_____

_____

Sentence: _____

Word:_____

Selection: _____

Page/Line: _____ / _____

Part of Speech: _____

Definition: _____

_____

_____

Sentence: _____

_____

Word:_____

Selection: _____

Page/Line: _____ / _____

Part of Speech: _____

Definition: _____

_____

_____

Sentence: _____

_____

Word:_____

Selection: _____

Page/Line: _____ / _____

Part of Speech: _____

Definition: _____

_____

_____

Sentence: _____

_____

Word:_____

Selection: _____

Page/Line: _____ / _____

Part of Speech: _____

Definition: _____

_____

_____

Sentence: _____

Word:_____

Selection: _____

Page/Line: _____ / _____

Part of Speech: _____

Definition: _____

_____

_____

Sentence: _____

_____

Word:_____

Selection: _____

Page/Line: _____ / _____

Part of Speech: _____

Definition: _____

_____

_____

Sentence: _____

_____

Word:_____

Selection: _____

Page/Line: _____ / _____

Part of Speech: _____

Definition: _____

_____

_____

Sentence: _____

_____

Word:_____

Selection: _____

Page/Line: _____ / _____

Part of Speech: _____

Definition: _____

_____

_____

Sentence: _____

_____

Word:_____

Selection: _____

Page/Line: _____ / _____

Part of Speech: _____

Definition: _____

_____

_____

Sentence: _____

Word:_____

Selection: _____

Page/Line: _____ / _____

Part of Speech: _____

Definition: _____

_____

_____

Sentence: _____

Personal Word List (continued)

Word:_____

Selection: _____

Page/Line: _____ / _____

Part of Speech: _____

Definition: _____

_____

_____

Sentence: _____

_____

Word:_____

Selection: _____

Page/Line: _____ / _____

Part of Speech: _____

Definition: _____

_____

_____

Sentence: _____

_____

Word:_____

Selection: _____

Page/Line: _____ / _____

Part of Speech: _____

Definition: _____

_____

_____

Sentence: _____

_____

Word:_____

Selection: _____

Page/Line: _____ / _____

Part of Speech: _____

Definition: _____

_____

_____

Sentence: _____

Word:_____

Selection: _____

Page/Line: _____ / _____

Part of Speech: _____

Definition: _____

_____

_____

Sentence: _____

_____

Word:_____

Selection: _____

Page/Line: _____ / _____

Part of Speech: _____

Definition: _____

_____

_____

Sentence: _____

_____

Word:_____

Selection: _____

Page/Line: _____ / _____

Part of Speech: _____

Definition: _____

_____

_____

Sentence: _____

_____

Word:_____

Selection: _____

Page/Line: _____ / _____

Part of Speech: _____

Definition: _____

_____

_____

Sentence: _____

Word:_____

Selection: _____

Page/Line: _____ / _____

Part of Speech: _____

Definition: _____
_____
_____

Sentence: _____
_____

Word:_____

Selection: _____

Page/Line: _____ / _____

Part of Speech: _____

Definition: _____
_____
_____

Sentence: _____
_____

Word:_____

Selection: _____

Page/Line: _____ / _____

Part of Speech: _____

Definition: _____
_____
_____

Sentence: _____
_____

Word:_____

Selection: _____

Page/Line: _____ / _____

Part of Speech: _____

Definition: _____
_____
_____

Sentence: _____

Word:_____

Selection: _____

Page/Line: _____ / _____

Part of Speech: _____

Definition: _____
_____
_____

Sentence: _____
_____

Word:_____

Selection: _____

Page/Line: _____ / _____

Part of Speech: _____

Definition: _____
_____
_____

Sentence: _____
_____

Word:_____

Selection: _____

Page/Line: _____ / _____

Part of Speech: _____

Definition: _____
_____
_____

Sentence: _____
_____

Word:_____

Selection: _____

Page/Line: _____ / _____

Part of Speech: _____

Definition: _____
_____
_____

Sentence: _____
_____

Personal Word List (continued)

Word:_____

Selection: _____

Page/Line: _____ / _____

Part of Speech: _____

Definition: _____

_____

_____

Sentence: _____

_____

Word:_____

Selection: _____

Page/Line: _____ / _____

Part of Speech: _____

Definition: _____

_____

_____

Sentence: _____

_____

Word:_____

Selection: _____

Page/Line: _____ / _____

Part of Speech: _____

Definition: _____

_____

_____

Sentence: _____

_____

Word:_____

Selection: _____

Page/Line: _____ / _____

Part of Speech: _____

Definition: _____

_____

_____

Sentence: _____

Word:_____

Selection: _____

Page/Line: _____ / _____

Part of Speech: _____

Definition: _____

_____

_____

Sentence: _____

_____

Word:_____

Selection: _____

Page/Line: _____ / _____

Part of Speech: _____

Definition: _____

_____

_____

Sentence: _____

_____

Word:_____

Selection: _____

Page/Line: _____ / _____

Part of Speech: _____

Definition: _____

_____

_____

Sentence: _____

_____

Word:_____

Selection: _____

Page/Line: _____ / _____

Part of Speech: _____

Definition: _____

_____

_____

Sentence: _____

Word:_____

Selection: _____

Page/Line: _____ / _____

Part of Speech: _____

Definition: _____

_____

_____

Sentence: _____

_____

Word:_____

Selection: _____

Page/Line: _____ / _____

Part of Speech: _____

Definition: _____

_____

_____

Sentence: _____

_____

Word:_____

Selection: _____

Page/Line: _____ / _____

Part of Speech: _____

Definition: _____

_____

_____

Sentence: _____

_____

Word:_____

Selection: _____

Page/Line: _____ / _____

Part of Speech: _____

Definition: _____

_____

_____

Sentence: _____

Word:_____

Selection: _____

Page/Line: _____ / _____

Part of Speech: _____

Definition: _____

_____

_____

Sentence: _____

_____

Word:_____

Selection: _____

Page/Line: _____ / _____

Part of Speech: _____

Definition: _____

_____

_____

Sentence: _____

_____

Word:_____

Selection: _____

Page/Line: _____ / _____

Part of Speech: _____

Definition: _____

_____

_____

Sentence: _____

_____

Word:_____

Selection: _____

Page/Line: _____ / _____

Part of Speech: _____

Definition: _____

_____

_____

Sentence: _____

Personal Word List (continued)

Word:_____

Selection: _____

Page/Line: _____ / _____

Part of Speech: _____

Definition: _____

_____

_____

Sentence: _____

_____

Word:_____

Selection: _____

Page/Line: _____ / _____

Part of Speech: _____

Definition: _____

_____

_____

Sentence: _____

_____

Word:_____

Selection: _____

Page/Line: _____ / _____

Part of Speech: _____

Definition: _____

_____

_____

Sentence: _____

_____

Word:_____

Selection: _____

Page/Line: _____ / _____

Part of Speech: _____

Definition: _____

_____

_____

Sentence: _____

_____

Word:_____

Selection: _____

Page/Line: _____ / _____

Part of Speech: _____

Definition: _____

_____

_____

Sentence: _____

_____

Word:_____

Selection: _____

Page/Line: _____ / _____

Part of Speech: _____

Definition: _____

_____

_____

Sentence: _____

_____

Word:_____

Selection: _____

Page/Line: _____ / _____

Part of Speech: _____

Definition: _____

_____

_____

Sentence: _____

_____

Word:_____

Selection: _____

Page/Line: _____ / _____

Part of Speech: _____

Definition: _____

_____

_____

Sentence: _____

_____

Acknowledgments

Curtis Brown: "Be Ye Men of Valour," from *Blood, Toil, Tears and Sweat* by Winston Churchill. Copyright © the Estate of Sir Winston S. Churchill. Reproduced with permission of Curtis Brown Ltd., London, on behalf of the Estate of Sir Winston S. Churchill.

Doubleday and Harold Ober Associates: "Civil Peace," from *Girls at War and Other Stories* by Chinua Achebe. Copyright © 1972, 1973 by Chinua Achebe. Used by permission of Doubleday, a division of Random House, Inc. and Harold Ober and Associates Incorporated.

Dutton Signet: Excerpts from *Beowulf,* translated by Burton Raffel. Translation copyright © 1963 by Burton Raffel, afterword © 1963 New American Library. Used by permission of Dutton Signet, a division of Penguin Putnam Inc.

Faber and Faber: "Preludes" from *Collected Poems, 1909–1962* by T. S. Eliot. Copyright 1936 by Harcourt Brace & Company, copyright © 1963, 1964 by T. S. Eliot. Reprinted by permission of Faber and Faber Ltd.

Harcourt: "The Duchess and the Jeweller," from *A Haunted House and Other Short Stories* by Virginia Woolf. Copyright 1944 and renewed 1972 by Harcourt, Inc. Reprinted by permission of the publisher.

Harold Ober Associates: "My Fight with Jack Dempsey" by Paul Gallico. Reprinted by permission of Harold Ober Associates Incorporated.

New Directions Publishing Corporation and David Higham Associates: "Do Not Go Gentle into That Good Night" by Dylan Thomas, from *The Poems of Dylan Thomas*. Copyright © 1952 by Dylan Thomas. Reprinted by permission of New Directions Publishing Corporation and David Higham Associates.

The New York Times: "Waiting for the A Train" by Randy Kennedy, *The New York Times,* March 5, 2002. Copyright © 2002 The New York Times Company. Reprinted by permission.

Penguin Books: Excerpt from the "Prologue" to *The Canterbury Tales* by Geoffrey Chaucer, translated by Nevill Coghill (Penguin Classics 1951, fourth revised edition 1977). Copyright © 1951, 1958, 1960, 1970, 1975, 1977 by Nevill Coghill. Reproduced by permission of Penguin Books Ltd.

Pollinger Limited: "The Rocking-Horse Winner" by D. H. Lawrence, from *Complete Short Stories of D. H. Lawrence*. Copyright 1933 by the Estate of D. H. Lawrence, renewed © 1961 by Angelo Ravagli and C. M. Weekley, executors of the Estate of Frieda Lawrence Ravagli. Used by permission of Pollinger Limited.

Random House: "Musée des Beaux Arts," from *W. H. Auden: The Collected Poems* by W. H. Auden. Copyright © 1940 and renewed 1968 by W. H. Auden. Used by permission of Random House, Inc.

Russell & Volkening: "Six Feet of the Country," from *Six Feet of the Country and Other Stories* by Nadine Gordimer. Copyright © 1956 by Nadine Gordimer, renewed © 1984 by Nadine Gordimer. Reprinted by the permission of Russell & Volkening as agents for the author.

Simon & Schuster: "The Second Coming" by William Butler Yeats, from *The Poems of W. B. Yeats: A New Cover Edition,* edited by Richard J. Finneran. Copyright © 1924 by Macmillan Publishing Company, renewed 1952 by Bertha Georgie Yeats. Reprinted with the permission of Simon & Schuster, Inc.

"Sailing to Byzantium" by William Butler Yeats, from *The Poems of W. B. Yeats: A New Cover Edition,* edited by Richard J. Finneran. Copyright 1928 by Macmillan Publishing Company, renewed 1956 by Georgie Yeats. Reprinted with the permission of Simon & Schuster, Inc.

Simon & Schuster and Jonathan Clowes: "A Sunrise on the Veld," from *African Stories* by Doris Lessing. Copyright © 1951, 1953, 1954, 1957, 1958, 1962, 1964, 1965, 1972, 1981 by Doris Lessing. Reprinted by permission of Simon & Schuster, Inc., and Jonathan Clowes Ltd., London, on behalf of Doris Lessing.

Cover

Illustration copyright © 1997 David Bowers.

Art Credits

36 *border* Sharon D. Siegel; **36** *bottom* From the Ellesmere manuscript, EL 26 c.9, fol. 153v, The Huntington Library, San Marino, California; **61** Photograph by Sharon Hoogstraten; **70** Photofest; **163** London (19th century), unknown artist. Colored engraving, The Granger Collection, New York.; **222** PhotoDisc/Getty Images; **230–231** *background* NASA; **258–259** *background* PhotoDisc/Getty Images; **266–267** *background* PhotoDisc/Getty Images; **266** Scala/Art Resource, New York; **300–301** *background* Evelyn Hofer, courtesy of The Witkin Gallery, Inc., New York; **320–321** all PhotoDisc/Getty Images; **354–355** *background* PhotoDisc/Getty Images; **362–363** *background* NASA; **370–371** *background* Copyright © UPI/Bettmann/Corbis; **385–386** *background* PhotoDisc/Getty Images; **400** Copyright © Jonathan Blair/Corbis; **400–401** *background* PhotoDisc/Getty Images; **411** all PhotoDisc/Getty Images; **442, 445** Copyright © Bettmann/Corbis; **447** PhotoDisc/Getty Images; **449** Bruce Ayres/Stone/Getty Images; **451** Thomas J. Peterson/Stone/Getty Images.